The Politics of
Cultural Performance

THE POLITICS OF
CULTURAL PERFORMANCE

*Edited by David Parkin, Lionel Caplan
and Humphrey Fisher*

Berghahn Books
Providence • Oxford

First published in 1996 by

Berghahn Books

Editorial offices:
165, Taber Avenue, Providence, RI 02906, USA
Bush House, Merewood Avenue, Oxford, OX3 8EF, UK

© David Parkin, Lionel Caplan, Humphrey Fisher 1996

All rights reserved.
No part of this publication may be reproduced in any form or by any means without the written permission of Berghahn Books.

Library of Congress Cataloging-in-Publication Data

```
The politics of cultural performance / edited by David Parkin, Lionel
  Caplan, Humphrey Fisher.
       p.    cm.
    Includes bibliographical references.
    ISBN 1-57181-898-7 (cloth : alk. paper). -- ISBN 1-57181-925-8
  (paper : alk. paper)
    1. Ethnology--Philosophy. 2. Culture--Philosophy. 3. Symbolic
  anthropology. 4. Rites and ceremonies.  I. Parkin, David J.
  II. Caplan, Lionel.  III. Fisher, Humphrey J.
  GN345.P633  1996
  305.8'001--dc20                                            95-26832
                                                                  CIP
```

British Library Cataloguing in Publication Data

A catalogue record for this book is available from the British Library.

Cover Illustration by Simon Cohen

TABLE OF CONTENTS

Preface	viii
Select Bibliography	xi
Acknowledgements	xiv

INTRODUCTION xv
The Power of the Bizarre
David Parkin

CHAPTER 1 1
Cultural Performance, Authenticity, and Second Nature
F. G. Bailey

CHAPTER 2 19
Political Ritual and the Public Sphere in Contemporary West Africa
Sandra T. Barnes

CHAPTER 3 41
Beyond Cultural Performance: Women, Culture and the State in Contemporary Nigerian Politics
Ifi Amadiume

CHAPTER 4 61
The Bantu Botatwe: Changing Political Definitions in Southern Zambia
Elizabeth Colson

CHAPTER 5 81
The Fusion of Identities: Political Passion and the Poetics of Cultural Performance among British Pakistanis
Pnina Werbner

CHAPTER 6   101
*Commensality as Cultural Performance:
the Struggle for Leadership in an Igbo Village*
O.A.C. Anigbo

CHAPTER 7   115
*Migrating Cultural Performances:
The Urhobo among the Ikale-Yoruba, Ondo State, Nigeria*
Onigu Otite

CHAPTER 8   125
On Avoidance
P. H. Gulliver

CHAPTER 9   145
*Fighting with Operas: Processionals, Politics, and
the Spectre of Violence in Rural Hong Kong*
James L. Watson

CHAPTER 10   161
*Cultural Performance and the Reproduction of
the Anaguta Symbolic Universe*
Adrian Collett

CHAPTER 11   181
Dance and the Cosmology of Confidence
Paul Spencer

CHAPTER 12   199
*Possession and Dispossession: Changing Symbolic Structures and
Meanings in Contemporary Nigeria*
Renée Pittin

CHAPTER 13   217
*Cultural Performance and Economic-Political Goals:
an Ethnographic Study of Blacksmiths in Kano
(Northern Nigeria)*
Philip J. Jaggar

CHAPTER 14 237
*Pilgrims and Genies: A Case Study in the Liminality and
Masquerade Politics of Cultural Performance, from
the History of Islam in West Africa, c. 1500*
Humphrey J. Fisher

CHAPTER 15 257
*A Cultural Given and a Hidden Influence:
Koranic Teachers in Kano*
J.A.McIntyre

Biographical Notes on Contributors 275

Index 281

Preface

A Tribute to Abner Cohen

This collection of essays has been brought together by friends, former students and colleagues of Abner Cohen to whom the book is dedicated.

To many – including his family – Abner often seems to have been 'born a social anthropologist'. He has devoted himself to teaching, exploring, writing and thinking about the subject through most of his working life. Moreover, it has informed his approach to life itself, and his dedication to social anthropology has not diminished despite a long, progressive and debilitating illness.

Armed with a first degree in philosophy from the University of London (external), Abner taught at and inspected schools in Teheran and Israel. This early experience gave him the teaching skills which were later appreciated by students at the School of Oriental and African Studies (SOAS).

It was during this period as school inspector in Israel that Abner's interest in social anthropology first began. After a long correspondence with Max Gluckman, founder of the 'Manchester School', a two-year scholarship from the British Council enabled Abner to begin his postgraduate career in 1956 in the Department of Sociology and Anthropology, University of Manchester. Abner was seduced into continuing his research by the Manchester School and the stimulus of those scholars who were to exert considerable influence on social anthropology in Britain. Max Gluckman and Emrys Peters played a significant role in his early thinking on the subject. In 1958 Abner embarked upon a study of Arab villages in Israel, which was to provide the data for his doctorate and for his first book.

Manchester also provided the foundation for Abner's family life. In 1960 he married Gaynor, a former undergraduate and fellow student of Emrys Peters. She later gained a doctorate in Social Anthropology. Sara, their first child, born in Manchester in 1961, has also followed her father into the subject. Both their other children – Tammy, born in Nigeria in 1963, and Simon, born on their return one year later – would also claim to have been influenced by their father's passion for his subject.

The diaspora of the Manchester School continued to influence Abner's subsequent career. In 1961 he was offered a research fellowship at SOAS by F.G. Bailey, who has continued to maintain friendly professional contact even though he now lives in California. The late Victor Turner also provided inspiration.

The whole of Abner's teaching career in social anthropology was spent in the Department of Social Anthropology at SOAS under the leadership of Christoph von Fürer-Haimendorf. Abner remained a teacher at SOAS for twenty-four years until his retirement in 1985. He rose rapidly through the ranks: Lecturer (1964), Reader (1970), Professor (1972). Abner has never failed to record his gratitude to SOAS and his colleagues there who offered him the stimulus, support and peace of mind to develop his studies and teaching.

In 1962–3 Abner made his first visit to Africa to carry out a study in a semi-urban community in south-western Nigeria. He also paid a brief visit to Ghana. The introduction to West Africa was the starting point for a lasting love for the region and for a continuing interest in its peoples and the social changes which they have undergone. Abner has addressed the problem of how small-scale societies, isolated during the colonial period, have been accommodated within the nation-state structures set up after independence and how they have coped with the processes of historical change. Nigeria provided rich material for the initial study: *Custom and Politics in Urban Africa* (1969), which quickly became 'a classic' and for which Abner was awarded the Amaury Talbot Prize (1969). A study of the Creoles in Sierra Leone continued this research theme, issuing finally in *The Politics of Elite Culture: Explorations in the Dramaturgy of Power in a Modern African Society* (1981). After returning from Sierra Leone, Abner embarked upon his study, sustained over many years, of the Notting Hill Carnival, which depicted the life-style of Africans of West Indian origin who have settled in London.

Ethnographic data collected in West Africa and the UK have provided generations of students of West African studies at SOAS with original material through which to approach the study of ethnicity and other major problems of social anthropology. Single ethnographies, however, have not been the sole outputs of Abner's work. *Two-Dimensional Man* (1974) provided a crucible for many of his ideas, making them applicable to a wide range of sociological problems arising in different geographical areas.

Throughout his career Abner's work has continued to interest U.S. social anthropologists, many of whom he has worked with and visited. He has taught at Cornell University, the State University of New York at Binghampton, Bryn Mawr College, Pennsylvania and the University of Washington, Seattle. This sequence climaxed in a year's fellowship at the Center for Advanced Study of the Behavioral Sciences at Stanford. The latter brought him into contact with international scholars from different disciplines whose ideas he was able to apply to his own work in anthropology. In 1980 Abner was awarded the Rivers Memorial medal by the Royal Anthropological Institute.

The material for Abner's latest book, focussing upon the Notting Hill Carnival, was collected over several years of observation and interviewing while he still taught at SOAS. It was published as *Masquerade Politics: Explorations in the Structure of Urban Cultural Movements* (1993). By that time Abner and his family were living in Oxford. He retired prematurely from SOAS in 1985 because of the debilitating effects of Parkinson's. Abner was awarded the title of 'Emeritus Professor of the Anthropology of Africa and the Near East' in the University of London.

The warm welcome which Oxford anthropologists extended to Abner has enabled him to take part in seminars such as that on Ethnicity and Identity organised by Shirley Ardener et al. at the Friday departmental seminar, thus sustaining his active involvement in social anthropology. His election as senior research associate at Queen Elizabeth House at the University of Oxford through which he has maintained regular contact with scholars from a range of countries and related disciplines has also provided him with moral and intellectual support in moving forward in social anthropology.

Select Bibliography of Works by Abner Cohen

Books

1965. *Arab Border-Villages in Israel: A Study of Continuity and Change in Social Organization*. Manchester: Manchester University Press. Reprinted in 1972.

1969. *Custom and Politics in Urban Africa: A Study of Hausa Migrants in Yoruba Towns*. London: Routledge & Kegan Paul, and Berkeley: University of California Press. Won the Amaury Talbot Prize in 1969.

1974. *Two-Dimensional Man: An Essay on the Anthropology of Power and Symbolism in Complex Society*. London: Routledge & Kegan Paul. Paperback edition published in 1976, Berkeley: University of California Press, with special forward. Also issued in a Japanese translation (1976), and a Portuguese translation (1978).

1981. *The Politics of Elite Culture: Explorations in the Dramaturgy of Power in a Modern African Society*. Berkeley: University of California Press.

1993. *Masquerade Politics: Explorations in the Structure of Urban Cultural Movements*. Berkeley: University of California Press.

Edited Works

1974. *Urban Ethnicity*. London: Tavistock Publications.

Articles

1965. 'The Social Organization of Credit in a West African Cattle Market', *Africa* 35(1): 8–20.

1966. 'Politics of the Kola Trade', *Africa* 36(1): 18–36.

1967. 'Stranger Communities: the Hausa', in *The City of Ibadan*, P.C. Lloyd, A.L. Mabogunje and B. Awe (eds). Cambridge: Cambridge University Press.

1968. 'The Politics of Mysticism in Some Local Communities in Newly Independent African States', in *Local Level Politics*, M. Swartz (ed.). London: University of London Press.

1969. 'Antropologia Hivratit Ve Tarbutit', in *Intsiklopedia Hinukhit*, Kerekh 5 Madae Haezer Shel Hahinnoukh. Yerushalyim: Misrad Hahinnukh ve Hattarbut ve Mosad Bialik. (In Hebrew)

——. 'Political Anthropology: the Analysis of the Symbolism of Power Relations', *Man* 4(2): 215–35.

1970. 'The Politics of Marriage in Changing Middle Eastern Stratification Systems', in *Essays in Comparative Social Stratification*, L. Plotnicov and A. Tuden (eds). Pittsburgh: University of Pittsburgh Press.

1971. 'Cultural Strategies in the Organization of Trading Diasporas', in *The Development of Indigenous Trade and Markets in West Africa*, Claude Meillassoux (ed.). London: Oxford University Press for the International African Institute.

———. 'Hamula', in *Encyclopedia of Islam* (New Edition), B. Lewis, V.L. Ménage, Ch. Pellat and J. Schacht (eds). Leiden: E.J. Brill.

———. 'Ibadan', in *Encyclopedia of Islam* (New Edition), B. Lewis, V.L. Ménage, Ch. Pellat and J. Schacht (eds). Leiden: E.J. Brill.

———. 'The Politics of Ritual Secrecy', *Man* 6(3): 427–48.

1973. 'People of Israel', in *People of the Earth*, Volume 17, E.E. Evans-Pritchard (supervisory ed.) and Ahmad Al-Shahi (volume ed.). Italy: The Danbury Press.

———. 'The Social Organisation of Credit in a West African Cattle Market', in *Africa and Change*, Colin M. Turnbull (ed.). New York: Alfred A. Knopf.

———. 'The Social Organisation of Credit in a West African Cattle Market', in *Sociology in Africa*, P.F. Wilmot (ed.). Zaria: Ahmadu Bello University.

1974. 'Introduction: the Lesson of Ethnicity', in *Urban Ethnicity*, Abner Cohen (ed.). London: Tavistock Publications.

———. 'The Politics of Ritual Secrecy', in *On the Margin of the Visible: Sociology, the Esoteric and the Occult*, Tiryakian (ed.). New York, London & Sydney: John Wiley and Sons.

1977. 'Symbolic Action and the Structure of the Self', in *Symbols and Sentiments*, I.M. Lewis (ed.). London: Academic Press.

———. 'The Social Organisation of Credit in a West African Cattle Market', in *Friends, Followers and Factions: A Reader in Political Clientelism*, S.W. Schmidt, J.C. Scott, C. Lande and L. Guasti (eds). Berkeley: University of California Press.

1979. 'Foreword', in *Pasture and Politics: Economics, Conflict and Ritual Among Shahsavan Nomads of Northwestern Iran*, Richard Tapper. London: Academic Press.

———. 'Political Symbolism', *Annual Review of Anthropology* 8: 87–113.

1980. 'Drama and Politics in the Development of a London Carnival', *Man* 15(1): 65–87.

1981. 'Variables in Ethnicity', in *Ethnic Change*, C.F. Keyes (ed.). Seattle: University of Washington Press.

1982. 'A Polyethnic London Carnival as Contested Cultural Performance', *Ethnic and Racial Studies* 5(1): 23–41.

——. 'Drama and Politics in the Development of a London Carnival', in *Custom and Conflict in British Society*, R. Frankenberg (ed.). Manchester: Manchester University Press.

1983. 'Drama and Politics in the Development of a London Carnival', in *Political Anthropology: Culture and Political Change*, M.J. Aronoff (ed.). New Brunswick & London: Transaction Books.

1988. 'The Politics of Ethnicity in African Towns', in *The Urbanization of the Third World*, Josef Gugler (ed.). Oxford: Oxford University Press.

1991. 'Drama and Politics in the Development of a London Carnival', in *Black and Ethnic Leaderships in Britain: The Cultural Dimensions of Political Action*, Pnina Werbner and Muhammad Anwar (eds). London: Routledge & Kegan Paul.

1994. 'La Lezione dell'Etnicita', in *Questione di Etnicita*, Acura di Vanessa Maher. Rosenberg & Sellier Materiali. (In Italian)

1996. 'The Lesson of Ethnicity', in *Classic Essays in Ethnic Theory*, Werner Sollor (ed.). Basingstoke: Macmillan Press Ltd.

ACKNOWLEDGEMENTS

The editors wish to thank the Nuffield Foundation for a grant which enabled many of the volume's preparatory costs to be met. We are also indebted to the SOAS Publications Committee and two anonymous donors for additional subventions. We would like to express our gratitude to Simon Cohen for the cover design, and to Constanze Schmaling for her invaluable secretarial assistance in the early stages of the project. This collection would not have come to fruition without the editorial, computing and organisational skills of Anna Debska nor, indeed, without the enthusiastic co-operation of the contributors.

INTRODUCTION:

The Power of the Bizarre

David Parkin

Dramatic Origins of a Concept

If power is immanent in all social interaction and not vested solely in leaders and the incumbents of formal office, then we need to ask what is special about power emanating from cultural events, ceremonials and customary practices. Abner Cohen's work (1969, 1974) first developed the idea of power and symbolism as distinct variables in dialectical relationship with each other, as when religious belief (or kinship or some other symbolic mode) becomes the medium through which people control others or, conversely, when people's attempts to influence others become expressed and legitimised through appeal to religion or kinship (1981). Later, Cohen emphasised the transformative qualities of these two dimensions, with, say, the symbolic or cultural becoming the political and vice versa: the Notting Hill Carnival begins as a small-scale, poly-ethnic local festival but develops into a political movement consciously mobilising Black Britishers in the struggle against racism (1993). Reverse cases also occur, as when political movements lose their strategic quality but remain ceremonially important, perhaps to assume at a later stage a new political or economic function.

Cohen thus proposed, as long ago as 1969, a concept of power as being not only immanent and comprising economic and political directives, but as also presentable to people in such a way that they would gladly submit themselves to social rules and authorities to the extent even of regarding them as desirable. This notion of mystificatory compliance or collusion, shading into the idea of hegemony, drew more from Marx than Foucault and points to a whole tradition of anthropological scholarship deriving from Max Gluckman and the so-called Manchester School which wrestled constantly with the dialectics of practical effect and ceremonial expression. Cohen was able to clarify the various, somewhat untidy, strands which made up this approach and undoubtedly advanced our understanding of its dynamics, doing so in a language whose clarity enhances its theoretical profundity.

To date no scholar working within Cohen's general theory has improved on it. Less obviously, it has also become absorbed in a broader treatment of the cultural as inherently political, as in more recent critical theory and the new field of cultural studies. By comparison, much so-called Foucauldian discourse theory has deliberately meandered, enrichening through insight but opposed to the neat, analytical conclusiveness that characterised Cohen's work. It seems unlikely that this post-modernist thinking will, so to speak, revert to the modernist agenda of grander theorising: they are now two species apart. It is however, important to ask, in the famed manner of Habermas, what unfinished business there is in Cohen's own dialectic and whether, indeed, it is not in fact a heuristic approach which we might all do well to adopt as the litmus test for further study. For all the talk of epistemological shifts and new paradigms, the continuity is, beneath the new language, more evident than the rupture. For this reason, we understand Cohen's theoretical importance not only today, but also for the future, by investigating its precedents.

As a subject of study, the politics of cultural performance can be traced at least to the famous article by Gluckman, written first in 1940, which examined one day in the life of workers building a bridge in Zululand (1958). Against the conventions of the time of long-term fieldwork studying a culturally and linguistically homogeneous people represented statically, Gluckman saw that cross-cutting ties of black and white, superviser and supervised, workers one moment and ritual performers the next, could be represented simultaneously in the single sphere of overlapping activities involved in the bridge-building. It seems that, rather than regarding the event as an explosion of seemingly conflicting and unmanageable information, Gluckman realised brilliantly that there was a kind of paradox: out of the plethora of acts making up a somewhat arbitrarily defined event, one could in fact abstract relatively constant principles, of race, of occupational specialisation, and of work and beliefs. Out of mixture came clarity but not simplistic reductionism.

In my view, this article – because of the colossal impact it generated, not all of it acknowledged – has been the most important single work in British social anthropology. Gluckman's openly marxist colleague, Godfrey Wilson (see Brown 1973), had cleared the way for a study of social change caused by the economic dislocations of labour migration in central Africa. Gluckman provided the template for a methodology based on what one might call the critical case-study, which allowed theoretical abstractions to be drawn from raw data.

I refer to this as a critical case-study approach in order to emphasise its resemblance to the analysis of a crisis which, once interrogated, reveals key interests and their value as perceived by the people themselves (Epstein 1967). Gluckman himself loosely referred to the Freudian case material approach as comparable to his own (cf. Epstein 1978).

What was perhaps not fully anticipated by Gluckman was the increasingly elaborated use by later anthropologists of the element of drama in the event to illustrate principles of social and cultural organisation. It is obvious that any culturally designated event is always in some way a piece of drama, and it was next left to Victor Turner to develop the notion of social drama as being central to his own methodology in his study of the Ndembu of central Africa (1957). To this innovation may be added Clyde Mitchell's 1956 study of the Kalela dance, Epstein's tracing of Zambian national and trade-union political development back to a seemingly minor but dramatically expressed boycott by African workers of White-owned butcher's shops (1958), Van Velsen's use of extended case studies (1964), Bailey's local, self-sealed history of the Orissa distillers (1957), and, more recently, Abner Cohen's concept of micro-history (1965, 1969) and dramaturgy (1981), which he acknowledges as belonging to this intellectual pedigree and as having a special provenance in Turner's notion of social drama. The dramaturgical metaphor has, of course, been much explored in the years since this period by a number of ex-Manchester scholars (e.g., Kapferer 1981).

Here, we return to the question of unfinished business in the evolution of this methodological trajectory. Possibly as a result of the post-modernist emphasis on the fragmentary nature of social life and its irreducibility to constant principles, or of classic structuralism's disregard of history or diachrony, a new generation of anthropologists has emerged who frequently employ case studies in the manner of 'apt and isolated illustration' (to use Gluckman's phrase) rather than extended case studies stretching over months or years and informing an ethnographic and theoretical argument throughout its phases. For this generation, it is as if the legacy of the Manchester School has, with certain notable exceptions, gone unrecognised.

In fact, the social drama or micro-history is ideally compatible with the presentation of society as fragmentary and as founded on fictions more than facts of social perpetuity. It ought, after all, to be the best method of portraying the inconsistencies which players in a social drama often claim as perduring principles. Society may be fragmentary but it is also continuous conversation and exchange. Its continuity lies precisely in people's performative attempts to bridge differences between one event and another. Whether they appeal to putative over-arching principles or to everyday objects, acts and phrases that link each other, people elide the anthropologists' distinction between the social and the cultural. For instance, wedding ceremonies may be compared by participants in terms of, say, their performative correctness and lavishness, but the same judgmental comments will also reveal the speakers' views on the social suitability of the partners and families marrying each other. Letting the subjects speak for themselves gives us cultural data, namely the overt beliefs and justifications behind practices. The outside anthropologist may, from his/her comparative perspective, be better at seeing these cultural data in terms of long-term trends in conflict with each other and so affecting social perpetuation. Cultural data removed from local histories are less able to reveal latent problems of struggle and survival over time.

American anthropology has usually been more cultural in the sense that it would seek to explain in meticulous detail the rationale of particular rites, ceremonial roles and cosmic beliefs, sometimes to the exclusion of even local histories, and was less concerned with the sometimes contradictory rules of social perpetuity. The British social became merged in the great American cultural. In his first major work in Britain (1957) Victor Turner developed the notion of *social* drama, which enabled social contradictions to be played out in terms of customarily acceptable disagreements, but which hid their ultimate irreconcilibility. Even so, later, and especially after his shift from

Manchester to the United States, he was a principal architect, perhaps the major one, in the development of studies of cultural and symbolic performance in which the play of power relations was certainly implicit but more as the interplay of discrepant psyches than of the social cleavages wrought by political and economic contradictions and conflicts (e.g., 1974, 1982, 1986). A recent study by Kratz (1994: 14–53) includes the most comprehensive theoretical summary to date of this and other approaches.

On the one hand, then, there is the British concept of social drama, with its performative emphasis, originating in Gluckman's study and developed by those working with or influenced by him, including Turner, and of marxist provenance. On the other hand, there is the recently much more influential American notion of cultural performance, originating in a rich blend of folklore interests and language use, dance, ritual and theatre, and also later developed by Turner, and, except perhaps for the later, highly distinctive work of Taussig (1980), essentially non-marxist (e.g., Hymes 1975; Bauman 1986; Fernandez 1986; Schechner 1993). The existence of these two fundamentally different approaches to cultural performance appears to have been missed by modern commentators.

In an instructive and extensive review of the field by Beeman (1993), Turner's influence is wholesomely acknowledged. However, no reference is made to the work which was the *fons et origo* of his concept of social drama, namely *Schism and Continuity in an African Society* (1957). The absence of this key work, and of any reference to, say, Gluckman, Mitchell or Abner Cohen, is perhaps to be explained by the concern in the review article to focus on the more literal understanding of theatre and spectacle. The review is not much interested in the idea of cultural performance as a methodological metaphor for exploring issues of conflict and contradiction in wider society. In this sense, then, Abner Cohen's approach and the intellectual line from which it descends stand alone. The approach starts from the assumption that human struggle is intrinsic to all forms of social organisation and that peoples seek non-explicit or diversionary, and therefore ceremonialised, ways of resolving the contradiction that comes from having to co-operate with neighbours and kin with whom they necessarily diverge, sometimes fundamentally, in their interests. Though much muted, the original marxist (or perhaps marxisant) inspiration can still be discerned. It nowadays asks whether a concept of social reality may be distinguished from its representation as cultural performance, and whether such performances hide, clarify or transform that reality.

Reality is a highly contestable notion. The usual question challenging it asks: how much is reality an objective condition that can be represented? However, this makes a false distinction. An event that is truly believed to have happened, and its representation in, say, ceremony or art, are both aspects of the same reality. They both have effects on the world, though of different kinds. To take a familiar example, it may historically be demonstrated, and therefore true, that a certain battle killed many civilians; but the media version may ignore this fact and tell instead of soldiers' bravery and heroic victories and so justify the government decision to have waged war. Moreover, while it may be obvious that a representation is dependent on the event that it denotes, an event is itself dependent on its later representation. For instance, when people discover, delineate and elaborate on the event in unprecedented detail, it takes on the possibilities of more formal representation. To be conscious of an event is itself to begin to represent it. The forerunner of this mutually transformative quality is to be found in Cohen's own two-dimensional view of power relations and symbolism: power informs symbols, but the process of symbolisation is never without new effect.

Repertory Cues and Constraints

The opening chapter in this volume is by F.G. Bailey, himself a product of the Manchester School and a scholar who has always focused on the way in which the small cultural performances of everyday life provide the outlines for the micro-politics on which all other politics are based. Bailey discusses the conundrum of the play within the play. Hamlet used a dramatisation of *The Mousetrap* to alarm and anger the King of Denmark by alluding to the latter's murder of Hamlet's father. Both Hamlet and the King know that it is only a play, just as we, the audience, know that *Hamlet* is also only a play. Plays, films, spiritualist performances, religious and seasonal festivals, or, as in Bailey's example from the Indian community of Bisipara, a prepared, almost ritualistic threat of entry by Untouchables into a clean caste temple, can frighten, anger and disturb spectators. Everyone knows the event is a pretence at, say, violence, yet it can still have an effect. For

Bailey, people's recognition that a play or drama is a pretence at something else, is evidence that they always distinguish a political reality from its dramatic representation. He goes further, and touches on the paradox of cultural performance: it is real in its effects but, because imagined, gives its creators and their audience a freedom of invention and interpretation that does not exist with regard to structured or positive reality. Politics and its representation are indeed both aspects of reality but, as we know if we carry our emotions from the theatre into everyday life as if there was no disjunction between them, they play on our consciousness in quite distinct ways.

Brecht understood this well enough to wish to make of theatre a forum for political and social argument and decision-making which could be carried out into the streets, and which would therefore necessitate cutting out all emotional engagement between actors and audience. The drama should be acted in a more matter-of-fact way, so that the disjunction between on- and off-stage is minimised. For Brecht emotional commitment on the part of either actor or audience deflects them from taking political decisions. Actors and audience should instead be involved in a mutual learning experience. The very fact that in bourgeois theatre it is emotional empathy which links the realities of the play and life off-stage, enables spectators to leave the problem back in the theatre: according to Brecht their emotionalisation of the social injustice depicted in the play obscures their reasoned judgement of it, and the fact that they themselves can, if they do so reason, attack comparable injustices in society itself (Brecht 1964; Fiebach 1986: 148–9, 290). We can argue that the Bisipara Untouchables described by Bailey in this volume were Brechtians, whose pragmatic and dramatically self-conscious threat to enter the clean caste temple did indeed oblige others around them to pay heed to what the Untouchables and other supporters of the new Gandhian Hindu morality had to say. It was a mutual learning experience *par excellence*.

Bailey emphasises that it was a feature of Bisiparans at the time to behave in such pragmatic ways. He concedes, however, that peoples do not always have this self-consciousness of pretence and so do not in all circumstances so easily separate imagined from positive reality. Certainly, the more common Western view, partly derived from the Aristotelian theory of catharsis or purging of the emotions through empathy or self-identification with actors, is that we may so merge what happens on-stage with what happens off-stage that the boundary between the two becomes fuzzy. Apologists for violent films and television may deny this, but it is difficult to resist the conclusion that many viewers imitate at least the life-styles that go with such performances, with live theatre curiously less subject to such mimesis, yet also capable of generating emotional identification between events in the play and outside.

Indeed, it seems unavoidable that dramatic effect will necessarily include emotional arousal. The question is how much and under what socio-cultural conditions. Here, Brecht himself was by no means consistent in his theatrical theories. He admitted that it was difficult to entirely eliminate emotion from that kind of theatre which he called epic and which, being unlocated in specific time, place or plot, could best serve as a learning play (*Lehrstück*) by appealing to the audience's reason more than their feelings.

We are left here with the question of whether the Aristotelian view of drama is but one cultural version, rooted in what we nowadays call the West, which privileges the role of emotions in performative activities, while in other societies, or in the same society at other times, a less emotionally charged and more pragmatic attitude is taken to dramatic and ritualised activities, such as appears to be the case in Bisipara.

If this is so, it raises a further question regarding the manner in which symbols, on which successful cultural performances so heavily depend, have their effect on participants' psyches. A symbol, after all, only exists as such to the extent that it is believed to more than simply represent an object or condition, but also to partake of that object or condition, and this can only be achieved through emotional identification with the symbol-object: a Westerner may appreciate Middle Eastern music but it does not necessarily evoke in him the intensity of emotions experienced by, say, people from the region who are currently obliged to live as exiles outside it. To appreciate a cultural performance is not to partake of it. The first is cognitive with minimal emotional empathy, while the second is sustained by a plethora of empathetic images and memories. It is this latter which creates the possibilities for that kind of mutual identification which we call a formal or informal political movement. Politics and political commitment are, after all, more than strategy, they are also passion.

For Abner Cohen there must be precipitating conditions which allow for this mutuality of symbolic and political identification:

the loss of legislative autonomy, a trading monopoly or land (see also Caplan 1970), or the development of discriminatory practices by the host society. At the same time, since nothing is made out of nothing, a particular society's cultural repertoire may provide ready-made templates for the symbolic complexes around which people may eventually rally.

Demonstrating this power of the cultural template, the account by Barnes contains one of the most significant hopes for the political future of Africa. It shows that, despite first colonial and then immediate post-colonial attempts to foster alien methods of political representation on peoples in western Africa, it is in the end an idea of ceremonially invested chiefship that persists and is now increasingly important. More than this, it is a form of chiefship that is neither co-terminous with government nor subservient to it, nor even simplistically to be regarded as exclusively a local-level political institution. Rather, the new chieftaincy that has emerged in, say, Nigeria draws on the reverence for titles bestowed on worthy dignitaries who are seen to have served their community honourably and materially. Chiefs may have abandoned profitable modern commercial or central government positions in order to apply for chieftaincies, seeking the prestige, influence and also local material advantage which goes with them. The Western-imposed assumption that men and women of ability and education will rise in a globally inscribed ladder of professionalism and wealth-accumulation has been reversed by this return to modernised traditional values in chiefs as local providers of community spirit and well-being, who are also able to mediate between the demands of central government and the people, and to transcend many of the ethnic and other boundaries artificially created during colonialism and after.

In many ways, these new forms of ceremonially titled chieftaincy constitute the civic society that many African states seek, in the sense that the chiefs provide an intermediary space between domestic groups and villages on the one hand and the force of central government on the other. Chiefs can interpret and convey government intentions but also allow for reflection on them, while at the same time representing local people's views to government more independently than if they were appointed by government or elected under government auspices. What is distinctive about this concept of civic society or space is that it is not the result of organised central government policy, nor presented by people as filling a gap in the hierarchy of a modern political machine. It arises from people's confidence in the efficacy of local-level rituals and personalised leadership.

The image of cultural template recurs in Watson's study of rural Hong Kong rites of renewal and their accompanying operas. Formerly the *jiao*, as these periodic rites are called, were associated with inter-lineage conflict, competition and violence. Nowadays, that competitive element remains but with regard, not to physical violence, but to operatic performances which have become even more lavish between communities. The dominant Teng lineage used to control satellite villagers through their monopoly of land, but the British colonial administrators gave ownership rights to tenants at the beginning of the twentieth century. The Teng have, however, retained hegemonic control by inducing the former tenant population to worship at the temple cult which the Teng administer, and which they have made especially powerful by placing the nationally important goddess, Tianhou, at its head.

As Watson puts it, it is through the enforcement of ritual ortho*praxy* rather than through ortho*doxy* that the Teng have remained influential, that is to say, by placing a ritualistic and symbolic premium on correct ritual practice more than on belief. The Teng *jiao* processions carry the representation of the goddess, Tianhou, and so reinforce the encapsulation within their temple sphere of the non-Teng villagers, who are therefore never able to rise above the Teng to positions of political importance. The hegemonic persuasiveness of correct ritual practice has its parallel in the verbal power of correct oral narrative, as described by Collett in his discussion of the fables of the Anaguta of Nigeria, or of skilful rhetoric, as is evident in Pnina Werbner's study of British Muslim Pakistanis. Pakistani leaders here do not reach out to each other through any bounded localisation of activities, such as occurs among the people of Hong Kong Ha Tsuen district described by Watson, or the Hausa of Ibadan studied by Cohen. These British Pakistanis make appeals rather to three domains of sociality, the moral, political and aesthetic, which travel verbally, so to speak, along the many scattered interpersonal lines of the Pakistani diaspora.

Werbner recognises that Cohen's theoretical approach to ethnicity rests a great deal on the idea of groups articulating their distinctiveness through a sense of overall boundedness, with the territorial, religious, moral and politico-economic tending to reinforce each other. Such groups might well be linked to each other in the nature of a wide-flung diaspora (a term which Cohen himself used long before it became fashionable), but the primary units of such a diaspora were irreducibly made up of close-knit and territorially distinctive, highly solidary communities. Much like Parkin's distinction between congregational and interpersonal ideologies (1974), however, Werbner wishes to emphasise a difference between this isomorphic, group-like boundedness of the communities studied by Cohen and the open-ended, multi-stranded, occupationally diverse and internally conflicting diasporas characteristic of British and indeed overseas South Asians generally. For such interpersonally linked diasporas, more is needed to create distinctiveness than the visible symbols of common prayer, locale, dress and residential assembly. Rather, it is necessary to evoke loyalty to what Watson would call orthodoxy, a common adherence to what are regarded as proper moral, aesthetic and political beliefs, more than visible practice.

The contributions by Watson and Werbner are thus interesting inversions of each other in their stress upon correct practice and correct belief respectively. The difference in orientation makes sense in the light of the contrasting conditions under which the two peoples operate. The Teng people of Hong Kong are necessarily limited in the elaboration of their cultural repertoire by the fact that they live in a restricted territory under colonial regulations and an openly consumerist and capitalist economy. For them, the most obvious means of communicating relative status is through lavish visible display. However, once they again become part of China in 1997, and despite the People's Republic of China's venture into its own brand of consumerism, they may not find the device of lavish and visible boundedness as useful as before and may need to draw on cultural templates other than *jiao* processions and operas if they are to secure interests beyond Hong Kong and into the mainland, much as the Man people had earlier articulated chain-relationships based on appeal to lineage membership in moving from Hong Kong and into restaurant-owning throughout Britain (Watson 1975). By contrast, British Pakistanis are so diverse, and moreover are linked through cross-cutting interests to other Pakistanis throughout the world and to other non-Pakistani Muslims, that collective visibility as the basis of communal solidarity and expression is an inadequate means of establishing extensive communication and interests. Much more generalised symbols, often cast in abstract form, must be used, as reformist Muslims are discovering in many parts of the world.

New information technology has made rapid and changing interpersonal communication possible over more extensive areas, to an extent that could never have been achieved through the visible Tijaniya assemblies gathered in individual mosques characteristic of the Hausa diaspora of the early 1960s (Cohen 1969).

Werbner's insistence on interpersonal and rhetorically invoked diaspora rather than visibly bounded group as nowadays the most appropriate unit for the analysis of social movements, whether ethnic, nationalistic or religious, is echoed in a number of chapters in this volume. Her insistence parallels the wider intellectual concern with the globalisation of communication and of the production and exchange of commodities, which may themselves become communicative symbols denoting alternative lifestyles and possible existences (the latter, in fact, being for most poor people in the world quite inaccessible).

Amadiume, for example, shows the shift in Nigeria from the ritual autonomy and relative cultural homogeneity traditionally enjoyed by many women's organisations, based in a core reverence for motherhood, to the multiplicity of factors needed by Nigerian elite women for organising themselves into associations. Although they are members of such associations, it is as individuals that these women 'manoeuvre through different cultures, using a multiplicity of symbolic forms and identities rather than being gelled by means of a common culture as in the case of diaspora Hausa communities or the Creoles of Sierra Leone' (*infra*: 45).

Otite also stresses the reality of an Africa in which many and in some countries, most, people are on the move, not always from one settled community to another, but from one labour-supplying area to another, characteristically rural-to-rural migration. His study of Urhobo in Nigeria raises questions about the normative weight placed by earlier anthropologists on settlement as against migration, for it is now surely more and more the case that, as a result of labour shortages, as discussed by Otite, and of famines, wars, floods, desertification and pestilence, the norm in Africa is tending towards rapid movement between areas rather than settlement in one locality. Yet, as Otite's work also shows, immigrants into Urhobo still marry among themselves for the most part. We have long been familiar with the norm among nomadic pastoralists to marry among themselves, but the new crisis-driven population movements characteristic of Africa and elsewhere are not usually within transhumance patterns or set landscapes as among pastoralists, but are often of unpredictable direction. Intra-marriage under such circumstances may be no more than what is possible, but, as a ready-made set of customary practices, another example of cultural repertoire, it may take on considerable symbolic power in communicating ethnic separateness which may not always be regarded positively by others.

Rational Actors

This issue of negative symbolism, or the adverse effects of set cultural performances, takes us to the heart of many examples of ethnic and other prejudices, and of inter-ethnic conflict. On the whole, Cohen's work has focused on the beneficial effects of cultural mobilisation. In addition, it is presumably true that no people would knowingly and willingly incur the disapproval of others without what it regards as good reason, an undeniable premise of human rationality. But, people are not always aware of the long-term implications of their actions, nor, as Cohen constantly emphasises, do they normally sit down and rationally calculate in advance the value to themselves of this or that form of cultural and political distinctiveness. For any one individual such separateness is something that happens and is not planned, and, until and if collective enthusiasm takes over, is regarded ambivalently, as it may also be by outsiders.

Let us take, for instance, the case of the Bantu Botatwe of Zambia, discussed by Colson. Is this a case of a newly formed cultural grouping seeking to establish and advance its interests, or is their emergence in fact yet another contribution to the problems of proliferating ethnicity that bedevil African states no less than others in the contemporary world?

'Bantu Botatwe' is a term first coined by a Jesuit priest in about 1920 to refer to the linguistic similarities of such numerous peoples as the Tonga, Ila, Totela, Subiya, Lenje, Soli and Sala, spread out over three different provinces of Zambia. By the 1990s the term has come to denote a powerful political grouping which sees itself as having to compete with other dominant ethnic groups. This process of ethnogenesis may eventually confer unitary political consciousness on a people but may first pass through phases which are non-political but which invent and celebrate a common past as well as linguistic similarity. The Bantu Botatwe did not traditionally have kings (though the Soli and Lenje had great chiefs) as did the rival Lozi or Barotse, Bemba, Ngoni and Lunda, whose major centralising ceremonies have become accentuated in recent years. It is contrary to the Bantu Botatwe egalitarian ethos to build major rituals or ceremonial around individual persons, and to have invented and celebrated kingship would not have had the positive effects that it carried among the more traditionally hierarchical societies of Zambia. Small wonder that, instead, the Bantu Botatwe created in 1967 a special egalitarian cultural association to carry forward their newly articulated sense of common identity and political purpose.

As discussed in the previous section, we note here again the performative constraints and limits, as well as encouragement, placed by a pre-existing cultural repertoire on a people's attempt to represent and advance themselves. As a result, we can see already a kind of polarisation in modes of representation in Zambia between those super-ethnic polities which celebrate hierarchy and those which abhor it. We have to wonder at the long-term possibilities of their future collaboration in a single so-called nation state (in which there have been attempts, as elsewhere, to create an overall Zambian cultural and national consciousness).

It is ironic that, while anthropologists have wished to remove the essentialism and exaggerated mutual boundedness implied by such terms as tribe and culture, the members and bearers of these same groups and concepts have themselves emphasised such qualities as being at the basis of their own beliefs and practices. At one level, then, people appeal to an alleged past cultural repertoire which constrains their use of modes of cultural expression. On another level, perhaps that of the observer more than the participant, there is also a current propensity to invent culture. Does the evident cultural dynamism that is witnessed throughout the world in media-reported performances as well as in political competition result, then, from this tension between the invented and the inherited and from the choices that have to be made between them? How is a people to know which cultural idiom to avoid and which to privilege or establish?

In this context it is salutary to look to Gulliver's ideas on various forms of socio-cultural avoidance. He distinguishes between the avoidance of disputes, where a precipitating quarrel has already broken out, and the avoidance of conflict itself, or of situations likely to produce conflict and disputes. The former tolerates the likelihood of disputes happening but will not allow them to continue, managing their resolution through established moots, as among the Arusha of Tanzania, or through morally reciprocal interpersonal relationships, as among the Ndendeuli of the same country. Conflict avoidance is more an explicit cultural style, as among hunters and gatherers or in American suburbia, and is even more cautious. It aims to quash even the possibility of a dispute breaking out. Of course, these are both aspects of all behaviour, but, as Gulliver points out, can each characterise the ethos of a society.

It would be intriguing to know what effect these different cultural sensitivities concerning conflict and its resolution have on the expression of ethnicity within states. Can there be a cultural distinction between ethnic-tolerant and ethnic-intolerant polities? Or are material stakes and interests so fundamental to the expression of ethnic distinctiveness that these in the end determine the degree of inter-ethnic ferocity? It is, in any event, clear how rapidly a situation may appear to be transformed in this respect. How could civilised German society of the 1920s have fallen into the anti-Semitic barbarism of the 1930s? How can British society of the 1990s tolerate more beggars and homeless on the streets of its capital than at any time in the previous fifty years and yet witness its Prime Minister expressing not sympathy nor a plan of action to help them, but instead criticism and contempt? Before the fall of Communism, who would have imagined the renewal of balkanisation and mutual persecution as likely to occur again in ex-Yugoslavia? The examples abound and point to the unpredictable conditions and consequences of such different kinds of socio-political distinctiveness, which are not always strategies of communal defence or advancement, but are sometimes imposed and result in involuntary ghettos.

The concept of strategy presupposes choice, although the concept of choice is not central to Cohen's analyses. His use of strategy is neo-Durkheimian rather than of the rationalistic Weberian kind. It rests on collective understanding of their predicament, or of their opportunity, that induces members of a polity to seek specific means to attain desired ends. An acceptable cultural idiom, backed up by the appropriate forms of performance and belief, becomes the means, and political and economic security the goal. There is, therefore, an underlying rationality in the long-term consequences of a polity's socio-cultural activities. But can a community make mistakes by choosing the wrong cultural idiom, the one that simply does not fit a wider environment of, so to speak, cultural spectators? Can it thereby cast itself into oblivion, having, by its mistake, acted irrationally?

Take the case of the Hausa blacksmiths in Kano, Nigeria, described by Jaggar. Many other blacksmith communities in Africa suffer low status, or are at least regarded as having a ritually and socially ambivalent position. But those of Kano appear to have surmounted negative cultural stereotypes. They are held in high regard and suffer none of the opprobrium commonly directed at members of their caste elsewhere. They straddle well the potentially divisive effects of Islamic and non-Islamic practices in this predominantly Muslim society and manage well the powerful and potentially incriminating, because dangerous, symbolism of fire and its uses. The smiths' weddings accentuate, in fact, their separateness from other Hausa groupings, giving an impression of supreme confidence and even of therapeutic and other ritual power.

How have the Hausa blacksmiths achieved this? Is the line between remaining respected and losing that respect a thin one? The question points, again, to the issue of what are the conditions under which these blacksmiths might commit the cultural mistake that leads to their social downfall. Jaggar notes the common recognition of blacksmiths as masters of fire, often associated with shamanism elsewhere in the world, and in this respect anathema to certain Hausa Muslims, who deplore the blacksmiths' frenzied fire-handling feats carried out to chant, dance and trance. Such Muslims regard the performances as trickery as well as paganistic. However, metalworking is incorporated in the famous Hausa pre-Islamic *bori* cults. Muslim clerics may condemn these cults, as Pittin notes in her chapter, but almost everyone turns to them, just as everyone needs the medicines and iron-working of the smiths. Mystical awe and admiration for one activity reinforces that for the other.

Discussion of the place of performance in Islam brings together a number of issues emanating from the distinction made earlier between orthodoxy and orthopraxy, or between correct belief and ideology on the one hand, and correct practice on the other. Islam has no more intrinsic purchase on stressing correct belief and practice than any other world religion. However, the current historical circumstances in which Islam finds itself, and the way in which it is portrayed by Western media, have imposed an apparent distinctiveness. Islam is essentialised, despite the many obvious internal sectarian and theological differences, yet is resistant to any but the most general descriptions. It might be argued that there are many Islams, each shaped in its details by local cultural circumstances and yet circumscribed by overarching premises rooted in the Koran and other religious texts. Even so, this definition no more than raises questions as to what are the different local conditions and what are the wider sectarian and school differences that make certain kinds of performance and belief acceptable. What is universal about Islam, and what is particular or local, and how are these resolved and their resolution communicated? It is clear from discussion of the cases presented that such questions cannot be answered in terms of the success or failure of conscious strategies undertaken by peoples, despite the fact that, for Islamic fundamentalists, it is precisely religiously correct and therefore rational practice and belief that ensure survival and advancement. Alongside the alleged logic of correct performance run the unintended effects of inspiration.

Experiencing Inspiration

McIntyre's and Fisher's papers are both concerned with the conditions under which legitimacy may be conferred on individuals seeking Islamic grace, knowledge or power. Both are also accounts of individuals' experience as they journey, so to speak, in time or place to their desired goals. McIntyre introduces the concept of idiolect to refer to the personalised culture of a Hausa malam (Koranic teacher) as it is shaped in conformity with overarching Islamic expectations. The malam's life history is a tale of successive performative achievements: as a boy learning some parts of the Koran by heart, moving after seven years to settle in another Hausa place of religious learning on recognition of his capacity to train to become a malam, completing his first full reading of the Koran, moving to yet other places of learning and eventually writing the text of the Koran twice from memory, building up his own circle of students and, finally, having a wealthy contractor build him his own mosque, an indication that he was now fully a malam and could marry. It is only through the personalised account that we are able to appreciate that this quest for Islamic legitimacy is highly competitive and subject to the demanding assessments of senior clerics. It is not enough for the novice to be pious, God-fearing and well-intentioned. The cultural performances involve physical and educational tests and hardships, and chronicle the play of power relations in the Islamic hierarchy. Knowing the texts satisfactorily is to have mastered a key performative element in being a malam. Orthodoxy and orthopraxy are here part of each other.

The same sense of the cultural and religious journey as struggle is evident in Fisher's description of the pilgrimage to Mecca of the Askiya Muhammed of Timbuktu, in the Songhay empire of West Africa, towards the end of the fifteenth century. The Askiya has to be recorded as having made this pilgrimage, despite many obstacles, in order to secure his position against the ruling dynasty he has overthrown.

However, despite the ostensibly rule-governed nature of such religious journeying, it is during his travels that the Askiya has numerous, unexpected dramatic encounters. Although unanticipated, they help legitimate the stories of his installation as West Africa's leading Islamic authority and thence, through some early nineteenth-century rendering, of the Muslim theocracy of Masina. Using the transitional and transcendental notion of liminality, which effects movement from one state to another (e.g., from secular king to Muslim caliph), Fisher also shows how the different encounters act like ceremonial masks. They may hide certain aspects of unpalatable reality (such as one story claiming that the usurper, the Askiya, had in fact killed the previous king), but reveal and so legitimate certain features of the new caliphate. Given the inevitably contradictory nature of the historical accounts of the pilgrimage, it is not surprising that they are punctuated by various dramatic encounters, such as meeting *jinn* in the Egyptian desert, a Cairo caliph, a Mecca sharif, and killing a servant who had turned into a snake. Narration, like history, can, then, be performative. Through its dramatic effects, it may confer position and power in the guise of being a disinterested tradition handed down over the generations, while in reality constantly being revived over time as competing narrators try to inscribe their own interests.

The Askiya's struggle for Islamic legitimacy is here on a manifestly political level, for his very rule depends on such religious inspiration and recognition and is a universal feature of all such theocracy. The question of whether the spirit *bori* cult can be tolerated in Islam, as discussed in detail by Pittin and referred to by Jaggar and Spencer, seems at first sight to be a local rather than universal problem of legitimacy, peculiar to the Hausa. But, if we note the central role played by *jinn* in the Askiya's journey described by Fisher, and by *jinn* and other spirits in accounts of Islam from elsewhere in the world, we realise that the *bori* cult is one of a number of manifestations of pre-Islamic polytheism, of *shirk* as it is known in Arabic, against which Islamic theodicy has struggled since its inception.

I would argue that this struggle against the worship of many gods remains a principal means by which modern Islam defines itself, extending into the various forms of Islamic fundamentalism. In other words, while McIntyre and Fisher stress pilgrimage and learning as unambiguously positive means by which Islam is embraced, we must recognise too that the various ritual performances and beliefs surrounding spirit worship also provide a basis against which 'proper' Islam may be defined, despite often being regarded negatively by senior clerics. For, while clerics control the interpretation of Islamic texts, non-human spirits threaten always to inspire worshippers with alternative ideas. Similarly, as Pittin notes, Koranic medicine achieves some of its reputation by being distinguished from *bori* medicine, which, while condemned as non-Islamic by some clerics, is nevertheless a viable therapeutic alternative both to the Koran and western medicine.

The caulking of past ideas onto present practices often reproduces the gender distinctions on which they may partly be based. Amadiume argues for the reinstatement of ancient ideas of matriarchy and motherhood in legitimating and giving power to modern Nigerian elite women's groups and what she calls the cult of the First Lady. Pittin discusses the local distinction made between public and and private *bori*, the former being sexually mixed and the latter consisting only of women. On the one hand, the *bori* institution as a whole is at times presented as being outside and opposed to Islam and is overall more associated with women than men. To this extent *bori* reverses the lesser role of women in the formal organisation of Islam. On the other hand, the distinction between mixed public and female private cults partly reproduces and reinforces the tendency within Islam for public mosque and religious displays to be dominated by men and for women to control domestic events. This metaphorical capacity of cultural performance to say things sideways, so to speak, highlights again the infinite symbolic malleability of religious beliefs and practices. Their reduction to propositional argument would eliminate not only their creative ambivalence but also make it impossible to believe in them as unquestionable tenets of existence, a point often made by Cohen.

We return here to another dimension of the problem of

rationality. Earlier, I noted Cohen's insistence that the symbolic is not rationally calculated by its exponents in advance of its effects, but that it is expressed in socially bestowed collective enthusiasm. This is not to say that the consequences of ceremonial or symbolic activity are necessarily inconsistent with social needs, but that there is a drive towards social and symbolic congruence, a neo-Durkheimian view taken by Douglas (1970) as well as Cohen, and illustrated by Collett's study of Anaguta fables which both interpret the people's symbolic universe and make it consonant with the everyday negotiation of power relations.

A rationalist, transactionalist approach to social interaction would regard this neo-Durkheimian claim as depending too much on a reified idea of society as having a determining force over and above the individual dispositions of its members. In fact neither the neo-Durkheimians nor their critics have proven their cases. We still know far too little about what happens in the gap between individual consciousness, inspiration, intention and the actions of groups. Individual tendencies may catch on in a larger population (the inspirational, emergent properties of social interaction), but it may also be true that pre-existing ideas and practices provide a ready mould, a cultural template as we called it, which shapes the performance of new activities. From observation, either seems possible.

Is it then unhelpful to distinguish here between rationally planned actions and fortuitous or non-rational, unplanned consequences and experiences? Propositional argument is certainly a property of human speech. A speaker plans what s/he wants to say and so reduces ambiguity as best s/he can. Ritual performers may not know quite what it is, if anything, that they wish to say, yet spectators can certainly infer messages from their performances. This is the proposition after the event rather than as part of it, as in speech, and to that extent is an imposed rationality. By this token all standardised, customary or ritualised behaviour can be judged rational *post hoc*, which is presumably why anthropologists as much as actors wish to see reason in cultural performances. Are, then, some kinds of cultural performance more given to the promulgation of reason than others? This seems at first unlikely, and would seem to depend on which performative media are most valued in a society: London privileges film and theatre, the Bisipara Untouchables prefer threats of temple entry, and so on.

Nevertheless, Spencer suggests that the universal capacity of dance to bridge inner feelings and social consciousness makes it distinct from other kinds of performance. He thus challenges our anthropological neglect of the socio-psychic aspects of dance. In particular, he argues that the experientially transcendental quality of dance may foster confidence in dancers both as individuals and as members of a group of a kind that could not be obtained by other more direct means of communication, and that this quality can be culturally recognised as legitimating social changes. He takes, among others, the case of the *lebarta* dance which Samburu young boys dance with increasing confidence as they get older, eventually reaching a point when they feel ready to challenge and usurp the older *moran* warriors' privileged position. This comes across as culturally a most rational form of legitimation, depending not on simple belief in the boys' capacity but on their performed demonstration of it. No spiritual claims are invoked to justify their new position. It is enough that they have shown to themselves and the society of spectators that they are the performative stuff of which warriors are made. Indeed, the absence of any evidently spiritual dimension reminds one of Marrett's claim that early religion is not believed but danced. Spencer also compares the Hausa *bori* cult's capacity through dance to inspire confidence in locally competing markets: if a market town is known to have excellent *bori* cult dances, then more people come to trade there. The religio-aesthetic here shapes the economic.

Masquerade dancing, which is a feature of Cohen's study of the London Notting Hill Carnival, is more propositionally explicit than the kinds of unmasked dances described for the Samburu and Hausa *bori* cult. For non-masquerade dancers, their bodies are their sole resource and yet also the means by which they unburden themselves of them. As Blacking has put it (1985: 72), they are danced as much as dancing. But masquerade dancing presupposes an elaborate structure of preparation, ranging from the actual design and manufacture of masks to planning when, how and by whom they should be worn. Anigbo ties in his description of Igbo masquerade dancing to the initiation of youths into the secrets of the *Omabe* festival, by which they learn the essentials of lineage differentiation and identity. The mask is a constant reminder to the dancer and spectators of social and cosmological responsibilities. S/he may hide as an individual behind the mask, but is unlikely to be able to vanish, to speak, in the space between self-abandonment and social awareness. For Anigbo, the huge Igbo ceremonial feasts and the great stress placed on reciprocal commensality give a rigorous social casting to ritual life. Far from constituting communal liminality, it provides an arena for leadership and chiefly struggles and so reinforces the obligations of political hierarchy. The Igbo seem rather like the people of Bisipara in their somewhat pragmatic attitude to ceremonial. Pragmatists are not, in Ardener's words (1989: 211–23), event-rich and are typically people who are aware of their close involvement in the flat and unceremonial humdrum of the world order and as not having, or no longer having, markedly distinctive cultural features. By contrast, those peoples who see themselves as remote from what we might nowadays call the homogenising effects of global culture, may regard themselves as rich in their own events which are marked by distinctive cultural ceremonial. These are notional nationalisms and yet inform, and are informed by, world media opinion on topics ranging from politics and finance to tourism.

Conclusion

As the contributors to this book show, ceremonial, ritual, symbolic, dramatic and other cultural performances sometimes convey the threat of external contingencies (and perhaps help in the making of plans to deal with them) or obscure such immediacy and engage in fantasy that makes for expressive ambivalence and elasticity. At times drama and ceremony clarify but sometimes mystify, yet are always enmeshed in a play of power. We are constantly having to make political decisions, even when we seek to avoid them, phrasing them instead in non-political terms, surely a Brechtian premise of human action. In Cohen's terms, there can thus be no political action which is not also in some way symbolic of other concerns. Symbolic interpretation is however, always contestable: consensus is rare or unlikely to last. As well as creating uncertainty, it is this symbolic contestability which makes political plans subject to so much reinterpretation and so unlikely to be fulfilled. Yet, alongside the recurrent disagreements as to what icons, plans and actions mean, cultural repertoires or templates are often invoked as final arbiters. Analytically this sounds like earlier theories of homeostasis or functionalist equilibrium, and it may well be that the repetitive patterns are more in the minds of anthropologists than real. On the other hand it is the peoples themselves studied by anthropologists who claim to respond to the extraordinary power of allegedly ancient as well as recent ideas and practices in, say, overturning attempts at political reform or government or re-shaping a community's interests and identity.

The rapidity of communication and influence from the producers of mass capitalism and popular consumerism throughout the world is said by some to threaten these older cultural outlines. Analysts may be falsely essentialising and reifying cultures in claiming to see cases of local cultures resisting or, conversely, embracing the newly global consumer capitalism and its baseball-cap, Coca-Cola values. But, while sharp cultural boundaries are indeed commonly over-drawn by outside observers, they may nevertheless be used by peoples themselves to justify collective actions and claims of common identity.

Anthropologists have the privilege of comparing such claims over time and with other places, and it is this comparative historical perspective that enables them to re-cast ethnicity as, say, the dramatic elaboration of momentary events into historical movements, or as the creation of predictable behavioural tendencies out of previously unpredictable and cross-cutting ones. They do not have to start at all with a concept of boundary.

It is the greatest legacy of Abner Cohen's work on ethnic and other groups that we are able to rethink the concepts of politics, culture and symbolism, which have been so central to his studies and to anthropology generally. It is interesting to note, for instance, that these terms are at present rarely highlighted analytically in socio-cultural anthropology. Politics has become part of a concern with the differential flow of power and human agency and capacity (Arens and Karp 1989); culture has been reconstituted as different forms of knowledge or of human knowledge in its diversity (Fardon 1995); and symbolism has become subsumed in the problem of representation and its alleged crisis in the social sciences and humanities (James, forthcoming).

Cohen has, in his most recent work (1993), already anticipated some of this conceptual shift, focusing on the masquerade as both performative and transformative, as both expression and effect, as creating knowledge and as enabling or empowering. Why is the masquerade so significant? It continues the perennial question that will always confront anthropologists. The ceremonial mask may be odd, out-of-the-ordinary and worn only on special occasions. Yet, when placed in a wider context of struggle and achievement, it may tell us more about those who wear it and their sense of their interrelationships than a study rigorously focused on their everyday, regular activities. In the idiom, wearing and play of the mask lie the questions of human agency, knowledge, justification and representation that will always in some form engage anthropologists. Cohen has always reminded anthropologists to give primary attention not to the routine but to the apparently bizarre, the better to understand the unexpected mystery behind the routine.

References

Ardener, E. 1989. *The Voice of Prophecy.* M. Chapman (ed.). Oxford: Blackwell.

Arens, W. and I. Karp (eds). 1989. *The Creativity of Power: Cosmology and Action in African Societies.* Washington and London: Smithsonian.

Bailey, F.G. 1957. *Caste and the Economic Frontier.* Manchester: Manchester University Press.

Bauman, R. 1986. *Story, Performance and Event: Contextual Studies of Oral Narrative.* New York: Cambridge University Press.

Beeman, W.O. 1993. 'The Anthropology of Theater and Spectacle', *Annual Review of Anthropology* 22: 369–93.

Blacking, J. 1985. 'Movement, Dance, Music and the Venda Girls' Initiation Cycle', in *Society and the Dance*, P. Spencer (ed.). Cambridge: Cambridge University Press.

Brecht, B. 1964 (orig. variously earlier). *Schriften zum Theater.* Bd. V. Berlin/Weimar.

Brown, R. 1973. 'Anthropology and Colonial Rule: the Case of Godfrey Wilson and the Rhodes-Livingstone Institute, Northern Rhodesia', in *Anthropology and the Colonial Encounter*, Talal Asad (ed.). London: Ithaca Press.

Caplan, L. 1970. *Land and Social Change in East Nepal: A Study of Hindu-Tribal Relations.* London: Routledge and Kegan Paul.

Cohen, Abner. 1965. *Arab Border-Villages in Israel.* Manchester: Manchester University Press.

———. 1969. *Custom and Politics in Urban Africa.* London: Routledge and Kegan Paul, Berkeley and Los Angeles: University of California Press.

———. 1974. *Two-Dimensional Man.* London: Routledge and Kegan Paul, Berkeley and Los Angeles: University of California Press.

———. 1981. *The Politics of Elite Culture: Explorations in the Dramaturgy of Power in a Modern African Society.* Berkeley: University of California Press.

———. 1993. *Masquerade Politics: Explorations in the Structure of Urban Cultural Movements.* Berkeley and Los Angeles: University of California Press.

Douglas, M. 1970. *Natural Symbols*. London: Barrie and Rockcliff.

Epstein, A.L. 1958. *Politics in an Urban African Community*. Manchester: University Press.

────── (ed.). 1967. *The Craft of Social Anthropology*. London: Tavistock.

────── . 1978. *Ethos and Identity: Three Studies in Ethnicity*. London: Tavistock, Chicago: Aldine.

Fardon, R. (ed.). 1995. *Counterworks: Managing Knowledge in its Diversity*. London: Routledge.

Fernandez, J. 1986. *Persuasions and Performances: the Play of Tropes in Culture*. Bloomington: Indiana University Press.

Fiebach, J. 1986. *Die Toten als die Macht der Lebenden: zur Theorie und Geschichte von Theater in Afrika*. Berlin (DDR): Henschel Verlag.

Gluckman, M. 1958 (orig. 1940). 'Analysis of a Social Situation in Modern Zululand', *Rhodes-Livingstone Papers* No. 28. Manchester: Manchester University Press.

Hymes, D. 1975. 'Breakthrough into Performance', in *Folklore: Performance and Communication*, D. Ben-Amos and K. Goldstein (eds). The Hague: Mouton.

James, A. (ed.). Forthcoming. *Representation and Anthropology*. Papers drawn from the ASA conference of the same title. Hull: Hull University.

Kapferer, B. 1981. *A Celebration of Demons*. Bloomington: Indiana University Press.

Kratz, C.A. 1994. *Affecting Performance: Meaning, Movement and Experience in Okiek Women's Initiation*. Washington and London: Smithsonian.

Mitchell, J.C. 1956. 'The Kalela Dance', *Rhodes-Livingstone Papers* No. 27. Manchester: Manchester University Press.

Parkin, D. 1974. 'Congregational and Interpersonal Ideologies in Political Ethnicity', in *Urban Ethnicity*, Abner Cohen (ed.). ASA Monograph 12, London: Tavistock.

Schechner, R. 1993. *The Future of Ritual: Writings on Culture and Performance*. New York: Routledge.

Taussig, M.T. 1980. *The Devil and Commodity Fetishism in South America*. Chapel Hill: University of North Carolina Press.

Turner, V.W. 1957. *Schism and Continuity in an African Society*. Manchester: Manchester University Press.

────── . 1974. *Dramas, Fields and Metaphors*. Ithaca, N.Y.: Cornell University Press.

────── . 1982. *Celebration: Studies in Festivity and Ritual*. Washington: Smithsonian.

———. 1986. *The Anthropology of Performance*. New York: Performing Arts Journal Publication.

Van Velsen, J. 1964. *The Politics of Kinship*. Manchester: Manchester University Press.

Watson, W. 1975. *Emigration and the Chinese Lineage*. Berkeley and London: University of California Press.

CHAPTER 1

Cultural Performance, Authenticity, and Second Nature

F. G. Bailey *

> '... various cultural forms differ in their potentialities for political articulation.'
> Abner Cohen, *Masquerade Politics*

Cultural Performance

Models, which are also known as conceptual frameworks, disciplinary matrices, paradigms, problematics, regimes, discourses, epistemes, discursive formations, and other exotic signatures, are intellectual devices for making sense of our experience in the world. They are used to explain what happened, after the event, or, a bolder claim, to predict what will happen. Where human conduct is concerned, metamodels are constructed to access the models people use to construe their world, and to describe how they put that understanding to use. In everyday terms, metamodels make sense of the notions (articulated or taken-for-granted) that people have in their minds (conscious or unconscious) to make them behave the way they do. My intention in this chapter is to treat *cultural performance* (or social drama, or ritual statement, or theatre, or narrative, or text – overlapping but not identical concepts) as one such metamodel and to ascertain the limits of its usefulness.

---

* I am indebted, for their comments, to Roy D'Andrade, Joe Masco, Michael Meeker, and Erica Prussing.

The noun *performance* carries with it a notion of publicity, something exhibited, something that is staged.[1] From a cultural performance, the model assumes, one can read off significant features of the values and beliefs of the performers. Indeed one can; but all models are limited in their applicability, because they must start from simplifying (unreal) assumptions about a more complicated (real) world. I will consider two limitations to the understanding that can be gained from a cultural performance metamodel, when the performance is staged in a political context. First, in that context, a performance is likely to generate a plurality of meanings that make interpretation difficult. Second, to read a culture from the symbols of a cultural performance may be to overlook another part of that culture, which, *for its bearers*, is its 'real' or 'authentic' part.[2] This part is manifested in actions and utterances but not in staged performances.

The Mousetrap, Shakespeare's play within a play, will set the scene, and provide a background against which to ask what assumptions are built into the cultural-performance framework. Hamlet intended *The Mousetrap* to 'catch the conscience of the King.' The play within a play was a weapon designed to impose on the King, and the Queen, and the royal court of Denmark, a definition of the situation off-stage. The definition, once accepted, would create appropriate attitudes and instigate appropriate action. In short, a cultural performance, when linked to politics, is intended to effect a course of events that are not themselves part of the performance. In *Hamlet*'s case, the situation off-stage was the death of Hamlet's father, to be redefined as murder.

The play did more than that; events ran wild. The King, 'marvellous distempered' by *The Mousetrap*, planned Hamlet's downfall; 'I like him not, nor stands it safe with us/ To let his madness range.' Actions, set in motion by the players, unfolded in overkill: death for Polonius, Ophelia, the Queen, the King, Laertes, and Hamlet himself. These several deaths, from the perspective of *The Mousetrap*, happened in the real world off-stage.

In this there is a paradox. The reality, off-stage, was the murder of Hamlet's father, but to make that reality known Hamlet used a

---

1 Where the line is drawn between staged and not-staged, public and private, can only be a matter of judgement in particular cases.

2 The phrase *for its bearers* indicates that I will not address the issue of 'objective truth'.

form that by definition is not real, a play. A play, therefore, is used to *make belief*. How can this be done? What features make a play persuasive? A play – what occurs in a theatre – is a form of *playing*: activity that is not real, not serious, not work. The two main senses of the word – a dramatic performance and playing a game – flow into one another. A play is not real, first, because it is always a *simplification* of reality. People presented in a performance are not particular individuals but roles, parts to be played, ultimately stereotypes. They instantiate a pattern. The same is true of dramatic situations. The dilemmas and the contradictions of the human condition are standardised, stripped clean of the 'irrelevant' attachments that would adhere to them in actual life, made comprehensible and persuasive by abstraction. This same analytical procedure must be used to make anything intelligible: it sets an item free from its encumbrances, placing what hitherto was unknown into a category and thus renders it knowable. It makes the shifting world stand still long enough to be understood.

However, more than cognition is involved. Theatrical performances, like any rhetoric, arouse affect by selecting features with an eye to asserting eternal verities, truths that are simple, uncontested, and permanent. These truths are presented without qualification or expression of doubt. 'God is good!' is persuasive: 'God is good, probably, most of the time, I think, if I could be sure what I meant by God', is rendered less persuasive by qualifications, especially by the conditional clause. The first expression is an assertion; the second is a proposition, anticipating contradiction. Plays make assertions. Performances assert a truth: something removed from the instability of time and the variation of particularity so as to make it authoritative.

The second kind of unreality is *make-belief*. A play has actors, who pretend to be what the audience knows they are not. The audience, if they are to accept the make-belief, must block the faculties they use elsewhere to distinguish *real* from *unreal*. The child at the Christmas pantomime who remarks that Peter Pan looks like a woman has not yet learned when to suspend the reality-principle. The signals that prompt an audience to forego reality-testing are called by Goffman (1970:9) and others 'framing'. Framing indicates that it would not be appropriate to react to what is going on, as if it were real. When Caesar falls murdered on the stage, something has gone wrong if the audience search the next day's newspapers for the obituary notice. On the other hand, when they hear Mark Anthony's threat – 'Woe to the hand that shed this costly blood!' – if all it suggests to them is the price of tomato ketchup, something else is wrong. They, the audience, are supposed to experience the emotion – fear, horror, pity, anger, exultation, whatever – that they would have done if the murder had been real. Plays seem to want it both ways; the audience should *know* that the situation is faked, but at the same time *feel* real emotion. Plays require a disconnection between reality and feeling.

Third, both play and plays include a component that contrasts them with *work*. For producers, authors, actors, scene-shifters, usherettes, critics, and other people who make their living out of it, a play or a movie is work, in the ordinary sense of that word. For the audience it is the very opposite of work: a visit to the theatre is 'play', that is, relaxation or entertainment. The state of mind that goes with play is not the state of mind that goes with work. Play commands *voluntary* assent; it stands apart from involuntary or purchased compliance; it is expected to be its own reward and becomes self-contradictory if grimly endured. Play, in a word, belongs with the 'consent' side of life, the side that is opposed to the calculation of utility and the use of force. In that respect it resembles morality.

Definitions of *play* produce a scatter-shot pattern, never a bull's-eye. One of my sources, an article in the Kupers' *Encyclopaedia*, having stated that the notion of play is impossible to define clearly, talks of an activity 'easily recognised in children or young domestic animals', and goes on to discuss 'motor patterns' in 'immature creatures' (1985: 601–2). These and other phrases suggest an absence of rationality, of calculation, a kind of mindlessness.

Stage performances likewise disconnect normal critical faculties. One is secluded from the real world, rationality is suspended, and emotions given free play. When a performance or a work of art enfolds a social commentary (not all do), a selected version of the real world is admitted into the frame and there subjected, so to speak, to emotional irradiation. Then the patients are released back into the real world, carrying with them an altered capacity for feeling about and acting upon that world. The message people get from a performance is not only informative, but also – primarily – attitude-shaping. They are told how the world is in order to make them feel about it and act in accordance with that feeling. The process in essence is brainwashing. This is the world of Turner's

Ndembu (1957) and their social dramas; performance creates a valued, but also imagined, reality.

The model of a cultural performance contemplates conduct that is profoundly *disintellectual*. As modeled, the performance is not, even when it purports to be (more on that later), an invitation to be rational, to doubt and to ask questions even-handedly. It is an enticement directly to feeling, to unquestioning belief; an implantation of values, and in that respect it is a form of diseducation. It is designed first and foremost to make people not-think, not-question, not-calculate, only to feel and ultimately to act on the 'truth' that has been presented to them. What, then, is modeled as the source of this power to inhibit normal rationality?

The effect comes from its form. The myriad rhetorical devices that are available gain their potency ultimately from patterning. A play, a speech, a military parade – any work of art that succeeds in being emotive – must be coherent; its parts must fit together, so that the viewer or reader has a sense of completeness, of perfection. There must be a perceptible internal logic between the parts (even a logic of disarray, as in carnival or in the metaphysical anguish conveyed in the theatre of the absurd); digression and irrelevancy are qualities that distract attention, confuse meanings, and so diminish the work's authority. In short, it is the constructed and contrived quality of a performance that allows it to be persuasive; and if it is not persuasive, a performance will not have an impact off-stage.

However, the venture off-stage into a political arena vastly complicates the situation, because the arena's circumstances are, at least in part, externally given; they are beyond the artist's control, they cannot be entirely contrived, selected by the playwright to conform with the canons of artistic unity. On the contrary, they inevitably activate a multivocality that makes the unity, on which persuasiveness depends, difficult to attain. Multivocality also hampers an interpreter's attempts to read back from the performances to the culture. To show the disruptive effect of entry into the political arena I will present a second narrative, more complex than Shakespeare's play within the play.

Multivocality

Some time after 1949, when the Orissa legislature passed a Temple Entry Act, making it illegal to deny Untouchables access to sacred places, there was a disturbance at the Shiva temple in Bisipara.[3] This happened before 1952, when I first went to the village. The occasion, I was told, was a major festival, probably the celebration of the deity's birthday, which takes place in November. It was the custom for households to bring offerings to the temple and to receive *prasad*, food dedicated to the deity and thereby made sacred. Clean caste people entered the temple's forechamber; Untouchables remained at the threshold. Bisipara's Panos, who are Untouchables, arrived all together, as happened every year, but on this occasion they demanded that the law be observed and they be allowed to enter the forechamber.

According to the tale told me, this confrontation occurred almost as theatre, in a manner that had become an approved political style in India. Advance notice was given to those likely to oppose the move. Just as Congress politicians, practising non-violence under Gandhi's inspiration, were careful to inform the authorities beforehand where they intended to stage their protest and court arrest, so also the Panos had let it be known that on this occasion they would demand entry into the Sibhomundiro. The Warrior response – they were Bisipara's dominant caste – was to mount a guard of men armed with battle-axes, the traditional weapon of the Kond hills, around the temple. The Panos though, had taken a further step; they had informed the authorities in the district headquarters, Phulbani (about eight miles away), of what they intended to do. The result was, late in the morning of the day of confrontation, the unhurried arrival in the village of a riot squad, which consisted of a sub-inspector of police, escorted by two constables, all three mounted on bicycles. If the authorities had felt a sense of urgency, it was evidently muted.

The Warrior guard stood down and the policemen were provided with refreshments (tea and *mudi* – a kind of popcorn made from rice) by the headman, a Warrior. Then the leading men of the village retired with the sub-inspector, who happened to be a Brahmin, to argue the case. They sat under a banyan tree, the Panos on one side of the officer and the clean castes on the other. I have only someone's remembered summary of what was said. The Panos argued they were legally entitled to go inside the temple. The Warriors did not directly dispute the law, but said that

---

[3] Bisipara, a village of about 700 inhabitants in 1952, lies in the state of Orissa in eastern India. It is described in Bailey (1957).

they were merely the trustees of the temple, not its owners, and while they themselves would stand down and permit the Panos to go inside, they could not in good conscience do so until the inspector had consulted all the other Hindus in the Kondmals, for, as everyone knew, the Sibhomundiro belonged not to Bisipara but to all the people of the Kondmals. They, the people of Bisipara, would surely abide by the verdict.

What the sub-inspector said to this I was not told; but I can guess. My guess is that he did not try to mediate, still less to risk arbitration and say who was right and who was wrong. He probably told the Panos that their proper course was to seek a remedy in the courts, if they thought their legal rights were being withheld. The Warriors could then, if they wished, counter-petition, arming themselves with evidence that they had made the necessary consultations and could speak for all the Hindus in the Kondmals. Then, as was a policeman's habit in places like Bisipara at that time, he would have told them all, Warriors and Panos alike, that the government (the *sircar*) was displeased and would not tolerate disorderly conduct, and if he heard more reports of bad behaviour he would station a couple of constables in the village and keep them there until the villagers learned not to cause trouble. The bite in that threat is the behaviour of constables billeted out in villages; they are extremely rapacious guests.

The sub-inspector and his escort cycled back to Phulbani that afternoon, having received gifts (rice, lentils, and a couple of chickens). There was no further trouble that year in Bisipara. The Panos staged no more confrontations. Instead they built a Shiva temple in their own street, under the leadership of Sindhu the schoolmaster, who himself conducted the worship there. It was a modest construction, mud walls and a thatched roof; but they did whitewash the walls, so that the building stood out from the khaki-drab houses that lined the street.

The clean castes punished their Panos by taking away their privilege of making music on festive occasions. All the time I lived in the village music was provided not by the Panos who made their protest at the Shiva temple, but by another group of Untouchables, also mostly Panos, but of a different origin. Thus, in this symbolic fashion, the clean castes signified that they no longer considered their original Panos a legitimate part of the Bisipara community. Economic links, however, in particular farm-labour (Panos working for Warrior landholders), continued unchanged.

These events can be modeled as cultural performances at two simple levels. The celebration of Shiva's birthday was an occasion for representing, in dramatic fashion, the caste hierarchy of Bisipara. Parties bringing offerings were always of one caste, coming as distinct groups, thus making a statement about caste separation. Caste hierarchy – not all its steps but a main division between clean castes and Untouchables – was marked by allowing clean castes to enter parts of the temple forbidden to untouchables. There were many other ritual occasions in Bisipara's year, both in sacred places and in everyday life, that symbolised this distribution of privilege.

The second level of performance symbolised resistance to hegemony. It was no less transparent. Panos demanded to enter the temple precinct and so signified the end of hegemony: they no longer accepted as natural and unquestionable their own inferiority in the context of sacred places.

Matters are already more complicated than in Shakespeare's drama. In Bisipara the play was contested, not off-stage by 'marvellous distempered' muttering and threats, but by mounting a counter-performance, using the stage, so to speak, to assert the adverse definition. It is as if the King, instead of sermonising about 'obstinate condolment' and 'unmanly grief', had hired the players to dramatise a natural death and its proper level of filial mourning. In other words, in Bisipara the cultural performance was a duality, two plays in contest, a debate, rather than the single definition of the situation that *The Mousetrap* imposes.

Debate is a familiar dramatic form. In many plays there are two or more points of view and the audience is led to choose between them. It should be noted however, in Bisipara there was neither an Ibsen nor a Bernard Shaw master-minding the debate, contriving dramatic unity and pointing to the ultimate truth. There were two different sets of performers, two authors, acting and reacting to each other. To the extent that they were disputing over a single issue, I suppose, a measure of artistic unity might have been forced upon them. It also is a truism that through encounters opponents find a common language. Even so, when one widens the perspective, there were other and more formidable obstacles in the way of dramatic unity.

If Bisipara people were not just playing but were putting on an act, it follows that they were calculating the effect of their performance on their lives off-stage. They were, in other words, adjusting the play (or plays) to what they saw to be the political context. What could have been involved in that context and their calculations?

The context certainly was complicated, even when one stays beside only one set of players. Consider the Panos. First, they did not have their act together, in the quite literal sense that they were not all agreed about the script they should use. That happened in part because the play was being put on simultaneously before different audiences, each with different expectations, and Panos had no consensus about the relative importance of those audiences. The main candidates for persuasion were: (i) Panos themselves (because they had incompatible agendas); (ii) Warriors and other clean castes (there were also differences among them, here disregarded); (iii) local officials; and (iv) politicians.

This however, is too simple, because the four audiences were not distinct. Membership cross-cut. For example, two Panos had been candidates for the legislature, and therefore belonged both in category (i) and category (iv). The Warrior headman was also, *ex officio*, a low-level bureaucrat and therefore fell into both category (ii) and category (iii). There were other cross-affiliations as well, all making it difficult to pin down the appropriate mode of persuasion.

Further complications existed because the audiences were active players in the performance, writing their own scripts according to their own running interpretations of the situation. Therefore, Pano designs had to respond appropriately to tactical responses both from other Panos and from the various non-Pano audiences. Furthermore, the different audiences were themselves directing cultural performances at each other: acting out, for example, the well-known antagonism between officials and elected politicians.

Let me unfold some alternative meanings that inhere in this pasticcio. First, there was a cultural performance defining caste hegemony: Warriors dominate and Panos are their subjects. Second, this hegemony was contested: Panos are not ritually inferior and have the right to enter temples. Third, this counter-performance at the same time made a positive claim: all people in Bisipara are citizens of India and equal in their subordination to the law. This was simultaneously a claim that Bisipara's caste system was no longer the framework that regulated political interaction between its inhabitants. A wider polity had taken over.

Fourth, the immediate representatives of this wider polity were the sub-inspector and the two constables. They stood for the authoritarian bureaucracy that had regulated this region for more than a century. The police in particular, in that area at that time, were a significant audience for any cultural performance that might be interpreted as lawlessness. Villagers feared the police, and Pano non-violent tactics owed as much to this fear as to Gandhian moral values. A complicating factor was the Pano reputation: they were a byword for unlawful behaviour. (Their street was flagged on a crime-map I saw in the police headquarters in Phulbani.)

Fifth comes the term *Harijan*. This was the name – it means 'Children of God' – that Gandhi gave to India's Untouchables. The word became a slogan, a war-cry in Gandhi's campaign to reconstruct Indian society and Hindu morality. (Orissa's Temple Entry Act was one kind of response to this appeal.) Gandhi's somewhat Whiggish design for independent India was a land of self-governing village communities, where the central government would have limited authority. The design also had a novel view of the caste system. Castes would divide labour between them, but would co-operate as *equals*, all equally serving the public good. It would be a caste system, but one happily devoid of the competitive spirit, and no longer disfigured by hierarchy. Untouchability, in particular, was to be abolished. (Letters I received at that time were franked with the sentence, in English, 'Untouchability has been abolished.')

This form of society was presented – as was almost everything that Gandhi campaigned for – as a moral imperative, an end in itself that could not be doubted or questioned, because it was – his favourite word – the truth. One did not ask what would be the pay-off, because the term *Harijan*, for the true-believing Gandhian, represented an ultimate value. For Warriors and Panos, on the other hand, the word did not at all stand for an authentic moral imperative; it was a weapon in a struggle for power and an indication that government might be manipulated into supporting Panos.

Evidently the different significances that can be attached to the Shiva temple brou-ha-ha did not all define the situation in the same way. There was, however, some overlap. For instance, Gandhian non-violence coincided with the policeman's and official's law and order, but only up to a point, because for a policeman *all* protesters were bad. The theme of equality, validated through citizenship, ran through all the interpretations except that of the Warriors, which assumed hierarchy. Almost everything else that was acceptable to one audience would be repudiated by another. *Harijan* was a term that excited contempt from Warriors and from most officials, including the police. True-believing Gandhians and the Panos welcomed it, but even they did so, as I noted, for quite different reasons.

In such discordancy the dramatic unity of action, time, and space, which makes a theatrical performance persuasive, is put in peril. This is no longer a performance valued intrinsically in aesthetic or logical terms for *what it is*. It has becomes a plurality of alternative means, rationally evaluated by *calculating what effect each will have*. The integrated cultural performance has fragmented into *many* performances, each aimed at a different audience, and therefore unlikely to be consonant. Messages then are liable to leak into one another, their persuasive efficiency being thus diminished.

Of course, that kind of polysemous communicative virtuosity is not unknown. *Gulliver's Travels* may be read at several quite different levels. Durrell's *Alexandria Quartet* is another instance. Novelists and script-writers cater for a relatively inert audience. They do not face the complexity of politically intended cultural performances, where there is a constant need to adjust to constantly changing audience-responses. If, moreover, one accepts the interpretive canon that abolishes authenticity and insists that there are as many meanings in a text as readers choose to find there, it seems that one must have overstepped the limit of tactical computation.

Does this confusion-of-many-voices model represent what was in the minds of the Bisipara people? Certainly they were well aware that different folks need different strokes, but I do not think that they were in the least uncertain about where reality lay. They did not live in a world of Derridaemonic confusion.

Authenticity

The performances address multiple audiences, and contain multiple themes, and each performer has to write and rewrite the script to counter what others are saying. If one's model focuses only on the performances, it is not easy to work out what was in people's minds when they chose one move rather than another. But this uncertainty diminishes when attention is shifted from the text – the performances – to the context, to what people did off-stage and what they kept off-stage.

Recall some of the events. The Panos followed the Gandhian strategy of non-violence; they could have done otherwise. Then there was the 'riot squad playlet', in which the sub-inspector and the constables were given refreshments and gifts, and in which the sub-inspector laid down the law. Those actions do not explain themselves. Again, no one was hurt; no property was damaged; conduct, by and large, was civilised. Also, quite inexplicable unless the sub-inspector really was totally intimidating, why did the matter go no further? The Panos did not try again to get into Shiva's temple, although there were many occasions on which they might have done so, and although the law was on their side. The Warriors might have counter-attacked in a variety of ways, but the revenge they chose did not materially harm the Panos. They took away the right to be the village musicians, thus matching symbolic protest with largely symbolic penalties. If they had been in the mood to go to extremes, they could have put a ban on employing Panos as farm labourers, thus inflicting considerable material harm. But they did not do so, because they would have hurt themselves almost as badly. The confrontation was seemingly construed by neither antagonist as a fight to the finish.

There are many other signs of an underlying rationality. The Warriors, confronted by the sub-inspector, did not invoke the caste system and the natural inferiority of Untouchables. Instead they put on the mask of citizens in a parliamentary democracy and paraded willingness to obey the law, at the same time insisting on the need to consult, democratically, all those who had property rights in the temple. Over the next two years there were other disturbances in Bisipara, which I have no space to describe, but, taken in the round, the conflict between Warriors and Panos was remarkable for the moderation and prudent self-restraint with which both sides carried on their 'war'. The model of political action that suggests itself to me, as I think back, is much closer to academic politics (Snow's *The Masters*, for instance) than it is to what goes on at the genocidal extremes of some present-day ethnic and religious conflicts.

In short, it seems that the temple-entry antagonists really were putting on cultural *performances*. They were like actors, who on occasion may lose themselves in a role, but generally know they are actors, playing parts. Warriors and Panos were not fighting to the finish; they were *putting on an act* of being ready to fight to the finish. For sure play-acting makes claims, and claims may affect the real world (as in the case of *The Mousetrap*). But a play, as I think the

Bisipara people well knew, is dangerous if confused with the offstage world. This is the great paradox of cultural performance: the reality that is celebrated and asserted is an *imagined* reality, and its creators have a freedom of invention that is denied to positive reality. Turner's Ndembu proclaim their essential commonality, their belonging together – what later he called *communitas* – but they do so only because there is a structured reality, which concerns power and conflict, and features backbiting and malice, and is itself what drives the Ndembu to celebrate their imagined unity (1957). This imagined community, as conceived here, is a step beyond Anderson's; it carries with it an uneasy awareness of its own falsity, an awareness that it is not only imagined but also *imaginary*. The Ndembu must know they have their nasty side (Anderson 1991).

Turner's rituals of solidarity function as collective Couéism; tell yourselves often enough that you are united, and you will be united. I see little of such auto-suggestion in the cultural performances around the Shiva temple in Bisipara. Certainly the performers presented various images of their world, ones that were, so to speak, pasted over an underlying reality. Possibly some of them believed that what they presented was gospel that would be accepted by any right-thinking person, but most of the time most of them, I am sure, did not see the situation that way. They saw themselves as actors on a stage, out to convince an audience. They also saw themselves as able, when it suited them, to step off the stage and say 'This is only a play', in the manner of Hamlet explaining *The Mousetrap* to the King: 'This play is the image of a murder done in Vienna... 'Tis a knavish piece of work, but what o' that? Your majesty, and we that have free souls, it touches us not. Let the galled jade winch; our withers are unwrung.'

The lyrical Geertz, rejoicing in Balinese royal ritual, wrote: 'The message is so deeply sunk into the medium that to transform it into a network of propositions is to risk at once both of the characteristic crimes of exegesis: seeing more in things than really is there, and reducing a richness of particular meanings to a drab parade of generalities' (1980: 103). My understanding of Bisipara's play goes the other way: there is more in things than can be seen (see Amadiume, this volume). The actors themselves were constantly engaged in (mostly unarticulated) forward-looking exegesis, and all the time tempering the medium and the message so as to get what they wanted. Bisipara's players were conscious performers, calculating the likely pay-off from their performance.

This does not mean, I hasten to say, that the pay-off they wanted was always crassly material. The Panos, after that one attempt to gain admittance to the Shiva temple, stayed away and built a temple of their own in their own street. I read several possible significances in this. One is that, being politically sophisticated, they seized an apparent opportunity to mobilise the government on their side, to raise their own self-respect, and to make the Warriors and the rest of the village grant them a respect that hitherto had been withheld. Some of their leaders may also have seen this as a chance to reinforce their leadership. Then, as events unfolded, they computed the cost of a court-case, factored in possible violence, weighed the risk of angering local officials and the police, and concluded this was not a cost-efficient way to claim respect.

Alternatively, there may have been some Panos who did not see the matter exclusively, or even at all, in terms of symbolising political power. They may have wanted equal access to the Shiva temple as we might want equal access to a health clinic or an educational institution. From that point of view, it was a perfectly rational decision to go off and build their own facility. Seen in that way, the attempt to get into the Shiva temple was not a cultural performance at all, but a direct demand for access to valued resources.

This sustained moderation and the rationality on which it is founded suggest to me that among the many possible interpretations of the Harijan drama's meanings one was authentic. I do not mean by this term that one version was objectively right and the rest objectively wrong, but rather that the people involved had an order of preference in the versions, believing one to be nearer to reality, and therefore more powerful, than another. (The Greek word that 'authentic' comes from means 'to have absolute authority'.) The authoritative value, as should by now be clear, was that set on prudent calculation.

Second Nature

Bisipara's Harijan drama is to be read as a statement about the way the villagers wanted their politics to be, and about their understandings of the natural way to conduct themselves. Both duty and interest feature in the Bisipara model, but interest comes first; it is the default mode. To understand how others will behave, one must assume they are looking first to their interests, even while they speak of their devotion to duty. Their interests are the normal basic human concerns: safety, comfort, and sufficient control over material resources to make life physically and emotionally tolerable.

These words should be read carefully. I am not saying that everything had a price and nothing was intrinsically valued. People in Bisipara, like people everywhere, cared for others beside themselves: for their families and kin, for others in their caste, and even for fellow-villagers when they faced a common opponent (the Administration occasionally provoked that kind of solidarity). Nor were they exclusively attentive to material things; self-respect and dignity, for example, for sure were sometimes ends in themselves. What I am saying is that Bisipara people were not easy targets for the rabble-rouser; mystification put them on their guard; they were suspicious of appeals to their moral sensibilities (Vinoba Bhave's propagandists got short shrift in Bisipara).[4] They were not given to the kind of uncalculating enthusiasm that is the basis of morality. I read all this as the unarticulated theme that dominated Bisipara's Harijan drama. This is the ultimate reality in their off-stage world.

I do not for a moment think that this is the case everywhere or that it will necessarily always be so in Bisipara. Certainly such calculated moderation has not been a feature of India's recent politics in urban settings. Nor am I judging it good or bad; it was simply the way minds habitually worked in Bisipara.

The attitude was the product of Bisipara's particular experience up to the time I knew it. Bisipara people, although they imagined a structured feudal past for themselves, as Lords of the Marches for the Hindu kingdoms on the plains around the Kondmals, in fact had always lived, politically and economically, on their wits. Even before the administration came to the area, Oriya villages like Bisipara were politically precarious communities, surviving by playing the market of political alliances with warring Kond clans. True, the Warriors were landholders and still in the 1950s land was the principal source of wealth, but certainly since the area came under British control (about the

---

4 Vinoba Bhave was a Gandhian social worker who ran a much-publicised campaign to persuade landowners to give up one fifth of their land to *Harijans*. See Tennyson 1955.

1850s), Bisipara had been an *entrepôt*, a place inhabited by traders, small entrepreneurial groups or individuals, accustomed to bargaining and negotiating and calculating the consequence of every move they made. My assumption is that Bisipara people never had the wealth and power to luxuriate in the kind of true-belief that goes with a sense of unlimited mastery. Nor, on the other hand, were they ever reduced to the point of desperation where mindless fanaticism seems the only course available.

I should add that (for different reasons) the same pragmatic scepticism pervaded the local levels of the administration and had, to a large extent, displaced in local politicians the moral fervour that had been the hallmark of the freedom fight. They all were programmed to recognise a cultural performance, in the context of politics, for what they thought it was: a tactical pretence that should be taken seriously to the extent that it might have a positive or negative effect upon the authentic cultural value, which was the rational pursuit of utility.

The interesting fact is that this rationalism, although certainly not in any deep sense unconscious, was never overtly advertised in Bisipara's Harijan dramas. I suppose it was enough entrenched to need no celebration in staged cultural performances. There were none that I recall. The nearest approach was a recurrent trope in their mythology about practising deceit (sometimes murderous) on the Konds. They did, of course, constantly act out their pragmatism in the exchanges of everyday life. Nevertheless, to ask them why they behaved that way would be to ask why they ate or defecated or breathed. Rationality in Bisipara was like the air: invisible, pervasive, and, if one did happen to think about it, surely seen as an unarguable necessity for the continuance of human life.

What, then, of the model of cultural performance? Actions taken off-stage, which are part of culture but are not theatre, may spring from the taken-for-granted part of culture, which is hard to discern because it is not normally articulated. Some of these unarticulated values and beliefs may be coded in the text itself and therefore discoverable by an imaginative hermeneut. But others are not; they remain non-lexical, internalised, incorporated, embodied, connectionist, or, in everyday terms, second nature.

They are however, discoverable. They can be read by going beyond the text, surveying off-stage action, and inferring from it which unarticulated values and beliefs must underlie the action taken. In practice this usually requires one to assume rationality, to hypothesise possible courses of action and work out why one was chosen and others rejected. This though is well known: actions speak louder than words.

References

Anderson, Benedict. 1991 [1983]. *Imagined Communities*. London: Verso.

Bailey, F.G. 1957. *Caste and the Economic Frontier*. Manchester: Manchester University Press.

Geertz, Clifford. 1980. *Negara*. Princeton: Princeton University Press.

Goffman, E. 1970. *Strategic Interaction*. Oxford: Basil Blackwell.

Kuper, A. and J. Kuper (eds). 1985. *The Social Science Encyclopaedia*. London: Routledge and Kegan Paul.

Tennyson, Hallam. 1955. *Saint on the March*. London: Gollancz.

Turner, V.W. 1957. *Schism and Continuity*. Manchester: Manchester University Press.

CHAPTER 2

Political Ritual and the Public Sphere in Contemporary West Africa

Sandra T. Barnes *

Introduction

One of the hallmarks of Abner Cohen's work is his exploration of the hidden ways in which people pursue political agendas using culturally distinctive practices and ideologies. In a distinguished series of studies, Cohen describes in remarkable detail a variety of groupings – ethnic, elite, religious, kinship, and ceremonial – that have no formal political roles but act in informal ways to achieve politically oriented goals (1965, 1969, 1981, 1993). In his view, an important consequence of this kind of activity is that the pursuit of collective interests promotes solidarity among participants and helps them maintain boundaries around their groups (1974: 65–75).

The elaborate civic ceremonies and titles associated with chiefship in many areas of West Africa produce a similar outcome in that locally distinctive uses of chiefly symbols and the construction and interpretation of ritual practices serve to separate one group from another. This is only half of the story, because at the same

---

* I wish to thank Olufemi Vaughan and Toyin Falola for their commentaries on this paper when it was first read at the 10th annual meeting of the Canadian Association of African Studies in Toronto, 16–18 May 1991; the members of the University of Pennsylvania Folklore Seminar who discussed it later; the editors of this volume; and especially Steven Feierman who provided an exceptionally careful critique.

time as civic rituals associated with chieftaincy establish culturally defined boundaries around local communities, they also make these boundaries permeable by providing a context in which local people make connections to the wider world and articulate their desires and opinions to governing bodies of the state. Chiefs help meet peoples' needs by acting as intermediaries between diverse sectors of their society, especially ruling and wealthy classes and common people or one ethnic group and another, and by using ritual as a means for carrying out this integrative role.

The ceremonies associated with contemporary chieftaincy are cultural performances with broad political and economic agendas. As shown in the pages to follow, they constitute a vital arena for the expression and transmission of symbolic capital as well as a crucial forum where grassroots opinion can be heard and accommodated. They provide a context where local-national dialogue can take place, where ordinary people can address governing elites, and where public values and opinions can be expressed and debated. Chieftaincy rituals take place outside the realm of the official structures of the state yet they are focused on them. In fact they are focused in such a way that there exists within the parameters of contemporary chieftaincy a kind of social space that Habermas has identified as a public sphere – a realm of social life where 'something approaching public opinion can be formed' (1974: 49; see also 1991: 236–50).

The institution of chieftaincy varies dramatically from one locale to another depending on historical and political circumstances. Here, I will concentrate on chiefs in Nigeria, some with pre-colonial roots, others created by colonial administrators, and still others reinvented by the people themselves during the transition to independence (Barnes 1986: 97–98). The proposition that post-colonial chieftaincy constitutes a public sphere in Nigeria and elsewhere in West Africa is predicated on the fact that this institution has undergone a dramatic transformation during these three periods. Chieftaincy and government were synonymous in pre-colonial times. It was one aspect of government during the colonial period – strong at various periods but weakened at others, especially in the waning years of foreign rule. Immediately after independence its constitutionally mandated roles were eroded to the point that the chiefly sphere was effectively separated from main decision-making bodies of government. Rather than disappear altogether, however, chieftaincy emerged as an interest group. The astonishing part of its survival was in how significant – to varying degrees – this sphere became. The power of chieftaincy today derives paradoxically from the fact that it operates virtually outside the formal purview of the state, yet it articulates informally with the state through rituals which mask a vast array of personal transactions among ordinary people and officials of the state and other national-level elites, especially those with great wealth.

The past decade has born witness to a growing debate surrounding the viability of chiefs in post-colonial societies.[1] It stems in large part from the failure of new nation-states to institute viable forms of political representation and a hope, on the part of some observers, that past forms of governance may be able to meet contemporary demands for democratisation. It is the generality of this struggle over political representation, and of the recurrent importance of chieftaincy in imagined pasts, that calls for scrutiny all across West Africa, while recognising the richness and variety of local historical experiences.

This does not mean chieftaincy thrives everywhere today. It is dying out in some regions and flourishing in others (Geschiere 1993: 169). Those who find chiefly institutions in good health have suggested they are an alternative source of power for the state, a political sector that should be re-empowered to serve the state at the local level (Jagun 1985: 118), or at the very least to serve as a sector that can influence representative forms of government (Guyer 1992: 70). For others, chiefs are exploiters – co-opted by elites and political parties to serve their ends – or they are oppressors of those whose interests diverge from their own. For the latter, chieftaincy is an institution that should be abolished (Cookey 1987: 145). Both sides, in taking either/or positions, miss a key point. As part of the political system – in the broad sense of the term – chieftaincy needs neither to be a functioning arm of government (or an alternative to government) nor does it need to be abolished.

The point is that the chiefly sphere is effective precisely because it has moved to a position of governmental marginality. Chiefs are politically effective because they occupy an indeterminate place which, because of its paucity of formally allocated power, now stands largely apart from the state yet functions in reference to it. The legitimacy of this sphere is derived from historic associations

---

1 E.g., Aborisade (1985), Bayart (1989), Geschiere (1993), Guyer (1992) and Vaughan (1991). A recent article by Guyer (1994) is especially insightful with respect to the viability and role of contemporary chiefs.

made between the accessibility and accountability of authority figures to the public,[2] and from the public's acceptance of and even reverence for their practices by virtue of credentials such as titles and other distinctive symbols which often have salience beyond the secular realm of everyday life. The popularity of this sphere is enhanced by the fact that chiefs themselves are often wealthy or have connections to sources of capital and other resources that can be tapped both by local communities and by individuals (Guyer 1992: 60).

The post-colonial public sphere of chieftaincy also is effective because it relies on the media to attain visibility and create an aware public that is knowledgeable about and sympathetic to its practices. In a single month the internationally distributed weekly news magazine *West Africa* published six articles on chiefly ceremonies, including a marathon rite staged by the Ooni of Ife during which forty prominent citizens were given honorary titles, another by the Alaafin of Oyo which similarly honoured a large group of citizens including the chair of a newly formed political party, and reports of a heated debate among leaders about these rites and the appropriateness of some honourees.[3]

The chieftaincy sphere makes use of civic ritual as a neutral arena for the expression and consolidation of society's values. Such was the case with hundreds of Ghanaian Queenmothers who attended a recent ceremonial *durbar* in which they exhorted one another to maintain harmony in their towns and districts. The illustrious audience included teachers, businesswomen, and numerous representatives of prominent families whose kinspeople held professional and governmental posts (Stoeltje 1991).

The chieftaincy sphere uses title-taking as a way of converting those individuals who meet culturally defined canons of success into public servants. Titles conferred at public ceremonies in Côte d'Ivoire acknowledge the excellence of townspeople in their occupational endeavours. Each title holder is assisted by numerous individuals who offer their services in return for the

---

2 Chiefs were held accountable by a variety of means reported frequently in the historical record such as deposition, exile, the out-migration of subjects, execution, or imposed suicide; secret societies, councils of leaders, or disaffected factions served as checks in various systems of checks and balances. See for example Atanda (1970: 213) or Ferguson and Wilks (1970: 338).

3 *West Africa*, 11–17 March 1991: 366; 18–24 March: 407–8; 25–31 March: 448.

public recognition and rewards that attend their and their chiefs' leadership in community affairs (Adams 1991). Similarly, Cameroonians compete for titles, including numerous elites who want them as a way of validating claims to leadership and local amenities, but who are thereafter expected to share their wealth, dispense favours, and provide ordinary citizens with connections to the wider society (Goheen 1992: 402). Title-taking is a vital aspect of public life because it seriously affects the informal ways political participation can be constructed and experienced by ordinary members of society.

The effectiveness of chieftaincy is largely dependent on the fact that there are two kinds of chiefly titles: hereditary titles (held by privileged descent groups and passed down from one generation to the next) and appointive titles (conferred as an honour and intended to last only for the lifetime of a holder). The significance of this dual system is that hereditary chiefs select honorary chiefs. This system provides a major source of symbolic capital to title-givers. It is a source of power independent of the state. As will be shown, this two-tiered system of holding titles and the selection processes surrounding it is central to bringing various segments of a polity together. It is a system that has deep historic precedence.

Pre-Colonial Chiefs

Chiefs were the backbone of pre-colonial governments. A vast range of authority figures have been lumped together under this rubric, from primary rulers to heads of small ritual, occupational, or kinship groups (Crowder and Ikime 1970: ix–x). All had important roles, from the few who were heads of autonomous communities to the many who were subordinate to higher authorities or who served in complex hierarchies of title-holders and chiefly councils. Ordinary people were connected to the apex of power through these leaders. Chiefs belonged to the same social groups, were familiar with the same range of values governing personal interactions as their followers, and therefore were obliged to represent their interests and opinions to higher authorities or deliberative councils. They were responsible for overseeing followers' well-being, enforcing rules, and resolving conflict. All of these duties were rooted in face-to-face, frequent interactions with followers or with other chiefs both in and outside their groups or communities. Chiefs provided a venue for the expression of their own people's needs and concerns, but the fora for doing so were not independent of the state, but a formal part of it.

The chiefly system of government in one of the largest of West Africa's pre-colonial polities is instructive, for it took hundreds of chiefs to administer the Kingdom of Oyo and its outlying tributaries at the peak of its powers in the mid- to late-eighteenth century (Asiwaju and Law 1985: 449; see also Law 1977). There were both hereditary chiefs, usually the heads of descent groups and the ruler himself, and appointive chiefs. More than seventy of the appointed title holders were military chiefs who were honoured because of outstanding qualities such as valour in battle, leadership skill, or wealth (Asiwaju and Law 1985: 449). An untold number of appointed title holders serving in the palace tended to be heads of important immigrant communities, priests of ritual groups, or slaves, clients, and friends who were selected for titles because of their expertise and mastery of various skills. The people who were appointed to chiefships tended to be successful members of a community; their accomplishments and followings marked them out as big men and women and thus of sufficient stature to be drawn into the constitutionally legitimated sphere of authority and to channel their energies into serving the state rather than paralleling or opposing it.

Another set of chiefs, both hereditary and appointive, governed provincial subordinate towns and small tribute-paying states. An important administrative arrangement for these outlier chiefs was that each was paired with a palace official, sometimes a woman, who looked out for the chief's community's interests and served as an intermediary at court and on overarching chiefly councils (Babayemi 1979: 15–19, 62, 139). This was a highly personalised system of administration in which a ruler had immediate and direct access to information concerning communities or residential quarters in his domain through an in-house intermediary chief whose responsibility was to represent that particular group of people and its views. Conversely any subordinate chief, and by extension the community he or she headed, had a permanent representative at court who had direct access to the king, royal resources, trade and marketing information, and a host of other state-level aspects of their political and economic system.

In various regions along the Atlantic coast, as in Oyo, the political style of chiefship was similar. Chiefs were the communications channels among various segments of a community, up and down the hierarchy of power, and from inside to outside. Through chiefly representatives ordinary citizens could make contact with and become knowledgeable about those who governed them and their policies. Through chiefs people could act on that knowledge. Chiefs represented various interests and thus they were in touch with shifts in the public pulse. They served not only as the checks and balances against the excesses of paramount rulers or dominant interest groups but also as the pivots around which dissent could be mobilised and redressive actions taken.

Colonial Chiefs

There were major changes in the chiefly mode of governance during the colonial period.[4] In the early years in Nigeria, indigenous rulers and chiefs remained in place; there were astonishingly few British administrators – one political officer for every 70,000 southern Nigerians in 1925 (Feierman 1995:490) – and therefore foreigners devised an indirect way of maintaining control through existing chiefs and principles of office-holding. In most parts of the French colonies and some areas under British control, new chiefs were appointed on the basis of loyalty, administrative abilities, or success in establishing contact with foreign powers but not on the basis of traditionally established claims or precedents (Crowder and Ikime 1970: xi). Self-made leaders could therefore be self-made in new ways – mastering the language, educational processes, and bureaucratic practices of their foreign overlords. In many cases this was a break with the past in terms of selection criteria but not in terms of the chief as a link to centres of power.

The differences between French and British systems of governance were pronounced in the legal mandates of chiefs, their powers, and the amount of supervision to which they were subjected.[5] Chiefs in both French and British colonies, from rulers to the most subordinate village sub-chief, were subject to foreign control in some way and were caught between the conflicting demands of the foreign powers, without whose favour they could not remain in

---

4 For general discussions of changes in West African chieftaincy practices from pre-colonial to post-colonial periods see Crowder and Ikime (1970) and Aborisade (1985).

5 Two close studies of contrastive styles of chiefship under French and British are Geschiere (1993) and Asiwaju (1970).

office, and the people, without whose compliance they could not be effective. The initial days of indirect rule saw a strengthening of kings and other paramount rulers, especially in British West Africa, and a lessening of the powers of subordinate chiefs. It was easier for foreign political officers to develop a relationship with one authority figure than to deal with several of them; it was also incumbent on the foreigners to prevent factional conflicts that could disrupt the smooth flow of administration (Atanda 1970 and 1973).

Under colonial rule the obligations of chiefs to represent the desires and opinions of followers were unchanged but their abilities to respond effectively to public initiatives and discontent were more constrained than in the past. Chieftaincy councils as fora for public discourse continued to exist, but colonial chiefs were officials of the state and not independent of its scrutiny and sanctions.

The reliance on chiefs declined in the latter days of the colonial period. At Oyo, for instance, the responsibilities and rights of chiefs gradually shifted to an elected district council modeled on British local government (Atanda 1970: 225–6). Elsewhere the rise of nationalism and preparations for independence brought new actors onto the administrative stage, consisting of the educated elites who began to control national economic resources and take over bureaucratic offices (see Colson, this volume).

The close of the colonial period saw the institution of chieftaincy, and its ability to link the common people and the larger world, in steep decline. The death knell was prematurely sounded in 1968 by scholars who were asked explicitly to deliberate on the changing status of chiefs and predict their future (Crowder and Ikime 1970). They believed West African chiefs had been blatantly used by colonial authorities to the extent that their credibility had been undermined and, later, misused by a new wave of politicians in mobilising grassroots support for election campaigns. The little prestige and influence chiefs still enjoyed could not survive the taint of politics unless they maintained a strictly neutral political stance. Even then, the experts felt, chiefs were being relegated to performing ceremonial functions and serving as tourist attractions.

Post-Colonial Chiefs

Predictions that chiefly institutions were disappearing were not fulfilled. At a second conference fifteen years later only one of twenty-five West African scholars saw chiefs in decline (Aborisade 1985). In great contrast to the earlier group there was now overwhelming agreement that chiefship would exist long into the future. The blame for earlier pessimism was placed on modernisation theory which equated contemporary change with Westernisation rather than with the realities of specific historic and cultural situations. The experts attacked unquestioned assumptions that the non-Western world was moving unidirectionally toward a homogeneous level of 'development'. For them, African citizens had experienced a widespread 'disillusionment with imported social values' which strengthened their faith in traditional institutions and made it improbable their societies would 'evolve in the style of the West' (Ayeni 1985: xxx–xxxix).

Modernisation practices and theories failed to account for the salience of historically based cultural conventions. They failed to account for peoples' needs for institutions and systems that were based on deeply ingrained notions of trust and accountability that were imparted in the socialisation processes and passed down from one generation to the next. Such notions were critical to building confidence in relationships, transactions, and the central actors in them. From the time of earliest records it was clear that feelings of political efficacy were grounded in practices based on personal interactions and an intimate knowledge of local political actors. Hence a realistic account of development depended on accepting the logic of these notions and their being expressed, at least in part, in the modern political scene through chiefs and chieftaincy practices. To West African scholars it was precisely this logic that modernisation theory had missed.

Nevertheless a significant historical transformation had taken place, in that in the years following independence governmental institutions based on chiefs lost virtually all of their remaining legally mandated powers. From time to time chiefs were nominally tied to the state through appointments to advisory councils – in a few, sporadic instances this took the form of a House of Chiefs – or by virtue of statutes that regulated chiefly succession procedures, but in real terms the formal prerogatives and duties of office all but disappeared, and in some cases they disappeared altogether only to be revived at a later time (Bayart 1989: 215). In the breach informal arrangements for conducting political business took their place.

Chiefs today are involved in political processes and practices that do not match their legal roles. They lobby business and government connections for goods, services, and amenities for their followers, communities, or neighbourhoods (Vaughan 1991: 27). A detailed study in metropolitan Lagos during a ten-week period revealed that a minor chief was involved in sixty-eight separate negotiations on behalf of his neighbours. In an unofficial way, he helped people find jobs, make contact with government officials, resolve land and housing problems, settle disputes, and even solve a flood control problem, to name only a few of the kinds of problems he was willing to address. In each instance the chief approached a higher level contact – a business owner, bureaucrat, judge, lawyer, town council member, and political party leader – in order to secure assistance. In return he was asked by officials to help them unofficially investigate neighbourhood boundary problems and settle a leadership crisis in a local market (Barnes 1986: 78–95).

The effect of all this is that large sectors of the public value these services – however extra-legal they may be – and see chiefs as legitimate actors in political life who represent their views and guide them through the vagaries and difficulties of unfamiliar systems and institutions. As with no other class of authority figures, chiefs are members of the local communities in which they serve and are trusted as life-long neighbours, friends, and helpers. As they are known on a face-to-face level, chiefs are sought after by civilian and military politicians in times of unrest, when communications with the grassroots are necessary, or when leaders wish to mobilise public opinion around critical issues and concerns. At the same time, as already indicated, they know what people are thinking and can serve as communications channels for their followers upwards to government officials (Bello-Imam 1985: 182). Whichever way communications flow, chiefs are accountable to the people of their localities and are constrained to represent their interests. The spectre of ostracism or deposition is still a real and present sanction, with the loss of legitimacy on a local level being tantamount to losing one's entree to higher circles.[6] Today's checks and balances so far as chiefly politics are concerned are weighted on the side of whether or not a leader is effective, and effectiveness is inextricably tied to the credibility of representation that a local leader can provide.

---

6 *West Africa*, 20–26 March 1989: 431; 24–30 June 1991: 1,033; 25–31 January 1993: 113; 2–8 August 1993: 1,355.

The popularity of chiefs as authority figures is considerable.[7] Some of this favour comes from the failure of government to make meaningful contact with the grassroots and some, ironically, from chiefs' very marginalisation which, thanks to the public's lack of confidence in government, works to their favour (Vaughan 1991: 28). Concern for this historic institution is not restricted to the news media. In his memoirs a former military governor of western Nigeria wrote after his term of office that executive councils devoted eighty-five percent of their meeting times to chieftaincy affairs, mainly succession struggles (Vaughan 1991: 25 n.47). State governments in Nigeria conduct enquiries into the history of chiefly families and their succession procedures to curtail conflicts; court cases are commonly reported in local and national newspapers with opposing sides taking out full-page advertisements to promote a succession claim. Some disputes are sufficiently intense that thrones are vacant and successors unnamed for years, even decades.

One of the incongruities of chiefship is that while many people see chiefs as vestiges of the past and therefore representatives of unlettered or traditionalist sectors of the society, the actual trend is for holders of titles to come increasingly from high-income, educated and occupationally prestigious sectors of society. As a West African journalist put it:

> What impresses the observer of the chiefly scene ... is how time after time since the 1950s a man called back to become a sarki or an oba has not for a moment hesitated to choose between cabinet or top bureaucratic, diplomatic or academic posts ... and to return to his chiefdom (not always the sophisticated social centre to which he has been accustomed) and accept the honour done to him by 'his' people.[8]

Thus the Oba of Benin holds a Cambridge degree in economics and resigned as a federal permanent secretary to assume office; the Nze-Obi of Egbema is an aeronautical engineer who until his appointment was the general manager of Nigeria's Rivers State Transport Corporation; the Sultan of Sokoto was First Secretary of Nigeria's foreign service as well as a federal permanent secretary when he left for chiefly office; the Tor Tiv was a lawyer and head of the Civil Service; and a British-trained PhD resigned from

---

7 See Vaughan (1991: 21, 28) and Oladosu (1985: 150). For negative views, however, see Cookey (1987: 142–7).

8 *West Africa*, 20–26 March 1989: 431–2.

his history post at the University of Ibadan to become the Olufi of Gbongan. None of these individuals nor a host of others who could be named – pharmacist, accountant, author-publisher, diplomat, federal cabinet secretary, owner of a shipping line, banker, and judge – was reluctant to leave an influential government post or lucrative career for chiefly office that legally and bureaucratically had few mandated powers or obvious economic rewards. Hereditary titles, for which there is intense intra-familial competition among eligible candidates, require holders to leave their professions and devote themselves full time to the office, although there have been a few exceptions, such as a wealthy steel magnate and president of a manufacturers' association, who accepted a title in the Fulani Emirate of Adamawa.[9]

Any list of appointive title holders would be equally, if not more, distinguished but here the appointees do not leave their careers. Indeed the point of awarding an honorary title is that the holder continues to be active on the outside, the extreme cases of which are the Ghanaian chair of the UN Statistical Commission[10] and deputy directors-general of the United Nations and the World Health Organisation.

The rewards for taking titles would seem too few given the costs. However, chiefships have compelling advantages that lie well beyond the tangible, material rewards that office-holding often brings. Chieftaincy titles are held for life, assuming the holders serve with a modicum of decency. Chiefs do not retire; they are not dependent on elections; they do not lose office if there is a coup d'état, rebellion, or change of ruling party. Once they are chiefs, they are recognised and treated as authority figures for the remainder of their days.

Hereditary chiefs benefit significantly from the ability to name honorary chiefs and through them gain important resources and connections. It is not incidental that the 1993 Nigerian presidential election (later nullified by the military head of state) was won by a man who received more than 200 honorary chieftaincy titles from communities where among other things he had helped citizens establish sixty-three secondary schools, forty-one libraries, and twenty-one water projects. From his personal wealth, amassed as

---

9 *West Africa*, 20–26 March 1989: 431–2 and 2–8 September 1991: 1,445; *Daily Sketch*, 25 March 1989: 13–14; and Vaughan (1991: 19–20).

10 *West Africa*, 19–25 April 1993: 633.

an official of a multinational corporation, he also provided scholarships to 1,000 university students and paid school fees for another 2,000.[11] While this is a dramatic example, the net result is that through titles people construct highly sophisticated networks that, as one observer starkly put it, lead to the 'strategic locations of power' (Ayeni 1985: xxxiv).

People who confer honorary titles and other awards control overwhelmingly significant sources of symbolic capital. Bourdieu has written that symbolic capital, in the form of prestige and renown, is possibly 'the most valuable form of accumulation' because it can be converted into political and economic benefits. The reverse is also true, since those who have relatively large amounts of material wealth can lay claim to symbolic honours (1977: 179)

For hereditary chiefs the ability to enhance the standing of individuals who have gained wealth, high office, knowledge and expertise in other walks of life is an investment in the latter's accomplishments and the resources they control. Conferring high status on such individuals is unparalleled in the capacity to forge a bond between those who give and those who receive (Barnes 1986: 38). It establishes debts on both sides. Those who give honour can lay claim to reciprocal favours, while those who accept titles bring honour to the givers and therefore they too can expect to be repaid in some way. Exchanges of symbolic and political-economic capital establish long-lasting ties and interactions in the ways Mauss (1970) clearly set out.

The awarding of chieftaincy titles is thus a kind of meta-investment. The dividends can be reaped in future transactions, and they can be converted into many currencies. The reciprocal nature of title-giving and receiving rebounds into the wider society. But above all, these practices provide a basis for establishing networks that have social, economic, and political potential, and that continue the historically validated task of carrying the demands and convictions of one segment of the society to another.

The Rituals of Contemporary Chiefship

The ceremonies surrounding chiefly affairs, particularly the conferral of titles, constitute a public dramatisation of these

---

11 *West Africa*, 12–18 April 1993: 590.

reciprocal relationships and networks. The rituals communicate the fact that high value is placed not simply on this institution but very importantly on the attainments of the actors involved and what they represent. The pessimists who predicted chiefs would be relegated to ritual roles were correct in the sense that ceremonial duties are a critical aspect of office-holding; they were thoroughly incorrect, however, in their ability to comprehend the informal political uses to which rituals could be put and the many meanings and agendas attached to their performance.

The discourse taking place in the contemporary chiefly realm resonates strongly with the past, in that high value is placed on economic success, occupational accomplishment and expertise, and the conditions that make success possible. Much of the content of contemporary chieftaincy revolves around public concern with creating and maintaining the political and economic conditions that enable successful people to emerge as big men and women. The historic evidence for the importance of big men and women in pre-colonial life has been demonstrated (Bayart 1989: 323; Barber 1991: 183–247). The warrior chiefs and palace officials were the big men and women of Oyo's past and they were recognised in much the same way big men and women are today, with personal titles validating their accomplishments and converting various powers derived from them to the benefit of society through public service as authority figures.

The larger outcome for today is that public opinion and the discourse created by chieftaincy practices centre on people's basic perceptions of power and authority and their wellsprings, the ways these aspects of a political system should be articulated with the grassroots, and how all of this plays itself out in terms of the wider society.

Communication about the content of chiefly ritual is largely encoded in language focusing on the aesthetics of staging ceremonial performances. Chieftaincy rituals are evaluated according to their success in exhibiting the symbolic capital that they, in fact, embody. Public taste demands ostentatious displays in the rituals and in the protocol attending the treatment of guests.

While no two ceremonies are alike, most of them place stress on the organisers' attention to formalities, observance of social differences, and attention to detail in symbolic representations. An exemplary performance in these respects was the capping ceremony for Chief Olu Holloway, staged before hundreds of people in the football field-sized courtyard of the royal palace of old Lagos in June 1986.[12] As the audience rose in greeting, Oba Adeyinka Oyekan II entered the gathering at the head of a procession of elegantly robed chiefs and took his place at the throne in the centre of a specially constructed dais, signalling that the ritual had begun. He was flanked on the right by more than ten hereditary chiefs and on the left by an even greater number of honorary title-holders, all prominent members of the Lagos community who had multiple ties to the major business and administrative institutions of the city and the country. The chiefs were seated facing the audience in upholstered chairs according to seniority, the formula for which was based on the importance of the chief's title and the date of his or her investiture. At the foot of the dais on the ground sat a large entourage of palace servants, musicians and other entertainers, courtiers, wives, and numerous young relatives of the Oba and chiefs. The most prominent invitees were seated in comfortable chairs beneath canopies erected to shade them from the noon-day sun; those of lesser status sat on wooden folding chairs beyond the canopy; other members of the community, not invitees, stood behind or to the sides of seating areas; and still others crowded outside the fences surrounding the palace complex.

Emblems of office were used to reinforce these notions of status and hierarchy and to remind the notables of the responsibilities of office. The candidate was led bare-headed to the dais by Chief Egbe, the senior warrior chief, and as he knelt before the Oba, members of a prominent secret society – a society which once had the ability to depose the *oba* and check the abuses of office by other leaders – paraded before the dais in full uniform. Only then were the sacred foods of investiture – water, gin, kola, bitter kola, and alligator pepper – fed to the candidate by the Oba, who proceeded to cap him three times with a garland of leaves which had been touched by each hereditary and honorary chief with both hands, capped three times with a boat-shaped white cap, and then encircled three times with a necklace of beads, all of which are only worn by chiefs. As a final gesture of his new authority, the chief was presented with a special type of umbrella, allowed only to title-holders, and a silver-topped cane.

Participants were dressed according to their rank and centrality to the ritual. The Oba and chiefs wore expensive, elaborate robes.

---

12 Discussion of Chief Olu Holloway's capping ceremony are from the author's research notes of June 1986.

Members of Chief Holloway's entourage, those nearest him such as spouses, family members, and close friends wore new outfits made from the same cloth, i.e., *asho ebi* (family cloth), to indicate solidarity and closeness. More distant male friends and relatives wore matching hats, and even more distant women and men wore matching scarves or buttons with the chief's name and picture printed on them. The uninvited public were not dressed in special clothing.

Entertainment appropriate to chiefly rites followed the capping and provided a backdrop for a long period of informal activities. Participants circulated around the grounds talking in groups, greeting one another, and meeting the luminaries among the invited guests and title-holders who constituted a virtual Who's Who of local celebrities. The new chief provided refreshments and gifts for guests; they responded with counter gifts of money by way of honouring him and contributing to the large costs involved in staging this kind of event. While food was served, praise singers worked the crowd, royal *gbedu* drums were beaten by palace musicians, and *igbe* choral music was performed by women of royal and chiefly families. They were joined by masqueraders, stilt-walkers, and an assortment of performers. A second phase of the ceremony, which also provided opportunities for visiting and circulating among participants, began later in the day at the new chief's residence and lasted throughout the night.

Post-mortem evaluations of this and events like it involve an audience far larger than the actual participants. The ceremonies are covered by the various media and discussed in social settings by a wide cross-section of the involved public. To a considerable extent discussions centre on the environment in which titles were bestowed. Were the canons of hospitality upheld? Were the rituals performed properly and witnessed by an auspicious set of authorities? Were the guests seated in socially correct groupings? And, finally and most importantly, were the 'right' people in attendance? In many ways, the audience – in the widest sense – makes the event.

The post-mortem discussion is stressed in order to make a more important point. It is that public opinion regulates what occurred, the way it occurred, and whether or not it was acceptable. The public at large, informed by the reporting of attendees and the media, evaluates the ceremonies and establishes standards for how they are produced and reproduced. The formation and management of public opinion involves a larger sphere of discourse than that held at ceremonies and in the localities where they take place. The fact that chiefly practices are sufficiently newsworthy to merit regular inclusion in internationally distributed publications assumes there is a vast constituency of observers and commentators who are currently populating this particular social space.

The civic rituals and activities surrounding chiefly affairs constitute a public sphere in that they take place in a socially interactive realm that stands between the private (domestic or familial) spheres of society and the state (the formal, legal, bureaucratic, juridical, military institutions of government). Habermas elaborated his insights regarding the public sphere, public opinion, and the social space existing between the private and the formal orders of society in relation to a time, a place, and a set of conditions far from Africa. He wrote about the bourgeoisie of Europe in the eighteenth century and about the formation and communication of public opinion via the printed word or informal gatherings in cafes and salons. The public sphere, as Habermas saw it emerging historically, was an in-between realm where private individuals gathered to express their needs to the state, particularly for free market conditions, and their demands for transforming certain aspects of power into 'rational' authority (1974: 53). Habermas's model was not intended to be applied to other regions of the world, either in the causative factors which gave rise to it or in the ways public opinion was formed and communicated. The brilliance of his insight was in the very 'space' he opened up for investigation and the challenges that comparative analysis might raise.

The questions Habermas's work poses centre on how we might locate a public sphere in post-colonial Africa, where we can find the milieux for the discussion and dissemination of public opinion, and where and when public action can be provoked. One answer to these questions was dramatically provided in 1994 during the Nigerian crisis over the failure of the military to recognise the results of the previous June's election and install a civilian regime. At some risk to their safety, chiefs held meetings after which they communicated the various views of their publics to the military leaders in a series of memoranda. Although their full contents were not revealed, they contained a critique of inequality under the military regime which was conveyed to and published by the media.[13]

---

13 *West Africa*, 7–13 March 1994: 402.

It is becoming increasingly clear that some positions of authority at the local level are key points from which the articulation of political opinion among various sectors of a society must emanate. Local government in the form of a district or town council is not a place where independent public opinion is generated since local government, after all, is a formally constituted agency that is both of and for the state. Instead, there is extraordinary ferment around the historically based systems of local authority that were systematically disempowered and largely de-linked from the state and that now provide an alternative, yet informal, arena in which public discourse and participation in political processes can and do occur.

Conclusion

There has been a slow transformation of West Africa's pre-colonial governmental systems into active and thriving post-colonial public spheres where informal political processes take place that are intended to shape the decisions and resource allocations of the formal sphere which is the state. Chieftaincy-based systems of governance have changed profoundly, but some of the actual roles of chiefs have not. There has not been a transformation in the style of relationships between chiefs and ordinary people or in the idea that people can participate in governmental affairs through them. It is openly acknowledged that chiefs have adapted to post-colonial government by representing and lobbying for their subjects' interests with legislators, bureaucrats, and other office holders (Jagun 1985: 118).

The most blatantly transposed aspect of chieftaincy involves the two-tiered title system. Hereditary chiefs are locally based while appointive chiefs tend to represent higher, more all-encompassing levels of economic and political activity. The historic positions of hereditary and appointive title-holders are therefore reversed, for now it is kings who link people to appointive chiefs and who serve as intermediaries rather than the other way around as was the case in pre-colonial systems.

The *sine qua non* of a public sphere is the ability of participants to influence, criticise, or inform governing bodies. To be sure, governments have the constitutional power to curtail or eliminate chiefly institutions, but whether or not they have the *de facto* authority to do so can be seriously questioned. To varying degrees West African governments tolerate this sphere of parallel political activity. But is this benign tolerance or do chiefly institutions influence and inform governments in ways that demand – even necessitate – their tolerance? The answers are found in the public values that are displayed in connection with chiefly rituals and chiefly affairs and in the actors who participate in them. The values to which title-holders and their followers overwhelmingly ascribe idealise the local community and the systems of authority associated with them. The message being communicated is that local authority in the form of chiefs is one place where public trust and accountability begin (Vaughan 1991: 9).

In the years following independence, national leaders have faced the formidable problem of linking people and localities to nation-states that were not naturally developed, but were arbitrarily created by European powers. The forging of national identities and loyalties among illiterate rural peasants and others of the grassroots has presented an abiding dilemma. Broad ethnic identities have not been difficult to keep alive, but identities that cross-cut cultural or linguistic boundaries and that have political salience have been slow to emerge. National governments have found it difficult to create from the top down the kinds of credible ideologies and governing bodies that are based on common concerns and that link disparate sectors of their societies to one another – the military being an exceptional institution because of its pluralistic basis for recruiting and integrating personnel.

Looking at this problem from the bottom up provides an entirely different assessment. The spheres where chiefly activities take place can and do tie individuals and localities to the wider overarching institutions of the state through individuals who operate on various levels of society. These types of linkages are concretised through local titles awarded to people who are thereafter nominally and symbolically attached to that locality and its people. These individuals can be outsiders, such as Nigeria's chief of state who was given a title by the Oba (king) of Lagos who was not of his own cultural or linguistic group (Fernandez 1992: 129–30), or insiders who operate on the outside. The ceremonial events involving title-giving provide a context where successful people – locally defined – are on public view as participants. Through the people they honour, local citizens experience the wider world, while at the same time those honoured experience the local situation.

Thus chiefs perform the vital function of integrating disparate sectors of the population into the larger society (Oladosu 1985: 157; Bayart 1989: 209, 215). Their ceremonies provide a special meeting-ground for individuals whose loyalties and activities often place them at the disempowered, grassroots end of the political spectrum or conversely at the empowered end of political and economic privilege. Chiefly activities and practices offer a public space between the two extremes – a sphere where individuals of either end of the political continuum gain access to one another and where, as part of the exercise of formulating public opinion, they exchange information on what they value and how their demands should be represented in and implemented by the various institutions that govern them.

The very existence of this way of representing people and providing avenues for participation in contemporary political processes means that deeply embedded cultural influences are shaping today's African political systems in profound ways. Equally profound is the fact that many of these aspects are hidden from view by virtue of their historic origins and the failure of certain ideologies, especially those associated with modernisation and development, to recognise and legitimate the significance of history in today's political processes.

The interdigitation of informal political processes, involving and even depending on the performance of culturally circumscribed chiefly rituals, with formal governmental practices, and the dynamics of political life that emanate from these interactive relationships, are unique to West Africa. The contemporary public sphere as it has emerged in this part of the world arises out of quite dissimilar historical contexts than the ones in which a public sphere emerged in Europe. Yet contrasts such as these reveal the complexities of contemporary political experience and challenge us to continue the search for the many informal dimensions of the political sphere.

References

Aborisade, Oladimeji (ed.). 1985. *Local Government and the Traditional Rulers in Nigeria*. Ile-Ife, Nigeria: University of Ife Press.

Adams, Monni. 1991. 'Formal Public Titles for We/Guere Women, Côte d'Ivoire', *Anthropos* 86: 463–85.

Asiwaju, I.A. 1970. 'The Alaketu of Ketu and the Onimeko of Meko: The Changing Status of Two Yoruba Rulers under French and British Rule', in

West African Chiefs, M. Crowder and O. Ikime (eds). Ile-Ife, Nigeria: University of Ife Press.

Asiwaju, A.I. and Robin Law. 1985. 'From the Volta to the Niger, c.1600–1800', in *History of West Africa*, Vol. I (3rd edn), J.F. Ade Ajayi and M. Crowder (eds). London: Longman.

Atanda, J.A. 1970. 'The Changing Status of the Alafin of Oyo under Colonial Rule and Independence', in *West African Chiefs*, M. Crowder and O. Ikime (eds). Ile-Ife, Nigeria: University of Ife Press.

——. 1973. *The New Oyo Empire: Indirect Rule and Change in Western Nigeria, 1894–1934*. London: Longman.

Ayeni, Victor. 1985. 'Introduction: Traditional Rulers in a Period of Transition', in *Local Government and the Traditional Rulers in Nigeria*, O. Aborisade (ed.). Ile-Ife, Nigeria: University of Ife Press.

Babayemi, S.O. 1979. 'The Fall and Rise of Oyo c.1760–1905: A Study in the Traditional Culture of an African Polity', PhD thesis, University of Birmingham.

Barber, Karin. 1991. *I Could Speak Until Tomorrow*. Washington, D.C.: Smithsonian Institution Press.

Barnes, Sandra T. 1986. *Patrons and Power: Creating a Political Community in Metropolitan Lagos*. Manchester: Manchester University Press for IAI.

Bayart, Jean-Francois. 1989. *L'Etat en Afrique*. Paris: Fayard.

Bello-Imam, I. B. 1985. 'The Paralysis of Traditional Rulers in Nigerian Politics', in *Local Government and the Traditional Rulers in Nigeria*, O. Aborisade (ed.). Ile-Ife, Nigeria: University of Ife Press.

Bourdieu, Pierre. 1977. *Outline of a Theory of Practice*. Cambridge: Cambridge University Press.

Cohen, Abner. 1965. *Arab Border-Villages in Israel*. Manchester: Manchester University Press.

——. 1969. *Custom and Politics in Urban Africa*. Berkeley and Los Angeles: University of California Press.

——. 1974. *Two-Dimensional Man*. London: Routledge & Kegan Paul.

——. 1981. *The Politics of Elite Culture*. Berkeley and Los Angeles: University of California Press.

——. 1993. *Masquerade Politics: Explorations in the Structure of Urban Cultural Movements*. Berkeley and Los Angeles: University of California Press.

Cookey, S.J. 1987. *Report of the Political Bureau*. Lagos: Federal Government Printer.

Crowder, M. and O. Ikime. 1970. 'Introduction', to *West African Chiefs: Their Changing Status under Colonial Rule and Independence*. Ile-Ife, Nigeria: University of Ife Press.

Feierman, Steven. 1995. 'Social Change in Colonial Africa', in *African History*, P. Curtin et al. London: Longman.

Ferguson, P. and I. Wilks. 1970. 'Chiefs, Constitutions and the British in Northern Ghana', in *West African Chiefs*, M. Crowder and O. Ikime (eds). Ile-Ife, Nigeria: University of Ife Press.

Fernandez, Abiola D.E. 1992. *Lagos: A Legacy of Honour*. Ibadan: Spectrum Books.

Geschiere, Peter. 1993. 'Chiefs and Colonial Rule in Cameroon: Inventing Chieftaincy, French and British Style', *Africa* 63(2): 151–75.

Goheen, Mitzi. 1992. 'Chiefs, Sub-Chiefs and Local Control: Negotiations over Land, Struggles over Meaning', *Africa*, 62(3): 389–412.

Guyer, Jane. 1992. 'Representation Without Taxation: An Essay on Democracy in Rural Nigeria, 1952–1990', *African Studies Review*, 35(1): 41–79.

——. 1994. 'The Spatial Dimensions of Civil Society in Africa: an Anthropologist Looks at Nigeria', in *Civil Society and the State in Africa*, J.W. Harbeson et al. (eds). Boulder: L. Rienner.

Habermas, Jurgen. 1974. 'The Public Sphere: An Encyclopedia Article (1964)', *New German Critique* 1(3): 49–55.

——. 1991. *The Structural Transformation of the Public Sphere*. Cambridge, Mass.: The MIT Press.

Jagun, Adedokun. 1985. 'Traditional Rulers and the Concept of Democracy and Local Government: A Paradigm of Harmony or Conflict', in *Local Government and the Traditional Rulers in Nigeria*, O. Aborisade (ed.). Ile-Ife, Nigeria: University of Ife Press.

Law, Robin. 1977. *The Oyo Empire c.1600–1836*. Oxford: Clarendon.

Mauss, Marcel. 1970. *The Gift* (translated by Ian Cunnison). London: Cohen & West.

Oladosu, S. Ade. 1985. 'The Role of Nigerian Traditional Rulers in Nation-Building: An Overview', in *Local Government and the Traditional Rulers in Nigeria*, O. Aborisade (ed.). Ile-Ife, Nigeria: University of Ife Press.

Stoeltje, Beverly. 1991. 'Asante Queenmothers: A Study in Female Authority', paper delivered at a conference on 'Queens, Queen Mothers, Priestesses and Power: Case Studies in African Gender', April 1991, New York University.

Vaughan, Olufemi. 1991. 'The Myth of Political Modernisation: Chieftaincy Politics and Social Relations in Nigeria', paper delivered at the 20th annual meeting of the Canadian Association of African Studies, 16–18 May, Toronto.

CHAPTER 3

Beyond Cultural Performance:
Women, Culture and the State in Contemporary Nigerian Politics

Ifi Amadiume *

Introduction

My concern in this chapter is with historical developments in African women's movements for structural political power as organised groups in contemporary Nigerian politics. My interest is not so much in the politics of identity, staged dramas or representation, but in rationality, pragmatism and action.

Political mobilisation in itself is not the same as a social movement. I have argued elsewhere (Amadiume 1994) that social movements have a structural impact or aim for structural change. I therefore subscribe to Bailey's objection (p.11 above) to the 'confusion-of-many-voices model' by insisting on authenticity, that is, a shift from performances or text to context. I understand this to mean economics and social politics, and in the case of contemporary Africa, the context defining the actors of modern-day cosmopolitan ethnic groups or 'imagined communities'.

It is therefore with rational intention that I choose to be guided by the deconstructive aspect of Abner Cohen's work which was concerned with unmasking the processes in the formation of what he called 'cults of eliteness' or 'mystique of eliteness'. This concern

---

* I am grateful to Humphrey Fisher and Lionel Caplan for useful editorial comments.

with the instrumental use of culture by the political classes, 'power groups', or elite groups was central to his work, particularly his earlier studies of diaspora Hausa communities manipulating their own version of Islam for the control of specific trades, and Creole Freemasons in Sierra Leone using the dead for the control of state finance. The key message was the link between symbols and organised power, in other words, culture and ritual in politics (Cohen 1965, 1966, 1969, 1971, 1974, 1981). In this chapter, I am particularly interested in the place of gender in Cohen's theorisation and its relevance to women and class politics in Nigeria, using more recent data.[1]

Cohen was one of the anthropologists who did fieldwork in Nigeria in the early 1960s, an important period in our history which saw the formation of various interest groups within the centrist movement competing for the huge space at the top vacated by the British, following Nigerian independence in 1960. During this period, it was still possible for Cohen to think of community in the Durkheimian sense of a morally bounded group. This is evident in his work on West African Hausa trading diasporas, (synthesised in Cohen 1965, 1966 and 1971) which form the basis of his ideas on ideology and ethnicity. The criteria used in his analysis were those of group distinctiveness and homogenisation in a horizontal view of the nation-state.

In a later publication, Cohen (1981) extended his interest to the study of elite culture within a pluralistic and hierarchical system in a modern African society. His subject matter here was the professional man, still forming only a small sector in the economy: by 1970 a Creole professional elite, only two percent of the total Sierra Leone population, was maintaining and running the entire state system. The criteria used in the Creole case study were those of a co-operating corporate group which achieved cohesion and autonomy through the operation of 'a special culture'. While with the Hausa study, women were used as moveable objects in marriage for group reproduction, in the Creole case, elite women were active as agents of cultural reproduction in their role as socialisers for a special lifestyle and the 'cult of eliteness'.

However, in spite of the obvious public activities of Creole

---

1 Data used in this paper were collected between November 1985 and April 1987, and more recently June–August 1994 in Nigeria. This involved direct participation and use of newspaper reports, magazines and journals. A more detailed book is near completion.

women, Cohen seemed to be arguing that there was a contradiction in Creole women's experiences of Creoleness, since their feeling of solidarity at a wider public level was negated by their victimisation at the personal private level. The private interest served was a male power interest. The women were therefore simply being used by what in effect was a male power system.

Although inspired by Cohen's analysis of power cults, I wish to argue that loss of organisational autonomy is a later development in African women's social movements. It had become necessary in my own work to use a historical perspective to get away from the idea of women as objects or victims, hence in *African Matriarchal Foundations* (Amadiume 1987b), and later publications, I have worked more with the concept of traditional African matriarchy, elaborating the idea of a dual-sex political system,[2] situationally shifting between contesting and complementary gender ideologies. In the Igbo case, I showed clearly that in spite of colonialism, African matriarchal heritage is still present in the deeper structures of kinship systems, in women's rituals, women's institutions, and indigenous women's organisations. With economic achievement or ritual approval, it was also possible to belong to various title societies – some open, some restricted.

Many of the women's organisations traditionally enjoyed the privilege of ritual autonomy, a factor which was important for the exclusive political organisations to function autonomously and effectively. Women made their own rules, sanctioned their own members, and devised their own strategies of action. I would agree with Cheikh Anta Diop (1989) that these institutions mirrored ancient African matriarchy, from which we have inherited goddess religions and mother-focused myths, legends, and folktales. We have also inherited an ideology of motherhood and its social rewards and, more importantly, the structure of our primary kinship system and its matricentric units as well as our kinship morality of the all-binding 'spirit of common motherhood', the closest bond of love and trust in our descent or clan systems.

The reverence of motherhood that this system has generated in African culture is also related to the fear of women's anger in indigenous African societies. Collectively the women also held the power of opposition through strikes, non-co-operation, or mass

---

[2] Studies on the gender character of traditional African political systems of African societies and community politics include Lebeuf (1963); Okonjo (1976); Amadiume (1987a).

exodus. We have a great deal of data on traditional African women challenging formal patriarchal authority, particularly about African women applying traditional strategies of rebellion to protest patriarchal systems imposed by either Islam or Christianity.[3] Surely, there is a history of a cultural heritage that would explain the general strategy of what has been described as 'sexual insult' used by African women during protest and war (Ardener 1975).

These women's strategies of collective action were most effective during the pre-colonial and colonial periods, when traditional African women's organisations were still autonomous and the traditional dual-sex political system with its own systems of checks and balances obtained. Both the strategies and patterns of African women's movements underwent a radical transformation as a result of colonisation, new class formations and the character of the contemporary state in Africa (see Amadiume 1994).

Nigeria – Parallels and Disjunctures in Cults of Eliteness and the Mystique of Excellence

Under Global Finance Capitalism, leadership in the neo-colonies no longer requires a broad social base, or direct involvement in economic production, since donor money can act as payment for agency and subservience to Western powers. This is a major difference between the 1980s political economy of Africa and the character of its state systems, and that of the 1960s and 1970s that Cohen described for Nigeria and Sierra Leone respectively. As I argue later, external financial 'aid' has had a direct effect on women's mobilisation in Nigeria.

Even by the 1960s and 1970s, tradition and Islam which were the social basis of emirate autocracy in northern Nigeria were being undermined through the production of Europeanised elites to serve in the post-independence Nigerian government. Through British training, a new generation of sons of the northern aristocracy emerged as administrators in the bureaucracy, factions of whom joined forces with southern petty bourgeois elements to form powerful exclusive 'mafia clubs'. These were bureaucrats and

---

3 See Lewis (1971); Strobel (1976); Onwuejeogwu (1969); Ritzenthaler (1960); Ardener (1975). For references on Igbo women, see Ifeka-Moller (1975); Amadiume (1987a).

technocrats who, through their position in the 1960s and 1970s, built a material base out of corruption and embezzlement. They later became established in business and were powerful enough to form alliances with other power groups and to finance military coups and military dictators.

Nigerian scholars and political analysts have found it difficult to pinpoint these 'mafias'.[4] However, regardless of the secrecy surrounding these power cults, it is well known that they are multi-ethnic and multicultural in composition, and seem willing to participate in individual members' cultural or religious ceremonies and events, thus establishing primary ties of friendship and trust without being necessarily bound to the same culture or religion.

In this situation, therefore, rationality and greed seem to be the determining factors as individuals manoeuvre through different cultures, using a multiplicity of symbolic forms and identities rather than being gelled by means of a common culture as in the case of diaspora Hausa communities or the Creoles of Sierra Leone. It was particularly under the Babangida regime (1985–1993) and its well-developed state instruments of coercion, that it no longer seemed necessary to mystify the contradiction between private and public interests. Having clamped down on radical unions and co-opted radical individuals, it proceeded to seek to institutionalise corruption.

The history of contemporary elite women's groups has followed closely the pattern of men's groups. In tracing the emergence of women as an organised force in contemporary Nigerian society, it is striking how similar the new women's groups were to Creole women's organisations. This is not surprising given the fact that in Nigeria, much as in Sierra Leone, 'cults of eliteness' were produced through the churches, schools, and various church-linked women's associations, particularly the Young Women's Christian Association (YWCA), whose first president was the wife of the colonial Governor-General. At independence, Europeanised Nigerian women took over the leadership. Prominent in all these organisations were upper-class women who were wives and daughters of the urban-based ruling elite. As ladies of leisure, they were bored and needed more public activities and so they turned to

---

4 For the debate on one such group, see Fagbola (1986); Takaya and Tyoden (1987); 'The core of Kaduna Mafia', *Newswatch*, 29 May 1989; Olukoshi (1994).

philanthropic work. Emulating European women, they too took on the job of 'civilising' their sister Africans with missionary zeal.[5]

In the 1960s, for example, the YWCA devised a programme called *practical design for modern living*, which was specifically aimed at young girls moving to the cities from the rural villages. The girls were taught the basics of modern life, including how to dress like ladies, how to straighten their hair and how to use the make-up in vogue. Upper-class Yoruba and Creole women had brought the culture of a new Western femininity - skin-lightening and hair-straightening, a different kind of romantic love to the new urban elite women. In the 1960s, these women in turn carried the new culture into the 'hinterland', the villages. The first set of educated Nigerian women were mostly members of the YWCA.

The 1940s and 1950s saw the dominance of individual Western-educated and town-based Christian elite women over traditional women's organisations which hitherto had met the local needs of women. With this dominance came the reinterpretation of identity, function and strategies of women's organisations. A major transformation was the speedy incorporation in 1959 of the many locally generated women's organisations from the various regions of Nigeria into a bourgeois-led national umbrella organisation called National Council For Women's Societies (NCWS).

From the background of the founding leaders and the organisations from which they emerged into the NCWS, we can see the influence of the Ladies' Progressive Club and its concern with welfare, charity, and philanthropy, on the one hand, and, on the other, the political activism of the militant market women and those from the Women's Party. Some of the founding members might argue that the fusion in NCWS marked the beginning of group articulation of women's interests and a recognition by the government of women's groups as part of the political process. I hope to show that this claim is questionable by considering the issues of class, representation, and participation, and, consequently, the effect that this trend has had on traditional women's organisations and women's participation in politics.

NCWS claims to be the only national women's organisation,

---

5 See The *Guardian*, 21 May 1986, for an extensive interview with Dr Irene Elizabeth Ighodaro, one of the early YWCA founders. She was a Sierra Leonean by birth. The *Guardian*, 4 March 1987, featured Lady Oyinkan Abayomi, the most outstanding model of the upper class elite women of this period. See particularly Nina Mba's tribute, 'Saluting the "Mother of Lagos" '; see also *Sunday Vanguard*, 26 April 1987, for an interview with Mrs Ayo Ogun, titled 'A Touch of Class'.

and from the outset it also claimed to be non-political, being concerned with welfare and educational matters. It received an annual government subvention and became, as far as the government was concerned, the organisation representing Nigerian women. It had branches in all the capital towns of the then three regions, including Lagos. There are now branches in all the states and membership is still on an individual basis or as members of other organisations. Most of its leadership of mainly elite, educated and wealthy women had already been co-opted by the new political parties, which had also used coercion and red-tape in co-opting the new women's organisations as women's wings of the various parties. The women's organisations had thus come under party and state control.[6]

The continued collaborative role of the NCWS with the state has been ensured through the practice of the wives of heads of governments assuming patronage of the Council. NCWS has also continued to become a stepping stone for government appointments of women. Most of the state and federal presidents of the Council have at one time or another served as ministers of state or state commissioners.[7]

To some extent one can therefore say that politically women had some representation in government, but only as tokens. This representation was not structural, in the sense that women so appointed were in power in their own right and not structurally as representing Nigerian women through NCWS, a marked difference from the structural power position of indigenous women's organisations and Women's Councils, and their accountable leadership.

I am arguing, therefore, that the new organisation provided elite women with an extensive network through which they could participate as individuals in politics, the economy, and the new elite culture. They could also pursue careers, albeit in the name of women. This individual self-interest undermined the traditional spontaneous mass actions which had previously led to political gains for women as a collective. The focus of publicity was shifted to the leadership role of individual elite women. More emphasis

---

6 Mba (1982). There is also reference to local authority and police harassment of Northern Muslim women political leaders in Cohen 1969: 62–3 and Mba 1982: 254–5.
7 See my press article, 'Women and the political debate', The *Guardian*, 19 May 1986, and the rejoinder by Theresa Ogbuibe, a spokesperson for NCWS, 'Women and Political Future of Nigeria', *Daily Times*, 27 May 1986.

was consequently placed on cultural performance and image-making. The establishment was now able to speak to the female masses through these 'leaders'. With both economic and political interests in the establishment, the 'leaders' saw themselves as accountable to the establishment and not to the women in the rural villages, from whom they were now cut off and shielded by state agencies. It marked the beginning of the present era, with its female tokenism in an establishment which is basically male in culture.

In this new development the associations of wives linked to the various male-dominated professions tend to exercise power and control money and other resources according to the importance of their husbands and their husbands' professions. It is in the context of this political culture of corruption that one can understand the emergence of Maryam Babangida as a formidable political figure, and the cult of power that surrounded this Igbo wife of a Northern Muslim army officer. Compared to the powerful image of Mrs Maryam Babangida, all the other previous First Ladies now seem quite insignificant. The career of Maryam Babangida is a good illustration of structural failings in the democratisation of gender in the contemporary state system in Africa.

Emergence of the Cult of the First Lady

As the Nigerian military moved away from the traditional role of defence and combat into politics and more economic and political power, so also did their wives grow in importance. The long rule of the army has seen the Nigerian Army Officers' Wives' Association (NAOWA), another colonial heritage, emerge as the most powerful women's organisation in the country. Mrs Babangida, wife of the military ruler of Nigeria, General Ibrahim Babangida (from August 1985 to August 1993) and generally agreed to be the most powerful Nigerian first lady so far,[8] traced her public career to the presidency of NAOWA.

When the association was formed in 1960, it was called the Army Wives Association (AWA). Its activities then were confined to the barracks. As army men grew in power, so also did their wives grow in importance. With this growing sense of their class (a multi-ethnic, multi-cultural, multi-lingual group of women of different

---

8 'Maryam Babangida, the Power Behind the Throne', The *Guardian*, 27 August 1986.

ages and different levels of education), the women changed the all-embracing name Army Wives Association (AWA) which they described as 'bland and non-descript' to Nigerian Army Officers Wives' Association, (NAOWA). They then established a secretariat in an officers' mess in Lagos, reviewed their constitution, and made it mandatory that the wife of the Chief of Army Staff assume presidency of NAOWA. They coined a logo, drew up a code of conduct, and issued an identity card for members.

In 1988, the publication and launching of Mrs Babangida's book, *The Home Front* (1988), gave the public a lot of insight into the activities of the association, as much as it also raised questions and debate.[9] During this launching occasion, as in others, the might of the establishment was at her command and behind her and full of praise for her. The chief launcher was Sani Abacha, a Lt. General and Chief of Army Staff. The chairperson was Hannah Idowu Awolowo, widow of the late chief Obafemi Awolowo. The Guest of Honour was General Yakubu Gowon, one-time head of state of Nigeria. Others present included state governors, Armed Forces Ruling Council (AFRC) members and many other eminent Nigerians. Moving from the particular to the general, Mrs Babangida claimed in her speech that the presidency of NAOWA had given her a 'fuller understanding and appreciation of the problems faced by not only the officers' wives, but by all women as mothers and wives'. [10]

Mrs Babangida's career and persona had, by 1988, gone through tremendous changes from descriptions of her in 1985 when her husband first seized power. She may have traced her public career to her presidency of NAOWA, but I want to argue that powerful as that organisation was, it was not the means by which Mrs Babangida succeeded in wielding structural power. This was done through her appropriation of the potential structural power of the leadership of the NCWS and later by setting up her own organisation at a formal level. She, in effect, instituted a 'co-presidency' (does this echo the fears expressed in the United States about the formal role given to Hillary Clinton?)

In the early stages in her career, the First Lady's credentials contained statements about wifehood, motherhood, her good looks, and the fact that she hosted society women and the wives of

---

9 *Newswatch*, 3 October 1988; *The African Guardian*, 26 September 1988.

10 Ibid.

diplomats to tea.[11] These informal regular social meetings gave Mrs Babangida a core group of supporters with highly developed primary relations.

Developing primary relationships within a core group that is informal and does not have a base in economic production or ownership of the means of production, however, can confer only limited power. Such a group may share out commissions from a deal, but cannot legitimately claim a share of government revenue. This is probably why Mrs Babangida found it necessary to first work through existing and formally recognised wider women's organisations, as for example the National Council for Women's Societies (NCWS). I use three examples to show how Mrs Babangida first dominated and finally appropriated this very powerful symbolic forum.

The first is her role during the introduction of the World Bank-prescribed Second-Tier Foreign Exchange Market (SFEM) in 1986. SFEM, which was a means of devaluing and externally fixing the value of the Nigerian currency, was a component of the Structural Adjustment Programme (SAP). The SAP was a conditionality laid down by the World Bank through the International Monetary Fund (IMF) to debt-ridden African and Third World countries. This was supposedly designed to effect economic reform and economic recovery through financial loans with interest repayment. The stringent measures in this package included currency devaluation, removal of certain state subsidies, de-indigenisation, and privatisation of state-owned enterprises, reduction in state expenditure, and trade liberalisation. These measures, in effect, spelt general economic and social hardship, particularly weakening the autonomy of the state. As many have claimed, this was the single most effective means of multilateral recolonisation of Africa in order to serve Western capitalist economic interests (Campbell and Loxley 1989; Onimode 1989; Mkandawire 1992).

In this case, this self-interest placed more value on budget balancing than on people's basic needs. Women as food producers, family carers, farmers and subsistence economy workers, dominant in the informal sector, would suffer very directly from loss of government subsidisation of imported goods, food, healthcare and education (Gladwin 1991).

---

11 Kelechi Onyemaobi, 'The Radiance of the Queen', The *Guardian Sunday*, 15 March 1987.

The introduction of SFEM by the Babangida regime, after the majority of Nigerians had rejected the loan option in a state-sponsored debate in 1985 on the theme, 'To take or not to take', was consequently very controversial and unpopular. Left to market women alone, through their control of the market-places and the fixing of prices on certain commodities, they could have hoarded goods and thereby precipitated a price hike that would have frustrated SFEM right from its onset. The government was aware of this and consequently used Mrs Babangida as patron of NCWS to check the opposition to SFEM from market women by calling a meeting and ensuring their co-operation. Invoking the myth of unity, she said, 'Our collective strength is in mutual support'. Market women must today regret that compromise, since SFEM marked the beginning of the fall of the naira, and unprecedented mass poverty and general economic decline.

During this controlled performance, the president of NCWS in her own speech claimed that the purpose of the meeting was to give market women an opportunity to rebut the accusation that they were hoarding commodities. She did, however, admit that the problem of hoarding and inflation lay with the middlemen and not the market women. This seems to suggest that the purpose of the meeting was to intimidate the women and diffuse opposition. This can be seen by the fact that the spokeswoman of the market women gave her promise that they would co-operate with the government on SFEM. This was a great betrayal.

Having disarmed the market women, these women 'leaders' then stepped aside and introduced men of the establishment for whom they had prepared a safe ground. The director of Budget, Federal Ministry of Finance, then explained the modalities of SFEM to the market women. So also did the director of Exchange Control at the Central Bank. These were men who had never before taken the trouble to explain monetary matters to women. The contradiction of course was that market women would never enter the Central Bank to bid for SFEM which at that time was only open to banks or big businesses through the banks.

Mrs Babangida Dominates and Regulates NCWS

The second example concerns the manner in which Mrs Babandiga controls the NCWS. Its 11th Biennial Convention in

Port Harcourt, held at the International Airport Hotel[12] is a case in point. It crystallised most of the contradictions in the very idea, character and aims of the Council. The theme of the Convention was 'unity, action and progress'. It was attended by over a thousand women. The stated intention was to discuss common problems, review past achievements, plan future strategies and elect new officers. The sub-themes of the Convention were: youth in action for progress; women in action for national development; and community in action for national stability.

In the usual format that this cultural performance takes, the NCWS Convention was opened by the host state's military Governor (always a man). The nation's First Lady and some states' first ladies, who have always been patrons of the organisation in their respective states, all read opening speeches. The Convention thus opened symbolically under the blessing and supervision of the establishment. The general messages from these wives of the establishment can be summarised as calling on the women to endorse and carry out fully government policies. In all this, the voice of grassroots women was only heard in their capacity to entertain with songs and dances during a roll-call of the different states!

Mrs Babangida, in her speech, stressed the Council's role in forging national unity, and that in order to do so, the women had to start from the home. She reminded the women that the Council's motto is 'Service in Unity'. According to Mrs Babangida, 'This objective is laudable, and must continue to be the guiding principle in all you do... As I stressed last year, now is the time for Council to be seen as a vanguard for the promotion of unity and progress amongst women of all ages in this country, and through your example, permeate the whole nation with the spirit of unity'.

She made suggestions involving structural changes both in the organisation, policy and constitution of the Council. Forging a myth of genealogy by naming some founding leaders of NCWS and historical women leaders, she referred to past struggles where Nigerian women have united and fought for their rights and went on to say, 'I therefore urge you, in like manner, to mobilise the women's societies to contribute and support all government and private programmes... As women, we should always identify

---

12 *Daily Star*, 23 July 1986; The *Guardian*, 18 July 1986.

ourselves with peace. There are many challenging divisive elements in our various communities, in each state and in the country as a whole, we should therefore use our feminine attributes of sympathy, intuition and tact to influence our menfolk and the entire nation to surmount these divisive elements and thus maintain peace, unity and stability'.[13]

As a result of an internal power struggle, the 1986 Convention failed to elect a new leadership. This meant another term of office for those already in power. This struggle for control of the leadership of NCWS took a more overtly violent turn during the next Convention which was held in August 1988, in the new federal capital, Abuja.[14] The Convention ended abruptly as a result of a violent struggle for power. There were both regional and ethnic dimensions to the struggle for power, as the 'northern' women seemed determined to seize the presidency of NCWS from the 'southerners'.

The conference was reconvened at the Durbar Hotel, Lagos, in November 1988. The northern candidate[15] did not attend and Mrs Emily Aig-Imoukhuede won the presidency. Both Mrs Aig-Imoukhuede and her predecessor were firmly grounded in the Christian mission tradition.

The third example concerns Mrs Babangida's successful attempt to undercut existing government-recognised informal national organisations for women such as the NCWS, and formal government structures for women's outreach work, such as the Committee on Women and Development, and set up her own structure for the management of women and development in her own office inside the presidential building. What began as an informal elite women's equivalent of a 'Boys' Club' was converted to power when, in 1988, it acquired an official status and grew into a national network of military governors' wives for managing women and development called 'Better Life for Rural Women'. The project was state and foreign aid sponsored. It thrived particularly on the distribution of commodities such as cash and farm fertiliser.

---

13 Ibid.

14 *The African Guardian*, 22 August 1988.

15 This northern candidate, Laila Dogonyaro, as I observed during my last visit to Nigeria (June–August 1994) is now president of NCWS, the first northern Muslim woman to hold this post.

The National Secretariat of the programme was directly headed by Mrs Babangida. The State Committees, on the other hand, had a chairperson, a co-ordinator, a director of women's affairs and appointed members. There was in effect a three-tier structure, namely, the State Organising Committee headed by the wife of the military Governor, the rest of the members being appointed from 'all relevant agencies/ministries'; the Local Government Committee headed by the wives of the Local Government 'Chairmen'; and the community/village level committee consisting of 'recognised opinion leaders within the community'.[16]

Conclusion: After the Performance – Voices of Resistance and Dissent

At the end of her first year in power, journalists were searching for a CV for their First Lady. After three years in power, they now had it: Maryam Babangida, Nigeria's First Lady, author of *Home Front* and prime mover of the better life for rural women programme.[17] Again, at the end of four years, it was said of her, 'she has toppled a whole volume of political assumptions and reinvented the idea of a Nigerian first lady: a first lady not just contented with her routine honorary status and boring titular functions... She has used her proximity to power to ensure not only the allocation of substantial resources to women development programs, but also the establishment by the Armed Forces Ruling Council, AFRC, of the Commission for Women and Development'.[18]

Listed among her achievements were: the construction of the multi-million naira Centre for Women Development in Abuja, later called Maryam Babangida Women's Centre; sponsoring and hosting the United Nations' Economic Community for Africa's Conference on the Integration of Women In Development; donating more than a million naira accruing from the launching and sales of her book, *The Home Front*, to disabled children's homes.

Popular language which dubbed Maryam Babangida's programme 'Better Life For Better Women' is proof that people read

---

16 *Newswatch*, 14 May 1990.

17 *Newswatch*, 13 November 1989.

18 *Newswatch*, 8 January 1990.

the reality beyond the performance and saw that these women were acting in self-interest. The launching of these programmes has provided an occasion for society ladies to show off their visible wealth and privileges in their clothes, the amount of money they are able to raise and the calibre of dignitaries who attend. Mrs Babangida's book launch in 1988 was aptly captioned 'Maryam's Day of Glory' in *Newswatch*, 3 October 1988, a special edition on the *Changing Lifestyle of Nigerians*. It takes us on a journey through the lives of Nigerians in the different social classes, painting a vivid picture of poverty and suffering: 'Hard time, hard luck, sins of the few and visionless shepherds of state have turned the wheel of fortunes away from most Nigerians'.

At the opening of the seven-day Better Life Fair in March 1990, this is how Mrs Babangida was described by the critical pen of a radical journalist: 'She was like a Roman empress on a throne, regal and resplendent in a stone-studded flowing outfit that defied description. Her head-gear, a rose-pink and white creation perched coquettishly on her head, was a statement of extravagant opulence. She took in the official ceremony with a permanent smile on her face'.[19] According to this writer, Mrs Babangida visited the stand every day, accompanied by a winding entourage, and '... dressed in captivating outfits, she clearly stole the show from the rural women. But they loved it as most of them look up to her as their motivator. In apparent appreciation of her contribution, some wore outfits with her portrait printed on them and turned the popular gospel chorus, "I have decided to follow Jesus" into "I have decided to follow Maryam".' I observed myself that during President Babangida's visit to Niger State in May 1991, this time, it was Mrs Gwadabe, wife of the military state Governor who had an outfit with a portrait of Maryam Babangida printed on it.

From Mrs Babangida herself, we learn that wives of the military establishment appear to have an illusion of power, or a lust for power in their aspirations inside their own parallel hierarchical organisations within NAOWA. According to Mrs Babangida, 'quite a good number of officers' wives have consequently invented for themselves the military rank a step ahead of their husband' (1988: 15).

Weeks after the election on the 12th June, 1993, when Babangida annulled the result and opposition forces were telling

---

19 *Newswatch*, 26 March 1990.

him to get out, Mrs Babangida was attending a conference in Abuja in which she was seeking to legalise the role of 'The First Lady' by having it inscribed in the constitution.

Given this high level of 'politicking', calculated negotiations, shifting alliances and alignments, it is not possible to see this class of women as victims of the male system, but as very much actively involved in this system for themselves. The issue therefore is whether Mrs Babangida only succeeded in serving male interest, that is, was simply being used, or did she in anyway manage to institute, at a structural level, something like the traditional dual-sex political system which, as I argued earlier, gave women structural significance and power in indigenous societies in Africa?

Maryam Babangida and her female allies were not just being used by the establishment to perform state universalistic functions for private interests. She had reinvented the traditional institution of a dual-sex political system which operated in distinct male and female spheres. The female sphere saw the power and authority of legitimate matriarchs invoking the ideology of motherhood and collectivism.[20] Mrs Babangida's cult of matriarchy was supported by coercion and corruption. Her *mystique of excellence* did not fool the African masses who have an amazing ability to praise their European-backed dictators one day, and the next day dance at their overthrow or murder! The ideologies of the ruling classes remain problematic in a context of imperialism such as the contemporary African states and the dictatorial rule of its elites.

The analysis of Maryam Babangida's cultural performance has served three useful purposes in this paper. First, it shows the limitations of focusing purely on the woman's persona. Like the radical journalists tracking and deconstructing her, I could easily have filled pages writing about images, allegories, metaphors and audience response. Secondly, simply focusing on identity politics would have overshadowed the more important bigger picture, the contexual issues and organised resistance in the coming together of various social forces in a movement for social transformation. While Mrs Babangida was still busy calculating likely pay-offs from her performance, it was an organised movement of both radical and liberal forces which forced her husband, General Ibrahim Babangida to step down from power on 26 August 1993, in effect overthrowing a dictatorial military

---

20 See Diop (1989); James (1978); Amadiume (1987b, 1989, 1993, 1994).

regime. Thirdly, Maryam Babangida's performance came to an end, as she was compelled to face audience rejection, while the issue of social justice for women remains on the political agenda.

References

Amadiume, Ifi. 1987a. *Male Daughters, Female Husbands: Gender and Sex in an African Society*. London: Zed Books.

———. 1987b. *African Matriarchal Foundations: The Igbo Case*. London: Karnak house.

———. 1989. 'Introduction', to *The Cultural Unity of Black Africa: The Domains of Matriarchy and of Patriarchy in Classical Antiquity*. Cheikh Anta Diop. London: Karnak House.

———. 1993. 'The Mouth that Spoke a Falsehood Will Later Speak the Truth: Going Home to the Field in Eastern Nigeria', in *Gendered Fields: Women, Men & Ethnography*, D. Bell, P. Caplan, and W.J. Karim (eds). London and New York: Routledge.

———. 1994. 'Gender, Political Systems and Social Movements: A West African Experience', in *African Studies in Social Movements*, M. Mamdani and E. Wambadia-Wamba (eds). Dakar: CODESRIA Publications.

Ardener, S. 1975. 'Sexual Insult and Female Militancy', in *Perceiving Women*, Shirley Ardener (ed.). London: J.M. Dent & Sons.

Babangida, Maryam. 1988. *The Home Front*. Ibadan: Fountain Publications.

Campbell, Bonnie, and John Loxley. 1989. *Structural Adjustment in Africa*. New York: St. Martin's Press.

Cohen, Abner. 1965. 'The Social Organisation of Credit in a West African Cattle Market', *Africa* 35(1): 8–20.

———. 1966. 'Politics of the Kola Trade', *Africa* 36(1): 18–36.

———. 1969. *Custom and Politics in Urban Africa: a Study of Hausa Migrants in Yoruba Towns*. London: Routledge & Kegan Paul.

———. 1971. 'Cultural Strategies in the Organisation of Trading Diasporas', in *The Development of Indigenous Trade and Markets in West Africa*, Claude Meillassoux (ed.). London: Oxford University Press.

———. 1974. *Two-Dimensional Man: an Essay on the Anthropology of Power and Symbolism in Complex Society*. London: Routledge & Kegan Paul.

———. 1981. *The Politics of Elite Culture: Explorations in the Dramaturgy of Power in a Modern African Society*. Berkeley: University of California Press.

———. 1993. *Masquerade Politics: Explorations in the Structure of Urban Cultural Movements*. Berkeley: University of California Press.

Diop, Cheikh Anta. 1989. *The Cultural Unity of Black Africa: The Domains of Matriarchy and of Patriarchy in Classical Antiquity*. London: Karnak House.

Fagbola, Patrick. 1986. *Kaduna Mafia*. Ibadan: Heinemann Frontline Series.

Gladwin, Christina (ed.). 1991. *Structural Adjustment and African Women Farmers*. Gainesville: University Press of Florida.

Ifeka-Moller, C. 1975. 'Female Militancy and Colonial Revolt: The Women's War of 1929, Eastern Nigeria', in *Perceiving Women*, Shirley Ardener (ed.). London: J.M. Dent & Sons.

James, Wendy. 1978. 'Matrifocus on African Women', in *Defining Females: the Nature of Women in Society*, Shirley Ardener (ed.). London: Croom Helm Ltd.

Lebeuf, Annie M.D. 1963. 'The Role of Women in the Political Organisation of African Societies', in *Women of Tropical Africa*, Denise Paulme (ed.). Berkeley: University of California Press.

Lewis, I.M. 1971. *Ecstatic Religion*. Harmondsworth: Penguin.

Mba, Nina. 1982. *Nigerian Women Mobilised: Women's Political Activities in Southern Nigeria, 1900–1965*. Berkeley: Institute of International Studies, University of California Press.

Mkandawire, Thandika. 1992. 'Adjustment, Political Conditionality and Democratisation in Africa', paper delivered at CODESRIA Seventh General Assembly.

Okonjo, Kamene. 1976. 'The Dual-Sex Political System in Operation: Igbo Women and Community Politics in Midwestern Nigeria', in *Women in Africa: Studies in Social and Economic Change*, N.J. Hafkin and E.G. Bay (eds). Stanford: Stanford University Press.

Olukoshi, Adebayo. 1994. 'Bourgeois Social Movements and the Struggle for Democracy in Nigeria: an Inquiry into the "Kaduna Mafia"', in *African Studies in Social Movements*, M. Mamdani and E. Wamba-dia-Wamba (eds). Dakar: CODESRIA Publications.

Onimode, Bade (ed.). 1989. *The IMF, the World Bank, and the African Debt*. London: Zed Books.

Onwuejeogwu, M. 1969. 'The Cult of the Bori Spirits Among the Hausa', in *Man in Africa*, M. Douglas and P. Kaberry (eds). London: Tavistock.

Ritzenthaler, R.E. 1960. 'Anlu: A Woman's Uprising in the British Cameroons, 1960', *African Studies* 19 (3): 151–6.

Strobel, M. 1976. 'From Lelemama to Lobbying: Women's Associations in Mombasa, Kenya', in *Women in Africa*, N.J. Hafkin and Edna Bay (eds). Stanford: Stanford University Press.

Takaya, B.J. and S.G. Tyoden (eds). 1987. *The Kaduna Mafia: A Study of the Rise, Development and Consolidation of a Nigerian Power Elite.* Jos: Jos University Press.

CHAPTER 4

The Bantu Botatwe:
Changing Political Definitions in Southern Zambia

Elizabeth Colson *

Introduction

Abner Cohen (1969, 1974, and 1993) has argued that ethnicity is basically a political phenomenon: it becomes salient in political struggles among groups contesting control over public resources. He has been concerned with ethnic mobilisation in urban settings, in West Africa and Britain, and with the devices used to mark-off, celebrate and legitimate contenders for recognition in such arenas. Epstein and Mitchell, who watched ethnic mobilisation in urban areas of Zambia in the 1950s, recognised that ethnicity was being used to sort people into categories, but at the same time they asked why people from different parts of the country, who formerly had little knowledge of one another, let alone any thought of having a

---

* This article is based on field research among Plateau and Gwembe Tonga extending from 1946 to 1992, during which period I have visited Zambia many times. Research in Zambia was supported by the Rhodes-Livingstone Institute and its successor the Institute for African Studies in the University of Zambia, the Joint Committee on Africa of the Social Science Research Council and the American Council for Learned Societies, and the National Science Foundation. The University of California, Berkeley, and the California Institute of Technology provided additional support. Research in Gwembe District has been carried out in collaboration with Thayer Scudder, of the California Institute of Technology, all field notes being held in common. I am also indebted to a large number of local assistants and other Zambians who have assisted me over the years.

common ethnic identity or ethnic loyalty, were being classed together (Epstein 1978: 1–40; Mitchell 1987: 241; see also Werbner, in this volume).

Once an ethnic category is established, it becomes a 'social fact'; in the Durkheimian sense with a life of its own, as Epstein says (1978: 109). The 'fact', as it is acted out in public contexts, becomes clothed in a symbolism that marks its members as belonging to a group similar to, yet different from, others operating in the same context. Contending groups therefore dress themselves in comparable slogans, ceremonies, claims to authenticity. They need occasions to display themselves to themselves as well as to others and that display must conjure with claims to a community of interest based on something other than a naked struggle for political power. Such display requires organisation, but an organisation once in place can be used for many purposes. Cohen, in his discussion of the Notting Hill Carnival, highlights the way in which a collectivity creates itself at the same time that it

> ... creates, revives, modifies, mobilises and integrates various cultural forms to deal with rapidly changing economic-political conditions. The evolving cultural structure defines the political identity and exclusiveness of the collectivity, serves as a system of communication between its members, uniting them and providing them with an ideology to guide their action. In the process the cultural forms undergo a transformation by being ceremonialised, ritualised, aestheticised, mythologised and thus appear as autonomous, irreducible, signifying functionlessness, detached from politics (1993: 148).

Here I examine the political arena within which a linguistic category, created in about 1920 by a Jesuit priest, has acquired salience among Tonga-speakers of the Southern Province of Zambia (formerly Northern Rhodesia) and speakers of related languages who have begun to appeal to a common heritage to create an identity *vis-à-vis* other people of Zambia. They proudly cite archaeological evidence that Tonga-speakers and their linguistic kin occupied southern Zambia prior to the arrival of other Bantu-speakers from Zaire, Malawi, and the south. Thereby they appeal to old premises about the ritual significance of first settlement and the role of descendants of such settlers as intermediaries with the land.

The Bantu Botatwe

Father J. Torrend, S. J., introduced the term 'Bantu Botatwe' to designate a cluster of Zambian languages including Tonga and Ila in Southern Province (with Tonga also spoken in neighbouring areas of Zimbabwe), Totela and Subiya in what is now Western Province (and Botswana), and Lenje, Soli, and Sala in Central Province. These languages share an -o- infix before numerals, a feature not found in other Bantu languages, and so use 'Bantu Botatwe' for 'three people' or 'three persons'. Torrend also regarded the languages of this group as 'the most archaic, on the whole, in the Bantu field' (Torrend 1921: 3). In 1931, Torrend published *An English-Vernacular Dictionary of the Bantu-Botatwe Dialects of Northern Rhodesia*, still the only dictionary available for any of the languages of the group, although various word lists have been published.

The term, 'Bantu Botatwe', was picked up by other writers, including the linguists Kashoki (1978: 12) and Lehmann (1978: 107-19) though the former calls the term obsolete and the latter suggests that since Tonga had most speakers it would be appropriate to speak of the Tonga group (1978: 119), as Doke did in his classification of southern Bantu languages (1934: 31). Others found it a useful inclusive term for various populations within southern/central Zambia though they did not necessarily agree on its coverage. Brelsford recognised an Ila-Tonga or Bantu Botatwe group comprised 'of about twelve tribes all speaking closely allied dialects' (1968: 61). The linguistic map provided by Langworthy for the volume *Zambia in Maps* (1971: 34–5) has Bantu Botatwe displayed across the outline of southern and central Zambia, into Western Province. Roberts, in his history of Zambia, comments that 'the present extent of Tonga and other languages of the "Bantu Botatwe" roughly corresponds to the extent of the Tonga Diaspora culture as defined by archaeologists' (1976: 72), and he, like others, implies that Tonga-speakers and their linguistic kin are among Zambia's earliest Bantu-speaking settlers. Mitchell, in his examination of regional and ethnographic effects on association among urban Zambians in the 1950s makes at least one reference to Bantu Botatwe as including Ila, Tonga, Lenje and Soli with the Kaonde more distantly associated (1987: 204). The Ethnographic Survey of Africa considers the Ila-Tonga-Lenje ethnographic group to be inclusive of Sala, Soli, Mbala, Lumbu, Lundwe, Leya, Subiya, and Totela (Jaspan 1953: 9–10).

Bantu Botatwe, therefore, has had a literary existence as a linguistic category, with somewhat hazy ethnographic and historical implications, since the 1920s but its scope has varied from writer to writer: only Ila, Tonga, and Lenje are always included.

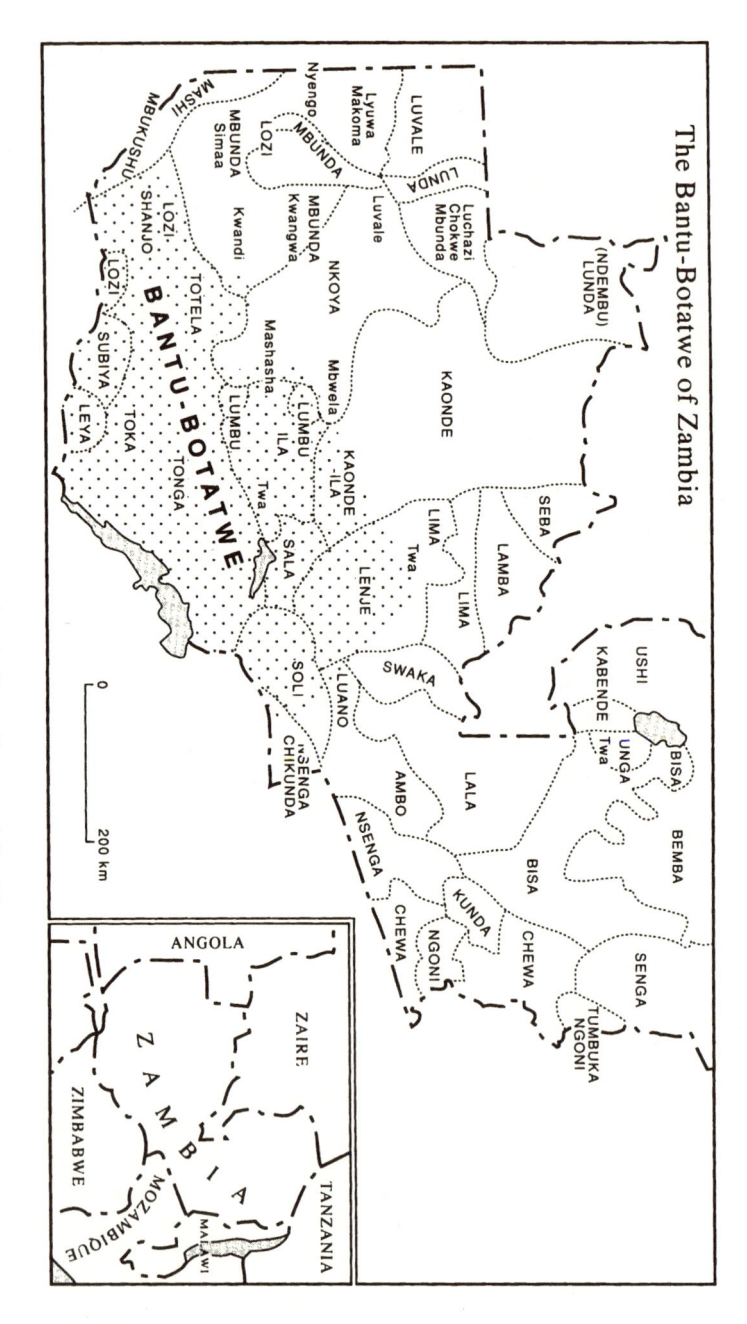

Figure 4.1 Map showing the Bantu-Botatwe of Zambia

Several historians have chosen to translate the term to mean 'three peoples', as though it were an old local term recognising some form of historic association of Tonga, Lenje, and Ila (Roberts 1976: 79n; Vickery 1986: 6). The term apparently did not enter local usage until after Zambian independence in 1964. Unsurprisingly it was first used by a few Zambians with secondary or university education. In 1967 The Bantu Botatwe Association was formed to contest what was seen as Northern Province control of the United National Independence Party (UNIP), the party in power (Chikulo 1979: 203). The Association appears to have been short-lived. It gained few adherents since few people from Southern or Central Province belonged to UNIP. I first heard Gwembe Tonga men speak of the Bantu Botatwe only in 1992. These were men of at least secondary education with ties to their peers elsewhere in Zambia. They were excited about the possibilities of an association uniting the peoples of Southern and Central Province in the context of future electoral politics. They saw the Tonga as too weak numerically to swing national elections without such an alliance. 'We are the oldest people in Zambia, we are the most numerous, the next president ought to be one of us.' Whereas Hausa traders in Ibadan turned to membership in the Tijaniya Brotherhood, and Creoles in Freetown turned to the Masonic order and participation in social gatherings to maintain old communal ties in the period immediately after the independence of Nigeria and Sierra Leone when 'tribalism' was decried as a political strategy (Cohen 1969: 1–6; 1981: 37–8), in the 1990s, with the coming of multi-party elections and freedom to organise and express dissent, Zambians reactivated or tried to establish overt ethnic movements. In 1992 the Bantu Botatwe was a newly emergent 'imaginary community' which had still to transform its potential members into an active support system.

I have no information on whether Bantu Botatwe has gained grassroots currency elsewhere: in Gwembe villages the term is still esoteric. Other members of the linguistic cluster might not choose to identify themselves with it. Even though they recognise that their language is classified with Tonga and Lenje, some Soli, certainly, align themselves with peoples to the north and west with whom they say they emigrated from the Luba Empire in Zaire (Manchishi and Musona n.d.). Although the Bantu Botatwe Ngoma Yamaanu Association, founded in 1991, was established first in Lusaka, the Zambian capital, and included Ila and Lenje among its members, I suspect its grassroots appeal is largely among Tonga who expect that their numbers will give them predominance within such an alliance.

Ethnicity and Language

Languages spoken in Southern Province are sufficiently similar so that Tonga informants in the 1940s found Ila and Toka-Leya no more difficult to comprehend than some dialects classified as Tonga. They also knew that Sala, spoken in Central Province, was much like Tonga. They were much less likely to claim linguistic affinity with other Central Province people, including Lenje and Soli, whose languages they said were very different from their own even though linguists have found a high agreement of basic vocabulary among all the languages of the Bantu Botatwe cluster (Lehmann 1978: 108–19). Such matters were of little interest.

In the 1940s, Tonga-speakers, whether they lived on the Plateau or in the Gwembe Valley, interacted little with people from Central Province and knew little about them. Nor, since Tonga rarely went north to work on the Copperbelt or in Lusaka, now the capital of the country, which drew workers from the north and east of the country, did they see Bemba or others from north and east as competitors. On the whole, if they knew of them, they spoke of them with respect. Since the 1920s Plateau Tonga had supported themselves by cash-crop farming and met other Northern Rhodesians primarily when these came to work in the towns and on the farms of Southern Province, after which they might settle in Tonga villages where they found easy acceptance (Colson 1970). Gwembe Tonga had to migrate to find wage work, but until Zambian independence in 1964 they travelled to Southern Rhodesia or further south, and there defined themselves, along with their fellow Tonga-speakers from Southern Rhodesia, against the peoples they encountered in Bulawayo and other employment centres. Towards these they felt little animosity, even against Ndebele and Lozi who had raided them during the nineteenth century. Instead, migrants boasted of the number of languages in which they could converse. They were much less tolerant of Tonga from elsewhere, whose dialects they derided. Although Plateau Tonga were less parochial, in the 1950s Gwembe villagers went so far as to reserve the name Tonga for themselves and their immediate neighbours, referring to other

Tonga-speakers, even within Gwembe District, by terms that emphasised their distinctiveness. The colonial government had earlier tried to generate attachment to larger territorially defined units when Tonga-speakers were allocated to three different divisions, each under its own 'native authority', the Plateau Tonga, the Gwembe or Valley Tonga and the Toka-Leya, but the majority saw these divisions as affairs of the colonial government.

The future, however, was signalled in the 1940s when a secondary school for African students was founded and the country's first radio station chose to broadcast programmes aimed at African listeners in only some of the country's many languages. Literacy and the necessity to choose among languages for purposes of education and official communication have sparked the emergence of interest groups throughout history and are seen as the seed-beds of nationalism (Anderson 1983: 106–28; Gellner 1983: 29–43; Kohn 1967 [1944]: 122). As Royce has written, 'The intellectual, whether writer, artist, or politician, is the one who articulates grievances, formulates nationalistic statements, and translates popular belief into a coherent ideology' (1982: 106). The formulation of an ethnic identity encompassing all Tonga-speakers and eventually speakers of the other languages classified with Tonga has largely been fostered by Tonga educated in the English language which they share with other Zambian elites.

In the 1940s, the major ethnic division within Zambia (then Northern Rhodesia) was that between Europeans, who dominated the colonial state, and the African majority who were beginning to challenge European privileges and power. However, those who challenged were also very much concerned about their own future status *vis-à-vis* Africans from other parts of the country whom they increasingly saw as competitors for available jobs. At the same time that they were learning to think of Northern Rhodesia as *their country*, they were also beginning to study the strategic position within that country of themselves and their home people. Young men from Southern Province who attended secondary school in the late 1940s did not complain about the use of English as the language of instruction in upper primary and secondary schools, since they went to school to acquire English, the indispensable tool for their own advancement. They were indignant that Bemba and Nyanja were being offered as examination languages along with Latin, since this gave students from Northern and Eastern Provinces what they saw as unfair advantage. They also signalled that they associated the provinces created by the colonial government with language and ethnicity when they argued (inconsistently) that Tonga should be a language of instruction at the recently founded Monze Agricultural Training Institute because, they said, Southern Province was Tonga country. It made no difference that the school was to draw its students from throughout the country. They took for granted that Tonga was used on Radio Lusaka and was one of the publication languages for schoolbooks, the government-sponsored African literature series, and the official newspaper, although some complained if the chosen Tonga dialect was not their own. Soli and Lenje students, I was told, asked why their languages were not equally favoured and resented the assumption that they ought to understand Tonga.

In the 1950s and early 1960s, as people mobilised politically to demand independence and contest subsequent control of independent Zambia, the idea of the solidarity of the people of Southern Province received additional emphasis. Tonga and Ila saw themselves as allied. Their political rhetoric played on the common interests of those who lived in Southern Province: rights in land *vis-à-vis* government and ex-patriate settlers, agricultural policies, and marketing arrangements (Chipungu 1988: 80 ff; Sikalumbi 1977: 102–3). From 1950 on they overwhelmingly backed the African National Congress (ANC), then headed by Harry Nkambula, an Ila and so a man of their 'own kind' (Mulford 1964: 128–30; Pettman 1974: 50–65). Tonga who seceded from the ANC in 1960 to join the newly founded United National Independence Party, were mostly men of education. They were accused of deserting their own people. UNIP was identified as a Bemba party, one of the grounds being that it was headed by Kenneth Kaunda, a Bemba-speaker although his parents had come as missionaries from Malawi, but it also represented the Copperbelt and urban workers. From then on, until it was abolished in 1973 when Zambia became a one-party state, the ANC continued to be what Mulford called 'a tribally based party deriving its greatest support from the Tonga-speaking groups in Central and Southern Provinces' (Mulford 1967: 327; see also Chikulo 1979).

By the late 1960s Central Province had emerged as a major agricultural area, overtaking Southern Province 'as the most productive agricultural Province in post-colonial Zambia' (Chipungu 1988: 139). Rural inhabitants of the two provinces therefore had comparable political interests in ensuring policies that favoured agriculture and the rural sector: the ANC spoke to their joint interests. Despite this, rural Tonga in these years continued to talk primarily of Southern Province, the focus of their own emerging Tonga identity. The people of Central Province, whatever their languages, were considered to have their own loyalties, even though the real opponents were usually identified as the people of Northern and Eastern Provinces, long dependent upon the copper industry and the urban areas to supplement subsistence agriculture. The few Tonga-speakers who joined UNIP and were involved in its internal contests allied themselves opportunistically with various others: in 1967 they joined the much more powerful Bemba faction to contest what they regarded as overrepresentation by Western and Eastern Province party members (Chikulo 1979: 202). But these were men and women whose careers were linked to the national system. The majority of Southern Province villagers continued to back the ANC which they identified as a party representing Southern Province interests against the nation (Pettman 1974: 79). Out of the political struggle, the Tonga had come to identify themselves as an ethnic group, distinguished by language, economic interests, and perhaps by other cultural factors from the rest of Zambia. For the time being, however, competition in ethnic terms had to be muted.

Nationalism and Ethnic Politics

When African states gained independence with the demise of the colonial order, strenuous efforts were made to combat what was then called 'tribalism', as the leaders of the newly enfranchised territorial states attempted to monopolise loyalties and economic resources to ensure their viability and to embark upon the goals associated with development. Adherence to old political loyalties or the use of linguistic or other cultural attributes to mobilise ethnic blocs were suspect as challenging the new order.

Old loyalties were not always easy to eradicate, especially when they focused on former states whose members were proud of their history and of symbols that spoke to their superiority over neighbouring peoples (Richards 1969: 23). Even so, in Zambia, as elsewhere in Africa, for the first decades after independence the official attitude, accepted by the majority of people, held that reference to one's own or another's origin was in bad taste, to say the least. In the first years of independence, which came in 1964, it was more or less taboo to ask people about their ethnicity because all were citizens of the one nation and this gave them their primary identity which took precedence even over close ties with kin and neighbours who might now live on the other side of an international boundary.

In Zambia, the ever-present slogan was 'One Zambia, One Nation', ritually recited at all political meetings. Gwembe school children by the 1970s delighted in associating themselves with the nation and proclaimed themselves Zambians even though their seniors backed the African National Congress and mourned when it was defeated at the polls by UNIP which came to power in 1962, before independence, and remained in power until October 1991. They continued to support ANC candidates until Zambia was declared a single-party state in 1972, and even later were covertly opposed to UNIP which they regarded as a party dominated by northerners who had usurped the independence movement.

Nevertheless, the majority were gratified that they now lived in a state governed by Africans and recognised the opportunities opened by independence and the rapid Zambianisation of the civil service and commerce. Until 1973 copper revenues gave the Zambian government the wherewithal to develop educational and other facilities, expand the job market, and otherwise reward its citizens. National policy favoured the towns, but there was also money for rural areas and in the early years of independence Southern Province farmers benefitted from the provision of credit, agricultural extension services, and other inputs. There is evidence, in fact, that Southern Province benefitted more than other provinces at this time, despite its failure to support UNIP (Chipungu 1988: 1978–9). Standards of living rose rapidly. In all provinces roads were built and schools and health centres opened. Many Southern Province children were able to complete primary school and many went on to secondary school with every expectation up to the early 1970s of being able to find a decent white-collar job and in turn assist parents, siblings, and other kin (Scudder and Colson 1980). Educated men and women aspired to live in the cities, preferably in the capital, and most succeeded in doing so. Even rural residents became urban and nationally oriented as they visited children and other kin in the cities and planned the careers of their children.

Government policy discouraged regional loyalties in the interests of the larger nationalism. Many school children found places in secondary schools located in distant provinces. School teachers and other professionals, including police and army personnel, were stationed if possible in provinces or at least districts other than their place of origin. Economic opportunities led to both rural-urban migration and inter-rural migration, with many Tonga farmers moving into Central Province while Lozi, Bemba, Nyanja and other fishermen settled along the shores of Kariba Lake in Gwembe District. Young educated men and women found work throughout Zambia. Zambian cities had multi-ethnic populations and although people from the same region tended to dominate in particular sections of a city, as did Tonga in portions of Old Kanyama in Lusaka, they also intermixed with people from other provinces. Their children were in the same schools where they were taught in English, the official national language. Intermarriage became common especially among elite families whose children modeled themselves upon the national and international elite and usually had little interest in any particular province or ethnic homeland.

Only in 1973 did Zambia pass the threshold where it had more secondary-school leavers than white-collar openings. This happened just at the time when declining copper prices, rising oil prices, and the dislocations associated with the struggle for African control throughout southern Africa sent Zambia's economy into a tail-spin from which it has not recovered. The full impact of the economic crisis hit the country in the late 1970s. Although government policy continued to favour the towns against the countryside, job seekers, and even those who had employment, began returning to the countryside in the 1980s to try to survive. Meantime government services declined everywhere and morale among government employees dropped noticeably. Emotional investment in the nation plummeted. By the early 1980s, Gwembe villagers boasted less of being Zambian and talked more of the failure of national leaders and of a general inferiority in comparison with Europe and the United States.

This disillusionment, shared with people elsewhere in Zambia, lay behind the discrediting of UNIP and its government from 1974 on (Chisala 1991: 33). In Southern Province both continued to be identified with Bemba, or northerners in general, although by this time UNIP drew its support largely from Eastern Province.

In 1972 one motive for transforming Zambia into a one-party state had been to prevent political parties from becoming the vehicles of ethnic politics. It is ironic that this move came just at the moment when the Zambian economy began its long decline which made access to jobs and other resources more problematic.

Under these circumstances personal networks acquired new importance as giving competitive advantage in a world where increasing numbers competed in a diminished resource pool. People became convinced that jobs, school places, and much else in Zambia flowed through patronage. Accusations of ethnic patronage were not new, but through the early 1970s it was 'not possible for any area or province to control the civil service' (Scott 1980: 154). Cabinet offices and membership on UNIP's Central Committee were allocated with an eye to regional and ethnic balance (Rothchild and Foley 1988: 244–5). Thereafter regional bias became more blatant. By the early 1980s, Tonga frequently commented that it was pointless to apply for jobs in such and such ministries or industries because they were controlled by members of other ethnic groups who looked after their own. People became alert to indications that others were being advantaged because of who they were. One sign of this sensitivity is the controversy over the amount of air time allocated to the seven Zambian languages given official status for broadcasting purposes (Kashoki 1990:44).

By the end of the 1980s, political discontent was endemic throughout Zambia. Opposition to UNIP and the one-party state was then spearheaded by a broad-based coalition that represented all regions of Zambia and included trade-unionists, university members and business men. In 1990, the regime was forced to agree to hold a multi-party election. In October 1991, UNIP was swept from power by the Movement for Multi-Party Democracy (MMD), the party of the coalition. The majority of people in Southern Province, including Plateau and Gwembe Tonga, saw this as a triumph. However, by early 1992, villagers were having second thoughts when economic conditions continued to worsen and they saw little change in the allocation of power. The new president came from Luapula Province and the Copperbelt, seen as Bemba strongholds, and so did many of those he appointed to ministerial and other positions.

Old ethnic claims were then reasserted throughout Zambia and new ethnic alliances began to be forged to claim either the right to participate fully in the national arena or to obtain local autonomy. Western Province under a Lozi elite, for instance, renewed an old battle to regain the special status that the Barotse Kingdom had held during the colonial period.

It is in this context that the Bantu Botatwe Ngoma Yamaanu Association was created to celebrate the ethnic identity of Toka,

Tonga, Ila, Sala, Soli, Lenje, Totela, and Subiya, who, if they acted together, could form a powerful political bloc. The Bantu Botatwe Association of 1967 had been activated for a particular struggle. The new organisation was to be placed on a firmer basis, fortified by an appeal to deeper emotions than short-lived political expediency. Its publicly stated mission was to serve as a cultural mechanism for celebrating the historic greatness of the Bantu Botatwe as primal settlers. It was to encourage literary, artistic, and ritual channels through which the Bantu Botatwe might celebrate their cultural uniqueness. Furthermore, potentially it provided a means of mobilising for the next presidential election. Some Gwembe men, who were enthusiastic about the organisation, said that while it might be desirable for Southern Province to become an independent Tonga nation, along the lines proposed by Barotseland, this was impractical. The alternative was for the Tonga to join with other Bantu Botatwe to become the predominant political force within the nation.

Fostering an Identity

It is interesting that this move towards political mobilisation took the form of a cultural association. It is consistent with the stress African leaders placed on African culture in the post-independence period and the encouragement given to Zambians to celebrate their past.

Audrey Richards (1969: 98) recognised early on that African leaders, while they stressed the need for centralisation and technological development, also felt 'a deep emotional need to reject things European and hence to glorify their own cultures and to prove that these are as admirable as the civilisations of Europe and superior to them' (see also Hyden 1993: 242). Kenneth Kaunda developed an ideology of Zambian Humanism as a distillation of values which he held to be characteristic of all its people (Kaunda 1974; Dillon-Malone 1989; Meebelo 1973), but placed the burden of development on the centralised state and its officials who replaced the old chiefs or native authorities of the colonial regime, now shorn of administrative and judicial functions. From now on the chiefs were to be paid and honoured as ceremonial representatives of Zambia's history. But this could only result in reminding Zambians of very different pasts (see also Barnes, in this volume).

Bemba, Lozi, Ngoni and Lunda were reminded of the power of their former kingdoms and their domination over 'lesser' neighbours. Soli and Lenje could make no boast of kingdoms, but they had memories of powerful chiefs and their moments of glory. The Tonga could not compete in this arena, and those who aspired to membership in the national elite felt disadvantaged by their inability to celebrate an ancient state. Their chiefs, for the most part, were regarded as created and empowered by the colonial government. The Tonga could and did boast of their egalitarian tradition and willingness to take individual responsibility: 'To the outsider this is a sign of social disorganisation and lack of national consciousness but to the Batonga themselves rallying around and "worshipping" one person is uncharacteristic of an independent person' (Chibalo 1983: 27). This, however, gained them little in the competition for recognition as historic forces within Zambia when others chose to celebrate chieftaincy and ancient centralised political power.

In the 1960s, chiefs were encouraged to dramatise their ceremonial roles and the past of their people through continuing to perform, or reintroducing, annual rituals celebrating their own particular cultural heritage. Having lost power, their continued justification lay in their ability to symbolise the former greatness of the various peoples who make up Zambia. When they regained a modicum of secular power in the 1970s through being given the right to allocate land, government continued to encourage enhancement of chiefly ceremonies as tourist attractions. Inevitably these occasions became rallying points for emphasising the importance of ethnic loyalties: the organisation of the elaborate ceremonies required the co-operation of a large number of people, including those from the area who now lived in cities or even in other countries who were applied to for funds and encouraged to return home to participate. As Cohen says: 'As a cultural movement evolves, it generates overlapping interpersonal networks of amity among the people actively involved in it and thus infuses the cultural form with moral imperatives, thereby consolidating and strengthening its central force' (1993: 154).

The Lozi ceremony of *Kuomboka*, the Luapula *Mutomboko*, the Ngoni *Nc'wala*, and the Ila *Shimunenga* have either been revived or embellished in recent years, while many other former political units have also created or refurbished similar ceremonies (Ngulube 1989: 162). These have become ethnic markers even among people who otherwise identify themselves with the emergent urban culture of Zambia which finds its reference point primarily in lifestyles associated with an international elite. The Tonga did not adopt *Shimunenga* as a symbolic representation of Southern Province although in many contexts they say Ila are really Tonga. *Shimunenga* celebrates the hunt while most village Tonga think of themselves as farmers whose interests are reflected in rituals that relate to the land and rain (Colson 1948; Machila n.d.). In the 1970s Tonga members of the Historical Association of Zambia, Southern Province Branch, attempted to transform the annual rain ceremony (*lwiindi*) of the Monzes into an annual provincial event of the Tonga on a par with the Ila *Shimunenga* and the Lozi *Kuomboka*. O'Brien, who was in the area at the time, was told that Monze, a rainmaker of the nineteenth century, whose successors were recognised as senior chiefs, had been chief over much of the Tonga-speaking region and that his shrine had received delegations from every part of that country (O'Brien 1983). The move to elevate the Monze shrine was an attempt to engage on equivalent terms with other ethnic groups. It was supported by some chiefs and those educated Tonga who had come to see the lack of an historic Tonga kingdom as invidious when Bemba, Lozi, and other Zambians could boast of former political might. The latter represented the first generation of graduates of the University of Zambia. They had also been exposed to the formation of associations for various purposes through their years in secondary school and the university.

Against them were many Christians or others who opposed recognition of any ancient spirits, adherents of other shrines who were not prepared to recognise the primacy of the Monzes, and those who still associated the *malende* (rain shrines) with powerful spirits and did not want them 'turned into a "play" and tourist attraction' (Machila n.d.: 112). The failure to establish a 'Tonga' annual ceremony, however, must also have been due to the Tonga dislike for overt hierarchy and the lack of concern of most villagers for such historic claims as other peoples of Zambia might make. They were interested in the present and the future.

The attempt demonstrates, however, that by the 1970s some Tonga intellectuals had decided that they needed to be able to field a range of collective symbols comparable to those that celebrate the unique histories of other peoples in Zambia. At that time acceptable collective ethnic symbols centred on regional annual rituals, and Tonga champions of the Monze shrine chose such a symbol. They may not have been trying to forge a larger ethnic coalition for political purposes, since the 1970s and 1980s were the years when the one-party state clamped down on overt political expression of ethnicity. Political manoeuvering and strategies used for the advancement of personal interests relied on patronage networks described in terms of kinship and home-ties rather than in ethnic terms.

Ethnicity in the Multi-Party State

When UNIP bowed to popular discontent and agreed that new parties might be formed to fight the 1991 election, the first response was a broad-based coalition that expressed the general will to be rid of UNIP and install a new government whose members would be responsive to public opinion which was to be expressed through public debate, a free press, and a legislature representing various parties and so free to criticise the workings of government. In so far as one can judge from a distance and from what people said a few months later, the election was not fought on ethnic lines.

Ethnicity became more salient when the new government failed to live up to expectations. Living standards did not improve; inflation skyrocketed as the government implemented the structural adjustment programme laid down by the World Bank and the International Monetary Fund. The civil service was cut, tightening the job market for those with education. Jobs in industry also vanished. Agricultural credit and marketing became chaotic. The central government turned over to the districts or local communities responsibility for services formerly financed by government, but did not give them the right to develop their own revenues. Both urban and rural residents saw such resources as the country still possessed being drained into the pockets of ministers and others in power, and since freedom of speech continued to be recognised, those aggrieved had no hesitation in accusing those in power of corruption. Many also said the government was staffed with people from the north.

People still retained a belief in the electoral process as a means of righting what they saw as bad government, but to use the electoral process to their own advantage they saw that they needed votes. Given local sensibilities, in a time when political patrons were seen as favouring people of their own ethnic group, emphasis upon the Tonga as a dominant group was a poor strategy in the search for allies. In these circumstances, a neutral term which privileged no particular group was desirable and the term 'Bantu Botatwe' existed to give recognition to a large number of people throughout Southern and Central Provinces and some in Western Province who had language, and perhaps some other characteristics in common. Those who founded the Bantu Botatwe Ngoma Yamaanu Association were appealing to such a constituency, which they were trying to bring into being as a conscious community. However, they have still to find songs and other insignia, or create 'traditional' occasions with which people can identify on the basis of being Bantu Botatwe rather than Tonga, Ila, Soli, Lenje, Sala, or a member of some other unit created under colonial rule, whose name is now part of the Zambian vocabulary. Some members of the educated elite are in the forefront of the movement, but they work against the desire of many Tonga and other Zambians to identify first with home people and then with the nation. Others prefer explicit political mobilisation. Few in Southern or Central Province without secondary education understand cultural associations, but all have been schooled on party mobilisation, with its manifestos and slogans, and on party organisation. This they understand. In 1993 as the coalition associated with MMD collapsed, Zambians began to form a large number of new political parties. Among them is the National Party, said to be dominated by Southern and Central Provinces, and so a candidate to carry on the tradition of the old ANC in which so much loyalty was invested. The appeal to a united Tonga past, indeed, is an appeal to the tradition of the ANC.

References

Anderson, Benedict. 1983. *Imagined Communities: Reflections on the Origin and Spread of Nationalism*. London & New York: Verso.

Brelsford, W. V. 1968. *The Tribes of Zambia*. Lusaka: Government Printer.

Chibalo, Esnart Chiyasa. 1983. 'Social Context and Literary Aspects of Muyabila Songs: A Study of Kuyabila as Performed by the Tonga of the Southern Province of Zambia', MA Thesis, University of Zambia, Department of African Literature. Special Collection, University of Zambia Library.

Chikulo, Bornwell. 1979. 'Elections in a One-Party Participatory Democracy', in *Development in Zambia*, Ben Turok (ed.). London: Zed Press.

Chipungu, Samuel. 1988. *The State, Technology and Peasant Differentiation in Zambia: A Case Study of the Southern Province, 1930–1986*. Lusaka: Historical Society of Zambia.

Chisala, Beatwell S. 1991. *Lt. Luchembe: Coup Attempt*. Lusaka: Multimedia Zambia.

Cohen, Abner. 1969. *Custom and Politics in Urban Africa: A Study of Hausa Migrants in Yoruba Towns*. Berkeley: University of California Press.

———. 1974. *Two-Dimensional Man: An Essay on the Anthropology of Power and Symbolism in Complex Society*. Berkeley: University of California Press.

———. 1981. *The Politics of Elite Culture: Explorations in the Dramaturgy of Power in a Modern African Society*. Berkeley: University of California Press.

———. 1993. *Masquerade Politics: Explorations in the Structure of Urban Cultural Movements*. Berkeley: University of California Press.

Colson, Elizabeth. 1948. 'Rain-Shrines of the Plateau Tonga of Northern Rhodesia', *Africa* 18(4): 272–83.

———. 1970. 'The Assimilation of Aliens among Zambian Tonga', in *From Tribe to Nation in Africa: Studies in Incorporation Processes*, Ronald Cohen and John Middleton (eds). Scranton: Chandler Publishing Company.

Dillon-Malone, Clive. 1989. *Zambian Humanism, Religion and Social Morality*. Ndola: Mission Press.

Doke, Clement. 1945. *Bantu, Modern Grammatical, Phonetical and Lexicographical Studies since 1860*. London: Percy Lund Humphries for the International African Institute.

Epstein, A. L. 1978. *Ethos and Identity: Three Studies in Ethnicity*. London: Tavistock.

Gellner, Ernest. 1983. *Nations and Nationalism*. Ithaca & London: Cornell University Press.

Hyden, Goran. 1993. 'The Challenges of Domesticating Rights in Africa', in *Human Rights and Governance in Africa*, Ronald Cohen, Goran Hyden, & Winston P. Nagan (eds). Gainesville: University Press of Florida.

Jaspan, M. A. 1953. *The Ila-Tonga Peoples of North-Western Rhodesia*. London: International African Institute.

Kashoki, Mubanga. 1978. 'The Language Situation in Zambia', in *Language in Zambia*, Sirarpi Ohannessian & Mubanga Kashoki (eds). London: International African Institute.

———. 1990. *The Factor of Language in Zambia*. Lusaka: Kenneth Kaunda Foundation.

Kaunda, Kenneth. 1974. *Humanism in Zambia and a Guide to its Implementation*, Parts 1 & 2. Lusaka: Zambian Information Service.

Kohn, Hans. 1967 [1944]. *The Idea of Nationalism*. New York: Collier Books.

Langworthy, H. W. 1971. 'Languages and Tribes', in *Zambia in Maps*, D. Hywell Davies (ed.). London: University of London Press.

Lehmann, Dorothea. 1978. 'Languages of the Kafue Basin', in *Language in Zambia*, Sirarpi Ohannessian and Mubanga E. Kashoki (eds). London: International African Institute.

Machila, Emmerson. n.d. 'A History of the Malende among the Tonga of Southern Province of Zambia: A Case Study of Chief Hanjalika's Area, 1890–1986', MA Thesis, University of Zambia, Department of History. Special Collection, University of Zambia Library.

Manchishi, P. C. and E. T. Musona. n.d. *The People of Zambia: A Short History of the Soli from 1500 to 1900*. Lusaka: Multimedia Publication.

Meebelo, Henry S. 1973. *Main Currents of Zambian Humanist Thought*. Lusaka: Oxford University Press.

Mitchell, J. Clyde. 1987. *Cities, Society and Social Perception: A Central African Perspective*. Oxford: Clarendon Press.

Mulford, David C. 1964. *The Northern Rhodesian General Election 1962*. Nairobi: Oxford University Press.

——. 1967. *Zambia: The Politics of Independence 1957–1964*. London: Oxford University Press.

Ngulube, Naboth M. J. 1989. *Some Aspects of Growing Up In Zambia*. Lusaka: Kenneth Kaunda Foundation.

O'Brien, D. 1983. 'Chiefs of Rain, Chiefs of Ruling: A Reinterpretation of Pre-Colonial Tonga (Zambia) Social and Political Structure', *Africa* 53 (4): 23–42.

Pettman, Jan. 1974. *Zambia Security and Conflict*. Lewes: Julien Friedmann Publishers.

Richards, Audrey. 1969. *The Multicultural States of East Africa*. Montreal & London: McGill-Queen's University Press.

Roberts, Andrew. 1976. *A History of Zambia*. London: Heinemann.

Rothchild, Donald and Michael Foley. 1988. 'African States and the Politics of Inclusive Coalitions', in *The Precarious Balance: State and Society in Africa*, Donald Rothchild and Naomi Chazan (eds). Boulder: Westview Press.

Royce, Anya. 1993. 'Ethnicity, Nationalism and the Role of the Intellectual', in *Ethnicity and the State*, Judith D. Toland (ed.). London: Transaction Publishers.

Scott, Ian. 1980. 'Party and Administration under the One-Party State', in *Administration in Zambia*, William Tordoff (ed.). Manchester: University of Manchester Press.

Scudder, Thayer, and Elizabeth Colson. 1980. *Secondary Education and the Formation of an Elite. The Impact of Education in Gwembe District, Zambia.* New York: Academic Press.

Sikalumbi, Wittington. 1977. *Before UNIP.* Lusaka: National Educational Committee.

Torrend, J. 1921. *Specimens of Bantu Folk-lore from Northern Rhodesia.* London: Kegan Paul, Trench, Trubner & Co.

———. 1931. *An English-Vernacular Dictionary of the Bantu-Botatwe Dialects of Northern Rhodesia.* London: Kegan Paul, Trench, Trubner & Co.

Vickery, Kenneth. 1986. *Black and White in Southern Zambia: The Tonga Plateau Economy and British Imperialism, 1890–1939.* New York: Greenwood Press.

CHAPTER 5

The Fusion of Identities:
Political Passion and the Poetics of Cultural Performance among British Pakistanis

Pnina Werbner *

Introduction

The anthropological gaze has shifted recently to a scrutiny of margins: of cultural encounters, hybrids or thresholds; of ethnic diasporas, global social movements and transnational communities; of travelling theories, boundary-crossing artifacts and footloose cosmopolitans or tourists; of global landscapes and local appropriations. One of the important strands in this trend has been the recognition that the people we study are not merely 'objectified' or 'essentialised' by our anthropological textualisations; perhaps more critically even, in their encounter with modernity and post/colonialism, they engage in acts of oppositional self-objectification, reflexive essentialising and the conscious maintenance of cultural boundaries (see, for example, Dominguez 1989, Friedman 1992, Carrier 1992, Thomas 1992, Eriksen 1994).

---

* The research on which this paper is based was conducted between 1987 and 1993 among British Pakistanis resident in Manchester. I am grateful to the Economic and Social Research Council, UK, for their generous support. An earlier version of the paper was presented at University College, London, and I am particularly grateful to Bruce Kapferer, Ruth Mandel and the other participants at the seminar for their comments.

A guiding truth of anthropological theory, at least since the publication of *The Nuer* (Evans-Pritchard 1940), has been that group membership is always relative. If social agents bear multiple (and sometimes contradictory) identities, these are typically highlighted or foregrounded situationally and selectively, in opposition. The further important insight contained in Evans-Pritchard's analysis, and one which bears directly upon current debates about identity and social movements, is that these sited identities are valorised in the last instance not by simple material interests or ecological exigencies, but by the moral values of sociality which constitute these interests and constraints within given contexts.

In the critiques of segmentary theory which followed the publication of *The Nuer*, a key point to emerge was that identities (and hence also interests and valorised socialities) grounded in different organisational principles, cannot always be kept separate as the theory had suggested. Men and women may be both lineage members and affines, spouses and siblings, and it is the fusion of these identities, with all the tensions and contradictions such a fusion implies, which shapes modes of mediation and overarching processes of dispute settlement.

The continuing relevance of these insights for the study of ethnicity in diasporic communities will become evident in the course of my discussion, which focuses on the imaginative construction of Pakistani diasporic discourses. A key aim of the analysis is to disclose both the situational *separation* of conflicting identities – and hence also of loyalties, sentimental identifications and communal imaginings – and their fusion, achieved through creative acts of cultural performance. Beyond segmentary theory, I argue further that what makes such fusings so powerful is their weaving of different types of identity – moral, aesthetic and political, to create a powerful grassroots basis for ethnic mobilisation.

My analysis reflects back to two classic *œuvres*. The first, *The Kalela Dance* by Clyde Mitchell (Mitchell 1956), drew upon segmentary theory to illuminate processes of situational selection among labour migrants on the Zambian (then Northern Rhodesian) Copperbelt.

In theorising Mitchell's case study, it may be argued that the fusing of identities – of urban and tribal aesthetics – was a mode of empowerment. Such a fusing drew its force partly from the improvised, and yet taken-for-granted nature of the conjunction. What made the Kalela dance so effective, in other words (and the dancers so irresistable), was the repeatedly renewed act of conjoining – the creative, humorous fusion of identities which remained, in principle, also discrete.[1]

The second set of studies is by Abner Cohen, whose work on political ethnicity anticipated the current *zeitgeist* by many years. Although our own conceptual schemata have altered somewhat, and we now talk of subjectivities, identities, empowerment, cultural encounters, hybridism, multiculturalism or modernity, the motivating quest of all Cohen's writings remains prophetically contemporary: to disclose how the articulation of identities – political, economic and cultural – is played out in the public arena. His interest in diasporas and transnational communities, in the fusion of identities and in the responsive creativity of ethnic cultures, raised a foundational set of questions for anthropologists which have come to be so taken for granted in the discipline that no reference to Cohen's work is usually thought to be necessary. I feel that it is important to set the record straight here, for latecomers into the newborn discipline of Cultural Studies have tended to assume that it is they who 'discovered' cultural politics and the politics of identity and that, stereotypically, anthropologists (the 'handmaidens of colonialism') have always focused on culture stripped of its politicised dimensions (for a critique which echoes this view, in relation to American anthropology in particular, see Ortner 1984). The movement in Cohen's four monographs (Cohen 1965, 1969, 1981, 1993) reveals an increasingly historicised, performative and dialectical approach to the study of cultural politicisation. His latest work on the Notting Hill Carnival (1993) stands out as moving towards a recognition of the ultimate irreducibility of

---

1 Mitchell's application here of segmentary theory and its associated principle of situational selection is, of course, an example of the more general approach to urbanism and the colonial encounter which became the hallmark of the Manchester School (see especially Epstein 1958). The sited nature of ethnic boundary maintenance was later developed by Frederik Barth in a celebrated essay (Barth 1969). In Britain two social anthropologists, Wallman and Banton, have both adopted this approach which stresses the situational nature of ethnicity, and have applied it to local British contexts (see Wallman 1986). Against this, I have argued, however, that the Manchester School situational approach as initially formulated and as later developed by Barth, glosses over the problem of how and why new social 'situations' are created and actively valorised by migrant groups in town (P. Werbner 1990). In relation to Wallman it may be argued, moreover, that her approach (unlike its Central African counterpart) fails to come to grips with the problem of racism, which is the issue addressed here.

culture to politics. If identities are fused and politicised, he shows, the aesthetic and the moral remain as truths in their own right which cannot ever be fully encompassed by the political.

The present chapter seeks to develop this point through an analysis of the powerful fusing of discrete cultural discourses which characterises, we shall see, the political rhetoric of aspiring, grassroots British Pakistani leaders. In their rhetoric the usual spatial and cognitive separations these immigrants observe between the sacred and the profane, the political and the aesthetic, are overridden for the sake of moving an audience. As elsewhere in the Muslim world, Pakistanis normally manage their multiple identifications through 'a radical disjunction between personal piety and [a secularised] public life' (Geertz 1968: 107). Being, simultaneously, British, South Asian, Pakistani, Muslim, Punjabi and Modern, the range of incongruous taken-for-granted identifications (and hence of identities kept in disjunction) they embrace is perhaps unusually large. It is, of course, a multiplicity which has its roots not simply in the recent migration process to Britain but in South Asia itself, a legacy of succesive imperial regimes and religious movements, of population displacements, the modern rise of nationalism(s), post-colonial wars and religious hostilities – all of which have conjoined to make the sub-continent, seen analytically, a vast, billion-strong 'borderzone' of social actors bearing multiple and often contradictory identities.

The situational management of these multiple identities is, in fact, quite consonant with classic segmentary theory. What creates the postmodernist, post-colonial *difference* is the further fact that the traditional is now essentially also modern: identity only makes sense, in a taken-for-granted way, within the modern. At the same time, as invoked by cultural mediators, it can also become highly reflexive or objectified in cultural goods. As Paul Gilroy argues in a recent book, black identities are rooted in slavery and in the black diaspora it generated. The cultural narratives created in response to this brutal encounter with modernity are 'deeply embedded' in modernity itself (1993: 190), woven into the very fabric of modernist discourses. This is falsified, in his view, by the current black movements which attempt to deny the experience of slavery by invoking a pure African, pre-slavery 'tradition'. Extending Gilroy's point, one may argue even further that the black diaspora itself is a modernist imagining, the creation of black metropolitan intellectuals seeking a common platform.

If diasporas are imaginative constructions, then there is no reason why exiles should not regard themselves as part of a whole series of quite *different* diasporas simultaneously. In their rhetoric, British Pakistanis evoke at least three diasporas, each of which valorises a different domain of sociality: moral, political and aesthetic. Nor are these diasporas merely the imaginatively *discursive* products of sentimental nostalgias. The diasporas 'exist' also as observable realities objectified through the global distribution of packaged 'culture' – culinary, visual and expert – ranging in its pretentiousness from high to mass popular. The culture industry supplying these diasporas reaches the very ends of the South Asian and Muslim diasporic worlds.

On the one hand, then, these multiple diasporas exist for Pakistanis as sites of sentimental attachment, imaginatively and actively constructed in local cultural performances; yet it is important to recognise that they also exist *beyond* the subjectivities of diasporic actors – in the aesthetic, political and moral products of a vast and increasingly transnational culture industry. The focus of the present paper is, however, on the local cultural performance of diaspora, seen as a moment in the emergence of a local ethnic social movement. The event presented here was itself a single episode in a continuing Mancunian social drama, in which local factions mobilised behind a changing constellation of grassroots leaders. Their ultimate aim was to capture the Central Mosque and with it the moral high ground of the Muslim Asian Pakistani community in the city. The performance described was thus typically, like most other such performances I attended, an embattled argument of identities intended both to mobilise support and to contest a range of aesthetic values and moral assumptions imputedly held by opponents.

The Performance: The Fables of the Blindfolded Ox and the Blue Jackal

On the 19 July 1987, Chaudri Muhammad Amin, an aspiring community leader in the Manchester British Pakistani community, celebrated his victorious election as an ethnic representative, a 'Community Rep', to the Municipal Council's Race Sub-Committee. The election had been a hard fought one and Chaudri Amin had vanquished a formidable foe and personal enemy, the current cleric or *maulvi* of the Central *Jamia* Mosque in Manchester.

Chaudri Amin was a man of honour. He had served for many years as a sergeant-major in the Pakistan army, working his way up through the ranks, before he deserted and immigrated to Britain. He had sweated on twelve-hour shifts in a textile mill before opening a small knitwear factory. A Punjabi of landlord peasant stock, he was dark, hard, and proud; not a man to be slighted in public. Always an aspiring leader, the public offence had fired him with a sense of mission (see below). He was determined that no servile *maulvi*, nor any of the latter's friends – cunning urban sophisticates and arrogant businessmen, would usurp the rights of the people. He was a representative of the people and he had triumphed. He savoured his victory. His speech, made to his supporters, mostly ex-factory workers like himself, at a dinner celebrating the victory of their 'party', was a rhetorical *tour de force*. It reveals some of the basic moral ideas which underlie ethnic community diasporic politics.

He began his speech, as virtually all community leaders do, by citing from Muhammad Iqbal, the revered Urdu poet, and by promising the opposition that he would represent them well, because 'as all our great leaders have told us, in a democratic system it is necessary to have an opposition party'. Hence, he continued, 'Now that the activities of the election have finished, we are all brothers. Therefore I pray ... that Allah will give us unity (*idhad*)'. Returning to Iqbal once more he went on: 'As the Eastern poet says: A man exists only in the unity of his nation as a wave is in a river, beyond the river, there is nothing [i.e., without a nation to lead there is no leadership].'

Having appealed to communal unity, he moved to the more serious business of demolishing the opposition faction and its *maulvi* leader, who, he claimed, was wasting public money by travelling around in taxis and watching videos, instead of performing his religious duties. The *maulvi* had called him an illiterate in public, an unforgivable dishonour and the basis for a perpetual personal feud:

> They call us *kolu-ka bail*, an animal without a brain [the ox that drives the oil press round and round with its eyes covered]. And whenever they want to they say, 'If that thing [person] does not remove itself we cannot start the *namaz*' [the prayers] [i.e., the *maulvi* refuses to conduct the prayer at the Central Mosque in his presence].
> It is strange to be called *kolu-ka bail*. You know what an ox of the *kolu* is? The ox that goes around and around [the oil press] all day [blindfolded]. And at night they give it something to eat, grass, and then it sleeps.
> We *are kolu-ka bails*. Yes, it means that we work hard all day. Islam does not

decree that we should not work. If it did, how could the schools be run? Or the mosque, without paying the wages and expenses of its employees?... This, to work, is not unusual or *haram* [forbidden] in Islam. It is wrong to call us *koluka bail*. The task of the [Mosque] committee is to supervise [the employees] and Committee members should not shut their eyes or ears [to the corruption of the *maulvi* and his allies]. When I asked one of the [Committee] workers: 'are you listening?' he replied: 'we are using our ears rightly'. 'What do you mean?' I asked. 'Allah created our ears opposite each other', he said. 'We hear with one ear, and clear the sound from the other'. [In other words, we ignore what is going on in the mosque.]

But we use our ears ... we listen both from this side and from the other side – which is why we have ears. Today we are not only saying but we are issuing a warning. They [the *maulvi* and his allies] should not take part in politics. They have a crystal ball and they gaze in it and predict what will happen to this or that [communal political] 'party'. Then they make propaganda and generate internal conflicts between members [of that group], and thus prevent them from doing anything about matters of real importance.

Today we are making clear that we shall break their crystal ball. Then they will no longer be able to perpetrate these things...

I learnt a lot during the day of my election – who is for me and who against. Who is a true supporter, and who a pretender. Where a person stands [in relation to me].

Having completed the fable of the Blindfolded Ignorant Ox, Chaudri Amin turned to a new fable, the fable of the Blue Cowardly Jackal:

Now we know about those *neelkanth*. Most of you wouldn't know the meaning of *neelkanth*. There was once a jackal (*geedar*) who was slightly bigger than the other jackals. One day he was hungry so he went to a village. But the dogs all chased him out of the village [at this point in the speech, the audience laughed uproariously]. He saw a man, a dyer, who was dyeing clothes. Because he was confused by what he saw, he fell into the big tub of dye. When he came out, the dogs all stepped back [in fear] so he thought he had become something special now. He went further and saw a lion eating his prey. The lion was surprised to see him. At that time, it was said, animals were able to talk. The lion asked him: 'Who are you?'. He said: 'I am a *neelkanth*'. The lion said: 'What is a *neelkanth*?' The jackal said: 'A *neelkanth* is a creature who, when he draws his claws over the earth, he tears it open. If he speaks loudly, all the trees fall down. If he calls once, a thousand voters come. If he clicks his fingers, four or five hundred voters come. And if he waves a big stick, two hundred voters come.' The lion was scared. He thought: 'If he draws his claws on the earth it will split, and where will I go then?' So he gave the jackal his prey – because he was scared. And for about a month the jackal went on eating this way. One day it rained, and the dye was washed away so that his real colour was revealed.

[Shouting] The lion saw the real thing and the jackal ran away in fear. Last Sunday [election day] it was raining and the dyed colour of the *neelkanth* was washed away. [*Neel* – blue, the colour of evil and cowardice] And they ran away like jackals. Those *neelkanths* ran away.

There is another verse from Dr Iqbal:

> Don't fear the strong wind, eagle
> For it comes to carry you higher.

['Isn't he a leader!' a member of the audience comments].

We come in truth, and we have the unity of truthful and sincere persons. With the help of these people we formed an organisation. And because we come in truth, people helped us. It is like this. If you do not abandon the truth, there is no power in the world that can overcome you...

Somebody told me: they are reading *dawas* (supplications) against you [in the mosque]... A famous *ulema* once said: 'Pilgrimage is true, but the pilgrim is false; fasting is true, but he who fasts is false; *namaz* (praying) is true, but he who prays is false.' So too, those *dawas*, supplications, which are read against us, those are true, but the people who read them are false. That is why they were not accepted [by God]. That is why those *dawas* came to us, came to the truth.

If someone wishes to answer my speech, let him do so in a public meeting and we shall answer in the same manner, in public. And if they answer us in the mosque [a place of prayer] then we have the right to answer them in that same place. And let them not say then that this is a place of prayer since they were the ones who brought it into disrespect [who desecrated it].

Finally, I embrace you all with an open heart and advise you that we should defend (*masba*) our good deeds (*emal*). That way we shall stay close to Allah. It should not come to pass that a voice descends from heaven [saying] that 'your *imam* is not true (*behazar* – without respect) therefore your *namaz* prayer cannot be heard [when you say your prayers behind the *imam*]. Follow (find) the good *imam*'.

I am so grateful to all of you who have spared your valued time and come here, and granted me the opportunity to thank you.

The fables of the Blindfolded Ox and the Blue Jackal tell a story of human passion and social morality: of individuals competing for honour and leadership in a battle of strategy, power and rhetoric; and of moral responsibility for the welfare of fellow countrymen and women, and for the cultural reproduction of the community as a moral community, a community of brothers and sisters who are beholden to one another. The passion of the battle is the passion of individuals who, in exile, away from home, seek status within the narrow public arena of diasporic politics. Despite the objective narrowness of this arena, however, it is, for the participants, a central life stage in which they act out their passions and rhetorical skills in a globalised drama of human encounters and social intrigue. As Levinas argues:

> Those animals that portray men give the fable its peculiar colour inasmuch as men are seen *as* these animals and not only *through* these animals; the animals stop and fill up thought... It is an ambiguous commerce with reality ... equivalent to an alteration of the very being of the object (1987: 6–7).

The fabled animal constitutes the man or woman as a coward or hero, as cunning and evil or strong and reliable. It reveals his or her exemplary, archetypal qualities, while retaining the reality of individual social agency. It naturalises his 'true', hidden identity.

What are the consequences of this intensity of political involvement? One obvious consequence is a passionate commitment to the communal political values fostered in the internal debate between contestants; the second is that the narrow stage of community politics is *globalised* as a world stage. The actors are perceived, and perceive one another, in vivid, dramatic terms. They are acting out a global drama, a drama in which people assemble to talk about democracy, power, nationhood, religion, the state and global politics. Such debates take place almost entirely hidden from the public eye, in a foreign language members of the wider society cannot understand.

Ethnic Social Movements

In his landmark discussion of social movements, Alberto Melucci makes the point that

> ... collective actors invest an enormous quantity of resources in an ongoing game of solidarity. They spend a great deal of time and energy discussing who they are, what they should become and which people have the right to decide that (1989: 218).

Social movements, he argues, live a 'double existence', partly performed in the 'invisible networks of civil society' and partly in the 'temporary mobilisations through which they become publicly visible' (ibid.: 228). The visible action is thus the other pole of the production of 'new cultural codes within submerged networks' (ibid.: 44, 70). Temporary public visibility occurs whenever collective actors openly confront an antithetical public policy (ibid.: 70). Otherwise, much of the activity of members of social movements is directed towards actualising collective values through distinctive lifestyles, within 'submerged networks'. Melucci draws both on the work of Touraine (1981) on social movements and, even more, on the theory of communicative action proposed by Habermas (1989). In the view of the latter, all forms of power ultimately draw their legitimacy from the everyday, taken-for-granted 'lifeworld'. He sees contemporary social movements as attempts to defend the erosion of the lifeworld, and the personalised identities it sustains, from a further encroachment of economic-administrative systems of control and profitability.

The point is, however, that social movements embody identity through performance, and such performances take place within the lifeworlds of participants. They do not separate different dimensions of their composite identities. On the contrary, the power of the performance is generated by the fusion of identities, discourses and modalities of knowing. The aesthetic, the moral, the intellectual and the political are blended. So too are the Islamic and the South Asian.

A further feature of performance is highlighted in Chaudri Amin's speech. Peformances reveal the conflicts and divisions preoccupying both speakers and their audiences. Performances are therefore not mere solidaristic events, expressions of a transcendent unity. The need is thus to theorise the relation between, on the one hand, the continuous ethnic arguments of identities which take place in invisible spaces, hidden from the public eye, and, on the other hand, the processes of ideological production and organisational mobilisation which reveal ethnic activists' submerged social networks and broadcast their collective voices periodically to a wider public sphere (see P. Werbner 1991a). My argument starts from the fact that ethnic participation is not limited to the spaces allocated by a dominant state or local state. It unfolds in the spaces and arenas created by members of the ethnic community themselves.

This, of course, begs the question of what is 'community'? Benedict Anderson's work on 'imagined communities' has released the sociological imagination from its fixation on community as *Gemeinschaft* – a traditional, face to face group of consociates (1983). To refine his heuristic concept further, however, the need is to elaborate on the fundamentally different senses in which community is imagined and, equally critically, is enacted and actualised through cultural performance, or incorporated through organisational mobilisation.

I want to suggest, in line also with my earlier work (1991a), that in ethnic groups three dimensions of community are publicly imagined and incorporated: the *moral* community, the *aesthetic* community (or the *interpretive* community) and the community of *suffering*. Each 'community' is a cultural world which is constructed through performative imaginings by networks of social actors whose membership in such imagined communities is continuously renewed by these performances.

In his speech Chaudri Amin articulated the moral dimensions of ethnic voluntary activity by engaging in a moral argument or dialogue with the opposition. He called for unity, truth, sincerity and the values of hard work and professional conduct. He also called for democratic public debate and recognised that such a debate was an essential feature of democracy. He made clear that people were locked in moral interdependency: a person cannot exist outside the community, as a wave cannot exist outside the ocean. He spoke in vivid images and tropes, appealing to Punjabi and Islamic cultural idioms and moral ideas to score his points and carry his audience forward with him. His rhetoric underlined the fact that an ethnic community is not only a moral community – it is also an aesthetic community, a community with a shared fund of tropes, symbols and images, associations and understandings.

The Aesthetic Community

If the moral community is defined by *khidmat*, unilateral giving, sharing and voluntary work for the public good, the aesthetic community is defined by cultural knowledge, passion and creativity.[2] The Pakistani community as an aesthetic community has its cultural experts: its orators, poets, clerics, saints and intellectuals. It shares common idioms of humour, love, tragedy, popular culture, festivals, cricket and myths of the past: of national or religious exemplary heroes, of great battles and victories, of oppression and freedom. It shares aesthetic ideas of spatial separations between the profane and the sacred, sensuality and spirituality, 'fun' and sobriety. To perpetuate and reproduce these, the community has incorporated itself in a myriad of associations: literary societies, religious organisations, orders and sects, sports clubs, women's cultural associations, and so forth.

Chaudri Amin's speech contains implicit acts of identification with several different aesthetic communities. The imagery in the speech is Punjabi, perhaps even pan-Asian. The *kolu-ka bail*, the blindfolded ox who grinds the oil seeds, is a familiar village sight;

---

2 Bauman (1992) attributes the notion of an aesthetic community to Kant, citing Lyotard (1988). The notion of an aesthetic community is more distinctively grounded, however, in my view, in postmodernist theory than in a Kantian aesthetics (see Geertz 1993, Chapter 5, for a superb account of what makes for an aesthetic community).

it evokes a far-away home community, agriculture, the dusty hot plains of the Punjab. Similarly, the fable of the Blue Jackal invokes the spaces between villages, the uninhabited jungles where lions and jackals live on the margins of humanity. Iqbal's Urdu poetry invokes heroic images of rivers and eagles, but also of the nationalist movement to create Pakistan as a Muslim independent homeland. The moral lessons are Islamic, but also Western-democratic. They evoke images of mosques, prayers and religious aphorisms. Chaudri Amin and his audience have complex identities: they are Punjabis, Pakistanis, socialists, democrats, British, and Muslim. The speech reaches them as an aesthetic performance in all these different dimensions. What Hall (1991) refers to as the 'silences' contained in each discrete identity are revealed through the rhetorical imagery, moving the audience to passion, touching their sentiments, the nostalgic yearning for another place with its smells and physical sensations. But also, at the same time, drawing *moral* lessons from these images which are much more specific.

The aesthetic community is thus intertwined with the moral community. Ideas about purity and pollution, good and evil, articulate the two and, as I have argued elsewhere (Werbner, in press), may generate moral conflicts about the legitimacy of aesthetic forms or, indeed, of a morality which rejects these valorised aesthetic forms.

Ethnic Organisation

To understand the organisation of moral and aesthetic communities we need to start from the recognition that such communities are not monolithic: they are internally divided by arguments between protagonists. In reality, arguments among Pakistanis occur along three major social axes: segmentary, class, and centre-periphery positioning. Each social division is the locus of different cultural mobilisations and each generates its own internal and external cultural dialogues.

First, the community is a segmentary group. It is not bounded by a single boundary, but contains boundaries within boundaries, revealed in situational opposition. Collective identities refer to moral communities on a rising social scale. To be a British-Pakistani-Muslim-Punjabi-Asian-Black-Mancunian-Sunni-Deobandi-Jhelmi-Gujjar is not necessarily, as anthropologists have long recognised, to bear contradictory or multiphrenic identities, since all these identities may never come into conflict in practice. Moreover, the most intensely passionate and all-encompassing moral conflicts may be 'internal' ones, such as that between Chaudri Amin and the *maulvi* – both Muslims, both Punjabis, both Sunnis although one less pious and more of a modernist than the other. What actually divides them thus is their political stance regarding the relationship between religion and civil society – the conflict surrounds the growing politicisation of religion and the control of this politicisation, expressed in the argument over democratic procedures at the mosque and the duties of religious officials in voluntary organisations. Neither protagonist would hesitate to mobilise allies well beyond his primary group in order to strengthen his side in the battle between them (see P. Werbner 1991b).

In addition to segementary, gender and class divisions which imply sited ethnic 'boundaries' – situationally operative cultural diacritica of exclusion or inclusion – the Pakistani community is very importantly also a social field, not a 'closed', bounded group in which actors are positioned differentially in terms of their access to symbolic, cultural and financial resources (see Bourdieu 1985). Processes of social exclusion and incorporation which sustain cultural boundaries are less critical to the reproduction of the group than the continuity of ethnic 'centres' (or 'cores'), producing 'high' (or, indeed, 'popular') cultural products. Hence, modern-day ethnic groups in capitalist societies tend to be defined by their centre or centres rather than by their peripheries. At the centre are the cultural experts and communal activists, the organic intellectuals like Chaudri Amin and the *maulvi*. The periphery consists of ethnic consumers, whose knowledge, commitment and identification vary a good deal, and who are differentially embedded in communal networks. These centres (for they are several) are sustained by their constitution as loci of high value, competed for in a game of honour and prestige, and by the continuous efforts of the cadres of intellectuals and experts that form them to achieve moral, cultural or religious hegemony.

Despite often very divisive conflicts within ethnic communities, such as the conflict between Chaudri Amin and the *maulvi*, the community forms a transcendent unity through the broader coalitions it builds up, centred upon the Prophet of Islam, the central communal mosque, and so forth. The cross-cutting ties within the community and the dense social networks cutting across factional, class and cultural divisions create the possibility of local communal ethnic mobilisation in response to a local issue about which there is widespread agreement. It is such coalitions which form the basis for the emergence of social movements.

The Formulation of a Common Ideological Discourse

Following Melucci, I have stressed the 'invisibility' of much diasporic public activity, of the cultural performances held in invisible spaces Pakistanis create for themselves. It is this 'normal' invisibility which made the British Muslim mobilisation, following the publication of *The Satanic Verses*, so shocking, and which highlighted also the need to theorise the bases for the emergence of ethnic social movements and to address the processes which lead to new public 'voices' breaking through a prior public 'silence'. Before the affair erupted, Pakistanis were virtually invisible as political actors, submerged in taken-for-granted networks of kin, friends and work or business partners. These networks were sustained by an elaborate ceremonial gift economy controlled by women, and by agonistic rivalries for status and power among men, embodied through cultural performances (see Werbner 1990). In 1987 Chaudri Amin was locked in factional battles focused around local political prizes. In 1990 he and his audience had mobilised, along with their opponents, for a mass protest rally in London to express their sense of moral outrage and public responsibility towards a global Islamic diaspora, the *umma*.

Crucially, the emergence of social movements depends on the formulation of widely shared discourses and emblems. The formulation of a common discourse of anti-racism was evident in Chaudri Amin's transformation into an anti-racist activist during his first year as Community Representative. At the end of the year, he was re-elected for a second year in a negotiated pre-election deal. His election speech in June 1988 concerned participation in Municipal committees and meetings, the intricacies of state rules and regulations, and the agendas for combating racial, as well as religious, discrimination. It was a new cultural idiom and Chaudri Amin was a new man, an expert, a man of knowledge and authority. For one thing, he spoke in English this time. His speech shows how anti-racist narratives are woven into the specific concerns of Pakistanis as Muslims and black people. Ethnic rights, anti-racist battles and communal predicaments are linked together and debated in English, the national political language. But, as in his earlier speech, Chaudri Amin made no attempt to keep the multiple identities and moral concerns of his audience apart.

After explaining the structure of the Council and listing a whole series of activities he had been involved in, he first called on the Council to increase the size of the Race Unit, to publish the MacDonald Report on the Burnage High School racist murder, and to increase the number of councillors on the Race Subcommittee. Although much of this left most of his audience bemused and puzzled, it also involved them in the very process of bureaucratic learning he himself had undergone, and this was reflected in the questions asked later. Chaudri Amin continued his speech, turning to issues of immediate concern to the audience:

> I have worked with various councillors on wide ranging issues. For example, I have held meetings with the councillors from the Market Committee to discuss issues relating to the difficulties faced by Pakistani traders in several Manchester markets. I've had discussions with councillors from the Police-monitoring committee when there have been policing issues affecting our community... *Halal* meals are now being served in Manchester city schools, and before long they will be available in all schools in the City Council's control. The Council spent a good deal via grants to community groups for the provision of playschemes during the summer holidays. We can now bury our dead in the traditional Islamic way without any extra cost.

Most remarkably, by contrast to his speech the previous year, this year Chaudri Amin explicitly highlighted the problems of racism:

> A big concern that I have is the safety of our community. We are subjected to all kinds of racial abuse and racial violence every day. Sometimes it is just taunting and name calling, but at other times it may be physical violence. I do not have to give you the details because you are all experiencing it all the time. When I've raised these issues with the police on many occasions, it has been clear to me that we are not getting the attention from them to which we are entitled. There is a long way to go but we must be resolute and we must ensure that our youngsters are good and strong in character, and also strong in body. Only then can we insure the safety of our community, as these young people will be in the frontline, defending themselves against these racist attacks. If the police are helpless to help us, then we have to help ourselves.

He ended his speech by thanking his audience: 'During the last year I have had a lot of support from all of you, without which I would not have been able to do any of the things I've tried to put before you today. Thank you all.'

In this speech Chaudri Amin evokes the existential problem

facing British Asian as well as Caribbean, African and other ethnic minorities in Britain – the fear of racial violence. The community is imaginatively constructed, in this sense, as a community of suffering.

Ethnic participation in the wider public sphere thus concerns two fundamental orientations: a demand for ethnic rights, including religious rights, and a demand for protection against racism. Different identities and identifications *empower* these two orientations, pointing to the critical difference between ethnicity and racism.[3]

Conclusion: 'Mosaics' or 'Collages'?

Personal, individual identities in a world of migrations, exilic diasporas and artificially created postcolonial nation-states constitute, it has been argued, composite 'mosaics' (Fischer 1986, Fischer and Abedi 1990). The metaphor of a mosaic evokes a created, coherent image, composed of bits and pieces taken from larger, absent wholes (see Strathern 1991: 110, Clifford 1988). Such wholes, it is implied, cannot, by definition, be abstracted or reconstituted merely from the partial assortment of fragments composing the mosaic. If, however, we look not to individuals but to broader collectivities – such as diasporic communities – we need to shift metaphors: larger collectivities may share multiple overlapping identities – moral, aesthetic, political – each of which can be celebrated separately as a coherent whole, in social spaces demarcated and 'framed' as separate and discrete. In Britain, Islamic piety, South Asian popular culture, Pakistani nationalism and British citizenship are foregrounded by British Pakistanis in separated social spaces they themselves create. Although multiple, these identities do not appear, in this sense, to

---

3 In asserting a major cleavage between racism and ethnicity, I am arguing, in line with recent debates in anthropology and sociology against a straightforward conflation of 'race' and 'racism' (see Anthias and Yuval-Davis 1992), and for a recognition that racism, quasi-nationalism or communalism are perversions of nationalism as citizenship (Kapferer 1988, R. Werbner 1991), and thus a feature of the modern nation-state with its Janus-faced orientation (see, for example, Geertz 1973, Anderson 1983, Giddens 1987). This is not to argue that 'ethnicity' is apolitical. As we have seen, the early work of Abner Cohen on political ethnicity anticipated subsequent work on cultural politics, the politics of identity and multiculturalism.

form a 'mosaic'; the play of identities is, like a painting by the German artist Esher, one in which figure and ground alternate, depending on perspective (see Strathern 1991; R. Werbner 1989, Chapter 5; Rapport 1993; Fischer and Abedi 1990, Chapter 5). Perhaps a more apt metaphor to describe this fusion of identities is 'collage' – a layering of wholes which are in principle also discrete. To single out or foreground a specific identity, relationship or role is equivalent to actively *dehybridising* what is essentially complex and multiplex. This is a feature of much symbolic ritual behaviour (Strathern 1991: 79; Gluckman 1962) and it is true of the behaviour of cosmopolitans or circulatory labour migrants, who switch identities when they move from one cultural space to another.

Separations and elaborations of particular dimensions of complex or multiplex relationships and identities cannot ignore, however, as Fischer recognises (1986), not only the inter-references but also the interferences between these acts of foregrounding which occur during actual performances. There is, as it were, a constant 'leakage' between domains and the identities/perspectives constituting them. Moreover, there are contexts in which fusion rather than separation is appropriate. Autobiography may be one of these (Papastergiadis 1993). I have argued here that mosaic, hybridised, identities infuse the *political* rhetoric of aspiring ethnic leaders performing for audiences of fellow co-ethnics sharing the same constellation of multiple identities. Rather than highlighting singular identities, these leaders combine and fuse their multiple identities in new creative patterns or mosaics in order to move their audiences to passion and fear. In their oratory they shift perspectives and scales, referring now to the utterly localised, now to the global, moving between moral and aesthetic arguments, from ethnic nationalism to citizenship, democracy or socialism, from one identity/ representation to another.

This public negotiation of identity by members of diasporic communities takes place in a hierarchy of progressively inclusive social spaces, from the domestic and inter-domestic to the mass cultural. At each scale of social inclusiveness different cultural narratives are negotiated in more, or less, inclusive cultural performances. Communal diasporic voluntary public culture lies at the point of greatest ambiguity between the utterly private and exclusive and the fully public and inclusive (see Habermas 1989). This is why diasporic ethnicities and religiosities are formed, celebrated and passionately debated within this sphere.

References

Anderson, Benedict. 1983. *Imagined Communities*. London: Verso.

Anthias, Floya and Nira Yuval-Davis.1992. *Racialized Boundaries: Race, Nation, Gender, Colour and Class and the Anti-Racist Struggle*. London and New York: Routledge.

Bhabha, Homi. 1994. *The Location of Culture*. London: Routledge.

Barth, Frederik. 1969. 'Introduction' in *Ethnic Groups and Boundaries: the Social Organisation of Cultural Difference*. London: George Allen and Unwin.

Bauman, Zygmunt. 1992. *Intimations of Postmodernity*. London: Routledge.

———. 1993. *Postmodern Ethics*. Oxford: Blackwell.

Bourdieu, Pierre.1985. 'The Social Space and the Genesis of Groups', *Social Science Information* 24 (2): 195–220.

Carrier, James G. 1992. 'Occidentalism: the World Turned Upside Down', *American Ethnologist* 19 (2): 195–212.

Clifford, James. 1988. *The Predicament of Culture*. Harvard: Harvard University Press.

Cohen, Abner. 1965. *Arab Border Villages: A Study of Continuity and Change in Social Organisation*. Manchester: Manchester University Press.

———. 1969. *Custom and Politics in Urban Africa*. London: Routledge.

———. 1981. *The Politics of Elite Culture*. Berkeley: University of California Press.

———. 1993. *Masquerade Politics: Explorations in the Structure of Urban Cultural Movements*. Berkeley: University of California Press.

Dominguez, Virginia. 1989. *People as Subject, People as Object: Selfhood and Peoplehood in Contemporary Israel*. Madison: Wisconsin University Press.

Epstein, A.L. 1958. *Politics in an Urban African Community*. Manchester: Manchester University Press.

Eriksen, T.H. 1993. 'In Which Sense Do Cultural Islands Exist?', *Social Anthropology* 1 (1B): 133–48.

Evans-Pritchard, E.E. 1940. *The Nuer*. Oxford: Clarendon Press.

Fischer, Michael M.J. 1986. 'Ethnicity and the Postmodern Arts of Memory' in *Writing Culture*, James Clifford and George Marcus (eds). Berkeley: University of California Press.

Fischer, Michael M.J. and Mehdi Abedi. 1990. *Debating Muslims: Cultural Dialogues in Postmodernity and Tradition*. Madison: University of Wisconsin Press.

Friedman, Jonathan. 1992. 'The Past in the Future: History and the Politics of Identity', *American Anthropologist* 94 (4): 837–59.

Geertz, Clifford. 1968. *Islam Observed*. New Haven: Yale University Press.

———. 1973. 'After the Revolution', in *The Interpretation of Cultures*. New York: Basic Books.

———. 1993 [1983]. *Local Knowledge*. London: Fontana.

Giddens, Anthony. 1987. 'Nation States and Violence' in *Social Theory and Modern Sociology*. Oxford: Polity Press.

Gilroy, Paul. 1993. *The Black Atlantic: Modernity and Double Consciousness*. London: Verso.

Gluckman, Max. 1940. *Analysis of a Social Situation in Modern Zululand*. Manchester: Rhodes-Livingstone Paper 28.

———. 1962. 'Les Rites de Passages' in *Essays on the Ritual of Social Relations*. Manchester: Manchester University Press.

Habermas, Jurgen. 1989 [1962]. *The Structural Transformation of the Public Sphere*. Translated by Thomas Burger. Cambridge: Polity Press.

Hall, Stuart. 1991. 'Old and New Identities, Old and New Ethnicities' in *Culture, Globalisation and the World System*, A.D. King (ed.). London: Sage.

Kapferer, Bruce. 1988. *Legends of People, Myths of State: Violence, Intolerance and Political Culture in Sri Lanka and Australia*. Washington DC: Smithsonian Institution Press.

Levinas, E. 1987. *Collected Philosophical Papers*. Translated by Alphonso Lingis. Derdrecht: Martinus Nijhoff Publishers.

Lyotard, Jean-François. 1988. *Peregrinations: Law, Form, Event*. New York: Columbia University Press.

Melucci, Alberto. 1989. *Nomads of the Present: Social Movements and Individual Needs in Contemporary Societies*. London: Hutchinson Radius.

Mitchell, J.C. 1956. *The Kalela Dance*. Manchester: Manchester University Press.

Ortner, Sherry. 1984. 'Theory in Anthropology Since the Sixties', *Comparative Studies in Society and History* 26: 126–66.

Papastergiadis, Nikos. 1993. 'The Ends of Migration', Keynote Lecture presented at the Art Gallery of New South Wales.

Rapport, Nigel. 1993. *Diverse World-Views in an English Village*. Edinburgh: Edinburgh University Press.

Strathern, Marilyn. 1991. *Partial Connections*. Marylands: Rowman and Littlefields.

Thomas, Nicholas. 1992. 'The Inversion of Tradition', *American Ethnologist* 19 (2): 213–32.

Touraine, Alain. 1981 [1978]. *The Voice and the Eye: An Analysis of Social Movements*. Translated by Alan Duff. Cambridge: Cambridge University Press.

Wallman, Sandra. 1986. 'Ethnicity and the Boundary Process in Context' in *Theories of Race and Ethnic Relations*, John Rex and D. Mason (eds). Cambridge: Cambridge University Press.

Werbner, Pnina. 1990. *The Migration Process: Capital, Gifts and Offerings Among British Pakistanis*. Oxford: Berg Publishers.

——. 1991a. 'Introduction' in *Black and Ethnic Leaderships in Britain: the Cultural Dimensions of Political Action*, Pnina Werbner and Muhammad Anwar (eds). London: Routledge.

——. 1991b. 'Factionalism and Violence in the Communal Politics of British Overseas Pakistanis' in *Economy and Culture in Pakistan: Migrants and Cities in a Muslim Society*, Hastings Donnan and Pnina Werbner (eds). London: Macmillan.

——. 1991c. 'The Fiction of Unity in Ethnic Politics: Aspects of Representation and the State among Manchester Pakistanis' in *Economy and Culture in Pakistan: Migrants and Cities in a Muslim Society*, Hastings Donnan and Pnina Werbner (eds). London: Macmillan.

——. In press. 'On Mosques and Cricket Teams: Nationalism and Religion among British Pakistanis' in *Sport, Identity and Ethnicity*, Jeremy McLancey and Jonathan Webber (eds). Oxford: Berg Publishers.

Werbner, Richard P. 1989. *Ritual Passage, Sacred Journey*. Washington DC: Smithsonian Institution Press.

——. 1991. *Tears of the Dead*. Washington DC: Smithsonian Institution Press.

——. In press. 'Human Rights and Moral Knowledge: Arguments of Accountability in Zimbabwe' in *Shifting Contexts*, Marilyn Strathern (ed.). ASA Monographs, London: Routledge.

CHAPTER 6

Commensality as Cultural Performance:
the Struggle for Leadership in an Igbo Village

O.A.C. Anigbo *

Introduction

We begin by noting that the principle of commensality is eating together for a purpose. Commensality is not a casual affair. It is a social scheme or design, through which some specific aspect of a relationship can be communicated (see Richards 1932: 187). The idea hidden beneath the exercise of eating together (or, indeed, of failing to do so) is the mutual interest or values which can be invoked through the activity, and the relationships thereby defined (Middleton 1960: 119–20). Common values or interests are therefore the lowest common denominator in the relationship.

One may also need to point out that commensality is not essentially about expressing love or intimacy even though they may not be excluded, for people who are opposed or even aggressive to one another in one sphere of human life might find themselves in total agreement in other spheres and use commensality to define their

---

* I obtained a Doctorate degree in Sacred Theology at the Urban University Rome before applying to read Social Anthropology at the School of Oriental and African Studies, University of London, where I came under the influence of Abner Cohen, who taught me how to develop commensality in alliance with politics. I first wrote a Master's thesis dealing with commensality across cultures (Anigbo 1972), before going on to write about commensality in an Igbo village community (Anigbo 1980).

ties (Anigbo 1987: 16). It can therefore be argued that commensality is an important aspect of universal cultural experience (see Anigbo 1972).

I discovered that these observations are valid for the Igbo in every segment of their social life. There, unity and peace in the domestic unit are assessed in commensal terms. This also applies to each segment of their lineage system as well as to their autonomous villages. For the Igbo, too, commensality is vital for the determination of a man's ultimate identity. This also applies to their descent groups or, indeed, entire village communities who maintain some patterned system of relationships. There, unity and separation as well as the identity of individuals within them are communicated through the idiom of sharing food (Anigbo 1987: 78–88).

The meals for such occasions must, however, be prescribed and would require definite responses which confirm the individual's standing as an insider or identify him as a total stranger. Such prescribed behaviour is time-dimensional or periodic, for it provides a focal point during which the drama of commensality is played out. However, time for the Igbo is not measured mechanically by the clock. It is their social events guided by their environment which signal the placement of a particular ritual action.

Linked to time is the issue of age. Age is important for both the individuals and their descent groups in the village community. Age can be understood in two senses: there is the physical age which has immediate reference to biology – the period in the day and the month of birth of the physical person, and his status *vis à vis* his ancestors. In this respect, rights, duties and social privileges accrue to the individual in a group because of his birth position. There is also the social age which operates in a mixed gathering, that is when different individuals from different descent groups or villages meet and sharing is involved. In that kind of setting, it is the ages of the descent groups or the village communities that govern the allocation of privileges and not the physical ages of those present (ibid.: 109). The four days – Eke, Olie, Afor and Nkwo – which make up the Igbo traditional week, and which are used to regulate socio-economic transactions, are also classified according to age.

The issue of time or period is also linked to territory, for a drama must be situated in a place. Thus a ritual meal ought to be bounded. For married partners, it is the principal meal in the day that provides clues to their identity and specifies whether there is peace or tension. For groups, whether descent or village-based, commensality is achieved periodically during traditional festivals.

At that time, various individuals respond to the call and they tidy up their social obligations (ibid.: 105).

In this chapter, an understanding of commensality is shown to be crucial for the analysis of a leadership crisis in an Igbo community. In this context, commensality serves as an expression of political culture. The analysis is presented under two broad headings – (i) commensality in the formation of allies, and (ii) the role of commensality in the historic leadership struggle.

Commensality in the Formation of Allies

In the Igbo village of Ibagwa Aka, *uno* (a house), can be defined as the smallest commensal unit in the community. This is so because for the Igbo *uno* can mean a woman; they say *nwanyi bu uno* which means that a woman is a house. In reality, it means that there is need for the presence of a woman to prepare food for those living in a house.

A house can be made up of a man and his wife together with their unmarried children. Its independence in matters of food supply is signalled by the ability of the group to feed its members. When a male child attains maturity, he is expected to contribute his effort towards this objective and any failure in this weakens the solidarity of the group. Similarly, it can be expected that individual members of such a group can sit down to a meal in the house as of right. There is no invitation to such a member to participate: to do so would in all seriousness be a clear indication that someone among the members has been aggrieved. Also, for any member of such a group to nose about for food during meal times is an indictment of both the individual and the group. It is therefore obligatory for the entire membership to ensure its unity and solidarity in all matters affecting its life.

The next larger meaningful potential commensal group is *ezi n'uno*. Literally, this means house(s) and path(s), or house(s) with so many married women. In short, it means a compound which is kept clean by the combined efforts of several women married to the men of such a unit. The father exercises authority or the oldest male if the father is dead (Anigbo 1987: 61). The joint efforts of these women can be seen as a kind of social thread which binds the group together. While the component households retain their respective unity and separateness in matters of food, individuals within them can take food anywhere in the compound without fear of indictment.

Several compounds socially linked form the *umu nna* – 'children of father'. The word 'social' is emphatic because, in some instances, houses can be situated close to each other without any kinship links between their inhabitants. The *umu nna* can also be the major lineage whose unity is defined by reference to a 'father' common to them all. It can also be analysed as a commensal group. Although its members can be too numerous to be accommodated under one roof, nevertheless, they achieve commensality because they worship together and share the food and drinks sacrificed at the altar of their ancestors.

The corporate nature of the major lineage can be discerned in some of its social features: the members live together on their land in a specific section of the village and each individual in the group can harvest the oil palm trees growing on their land. The lineage is headed by an *Onyeishi*, the oldest surviving male of the group, who holds their *ofo* and keeps their *arua*;[1] and within it marriage is completely exogamous. The *Onyeishi* also presides over religious and secular transactions and represents the group in meetings of persons of similar status in the village.

Another aspect of commensality which dramatises the unity, the inter-relatedness, and even the separation of the major lineages occurs during traditional festivals. By returning to their respective villages during these festivals, people reaffirm, through commensality, the identity of the village. It also demands a rekindling of the hearth as well as the preparation and serving of prescribed and prized food, and thereby confirms anew the unity and autonomy of the household unit. At that time commensality refocuses the major lineage (and ultimately the maximal lineage which is a confederation of major lineages and socially marked by the principle of exogamy). An important aspect of traditional festivals is the religious worship which rehearses the corporate nature of the lineage through time, involving the living, the dead and the not-yet-born of the group. Finally, some traditional festivals, like those featuring masquerading, emphasise the territorial boundaries of the village, because the mask-dancers cannot perform beyond it at that time (ibid.: 196).

In this chapter three such festivals are mentioned and briefly discussed because each of them stresses a different relationship of the individual to the major lineage.

---

1 *Ofo* – a jointed piece of wood representing justice. *Arua* is a staff of office.

Egba Eze – *Reunion Festival*

Egba Eze is a reunion festival held each year in February/March. The festival lays emphasis on the importance and identity of married daughters, for at that time they must return to their natal homes to meet brothers and unmarried sisters and together demonstrate the numerical strength of the major lineage. Issues which constitute serious threats to the peace, unity and solidarity of the group, whether promoted internally or from external sources, are discussed and measures taken to prevent future occurrences. The ne'er-do-wells are rebuked and encouraged to improve while those who have achieved some significant status such as marriage are congratulated.

There is also the issue of time or the order of doing things according to the days in the Igbo traditional week which are Eke, Olie, Afor and Nkwo. These are the days when their markets are held. Who does what and in what order or on what day of the week can be important for the individual as for the members of his group.

Nkwo is the day when the Ibagwa market is held and on that day all roads and footpaths in the community lead into it, thus effectively crippling any social event that may be contemplated in the community on that day. This economic arrangement affects the Egba Eze celebration. There are three maximal lineages in the community which are traditionally represented in order of seniority: Amebo, Echara and Ezema. In order to promote hospitality and reciprocity in the festivity, each of the three maximal lineages is scheduled to host the reunion with its sisters and daughters on a specific day, thus allowing the members of other maximal lineages to attend as guests. Amebo, which is the most senior in rank, hosts the celebration on Eke day, Echara and Ezema on Olie day, while Idi, a major lineage of Echara, alone celebrates on Afor day. This lone celebration is in itself significant (see p.111). On the Nkwo day which comes after Afor, market activity is suspended for the general exhibition of all the mask-dancers of the community.

Onwa Asaa – *the Seventh Month*

Onwa Asaa is the official date for the eating of new yams in Ibagwa Aka. It is held in the seventh month of the year, following the local calendar of events in the community. The festival focuses on the adult males of the major lineage and identifies those among them who are responsible. It also uses the presentation of yams as gifts to inculcate the value of seniority in the culture, for at that time, adult males have to acknowledge their birth order within the major lineage, juniors making presentations of new raw yams to their seniors. They also validate the unity of the group when all the adult males make such presentations to honour their *Onyeishi*, who is the oldest male among them, and who does not go out to work nor leave his compound except on prescribed occasions.

Although the festival is not marked by lavish entertainments, commensality revitalises the major lineage when all its members assemble with their *Onyeishi* presiding. The kola-nut, palm wine, meat and roasted new yams are served to the ancestors; then the *Onyeishi*, and finally all those present take their shares in turn. After this, each person proposes a vote of thanks to God and to their ancestors for having been allowed to live through the planting season to eat new yams.

Unity and autonomy of the Ibagwa community is communicated in the initial step leading to the proclamation of the feast. Custom prescribes a meeting of the representatives of the three senior-most maximal lineages that make up Ibagwa Aka. These are the *Onyeishi* of Edem Ani (representing Amebo), the *Onyeishi* of Echezema (representing Echara), and the *Onyeishi* of Owerre Ibagwa (representing Ezema).

The meeting is held at the court of the *Onyeishi* of Edem Ani whose privilege it is to invite the other three. Needless to report, it is obligatory for them to accept, and honour the invitation because custom says it should be so. One may also recall that the *Onyeishi* does not leave his compound. Where it is necessary for any of them to leave, as for such a meeting, then it is the privilege of the oldest of them to stay in his court while those younger in social age would have to move, thus endorsing the importance of seniority in the culture.

The main item on the agenda for the meeting is to fix the date for the community to celebrate the feast which permits the eating of new yams without fear of reprisal from the ancestors. The proceedings are fixed by tradition: there is, for example, the kola-nut sharing, which indicates unity among those involved in the activity (see Uchendu 1964). Prayers are also addressed to the founding ancestor (named Ozizikoko Owegu) of the maximal lineages that make up Ibagwa Aka, then to the ancestors of each of the lineages, in order of seniority – Amebo, the most senior of them, followed by Echara and Ezema. They are requested to guide the proceedings.

The sharing of yam fufu, produced from the old stock of yams, as well as palm wine, lavishly displayed for the occasion, are also part of this exercise celebrating the unity of the community. Finally, we should note that the festival is set for Afor day in accordance with the custom of the people, a point which adds dignity to Afor day in Ibagwa Aka.

Omabe Traditional Festival

Omabe is a masquerade feast which features the initiation of youths into the secrets of the mask-dancer in Ibagwa Aka. It emphasises the distinct nature of the three maximal lineages into which the community is grouped. How it achieves this distinctness needs some explanation. The feast used to rotate among these three maximal lineages and allowed a period of three years between the celebrations. Since the festival lasts for a whole year, it would take twelve years to complete a cycle.

Potential initiates into the secrets of *Omabe* are assembled before the *Onyeishi* of their respective major lineages who empowers the *ama* title-holders[2] of the group to scrutinise them and establish their capability to keep secrets. Having passed the test, the learning process leading to the production of the mask-dancer begins.

Features of commensality at the *Omabe* feast differ from what has been observed for *Egba Eze* or *Onwa Asaa*. *Egba Eze* defines the identity of married daughters while *Onwa Asaa* projects the image of the adult male. *Omabe*, on the other hand, highlights friendship as an important feature of social relationships in the community. A relevant friendship is negotiated and ratified with the approval of the lineage because it involves a high degree of reciprocity. Lineages are careful to scrutinise the character and creditworthiness of a potential friend. This is because obligation incurred as a result of the relationship must be met by the collective effort of the lineage should a member die or default. During the *Omabe* festival, friends are invited. Such invitations are known as *obe*. *Ndi ebere obe* are those invited to the feast.

The peak points in the celebrations are the *uda maa*, which means the emergence of the mask-dancers from the spirit world when they begin to perform for a whole year. The other is the *ula maa* which signifies the return of the spirits to the spirit world.

---

2 The *ama* title is gained or achieved through a demonstration of wealth. It gives the individual automatic right to share in the decision-making processes of his major lineage.

During the interval between the *uda maa* and *ula maa*, many important activities are expected to take place. Some of these are the various processes leading to the initiation of youths into the secrets of *Omabe*: there is, for example, the learning process which take place in the *otobo* – a hall erected in the middle of the square belonging to the lineage. The square can be seen as a symbol of the unity of the group. It is the duty of the women married to the men of the group to sweep clean the hall and ground on every Olie day in the year. The only possible exceptions are the Olie days during the *Omabe* season when potential initiates use it as a training ground for all kinds of activities leading to the successful performance of the mask-dancer.

It is necessary to emphasise certain behaviour patterns associated with different segments in the social organisation during the *Omabe* season and which emphasise the quality of commensality in the village. On Eke day, which opens the celebration, every household unit must cook *achicha* meal. *Achicha* is processed from *ede* coco-yam, generally grown by the women and eaten by the Igbo when yam, their staple food, has run out. In the context of prized food, *achicha* is low grade, and having to cook it at that time confirms that a man is married and lives with his wife.

Other symbols of the festivity are ashes, pigs and ropes to which pigs slaughtered for the festivity are tethered, for not to display them indicates a failure to participate and marks one as an 'alien'.

Marriage and friendship are social institutions which cut across the boundaries of descent and promote relationships that respond to the claims of commensality. Such relationships can be significant when struggles for leadership occur in the village, and commensal groups are manipulated by the contestants to achieve coveted leadership positions.

This was precisely the case in Ibagwa Aka in 1976, when the position of 'chief' of the town was hotly contested by two individuals from different maximal lineages in the community. The government did not encourage an election to establish who had the majority following in the community. Instead, it stipulated that the 'traditions' of the people should be the basis for recognition and appointment.[3]

---

3 See Supplement to Anambra State of Nigeria Gazette no. 31, vol. 1, Edict No. 8 of 1976, para. 3(3) no. 2.

Commensality in the Leadership Struggle in Ibagwa Aka

During the course of my research in Ibagwa Aka, the issue of recognition of chiefs came to the fore in the Igbo area of Nigeria. The Igbo people, numbering between three and seven million, and who are found in south-eastern Nigeria, live mainly in several hundred quasi-independent and semi-autonomous village groups or towns which, in their traditional social organisation, lacked any form of centralised leadership (see Uchendu 1965). The 'chief', as head or representative of the village, appears to have been thrust upon them by the colonial administration.[4] But the institution had a checkered history in the area for, at one time, there was the warrant chief who was hand-picked by the colonial officials and made to work with the administration. This was later replaced by the 'Best Man' system, whereby communities were encouraged to participate meaningfully in the transactions of local government,[5] and so to choose persons they considered acceptable, popular and intelligent as their representatives to Native Administrative bodies.

However, before Nigeria obtained independence from Britain in 1960, inquiries into the status of chief in Eastern Nigeria led to the promulgation of the Classification of Chiefs Law (1959), which divided chiefs into First, Second, Third and Fourth categories. After the civil war, the Administrator of the East Central State recognised three traditional rulers as the chiefs of their respective communities but denied the privilege to the rest, an action which caused much agitation among many Igbo communities. In time the government changed its mind and established an Edict which provided room for recognition for any community that met the following conditions:[6]

> Subject to the provision of Section 6 of this Edict, where on the date of coming into force of this Edict, there is in a town or community a person who is the chief of the town or community such community may, at any time thereafter and in accordance with the provision of this Edict, present such a chief to the Military Governor for the purpose of his being recognised by the Military Governor as the chief of the town or community.[7]

---

4 See Anambra/Imo States of Nigeria Government white paper on the Report of the Committee on Chieftaincy Matters Number 5, para. ii.
5 Ibid., para. iii.
6 See Edict No. 8 of 1976, para. 3(2).
7 Ibid., para. 3(1).

Ibagwa Aka had such a person, who met the conditions for immediate presentation for recognition. He had served the community as chief since 1960 and was publicly acknowledged. This man became interested in the publicity inviting communities to present their qualified candidates for recognition or apply for it. Accordingly, he presented his application for recognition to the Secretary of Igbo-Eze South Local Government. Also, in order to get the approval of the community, he appealed to the *Ndiishi* (plural of *Onyeishi*) of the oldest three major lineages who ordinarily would represent the unity of the community where they act together.[8]

This applicant would have been successful but for the public displeasure about his alleged misconduct in office. All kinds of indictments were produced to discredit him. Even the support of the elders (*Ndiishi*), who represent the unity of the community and which he won, was being ridiculed by the new elites who refused to allow this kind of gerontocratic principle to operate in the new democratic system. It was felt that such people were too old to promote the unity of the people, especially in a changed situation. Efforts were therefore mobilised on the community level to damage his chances. A new candidate was chosen by the community elites but the first contender stood his ground. There were therefore two candidates vying for the position of leader of Ibagwa Aka, the first from Idi, a major lineage of Echara, while the challenger was from Edem Ani, the oldest major lineage in the entire community.

It should be pointed out that in most Igbo communities, there is an accepted method of sharing things peacefully; the value of the commodity notwithstanding, it is the right of the oldest to pick first. Where there is doubt as to the order of seniority among those involved it is obligatory for them to resolve this before continuing with the business in hand.

In the context of the disputed leadership position in Ibagwa community, the challenger invoked the right of Amebo, as the

---

[8] It will be recalled that these elders can constitute the organ of unity for the entire community. This happens every year prior to the commencement of the feast of yams through which the identity of the adult males can be projected. At that time, they formally meet at the court of the *Onyeishi* of Edem Ani which is the oldest major lineage in the community. After eating and drinking and with due deliberations on the progress of agriculture in the community, they produce the calendar of events which will govern communal activities for the current year.

oldest maximal lineage in the village, to choose first, now that the 'tradition' of the community must be invoked. He also cited the order which is observed during the *Egba Eze* celebration when Amebo, the oldest maximal lineage, opens the feast on Eke day and others follow. He reinforced his argument by alluding to the position of Edem Ani, his own major lineage and the oldest in the community, during the feast of yams, when the privilege of the *Onyeishi* is annually emphasised by obliging the representatives of the maximal lineages to assemble in his house for the performance of their duty to the community.

While the claims of the challenger were valid, he also appeared to have over-reached himself. By referring to the customary patterns of behaviour followed during the traditional festivals to bolster his candidacy, and especially those which accord pre-eminence to men of his lineage, he denied the possibility of change in the village. This would imply that men from the other two maximal lineages in Ibagwa Aka could never assume the mantle of leadership of the village – an implication which the people from these lineages would not accept. Consequently, they withdrew their support from him and rallied to the original claimant.

The first contender fought back by reinforcing his argument for aspiring to the leadership of the community. He did this by referring to the same source – tradition – as his challenger. He claimed that his lineage was a privileged group in the village and therefore alone celebrated the reunion with married sisters and daughters on Afor which is considered solemn in Ibagwa Aka. He added that Afor is the only day when the feast of yams can be celebrated in the community. It will be recalled that the feast of yams marks an important point in the cycle of agriculture, which is the traditional occupation of the people.

The challenger rejected this line of argument outright by questioning the very legitimacy of the original contender's ancestry. He pointed out that the latter's major lineage (Idi) should not be hosting the reunion with married sisters on Afor day. According to him, if Idi were a true descendant of Echara and not a fictitious one, it would be celebrating its unity with the other members of the Echara lineage on Olie, the day allotted to it by tradition (see p.105). He suggested compromise and not privilege as the reason for compelling the Idi group to organise its reunion alone on Afor day, thereby alluding to its 'foreign' origin or late arrival in the community. The challenger argued that a member of such a lineage should not be the first to aspire to a leadership position of the village, especially where the tradition of the people has clearly established a method of doing things in the community.

The war of nerves between the two contenders in the leadership struggle in Ibagwa Aka reached its peak during the *Omabe* feast. It will be recalled that the *Omabe* festival celebrates the initiation of youths into the secrets of the mask-dancer. In 1976, the festival was resumed after a long disruption caused by the Nigerian civil war (1967–1970) which derailed many political and social events in Igboland. There was also unanimous agreement in the community to end the cyclical pattern which characterised the feast before the civil war, thereby introducing a communal celebration which would enable the youth of the entire village to be initiated together into the secrets of *Omabe* at the same time and place.

The first contender, in his capacity as 'chief' of the community, though not yet recognised by the current administration, took a significant step and fixed the date for the communal celebrations. His rival for the leadership repudiated the action on the grounds that it was contrary to the tradition of the people for a chief to proclaim a traditional festival. He insisted that such a privilege is reposed in the *Onyeishi* of the oldest major lineage in the community, and should be preserved. His supporters upheld this view. The division in the village was renewed.

The chief and his supporters proceeded to host the celebrations but the rival and his group boycotted the festivities that day. The performance took place at the *nkponkpo*, a traditional ground which is a parched piece of land on the outskirts of the village. I was there and watching. The supporters of the chief were there *en masse*. Traditional music and all the paraphernalia that would accompany the initiation were also there. As the initiates, clad in their masks, made their momentous exit from their hiding places, their supporters cheered and fired guns in respect.

The supporters of the challenger were also there, but instead of cheering as others did, they mocked and mimicked the guttural utterances of the mask-dancers, a spectacle which heightened the division between some of the onlookers. They also made derogatory remarks about the number of the chief's supporters. This kind of behaviour would have degenerated into an open fight but for the police whose presence kept the two parties apart.

Eight days later, the supporters of the challenger conducted their own ceremony of initiation on the same site as their opponents had previously. There was no visible difference in the style of their performance for I was there and made detailed observations. The music and other forms of entertainment were lavishly displayed. The only difference between the two was in numbers, both of the supporters and the initiated youths who formally put on the mask for the first time. The spectators were also more numerous than those attending the previous exercise. The enlarged attendance at the scene can easily be explained. More publicity was given to the show, and higher numbers also reflected the population of Amebo, the home base of the challenger and most of his supporters.

The supporters of the rival chief appeared to be very satisfied with the attendance. However, numbers are not crucial in the final decision since head counts are not an acceptable measure of success in the pursuit of a leadership position in the community (see Barnes, this volume). Moreover, the counting of human beings is proscribed in the culture of the Igbo.[9]

Summary and Conclusion

Commensality in Igbo social life demonstrates the various levels of interacting groups within the village. The basic operational unit is the *uno*, a house which is rooted in lineage land. The major lineage is an expansion of this and functions as a corporation, while the maximal lineage is marked by the principle of exogamy. The village group, which is autonomous, binds them all through a definite territory recognised internally and externally. This base is crucial to the individual, for without it he cannot participate in the various alliances which form the essence of the political process in the village.

Igbo communities have definite principles of commensality which guide the mechanism of avoiding and/or resolving discord when there are things to share in the village. One such principle is '*kedu kanyi si eke ife enwekoronu*' (how do we share common goods or services in the village?) Such a rule should have been evoked and respected in the early stages of the leadership struggle in Ibagwa Aka. It appears not to have been.

---

9 The Igbo people frown at counting their offspring. It is believed that such an exercise will attract evil spirits who can inflict death on the family.

It can therefore be claimed that the failure to resolve the conflict cannot be traced to the mechanism of commensality but to the failure of men to honour its dictates. However, when commensality at the village level failed to determine the fate of the contest, another layer of commensality appears to have surfaced. The new form of commensality has a base outside the village, and is achieved through sharing holy communion in a church (see Kolanut 1969: 236).[10] It was a common view that the rival lost to the chief because the latter and the Secretary who processed the application for recognition and appointment share the same faith.

References

Anigbo, O.A.C. 1972. 'Some Political Aspects of Commensality', MA Thesis, University of London.

——. 1980. 'Commensality and Social Change in Ibagwa Aka, Anambra State, Nigeria', PhD Thesis, University of London.

——. 1987. *Commensality and Human Relationship Among the Igbo.* Nsukka: University of Nigeria Press.

Kolanut, N.C. 1969. 'Igbo Symbol of Love and Unity', PhD Thesis, Rome Urbaniana.

Middleton, J. 1960. *Food Habits* Doc. No. 647. London: The Tavistock Institute of Human Relations.

Richards, A. 1932. *Hunger and Work in a Savage Tribe.* London: George Routledge and Sons Ltd.

Uchendu, V.C. 1964. 'Kola Hospitality and Igbo Lineage Structure', *Man* 53: 47–50.

——. 1965. *The Igbo of South East Nigeria*: Case Studies in Cultural Anthropology. New York: Holt Rinehart and Winston.

---

10 Contact with Europeans opened up the missionary enterprise in Igbo country and paved the way to denominational cleavages. Anglicanism and Roman Catholicism have made their impact in Ibagwa Aka.

CHAPTER 7

Migrating Cultural Performances:
The Urhobo among the Ikale-Yoruba, Ondo State, Nigeria

Onigu Otite

Introduction

This chapter, which deals with Urhobo rural-to-rural immigrants in Ikale-Yorubaland, seeks to show how cultural performances serve as important markers of cultural identity. At the same time, in the context of scarce political and economic resources and the ethnic pluralism which characterises Nigeria, the very mechanisms which sustain these boundaries can, ironically, lead to their fracturing, as increasing interactions generate new forms of cross-cultural performances. This argument builds on Abner Cohen's insights into the politics of cultural symbols and his most recent work which demonstrates how these are manifested in modern cultural movements (1993).

Urhobo Rural Immigrants in Ikale-Yorubaland

With a 1963 population of 0.6 million growing to about 1.1 million according to the 1991 census, the Urhobo people constitute the largest ethnic group in the former Bendel and now Delta State of Nigeria. They are divided into twenty-two polities, each defined by dialectal differences and micro-political and religious symbols. Most of the polities are organised around kingship, with the king, called *ovre*, chosen rotationally from descent groups or town units, such as in Agbon and Okpe, or through primogeniture, as in Ughelli and Ogor. A few of the polities have gerontocratic structures at the centre, as in Ephreon-tor, while others have central institutions in which senior members of title-associations officiate, as in Ughienvwen. Generally, each polity is also constituted by several towns and villages, where kinship symbols and sentiments determine, to a large extent, the character and operation of indigenous council democracies.

The Urhobo regard themselves as one people, principally because they share a system of common political, religious and kinship symbols and speak the same language. Thus there are several levels of differentiation characterised by the use of symbols and cultural performances. The dramatisation and even ritualisation of socio-cultural differences are critical in the political and economic relationship between some Urhobo entities and neighbouring ethnic groups inhabiting the same or adjacent settlements, for example in the urban areas of Warri and Sapele. Conflicts between the Urhobo and Itsekiri ethnic groups in Warri, for instance, over land and settlement space, on the one hand, and indigenous and modern political supremacy, on the other, provide the social spheres for manipulating and instrumentalising cultural performances in the urban setting.

This Urhobo experience of changing levels of symbolic identifications, which may be explained further in terms of the theory of segmentary opposition, forms part of their strategy of co-existence with members of other ethnic groups away from their own territory. Emigrants from rural backgrounds move to other rural areas where the abundance of oil palm trees and forest environment provide opportunities for the exploitation of resources for their socio-economic survival. Ikaleland in Okitipupa division, a rural Yoruba territory, offers such opportunities.

From the eighteenth century individual males or small male-headed households took the decision to migrate to Okitipupa and other parts of Yorubaland, a distance in this case of about 270 kilometres from their natal homes. Oil palm production is an enervating occupation which requires the co-operation of men, women, and children as working units. A rural Urhobo household can survive wherever oil palm trees grow in abundance.

On arrival in the area, immigrants were introduced to Ikale

rural landlords through friends or kinsmen who had arrived earlier, and paid a fee, or promised to do so, for a tenancy to exploit the land and oil palm resources. They then established camps or villages consisting of an average of seven households. A household was the smallest unit of social organisation, and each village was an exclusive Urhobo settlement. I studied six of these camps-villages in great detail, and found that everything was done according to Urhobo culture. Also, Urhobo expertise in palm oil production was preserved in the villages. Before the arrival of the Urhobo immigrants the local Ikale population had had no technology for climbing the tall oil palm trees to cut regimes (bunches of oil palm fruits). They could only cut fruits for food and domestic use from those short trees which did not require climbing with the rope girdles manufactured by the Urhobo.

The villages are organised and shaped after the Urhobo home villages in the Delta State, but with elements of impermanence which betray the target character of their migration and temporary settlements. The language and dress forms are Urhobo; just as their trough-factory, called *oko*, rope girdles, specially shaped slicing knives and axes, rafters and filters etc., are symbols of an exclusive occupation and manner of economic survival and prosperity in the locality.

Within this context of an exclusive lifestyle, the Urhobo immigrants work from about 7 a.m. to 5 p.m. daily except on Sunday (for Christians) and the indigenous resting day called *edewo* (for all immigrants). When not engaged in palm oil manufacturing, the immigrants do farmwork. The products of these two occupations bring the Urhobo face-to-face with members of Ikale society in the market places. Here, the Urhobo sell their palm oil and the kernel cracked and extracted by the women from the dried fruits. While the Urhobo have learnt the local language to facilitate their economic transactions, they maintain their identity, and in their camps follow their exclusive lifestyle and socio-economic activities.

The earlier immigrants apparently maintained friendly relationships with their hosts, and hence later arrivals were willingly accepted by local Ikale landlords. The Urhobo immigrants were target migrants, aiming to accumulate money and materials for a variety of needs – bicycles, wives, furniture, capital for urban businesses or trade, houses in Urhoboland or in a nearby town, etc. The failure or success in achieving these targets determined the rate of immigration and consequently the numbers of Urhobo in Ikale territory from year to year. The Urhobo immigrant population changed from 25 percent of the total population in the locality in 1931, to 22.3 percent in 1952, to 14.7 percent in 1963. Other immigrants in the area were Ijo (Izon), Igbo, Bini, Isoko, Itsekiri, Hausa, Effik and Ibibio, constituting between 1 percent and 8.2 percent of the population. The Urhobo are thus quite visible carriers and manipulators of a separate culture in this heterogenous rural locality.

The Urhobo camps are identifiable not only from the lifestyle of immigrants but also from the architectural design and structure of the settlement. Each camp consists of an average of seven family/household units, totalling some forty people related to one another through kinship and descent. Their government is gerontocratic. The eldest man, who is generally the father or uncle of the rest, has an intensively ritualised socio-economic authority, and intervenes during quarrels to ensure co-operation and peace both within the group and in relation to the host society. The success of oil palm production requires this peaceful co-operation (Otite 1979: 228). My calculations from observed working situations in the first half of the 1970s showed that 'it took a household twenty-one days to complete the process of extracting oil from the palm fruits. On average, a kerosene tin of 18.2 litres of oil was produced from 18 regimes of palm fruits, thus giving a total of sixty tins of palm oil produced yearly by a typical immigrant. In addition to this, an immigrant's wife or wives got 1,097.2 kg of palm kernel a year' (ibid.: 229). Fluctuating earnings were made from these products from year to year.

Immigrants, particularly those who have made substantial economic progress, have also set up shops manned by adult sons or relatives in Okitipupa or any nearby town. In 1972, immigrants engaged in several enterprises in Okitipupa town, involving textiles and clothes, tailoring etc. Single commodity shops were also run in Okitipupa for the sale of palm oil and kernel. It should be recalled that none of the immigrant camps is viable as a commercial or market centre, and this fact brings many immigrants face-to-face with other members of the local, non-Urhobo population on market day.

Such days are also the Urhobo resting day called *edewo*. They provide occasions for cultural performances focussed on *igbe* religious worship. In Urhoboland, the *igbe* as a religious movement is believed to have begun ages ago and became a very visible religion in about the eighteenth century. It is patronised in the Delta State and other areas where the Urhobo are found. Urhobo and non-Urhobo (such as the Isoko) believers in *igbe* religion in Nigeria (mainly in the Delta State) were estimated to be about one million in 1982 (Nabofa 1982: 249). The *igbe* religious worship was apparently alien to the Ikale in Okitipupa area. Only the Urhobo immigrants constituted the membership at the time of my first study. On *edewo* days, members, both male and female, assembled in the house of their leader, as early as 8 a.m. The overall colour scheme and background was white: white blouses and white wraps for women, white singlets and white wraps for men. Small white thread or beads might be tied round the necks, wrists and ankles of members, and white powder or chalk rubbed on the face and neck, although these were soon dissolved by sweat during the dancing. White, to the generality of *igbe* worshippers, as to the Urhobo generally, symbolises purity, peace and joy.

The 'congregation' in each case was not too large, that is, about twenty people. They formed lines of three members each, or constituted themselves into a small circle for the ritual dance. Though not compulsory, each member held a small skin fan with the right hand and, following the rhythm provided by the songs and bare-foot stamping, clapped it on the left palm or on the right leg. The *igbe* meeting and dance required energy to perform and could last until 4 p.m. or even later, so members found it advisable to eat their breakfast, usually consisting of starch and carbohydrates and some protein derived from cassava, yam, plantain, fish or meat, before it began. There were intervals necessitated by exhaustion. Occasionally, during such rest intervals, the leader or another member would get possessed by a spirit. Such occasions of spirit possession and mediumship provided more drama, and sometimes suspense, since at these times revelations and prophesies would be revealed about the life of an individual or the fortunes of the group.

In addition to the four-day *edewo igbe* meetings and worship, members organised yearly festivals or religious outings with dances through some streets of the town. On such occasions, which occurred between October and December, members would carry foodstuffs – yam, plantain, large fish, oil, etc., as gifts to the leader. In their natal Urhobo land, members from several of the twenty-two Urhobo polities assemble in the compound of their founders, for example, in Chief Agege's compound in Orogun polity. In such central places in Urhoboland, halls of worship (called *ogwa*) are constructed and decorated with white cloth, native chalk (*orhe*), carvings, hand skin fans etc. Such halls are absent from *igbe* arrangements in Ikaleland. In Urhoboland, as in Ikaleland, some of the foodstuffs are carried, while singing and dancing in their white dress, to the riverside where they are thrown into the river, ostensibly to be eaten by the water goddess, called 'mammy water' by some Urhobo adherents.

Igbe membership is voluntary, but the religion is also believed to provide sanctuary for confessed witches and wizards who thereafter profess to be benevolent (practising positive witchcraft) instead of harming victims. Members also include those who seek protection from bewitchment and anyone who 'gives his or her head to God for safekeeping'. Although they are not Christians, *igbe* worshippers also pray to God, known as *Orise*, to be saved, and to have good health and prosperity. Besides, the *igbe* is also a 'hospital' where those who are affected by illnesses, poisoning or mental and chronic health problems are treated with herbs, tree bark and prayers. This occurs after divination, to ascertain the involvement of superhuman, and spiritualised forces. Members' major precepts are love, charity and purity. Thus, although *igbe* is significant as an entertaining cultural boundary marker, its hidden meaning is the search for inner purification by purging the mind of evil deeds or thoughts.

The *igbe* religion in Ikaleland is an Urhobo affair, and the spectators and non-believers are Ikale and non-Urhobo immigrants. The *igbe* leader's compound, as theatre, provides an exclusive place for the dramatisation of Urhobo culture and belief system. The four-day *edewo* occasions, like the yearly gatherings, are thus critical events for manifesting and sustaining Urhobo migrant culture in Ikaleland. They symbolise an important aspect of Urhobo migrant social structure in the host society. The *igbe* is not in competition with any local religion. For the Urhobo, it provides a refreshing break and refrain from hard work and hazardous activities associated with oil palm production. It enjoins friendliness and co-operative living.

The two powerfully distinctive forms of cultural performance described above are mutually reinforcing and promote one identity. On the one hand, there is the exclusive identifiable economic organisation for individual and group survival and improved standard of living in a recreated Urhobo physical and architectural environment. Activities in this sphere of life are complementary in Okitipupa society and do not compete with those of the Ikale indigenes. On the other hand, *igbe* religion is not only spiritually and psychologically satisfying, but is also a visible cultural-religious drama with a distinctive Urhobo label. The potency of this cultural performance is increased by the need to ensure peaceful co-existence in the locality and economic well-being.

Together, these two forms of exclusive culture-bound performances have the effect of identifying a political category of Nigerians with local second-class citizenship. They are manipulated to get their votes during elections to the Local Council or State and National Assembly, but hardly ever compete or expect to be voted for as candidates on behalf of Ikaleland for new state political positions. In this sense, cultural performances convey political messages of disabilities. They are ready-made natural-cultural displays and exhibits for man-made political discriminations in the local setting. Yet the immigrants adhere to their 'Urhoboness', despite the evils of the widespread phenomenon of local dual citizenship in Nigeria, hoping that at some point in time they will achieve their targets: to acquire enough wealth and financial means to contest elections or be vocal and visible in politics as first-class citizens when they return to their natal homes in the Delta State of Nigeria.

The immigrant Urhobo cultural-social organisations, though exploited for political gains by Ikale-Yoruba political seekers, nevertheless remain together; politics from 'outside' does not have the effect of factionalising or segmenting them. Two reasons account for this phenomenon. First, the camp-villages are small and tightly held together as moral communities by ties of kinship and the cultural value of respect for elders as headmen. Second, immigrants are concerned with, if not committed to, their survival and the achievement of their targets, which they conceive of as economic, not political. Thus, for the Urhobo immigrants, ethnicity is not a political phenomenon in the sense of struggles, competitions, and confrontations in respect of local and national positions. Rather, it is essentially an economic phenomenon involving the dynamics of cultural exclusivity in a friendly host environment.

In the above senses, cultural performances reveal the differences between the Urhobo incomers and Ikale-Yoruba hosts and non-Urhobo immigrants. They maintain the content of Urhobo identity, and facilitate their link, one way or the other, to the local council, state and national politics and government. As processes of promoting their homogeneity, Urhobo cultural performances are symbols of exclusion. They also constitute an unintended means of maintaining cultural pluralism in the rural setting of Okitipupa. Ikale-Yoruba cultural performances are less visible, and less assertive. Yet both the hosts and immigrants are just as 'ethnic-conscious' in this Okitipupa rural environment as are the Hausa of Sabo and the Yoruba in the Ibadan urban setting.

Some Areas of Social Change

My seventeen years of continuous study of these immigrants from the 1970s (Otite 1994) reveals that the basis of Urhobo exclusivity has become gradually punctured following the introduction of oil palm plantations and a modern palm oil mill built in Okitipupa town in October 1974, to extract palm oil and process palm kernel. A large part of the land on which the exclusive villages were built, like the Ikale settlements, have been converted to oil palm plantations through the Small Holders Oil Palm Project. In a similar manner, a Nigerian Army Unit, established in Okitipupa, has occupied a large space from which the immigrants have had to re-emigrate. Furthermore, several sources of urban concentration (Otite 1988) have increased the population of Okitipupa creating more socio-cultural diversity. The town has 'set up new cycles of rural-urban dependencies with new phases of immigration and potentials for further development in the countryside' (ibid.: 26).

According to my earlier finding, 'real value was derived from the maintenance of exclusive ethnic identities and organisations. In this respect ... 100 percent of the total number of immigrant parents interviewed would not give their daughters in marriage to Ikale landowners and thereby change the pattern of ethnic exclusiveness in the future through filiation and dual local citizenship' (Otite 1975: 123). This preference for Urhobo marriage and family symbols has changed, and Urhobo-Ikale marriages have occurred in the latter period of my study.

Also changed is the Urhobo monopoly of palm oil manufacture technology. Young Ikale people have learnt to climb tall oil palm trees using rope girdles made by Urhobo immigrants. This Ikale acquisition of aspects of Urhobo technology has been possible because of its open practice. Nothing was done in secret, and the Ikale freely observed from time to time how the immigrants climbed the tall trees. The incentive for this Ikale adoption of the technology has been due mainly to the increasing market prices of palm oil and kernel. However, the Urhobo girdles made from oil palm fronds have gradually been replaced by new iron (woven wire) types made through Western technology and imported into Ikaleland. These are now used by the Urhobo and the Ikale alike.

Thus Urhobo immigrant socio-economic organisations are being reduced as a result of urban and industrial incursions into the rural areas, thereby forcing Urhobo immigrants to re-emigrate, become absorbed as physical labourers in the new oil palm plantations, or return home. In addition, those that remain in the Okitipupa urban environment find their exclusive organisation to be an unnecessary strategy of coping with the local economy and changing patterns of life. Although the Urhobo are still easily identified as Urhobo through their language, dress and lifestyle, they have become part of the growing urban heterogeneity and anonymity. The Urhobo answer to their disappearing village organisations has been the formation and invigoration of their ethnic associations and home town unions in Okitipupa and other large settlements.

Changes in the rites and membership of the *igbe* religious organisation have also occurred. New types of members have joined the religion as a result of Urhobo-Ikale marriages and affinal kinship links, and as a result of the desire of convinced local patients to be cured of certain 'imponderable' diseases. Yet, the essential content of the religion remains unchanged in the rapidly urbanising Okitipupa town.

In many respects, this Okitipupa rural situation contrasts with the urban Hausa in Sabo, Ibadan, described by Cohen (1969). Sabo is an ongoing permanent area set aside in 1916 by municipal law, for Hausa settlement. Since then, Hausa exclusive symbols have been maintained and recreated to meet the changing needs of cattle and kola traders, as well as of an endless stream of visitors and settlers with new and diverse occupations such as tailors, craftsmen, middlemen, currency dealers, and transport owners and drivers. The dynamics of Hausa cultural performances and exclusivity are still central in Ibadan politics today. Thus, while the Urhobo rural immigrant organisations are being reduced, much of Sabo today is still the Sabo that Cohen knew in the 1960s.

Conclusion

Symbolism and 'the politics of cultural performance' are never absent from the social life of either the Urhobo target migrants or the Hausa immigrant settlers. In this respect, Cohen's insights have contributed substantially to my work on Urhobo immigrants in Okitipupa, and to the study of their politics, symbols and cultural performances.

References

Cohen, Abner. 1969. *Custom and Politics in Urban Africa: A Study of Hausa Migrants in Yoruba Towns*. London: Routledge and Kegan Paul.

——. 1993. *Masquerade Politics: Explorations in the Structure of Urban Cultural Movements*. Berkeley and Los Angeles: University of California Press.

Nabofa, M.Y. 1982. 'Igbe Religious Movement' in *The Urhobo People*, Onigu Otite (ed.). Ibadan: Heinemann.

Otite, O. 1975. 'Resource Competition and Inter-ethnic Relations in Nigeria' in *Ethnicity and Resource Competition in Plural Societies*, Leo Despres (ed.). The Hague: Mouton.

——. 1979. 'Rural Migrants as Catalysts in Rural Development. The Urhobo in Ondo State, Nigeria', *Africa* 49(3).

——. 1988. 'Sources of Urban Concentration in the Nigerian Countryside', *African Studies Review* 31(3).

——. 1990. *Ethnic Pluralism and Ethnicity in Nigeria*. Ibadan: Shaneson C.I. Ltd.

——. 1994. *On the Path of Progress: A Study of Rural Immigrants and Development in Nigeria*. Lagos: Malthouse Press (forthcoming).

CHAPTER 8

On Avoidance

P. H. Gulliver *

Introduction

One late evening in 1980, after a meeting ended, I walked along the main street of a small Irish town with a local man as we had agreed to take a drink together. Suddenly, as it seemed to me, my companion said that we should cross the street and began to do so without waiting for me. It was early days in my research in the town and I forbore to question this unexpected action. (It was weeks later, as our rapport developed, that I discovered that my companion was following a common practice by avoiding an encounter with a man who was approaching on that side of the street. My companion had been in dispute with the man, the matter remained unresolved, and the two men were avoiding any interaction.) However, on the side of the street to which we had

---

* Whilst we were everyday colleagues at SOAS, Abner Cohen sometimes reminded me that political behaviour occurred, and could therefore be studied, wherever people interacted. From his proddings, I realised more clearly than hitherto that people engaged in dispute management were involved in political action. He also encouraged me to carry out comparative, cross-cultural analysis and, in so doing, to take advantage of the several and contrasting societies in which I had worked. This, he maintained, was both an opportunity and an obligation for a more senior anthropologist. His influence was salutary. The present chapter is in recognition of his contribution to, and stimulus in, the study of political behaviour.

crossed there was a convenient pub. Nearing that pub, as I said something about getting a good pint there, my companion declined and we crossed back over the street and went to a pub in a side street. After we had got our drinks, I expressed surprise that we had not patronised the first pub. My companion explained that a small clique of men had recently taken to heavy drinking there. Their leader was a 'troublemaker' and already under police warning for after-hours drinking and drunkenness: it was well, said my companion, to keep away from him so as to avoid being involved in any troubles that might arise.

In this chapter, I examine the concept of avoidance and avoidance behaviour from a comparative perspective and with particular attention to processes of dispute management. In the social science literature, reports of so-called, deliberate avoidance in social relationships and social interaction have been manifold in kind and ethnographic provenance. With no attempt to be exhaustive, a few examples can indicate the wide variety of references. In doing this, it is useful to distinguish at least two kinds of avoidance. One is *dispute avoidance* which follows directly from the outbreak of a dispute between individuals or groups. The second is *conflict avoidance* where the intention, more or less consciously, is to prevent disputes occurring or to circumvent involvement in those which do occur.

Dispute avoidance occurs when a disputant (whether a group or an individual) takes practical action to curtail interaction with the opponent (and, possibly, the latter's supporters) rather than seeking confrontation of some kind, at least immediately and perhaps permanently. For example, a sub-group, such as a subsidiary lineage or political unit, may secede when dispute occurs over the distribution of power and resources. An individual may resign from office or from a group or association because of sufficiently severe differences with others. Shoppers or businessmen may shift their purchasing away from a supplier because of unacceptably low quality of goods and services. Avoidance has sometimes been used to refer to the actions of slaves who ran away from their masters or to victimised spouses or employees who left their oppressors. Groups may sever or limit relations with each other, as in the case of states withdrawing their diplomatic representatives. Members of a group sometimes ostracise one of their number because of disapproved behaviour. A person may 'lump' or tolerate some injury because of unwillingness to take positive, ameliatory action.

Conflict avoidance may be an explicit cultural style or an implicit possibility. Thus, in some contexts it may be prescribed by formal rules which require individuals to abstain from or limit contacts with certain other persons with whom interaction is considered potentially dangerous: for instance, daughter's husband and wife's mother, or classificatory brothers and sisters.[1] Less formally, but often in a culturally stylised way, individuals practice avoidance in order to prevent dispute arising or to minimise involvement in situations where dispute already exists or seems imminent. For example, in rural Ireland (County Kilkenny), individuals often chose not to frequent places or to engage in activities where troublesome situations and people would be encountered, or they crossed the street or took another route so as not meet certain individuals. When unavoidable meeting occurred and straightforward ignoring was undesirable, interaction was kept to conversation on superficial topics, such as the weather or non-local gossip. In this way, people avoided intimacy or controversy or matters of importance.

Dispute Avoidance

Anthropological attention to dispute avoidance has been slight. Some general works in the anthropology of law and society did not include consideration, or even mention, of it.[2] Probably this occurred because, with a prime concentration on 'law' and on dispute resolution, avoidance was overlooked since it was seen as the antithesis of confrontation and seemed not to lead to an endeavour by disputants to move towards a practical resolution of their problems. However, if we broaden the field to include the 'management' of disputes and accept the palpable fact that not all disputes are 'resolved,' 'settled' and ended, then avoidance can be seen as a relevant and empirical mode of operation.[3] Individuals do not always want to settle and end a dispute and sometimes they

---

[1] This kind of rule-based behaviour was taken to be the prototypical form of avoidance by earlier anthropologists: e.g., Lowie (1931).

[2] For example, Hoebel (1954), Bohannan (1967), Nader (1969), Pospisil (1971), Roberts (1979).

[3] By dispute I mean open disagreement between persons in which the alleged rights and interests of one party are claimed to be infringed, interfered with or denied by another party (Gulliver 1969: 14, and 1979).

cannot; but they can still do something in the situation in which they find themselves.

Dispute avoidance involves deliberately restricting the relationship (if any) and interaction with the opponent and, perhaps, with the latter's supporters.[4] The degree of restriction ranges from complete cessation of all interaction, possibly including denial of any remaining relationship, to continuing limited interaction but without further reference to the issues in dispute. Essentially, avoidance is non-confrontation. It is, however, a *positive* and more or less deliberate choice of strategy and action by which to deal with – to manage – the dispute. It is not merely resignation because of perceived inability to do anything in the situation as the opponent appears to be overwhelmingly stronger, or out of reach, geographically or socially, or where the costs of any conceivable action are too high. By avoidance, nothing is done directly to attempt a resolution of the issues. The action may be, and may be intended to be, temporary whilst the party reconsiders the case and/or gathers resources for action – supporters, specialist advice, material assets. It can also be used – though this appears to be less common – as a pressuring sanction against the opponent who, finding avoidance to be disadvantageous, may come to agree to confrontation. Avoidance may be prolonged. By intent or not, it can become virtually permanent, even being continued in due course by the disputants' heirs. Alternatively, the dispute itself may be gradually forgotten within a new, restricted relationship between the parties or as the relationship returns to something like its former condition because the mutual advantages it offers are not sufficiently available elsewhere.

It would be incorrect to assume that some societies 'have' (or their members practice) dispute avoidance whilst other societies do not. Such avoidance is possible and occurs everywhere, but the frequency of the choice to take such action, and its sociocultural concomitants, vary cross-culturally: in some societies and social contexts, it is unusual and in others it is commonplace. It is necessary, of course, to describe and analyse this choice and its frequency within particular ethnographic contexts; it is also important to examine it as one option within a range of possible actions when dispute occurs. The range includes some or all of the following: resort to some form of third-party adjudication,

---

4 One Irish informant described persons in an avoidance relationship as 'bad friends'.

negotiation with or without mediators, self-help and violence, toleration or 'lumping', diversion to some other activity (such as appeal to the supernatural or confrontation in a contest) and avoidance.

The point is that, when a dispute occurs, the disputants have to make a *choice* of consequent action. The choosing may be quite deliberate and conscious as relative advantages and disadvantages are assessed: for example, which strategy in the context is most likely to lead towards the preferred resolution and outcome, taking account of resources that are available and the supposed costs of actions; which strategy seems likely to produce a quicker (or delayed) outcome or a less (or more) publicised one, if those are desirable ends; which will gain public approval and support, if that is important, and do least damage to or even enhance a person's reputation. Felstiner (1975) emphasised disputants' deliberate assessment of the economic and psychological costs entailed in the various strategies; but that is rather too simple. High costs may be worthwhile if the expected outcome is considered preferable. In any case, such premeditated calculation often does not occur at a time – the outbreak of dispute and rising frustration and hostility – when emotions may overrule rationality or when rational calculation seems to be (and actually may well be) impossible with variables of unknown magnitude. Moreover, the choice may be a more or less standardised response based on firm normative ideas or a disputant's previous experience, or the choice may be to follow the influential example of someone else.

In some circumstances, choice may be effectively limited within the range of the socially possible and not include what a disputant might consider to be most satisfactory. For instance, it may be culturally prescribed that, to maintain his public reputation, a man should resort to violence (or at least the threat of it) although he might consider that he could gain more advantage, for the moment, by avoidance. Conversely, in another context an injured party might prefer to seek confrontational action where the cultural norms and associates' expectations require restraint and avoidance.

Cases and Hypotheses from U.S. Suburbia

During the last two decades, our understanding of avoidance behaviour, in both senses of the term used here, has been extended by research and reporting on U.S. middle-class suburbia. There, such behaviour has been shown to be prominent and pervasive – indeed, the primary resort both when actual dispute emerges and when potential involvement is to be evaded.[5]

In addition to descriptions of avoidance behaviour in that context, a number of explanatory hypotheses have emerged, relating to questions of why and when avoidance is a common choice and form of action and the cultural meanings associated with it. To a limited extent, authors have made cross-cultural comparison, referring to non-Western cases where avoidance is common and which, it is claimed, have morphological similarities with the U.S. case. Since there is both empirical data and some broad agreement of interpretation, the results warrant serious attention.

Felstiner was the first to propose an explanatory hypothesis. He posited that there is 'less avoidance where avoidance costs are high' (1974: 77) and the 'cost of avoidance is always a reduction in the content of the relationship which has been truncated or terminated.' (1974: 76) Thus, where there are 'relatively weaker bonds of family, of friendship, of job and of place' (1974: 83), the negative consequences (costs) of avoidance are correspondingly low. Later, Felstiner added that 'the degree to which avoidance is used ... will depend upon how individual disputants evaluate its efficiency [to manage the dispute] relative to other responses.' (1975: 699)

Felstiner's basic reference to the costs of avoidance becomes less economistic (as, no doubt, he intended) when re-phrased in terms of the kind of social order and social relationships which allow avoidance because ties with, obligations to and claims against other people are weak and, if necessary, dispensible – both when dispute occurs and in the effort to evade involvement in dispute. Summarising, and drawing on Baumgartner's work in a New York suburb, Black (1987: 13–20[6]) proposed a number of conditions which are associated with and conducive to frequent avoidance behaviour. These, in effect, are the identified characteristics of U.S., middle-class, suburban life. They refer primarily to dispute avoidance but most probably also apply to conflict avoidance. In slightly revised form, these are:

---

5 Of particular note are Baumgartner (1984 and 1988), based on research in a New York suburb; and Greenhouse (1986 and 1992) on a suburb of Atlanta. See also, *inter alia*, Felstiner (1974 and 1975), Merry (1979), Ladinsky and Susmilch (1983), Black (1987).

6 An abridged version is in Black (1992).

- an absence of hierarchical authority
- easy and frequent entering and leaving relationships
- a dominance of single-stranded relationships
- loose-knit social networks
- a high degree of functional autonomy and capacity to decide and act alone.

In addition, Baumgartner proposed the concept of 'moral minimalism' which, 'with its aversion to conflict and its preference for restraint, will be found wherever social life approximates the suburban model.' (1988: 129) Thus, it was claimed, an essential moral idea lies behind, supporting and supported by, frequent avoidance behaviour. In similar fashion, Greenhouse proposed the concept of an 'avoidance ethic': 'an ethical preference to self restraint' (1992: 249) and a 'culturally appropriate means of resolving contradictions between the self interests and the collective good' (1992: 242). The ethical character of avoidance was clearly fundamental for both authors and their respective suburbanites; and both specifically related the ideas and values involved to the people's perception of the good and proper social order. Greenhouse went further, privileging the cultural content, when she claimed not to 'equate the avoidance ethic with avoidance behavior, though in some contexts they may be related' (1992: 248). Yet she found it useful in her exposition to refer to actual behaviour and, of course, the very word itself implies action and not merely thought and feeling. It is beyond credibility that a complex cultural ideology, of the kind that she well describes, should float in mid-air, as it were, rather than operating in a dialectical relation with interests, behaviour and social process. That is to say, the ethic, the cultural norm, must be linked with actual conflict avoidance in everyday life; and, despite the strength of the moral ideas surrounding conflict avoidance, real life 'grievances arise with regularity' (Baumgartner 1988: 73), thus bringing dispute avoidance into play.[7]

---

7 To what extent avoidance is similarly common and morally approved in U.S. suburban and urban neighbourhoods which are not upper-middle class is unclear. Greenhouse referred to the 'elitism' of the avoidance ethic but claimed a much wider provenance for it (1992: 237). Baumgartner (1988) noted that the working-class people (largely Italian-American) in her New York suburb did not practice and value avoidance and restraint in the way and to the degree that she found amongst the middle-class suburbanites. However, she did not explore this and its implications fully nor with empirical detail.

Comparisons and Contrasts

Of course, frequent and pervasive avoidance behaviour has not been peculiar to U.S. middle-class suburbia. It has been reported amongst some hunters and gatherers where the ease of geographical movement appears to have reinforced sociological conditions similar in principle to those prevailing in suburbia, together with an ethic of restraint and dislike of confrontation.[8] Indeed, Baumgartner suggested that regular avoidance behaviour is largely confined to modern suburbanites and hunters and gatherers (1988: 11) Empirically, this is not the case. Although such behaviour is most probably less common in other kinds of social systems, it has been reported as characteristic of some pastoral and some agrarian peoples. From my own research experience, for example, avoidance was frequent and universal among the Turkana pastoral nomads of Kenya (Gulliver 1975: 374 ff.) – although this was not the case amongst all nomads, for example the Somali of the Horn of Africa (Lewis 1961). However, the Turkana had no avoidance ethic: for them, avoidance was a purely pragmatic policy. In rural Ireland, among a sedentary population in County Kilkenny, only a minority of whom were farmers, avoidance behaviour was endemic and was associated with an ethic of restraint which was embraced by a wider-ranging idea of respectability (Silverman 1989).[9]

There is, obviously, much room for further enquiry and cross-cultural comparison, both in field and library research. However, here I want to use a contrasting form of comparative analysis. I make the assumption that if certain socio-cultural conditions are intimately associated with frequent and approved avoidance behaviour, then the absence of such conditions should be reflected in infrequent and disapproved dispute avoidance. For this purpose, I briefly describe conditions in two African societies where I have conducted and reported on research and where dispute avoidance is uncommon.

---

8 Following Baumgartner (1988), some examples are Pygmies of Zaire (Turnbull 1961), Hadza of Tanzania (Woodburn 1979), Chenchu of India (Fürer-Haimendorf 1967) and Inuit (Balikci 1970) – although in at least some Inuit groups confrontation by violence or contest has also been noted (Hoebel 1954).

9 Scheper-Hughes (1982: 13) reported a similar prevalence of avoidance in western County Kerry; but Shanklin (1985: 75) seems not to have found it in Donegal.

Arusha Sedentary Farmers

The Arusha occupied the lower slopes of Mt. Meru and the adjacent plains in northern Tanzania.[10] Small-scale subsistence farming, together with quite recent cash cropping, was almost the only form of livelihood. With a population density exceeding 1,000 people per square mile on the mountain slopes, farms were small and intensively cultivated.

An adult male, from initiation in middle to late teens, belonged for life to an age-group comprising men of similar age within a range of a dozen or so years. Within each local territorial unit ('parish'), age-groups were ranked by age and each gradually, and with ritual markings, gained increasing seniority. At any one time, there were five extant age-groups ranked in ascending order as junior and senior *murran*,[11] and junior, senior and ancient elders. Alternate groups – ancient elders with junior elders with junior *murran*, and senior elders with senior *murran* – were linked in the idiom of supervising fathers and subject sons. Competition and conflict between adjacent groups were endemic as the junior men endeavoured to demonstrate equality of esteem and abilities with their immediate seniors and sought to displace them by taking their rank and functions. Also, an age-group in the status of 'sons' sought to evade the claimed superiority and supervision of their 'fathers', although making alliance with them against the intervening group. Within an age-group, there was a marked emphasis on fraternal equality and mutual help. Members supported, assisted and joined with each other in political, ritual and leisure activities.

One particular characteristic of group membership was that when a member (or his dependant)[12] came into a dispute, the

---

10 This account refers to the 1950s when field research was carried out. Fuller analysis is in Gulliver (1963).

11 This word should be glossed as 'young men'. The sometime translation, 'warriors', possibly correct for pre-colonial times, is inappropriate for the Arusha in the mid-twentieth century. The Arusha age system, although structurally similar, operated rather differentiy from that of the pastoral Maasai (see Spencer, this volume). Arusha have long been sedentary farmers, with high population densities; they were heavily defeated by German colonial troops at the end of the nineteenth century and since then have been closely monitored by colonial and post-colonial administrations.

12 In this male-oriented society, public actions were monopolised by men, acting on their own behalf or that of dependent wives, sisters and children. Women only appeared in a public dispute process if they were required to give evidence, although of course they often privately influenced their male guardians and kinsmen.

group took action on his behalf and in his support. This was done primarily through the agency of institutionalised leaders – four or more 'spokesmen' – and other prominent members. If the opponent in the dispute were a member of a different age-group, the dispute became an inter-group affair, being fed, as it were, into the ongoing inter-group rivalry. Thus, inter-group confrontation concerning members' disputes was one form of expressing difference and conflict and, as such, was a continuing contribution to its persistence. If the opponent were a fellow member of the age-group, the dispute became an intra-group matter, with the express intention of preventing the interference of other groups, restraining internal conflict and maintaining idealised fraternal unity. Men were, therefore, constrained to accept group intervention and seldom sought to avoid it. Indeed, in practice, the initiative commonly came from the individual disputant himself, as he sought assistance and support. On a set day each week, a parish moot assembled, attended by age-group spokesmen, acknowledged men of influence and others who chose to be present. A man could present to the assembly his case against a man of another age-group with the confident expectation of support from his coevals. When it was thought to be more convenient, an ad hoc assembly could be arranged on some other day to give singular attention to a more difficult and complex dispute. Thus, a disputant rarely had difficulty in gaining a hearing; and despite the inter-group rivalry, tempered by the intervention of 'fathers', these assemblies were practical and efficient ways of managing disputes by public negotiations within the parish.

Beyond the parish, the age-group system was generally ineffective because, although all parishes had the same set of named age-groups, there was no organised means by which coeval groups could co-operate. Instead, when a dispute involved men of different parishes – as also where the issues involved important kinship matters such as bridewealth or inheritance – the operative group was the maximal patrilineage, based on the earliest known ancestor. Although its members were dispersed over several parishes, mutual assistance was maintained in all aspects of their lives. In this wider context, lineages operated in similar fashion to the age-groups within a single parish, but without the persistent inter-group conflict. Each lineage had one or two 'spokesmen' and inter-lineage moots or intra-lineage conclaves were convened on an ad hoc basis as disputes arose.

Spokesmen of age-groups or lineages were selected by their

fellow members and retained their role conditional on continued confidence and acceptable performance. They were expected to take the initiative, to express opinion and give advice and to act as advocates when a member of the group became involved in a dispute. They were not, however, possessed of authority and, indeed, authoritarian tendencies aroused quick criticism and mistrust. Whilst a spokesman was expected to take the lead, he operated by careful persuasion and tactful influence. Very few were secure enough to be able to dictate or over-ride differences of opinion. Insofar as there was 'authority', then, it was that of the group over its individual members. Arusha did not perceive it so: rather, they accepted the group (age-group or lineage) as, inter alia, a ready, practicable and reasonably efficient agency to manage disputes. Empirically, almost all disputes were managed and commonly resolved by tolerable, workable outcomes through negotiations between groups, led by the spokesmen and other representatives of the relevant groups.

Negotiations were virtually the only process of dispute management. Recourse to state courts was rare – the state's institutions and officials being seen as alien, imposed and untrustworthy – and only as an occasional last resort when successive attempts at negotiations had failed to produce acceptable outcomes. Arbitration was unknown, there being no credence of the virtue of a third party. Violent self-help was also rare although elders were always ready to accuse *murran* of inclinations to violence. It is important to emphasise, therefore, that dispute management was almost entirely accomplished by negotiations, through the effective agency of strongly organised groups.

To recapitulate and emphasise: through the age and lineage systems, a man (and so his dependants) seldom had difficulties in pressing a dispute and engaging in negotiations with the intent and expectation of gaining a tolerable outcome. A forum was always available, as were advisors and supporters who could scarcely be ignored. Older men, members of more senior age-groups, and therefore often also influential lineage members, regularly advocated the virtues of managing disputes by negotiations and condemned resort to violent self-help. This was largely directed against members of junior age-groups who were accused of propensities to unruly violence when disputes occurred. No doubt, this was an expression of senior superiority. Perhaps, too, there was still some tendency of juniors towards violence: the old idiom of warriorhood persisted although practical warrior activities had ceased at least two generations previously. However, the condemnation of violence within the dynamics of the age system also had the effect of promoting the necessity and effectiveness of the peaceful negotiation of problems. Moreover, this was associated with the strong moral idea that all disputes should be brought into the open and dealt with. Neither lumping nor avoidance were tolerable: they were perceived as secretive, dangerous and unethical.

What does all this mean in comparison with the U.S. findings and the proposed conditions under which avoidance is prevalent? Among the Arusha, there was a highly structured social system of strong groups, based on age or agnation, membership of which was both involuntary and permanent. These and their systemic organisation produced close-knit social networks of multiple stranded relationships. They also provided readily available and fairly effective means of dispute management by negotiations and a rationale for the rejection of avoidance. Although there were no roles of authority and the idea of authority was rejected – authority being typified by the alien and seemingly arbitrary power of the state – there were key roles of leadership, influence and advocacy. In those particular socio-cultural conditions, avoidance was not only seldom practiced but it was also perceived as illegitimate behaviour which denied the integrity and importance of groups and of a person's membership in them as well as the efficacy of peaceful negotiation through group intervention.

Whereas in the U.S. suburban case, avoidance was related to a high degree of functional and decision-making autonomy and loose-knit social networks, in the Arusha case such autonomy was low and networks were close-knit. The key to the rarity of avoidance amongst the Arusha, then, would seem to lie in the presence of strong groups and their effective, systemic organisation. However, this is not necessarily always the case, for avoidance can also be rare and disapproved where strong groups do not operate and where, therefore, an apparently different explanation is required. I take, as an illustrative case, the Ndendeuli.

Ndendeuli Shifting Cultivators

The Ndendeuli of southern Tanzania lived in small local communities of no more than thirty or forty dispersed households.[13] Each

---

13 This account relates to 1952-54 when field research was conducted. Fuller analyses are in Gulliver (1969 and 1971).

household – man, wife and unmarried children – cultivated a few acres of land for two or three years: these were abandoned as fertility fell and new fields were cleared in the surrounding bushlands. Formerly cultivated land was seldom re-used since natural regeneration was slow. Therefore, after a dozen or more years, a community exhausted locally available land and its members were forced to shift elsewhere.

Kinship was the idiom for the expression and explanation of active social relationships. It was traced bilaterally and affinally without notions of unilineal descent and without kin groups of any kind. Genealogical memory was shallow – seldom more than two generations prior to the older, living people. A man's acknowledged kin were dispersed geographically in several local communities with no more than a dozen (often fewer) kinsmen – household heads – as neighbours in his own community. Nevertheless, a man (and so, his dependants) was linked indirectly with all of his other neighbours. This fact was the logical result of the process of recruitment. A community was founded in untouched bushland by a pioneer leader and a set of household heads all of whom had some kinship link to him. They were not, of course, all directly linked to each other by acknowledged kinship – for example, the pioneer's brother-in-law and his mother's sister's son – but they were indirectly linked through him and others. Later, newcomers to the community were, virtually invariably, kin to at least one or two existing residents. This was so because a newcomer needed sponsorship by resident kin and, most importantly, he needed support and assistance from those kin in establishing his new fields and hamlet and in ongoing social life. Thus, newcomers fitted into the network of neighbours who were kin, kin of kin, kin of kin of kin...

A household head had regular, repetitive need of the assistance of his kin-neighbours: in work-parties to clear, cultivate, plant, weed and harvest his fields, to repair the mudded, thatched house, to perform therapeutic rituals and to support him when he came into dispute with a neighbour. On each occasion for these purposes, a man recruited a temporary action-set: his acknowledged kin-neighbours who were available at the time and such of their kin-neighbours who could be persuaded to join. Their participation was gained on the implicit understanding that they could obtain the man's assistance when they had need. Reciprocity was a prime ethical norm for the Ndendeuli; it was also a prime organisational practice.

More or less constantly, a household head endeavoured to expand the number of neighbours on whom he could call with fair confidence and to whom he would be able to reciprocate. Empirically, a man had several kin-neighbours on whom he could rely with a high degree of certainty and most of these had reciprocal obligations with each other – thus forming small, tight-knit networks of a dozen or fewer men and their dependants. They were clusters within the kinship-based network of the whole local community.

Yet, at the same time, it was a matter of particular practical importance to obtain enough neighbours for work-parties in the fields, taking on the obligations to work in theirs, during the short and congested periods when such work had to be accomplished. Some men found themselves in an intermediary position, linked to men in different clusters. This raised logistical problems as they were faced with requests for their participation in action-sets from both sides.

A cluster was associated with a 'big man': one of its members who had played a leading part in sponsoring newcomer-kinsmen and in organising schedules of work-parties and the like. The big man took the lead and gave advice when one of the members of the cluster came into dispute with some other neighbour. However, the role of a big man was scarcely institutionalised: the appellation itself was also given to the leader in any kind of enterprise such as ritual performance or a beer drink. Nor did the big man of a cluster acquire authority. His leadership was gained and retained from his acceptability by members as he proferred advice and acted as organiser and advocate. In fact, many men were a little sceptical of the big man's intentions and ambitions and he had no means of retaining his position other than by making himself useful and effective.

In the frequent recruitment of action-sets for various purposes, the fact that all men of the community were directly or indirectly connected was crucial. In seeking the assistance not only of kin-neighbours but also, as far as possible, of the kin of kin, there was often competition for the participation of those indirectly linked neighbours. This can be shown in a simplified diagram below. There, arrowed lines show direct links between men (A to B; B to C, etc.) based on acknowledged kinship and regularity of reciprocity. These men also had indirect linkages (kin of kin) as shown by the circular lines.

Thus men A and E were linked, though most indirectly.

However, their fields of social action in recruiting neighbours in action-sets could impinge and overlap and be, therefore, mutually limiting. The most obvious case was their competition for the participating assistance of C when both recruited action-sets at the same time. However, A might have attempted to recruit both C and D if, at the time, E were inactive. Were B and E recruiting action-sets simultaneously – as they certainly did, for example, if they were in dispute with each other – then both C and D faced divided loyalties. In the same way, but more intricately in the complex network of real life, neighbours were interlinked and interdependent, whether in competition or co-operation, within a close-knit network.

Figure 8.1.

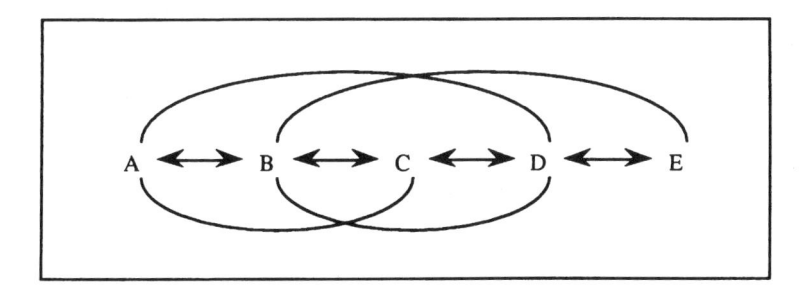

When he came into dispute with a neighbour, a man (on his own behalf or that of a dependant)[14] looked to his kin-neighbours and the big man of his cluster for support against a similar set of his opponent's supporters. In an ad hoc neighbourhood moot, the two sets of men met to negotiate, with the big men acting as advocates. Neighbours who were linked to both parties might take the active role of mediators; but, when the problem of divided loyalties and the responsibility of mediation were too intolerable, men evaded that role by absenting themselves temporarily from the community – often with the stylised excuse of being called by a mother's brother living elsewhere.

By such a neighbourhood moot, any dispute could fairly readily be treated and without going outside the local community. The support process was, of course, part of the larger system of mutual

---

14 This society was male-oriented and the comments on the Arusha apply also to the Ndendeuli: see note 12.

assistance. Each occasion when an action-set was recruited, for dispute management or any other purpose, became a reaffirmation of the inter-personal linkages which, people thought, were vital to many social activities. Avoidance behaviour was contradictory to these linkages – indeed, a virtual denial of them and a threat to other men's expectations of assistance in their times of need. I never heard Ndendeuli discuss the possibility of avoidance per se – nor did I think to enquire – but retrospectively it seems that it was a kind of action beyond credibility to these people. Moreover, negotiations in a moot most usually were both therapeutic to the participants and produced tolerable outcomes. Virtually all disputes between neighbours were managed in this way. The nearest state court was more than a day's walk away and was, in any case, mistrusted as part of weakly imposed government. Arbitration was an alien idea. I knew of no disputants resorting to violent self-help and there was disapproval of violence in general.

Some Conclusions

The Ndendeuli very rarely engaged in dispute avoidance behaviour. It was not necessary since effective means for managing disputes were readily available and it would have denied fundamental social relationships and the practical and moral idea of reciprocity. In contrast with the Arusha, this was a case without strongly organised groups. The key, in the Ndendeuli case, was a close-knit network of essential, multi-stranded relationships, together with non-authoritarian, scarcely institutionalised leadership. Much the same can be concluded in the Arusha case, however, if the emphasis is put not on the strongly organised groups as such but on the close-knit network of relationships in which the people were enmeshed within the group system. Thus, Arusha groups can be seen as a particular way in which close-knit networks were engendered and maintained. The Ndendeuli, with a notably different socio-cultural system, were enmeshed in dense networks differently engendered. In both cases, then, the conditions under which dispute avoidance was rare were the converse of the conditions in U.S. suburbia where such avoidance was common: close-knit social networks, multi-stranded relationships and little functional autonomy – in contrast to loose-knit networks and a high degree of autonomy.

One feature requires some amendment, however. A condition

of U.S. suburbia that was said to promote avoidance was the absence of hierarchical authority. The implication is, therefore, that infrequent dispute avoidance occurs where such authority is present and active. However, amongst neither the Arusha nor the Ndendeuli was this the case if by 'authority' is meant something like Weber's 'imperative control' and the sanctioned ability of an individual to compel others to act in a certain way. Yet, in both cases, there were recognised leaders – clearly institutionalised among the Arusha, much less so among the Ndendeuli – who acted as advocates and advisors, using influence through persuasion. Tentatively, I suggest that, where avoidance is uncommon, such leadership – not necessarily authoritarian – is a minimal condition, in conjunction with tight-knit networks. Hierarchical authority is, then, only one form of leadership. Thus, one condition where avoidance behaviour is common can be re-phrased as an absence of recognised leadership and, of course, of the social order which engenders, in one way or another, that leadership.

In this chapter, my principal concern has been with dispute avoidance – a pattern of behaviour more readily observable by the enquiring outsider than conflict avoidance. Less well studied, conflict avoidance is also more problematic. A common-sense assumption might be that frequent conflict avoidance is directly correlated with dispute avoidance where the latter is the prevalent form of dispute management. That assumption is, in fact, fairly well borne out in U.S. suburbia, in rural Ireland, amongst Turkana nomads and, probably, in hunter and gatherer bands. The converse, however – infrequent dispute avoidance and infrequent conflict avoidance – is unlikely to be so clear, if indeed it holds at all; and, of course, much will depend on measures of frequency. It was not the case amongst the Ndendeuli. I have already referred to the stylised avoidance behaviour of men who, confronted with divided loyalties, opted out of making choices or acting as mediators in disputes by temporarily absenting themselves from the local community. I do not know how carefully, or deliberately, individuals avoided or minimised contacts with disliked or troublesome neighbours. Certainly it sometimes happened and perhaps often. There were also a few extreme cases of such strong personal antagonism between two men that one refused to attend a beer-drink or to join a work-party where the other was to participate – creating a serious dilemma for their neighbours.

My evidence for Arusha is also inadequate in this respect. Some men did reduce interaction with and avoid co-members of their age-group or lineage whom they saw as troublesome or with whom there was personal animosity. I do not know how frequent or deliberate such action was. However, in keeping with the structured antagonism and competition between age-groups, at least sometimes men aggressively did not avoid a disliked man of another group; instead they invited and even relished the consequent expression of conflict. This was more common between men of adjacent groups in the age hierarchy. Such behaviour, no doubt, lowered the frequency of conflict avoidance as compared to the Ndendeuli, let alone U.S. suburbanites. Nevertheless, it would be an error to conclude that Arusha infrequently practiced conflict avoidance. Indeed, it is most unlikely that such a conclusion would hold true for any society. Whilst it would be useful to know more about conflict avoidance, I suggest that almost certainly it occurs irrespective of whether or not dispute avoidance is common and with a narrower range of variation cross-culturally than is the case with dispute avoidance.

References

Balikci, Asen. 1970. *The Netsiluk Eskimo*. Garden City, N.J.: Natural History Press.

Baumgartner, M.P. 1984. 'Social Control in Suburbia' in *Towards a General Theory of Social Control*, vol. 2, Donald Black (ed.). Orlando, Florida: Academic Press.

———. 1988. *The Moral Order of a Suburb*. New York: Oxford University Press.

Black, Donald. 1987. *The Elementary Forms of Conflict Management*. Tempe: Arizona State University, Distinguished Scholar Lecture Series, School of Justice Studies.

———. 1992. *The Social Structure of Right and Wrong*. San Diego: Academic Press.

Bohannan, Paul (ed.). 1967. *Law and Warfare: Studies in the Anthropology of Conflict*. Garden City, N.J.: Natural History Press.

Felstiner, William. 1974. 'Influences of Social Organization on Dispute Processing', *Law and Society Review* 9: 63–94.

———. 1975. 'Avoidance as Dispute Processing', *Law and Society Review* 9: 695–706.

Fürer-Haimendorf, Christoph. 1967. *Morals and Merit: A Study of Values and Social Control in South Asian Societies*. Chicago: Chicago University Press.

Greenhouse, Carol. 1986. *Praying for Justice: Faith, Order and Community in an American Town*. Ithaca: Cornell University Press

———. 1992. 'Signs of Quality: Individualism and Hierarchy in American Culture', *American Ethnologist* 19: 233–54.

Gulliver, P. H. 1953. *Social Control in an African Society: A Study of the Arusha*. London: Routledge and Kegan Paul.

———. 1969. 'Dispute Settlement Without Courts' in *Law in Culture and Society*, Laura Nader (ed.). Chicago: Aldine.

———. 1971. *Neighbours and Networks: the Idiom of Kinship in Social Action among the Ndendeuli of Tanzania*. Berkeley: California University Press.

———. 1975. 'Nomadic Movements: Causes and Implications' in *Pastoralism in Tropical Africa*, Theodore Monod (ed.). London: Oxford University Press.

———. 1979. *Disputes and Negotiations: A Cross-Cultural Perspective*. New York: Academic Press.

Hoebel, E. Adamson. 1954. *The Law of Primitive Man*. Cambridge, Mass.: Harvard University Press.

Ladinsky, Jack and Charles Susmilch. 1983. *Community Factors in the Brokerage of Consumer Product and Service Problems*. Madison: University of Wisconsin, Dispute Processing Research Program, Working Paper No. 1983-14.

Lewis, I. M. 1961. *A Pastoral Democracy: A Study of Pastoralism and Politics Among the Northern Somali*. London: Oxford University Press.

Lowie, Robert. 1931. 'Avoidance' in *Encyclopedia of Social Science*.

Merry, Sally. 1979. 'Going to Court: Strategies of Dispute Management in an American Urban Neighbourhood', *Law and Society Review* 13: 891–925.

Nader, Laura (ed.). 1969 . *Law in Culture and Society*. Chicago: Aldine.

Pospisil, Leo. 1971. *Anthropology of Law*. New York: Harper and Row.

Roberts, Simon. 1979. *Order and Dispute*. London: Penguin Books.

Scheper-Hughes, Nancy. 1982, ' "Ballybran" Letters', *R.A.I.N.* No.51: 12–13.

Shanklin, Eugenia. 1985. *Donegal's Changing Traditions*. New York: Gordon and Breach.

Silverman, Marilyn. 1989. ' "A Labouring Man's Daughter": Constructing "Respectability" in South Kilkenny' in *Ireland from Below*, Chris Curtin and Thomas Wilson (eds). Galway: Galway University Press.

Turnbull, Colin. 1961. *The Forest People*. New York: Simon and Schuster.

Woodburn, James. 1979. 'Minimal Politics: the Political Organization of the Hadza of North Tanzania' in *Politics in Leadership*, William Shack and Percy Cohen (eds). Oxford: Clarendon Press.

CHAPTER 9

Fighting with Operas:
Processionals, Politics, and the Spectre of Violence in Rural Hong Kong

James L. Watson

Introduction

This chapter is inspired by Abner Cohen's investigations of political performances, specifically periodic rites associated with renewal, revitalisation, and rebirth. Carnival is, of course, the quintessential example of this genre and it is surely no accident that Cohen chose this topic for his most recent research (1993). Just as the London carnival draws much of its interpretative power from an underlying theme of barely controlled violence, the Chinese ritual discussed in the following pages is best understood as a reenactment and celebration of violence.

Background

This paper is based on fieldwork carried out in the Hong Kong New Territories during the past twenty-five years, with extended periods of residence in 1969–70, 1977–78, and 1994. The site is a rural district (*xiang*) controlled by the Teng lineage which has been settled here for over six hundred years (see R. Watson 1985). The Teng live in Ha Tsuen ('Mansion Village'), a community that in 1970 had a population of approximately 2,500. Ha Tsuen is a single-surname/single-lineage village; all resident males – save for a handful of shopkeepers – trace descent to ancestors who pioneered this region. The vast majority of people in Ha Tsuen District are Cantonese speakers.

The Teng are representative of the rural elites that controlled much of rural south China prior to the Communist land reform campaigns of the 1950s. They owned the best agricultural land, dominated marketing and commerce, and monopolised local industries.

Ha Tsuen District also contains nine smaller communities, known as 'satellite villages', that were inhabited by former tenants and workers who were dependent on the Teng. Satellite villagers were rarely allowed to play more than a passive role in local politics.

In 1898 Ha Tsuen and its dependent satellites became part of the British Crown Colony of Hong Kong; the district has been administered by colonial officials since that date. The arrangement expires on 30 June 1997, at which point Hong Kong reverts to Chinese government control. The most radical action carried out by the colonial administration was a 1905 land reform that granted full ownership rights, in an English legal sense, to sitting tenants – including satellite villagers near Ha Tsuen. This did little, however, to raise the political status of Teng dependents. They remained clients of their former landlords until the 1950s and even into the 1980s the legacy of dependency coloured many aspects of satellite villagers' lives.

One of the primary means of maintaining political control was the promotion of a district-wide temple cult dedicated to the goddess Tianhou ('Empress of Heaven'), south China's most popular deity (see J. Watson 1985). The Teng, as outlined below, enforced a kind of ritual orthopraxy in their territory, ensuring that satellite villagers participated in periodic rites celebrating Tianhou's hegemonic position. The remainder of this chapter explores the complex interrelationship between political power and ritual performance in Ha Tsuen District.

Rites of Renewal

Tianhou's role as a guardian deity is clearly expressed in a set of periodic rites known as *jiao*. *Jiao*, perhaps best translated as 'rites of renewal', are performed every tenth year in Ha Tsuen District: 1904, 1914, 1924, ... 1964, 1974, 1984, and (just completed)

1994. Elaborate *jiao*, and the operas associated with these rites, have become ever more lavish in recent decades and now constitute the principal form of competition among New Territories lineages. It is surely no coincidence that the time, labour, and money devoted to *jiao* performances have increased as the frequency and ferocity of inter-lineage violence has declined. A similar pattern of ritual involution occurred in the New Guinea highlands, where 'fighting with food' has displaced warfare as a means of verifying status (see Strathern 1971; Young 1971). There is, as I shall argue below, a close relationship between the performance of *jiao* rites and the re-enactment of past conflicts.

Cantonese *jiao* take several days to perform and are distinguished from ordinary, household-based rituals by the fact that the entire community (or district) participates. The Ha Tsuen rites are widely recognised as the prototypical *jiao* of the New Territories; the celebrations are featured on Hong Kong television and, in 1974, a B.B.C. film was made of the proceedings. The Teng respond to this attention by investing time and money to ensure that their next performance will be even more elaborate. The *jiao* itself lasts for five days and six nights; the more esoteric aspects of the rites are orchestrated by paid professionals who do not live in the district.

Tianhou is 'invited' to preside over the festivities; she is represented by a portable statue that is escorted by Teng elders from her home temple to a special reviewing stand four miles away in Ha Tsuen Village. For the duration of the *jiao* participants eat vegetarian foods and avoid contact with meat. The highlight of the rites is a procession that marks out the territory of the Teng lineage and acknowledges political allies in neighbouring districts. This procession also has the ritual effect of sweeping the region clear of wandering ghosts and unlucky influences. On the last night of the *jiao* the names of participating villagers are posted for public inspection; families peruse the list with the aid of special lamps to make certain all contributors, including emigrants, are duly recorded. The rites of renewal are completed that evening and a series of banquets – featuring pork, chicken, and fish – begin the next day.

Smaller communities often hold an opera (or, in the past, a puppet show) concurrently with the *jiao*. The Teng have made a conscious effort to distinguish themselves by hosting a five-day opera after the rites are completed. The rationale, according to a local leader, is that this allows people 'to enjoy themselves by eating meat while they watch the opera'. The separation of opera from renewal rites also adds significantly to the costs and doubles the time involved.

It is the quality of the opera that matters most in the competition among communities. The audience bases its judgement on the number of days performed, reputation of the troupe, popularity of the stories selected (some are more expensive to perform than others), and the size of the temporary auditorium erected specifically for the event. In 1970 the Man lineage of San Tin sponsored a lavish opera to celebrate the renovation of their local temple. Although the Man ceased holding a periodic *jiao* in the 1940s, the renovation provided an opportunity to re-enter the competition for status among Hong Kong's older lineages. The Man produced an extravaganza that cost well over £50,000, most of which was donated by overseas emigrants (J. Watson 1975: 141–3). It was clear from my interviews at the time that the Man were judging themselves against the standard set by the Ha Tsuen Teng in 1964. The Teng, in turn, were determined to eclipse the Man and did so – at great cost – during the opera associated with their 1974 *jiao*.

Violent Death, Martyr Shrines, and the Origin of *Jiao*

Among the Teng it was generally agreed that the decennial *jiao* serves two purposes: (1) It placates the spirits of people who died under unusual circumstances in Ha Tsuen District and, by so doing, (2) it cleanses the region of baleful influences and allows participating communities to renew themselves for another ten-year cycle. Thus, from my consultants' point of view it is appropriate to translate *jiao* as 'rite of renewal', following Saso (1972).

The participants' own representations of the rites are replete with metaphors of violence, inter-lineage conflict, and territorial control. A local geomancer, one of the most highly educated and respected members of the Teng lineage, maintained that the *jiao* originated centuries ago as a means of placating the spirits of militiamen who were killed during battles with neighbouring lineages. He emphasised that satellite villagers also lost their lives in these confrontations, and they too were commemorated in the rites. Having died before their allotted time, the geomancer continued, the spirits of these men can never be entirely settled and, if not treated properly, might harm the living. Thus, the main purpose of the decennial rites, in his opinion, is to soothe the spirits of these martyrs and honour them by eating vegetarian foods.

Processionals and Ritualised Violence

From the participants' point of view the most important part of the *jiao* is the procession that traces out the boundaries of Teng territory. In many respects the procession resembles a military exercise. Young men and guardsmen spearhead the march, throwing firecrackers in all directions to clear the path of ghosts (and, incidentally, hostile neighbours). In recent decades over 2,000 men have taken part in the Ha Tsuen procession and walked for three days to mark out territory and visit allies. Women do not participate in this aspect of *jiao* ritual; they stay in their home villages and attend to rituals associated with the household. Male consultants argue that the march is too dangerous and arduous for women. The women themselves give a different explanation for their non-participation: 'If we went along it would be an unlucky occasion', said a seventy year-old Ha Tsuen woman – implying that the ritual pollution of menstruation and child birth would bring bad luck to the event (see Ahern 1975 on beliefs regarding women's pollution). Concerns about pollution also affect male participants: men who are in mourning, and thereby contaminated by death pollution (J. Watson 1982), cannot take part in the march.

The decennial processions invariably provoke trouble with the neighbouring community of Ping Shan – Ha Tsuen's ancient rival. In 1924 Ping Shan residents tried to block the march as it passed near their village. Ha Tsuen youths retaliated by destroying crops and burning buildings. The Hong Kong Police began to patrol the route in 1954 but this did not put an end to the violence. Police reinforcements had to be brought in from Kowloon (25 miles away) to deal with a serious confrontation that developed during the 1964 procession – again involving Ping Shan. Many Teng elders and middle-aged men spoke of the decennial marches with obvious nostalgia: 'There were so many of us we could go anywhere and no one could stop us', reminisced one man in his sixties. For most participants, therefore, the *jiao* procession is an act of barely controlled aggression performed in a ritual context. The event might be usefully compared to the annual Orange Day parades held in Belfast, where Protestant men – led by strutting, posturing youths – march through Catholic neighbourhoods. Both parades re-enact a history of territorial conflict, keeping the past alive in the present.

Disputes also arise among the Teng regarding the order of the march. Participants walk in groups corresponding to their village of origin. Cheong Gong Wai, the oldest Teng settlement, always takes precedence but there is no general agreement about the sequence for the ten remaining Teng hamlets. The men of San Wai, Ha Tsuen's largest and wealthiest hamlet, invariably claim the second position – much to the irritation of everyone else concerned.

In 1974, a serious dispute arose over a related issue: which dragon dance team would lead the procession? This 'dance' is, in fact, an athletic performance requiring expert co-ordination from a team of up to 130 men who manipulate a huge effigy that stretches for nearly one hundred yards. The dragon is made to bob and weave by moving a set of poles in unison. Given that the creature only comes alive when the handlers move at a fast trot, it takes weeks of dedicated training to perform the dance properly.

Ordinarily, the larger *jiao* processions are escorted by a single dragon team that represents the entire district. But, in 1974 the residents of San Wai sponsored their own dragon and found themselves in competition with the team recruited by the *jiao* organising committee. On the first day of the festivities both teams claimed the right to lead the procession and nearly came to blows. The San Wai contingent only backed down after the chairman of the *jiao* committee threatened to resign; he became so angry that he burst an artery in his nose, causing a serious loss of blood. The event was interpreted by many elders as a bad omen for the future of the lineage, coming as it did at such a critical time. In the past, they pointed out, Teng men were expected to shed a little blood during the procession, but only when fighting outsiders. This case was particularly inauspicious because the victim and his antagonists were members of the same lineage.

Processionals and Territorial Claims

All rituals associated with the *jiao*, including the procession, stress residence over kinship. Marchers halt along the route to pay their respects at temples and earth-god shrines – all of which represent deities that control a specific territory. No efforts are made to recognise ritual stations associated with lineages or surname groups (for example, ancestral halls or tombs).

Each morning the marchers assemble in a field just outside the village of Ha Tsuen. The first two days are devoted to a tour of Ha Tsuen District, stopping at satellite villages, commercial centres, and temples. In recent decades this part of the march has gradually diminished as former tenants have withdrawn from the *jiao*, but the basic outline of the procession has remained fundamentally intact. At every stop local villagers welcome the marchers and provide them with refreshments (cold drinks and vegetarian buns). The cost of feeding over 2,000 tired and hungry people is an additional burden for satellite villagers who have already contributed to support the *jiao*. Even so, the refreshment stops are an important part of the proceedings and help maintain a sense of shared identity within the district.

In 1954 residents of a small neighbouring village decided it was time to improve relations with the Teng after nearly two decades of estrangement. Village leaders invited the assemblage to stop for refreshments when – as usual – they passed nearby. On the appointed day local elders dressed in their ceremonial gowns and prepared three large tables, laden with expensive snacks and bottled soda (rare at that time). The procession, led by Teng youths and guardsmen, swept through the village without stopping or even acknowledging the proffered food. The intended hosts were so deeply offended that they vowed never again to make conciliatory gestures toward the Teng. Years later, a man who had taken part in the 1954 march confessed that he regretted his actions: 'We were young and hot-headed but we should have stopped. Now they will never forgive us and relations between our two villages will always be bad.'

Subjugating the Gods

When the territorial procession is completed, Ha Tsuen men turn their attention homeward and settle in to enjoy the opera. The opera itself is said to be performed primarily for the benefit of their patron deity, Tianhou. Normally the goddess resides in a temple four miles from Ha Tsuen, but during the decennial rites her spirit is 'invited' to enter a portable statue which is carried to the opera site. There she takes up temporary residence on a viewing stand that faces the stage. Tianhou is treated as the guest of honour by everyone who performs during the ten-day festival: opera stars, musicians, puppeteers, priests, and (more recently) pop singers. Important visitors are brought to pay their respects to the goddess before they tour the exhibits or enter the opera auditorium. In sum, the goddess presides over the festival as if she were a living patron – accepting gifts, receiving guests, and dispensing favours. The opera could not begin without her blessing and during the performance no one dares block her view of the stage. Tianhou's statue is placed in the centre of a temporary altar on the viewing stand. Deities from other temples and shrines in the district also share this altar and are ranked according to relative status (those closest to Tianhou are considered to be more important). Residents of Ha Tsuen District ordinarily worship only a handful of popular deities but, during the *jiao*, dozens of obscure gods and goddesses make their appearance.

Teng elders explain that they dare not risk offending even the most insignificant of deities during the *jiao*. Many were the founders of surname groups that the Teng ousted from Ha Tsuen District centuries ago. Called 'pioneer ancestors', these former enemies have been elevated to the status of minor gods. They must be placated to ensure that crops will continue to grow on fields that were plowed, or 'opened', prior to Teng settlement.

The other deities invited to attend the Ha Tsuen *jiao* are members of the nationally recognised pantheon: Beidi (Emperor of the North), Guandi (God of Justice), Guanyin (Buddhist Goddess of Mercy), and Hongsheng (Great Sage) to name only a few. Most are brought from minor temples scattered throughout the district. The Two Emperors Temple in a nearby satellite village is a good example: its two deities, Beidi and Guandi, never leave their home except to make the decennial trek to Ha Tsuen. Like their human devotees, therefore, the patron gods of satellite villagers are subject to a superior authority – in this case Tianhou.

In recent decades the people of this community have attempted to turn what was essentially a rite of supplication into a triumphant display of new-found wealth and power. The two Emperors are escorted to the *jiao* by local youths dressed in uniforms of imperial guards; their performance makes a colourful spectacle and has been featured in numerous films and photographic collections.

Judging from interviews in 1978, the people of this community were conscious that their continued performance of the transfer rite placed them in an ambiguous position. They justified their actions, in part, by stressing the power of their gods – especially Beidi (Emperor of the North). 'A long time ago', they claimed, the Ha Tsuen Teng forgot to invite Beidi to the *jiao*; on the first night of the festivities a terrible storm destroyed the opera stage. Ha Tsuen leaders recognised their error and sent a delegation of elders to beg forgiveness; a statue of Beidi was escorted to Ha Tsuen and there was no more trouble. Since that time, the story concludes, 'the Ha Tsuen people depend on our Beidi to ensure a safe *jiao*.'

Teng elders are aware of such stories and agree that Beidi has certain powers of intervention, but this does not affect their own conviction that Tianhou is the district's supreme deity. For the Teng, the physical transfer of local deities to the *jiao* arena in Ha Tsuen is confirmation enough of Tianhou's divine authority: she commands all other deities in her realm to sit by her side during rites which are performed in her honour. In one important respect, therefore, Tianhou is an analog of the Teng lineage. The parade of subjugated deities and vanquished enemy ancestors recreates, in ritual, the history of Teng territorial conquests.

Sanctioned Violence and Temple Festivals

The political dimensions of the Tianhou cult are even more salient in the rites performed during the goddess's annual festival (*dan*, sometimes translated misleadingly as 'birthday'), on the 23rd of the third lunar month. In this part of China the festival was previously celebrated by a colourful and often violent competition. Small associations, known as *huapaohui* (lit. 'flower cannon societies'), were represented by young men who fought over lucky coins fired from small cannon. The prizes were elaborate altars, made of bright paper, which were brought to the temple by participating associations. Each altar was numbered and therefore ranked in order of 'luckiness' (competition for numbers three and seven was particularly fierce).

In 1970 I witnessed one of the last festival competitions to be conducted in the traditional manner. The Hong Kong Police had banned the use of 'flower cannons' (special fireworks made exclusively for this purpose) in the early 1960s, citing the fact that these events often turned into near riots. A tame and rather boring lottery had been substituted for the cannons in most parts of the New Territories (see G. Johnson 1971: 141–2). Given their independent nature, however, the San Tin Man ignored these legal restrictions and continued to stage a traditional-style competition at their Tianhou temple. Of the forty young men who assembled for the event in 1970, one suffered a broken leg, several lost teeth, and hardly anyone escaped without bruises or a black eye.

Merchants, wealthy emigrants, and lineage leaders stood on the sidelines cheering for their designated 'catchers' who had been paid to retrieve the luckiest coins – which were later redeemed for the altars. Each winner (rarely an actual competitor) placed his prize in a public hall or in a place of business. The centrepiece of each altar was a mirror representing the goddess and, to ensure good fortune, it was worshipped throughout the year. Certain altars were thought to bring success in business while others conferred the blessing of male offspring. Those who entered the competition – both as catchers or as sponsors – were exclusively male; women did not participate in this aspect of the Tianhou cult.

In Ha Tsuen District the competition was not entirely open and there were unstated rules of engagement. It was understood, for instance, that altars number three and seven (being the luckiest) were reserved for members of the Teng lineage. Satellite villagers were, of course, expected to compete – but only for the altars that did not engender much interest. In the early 1950s young men from one of these satellite villages caused a sensation (and a bloody brawl) when they defied convention and fought openly for the coin representing altar number seven. Soon after this incident, the men involved withdrew from the annual competition in Ha Tsuen District and began attending the Tianhou festival in a neighbouring district.

During its heyday (1850–1940) the Tianhou festival in Ha Tsuen was attended by representatives of all nine satellite villages in the district. Temple managers ensured that the altars were collected – and paid for – on time (a fee always went to the temple committee). The organisation of regional cults made it impossible for satellite villagers to attend more than one Tianhou festival. Among land people (as distinct from boat people) in the Hong Kong region, the goddess's annual rite (*dan*) was observed on the same day in every district. Local cults were thus mutually exclusive and temples were not linked together in a hierarchical system, as was often the case in Taiwan (Sangren 1988). It would appear that Cantonese men in this region did not embark on regular pilgrimages to Tianhou temples outside their own district. This, more than anything else, explains why Tianhou was perceived as a jealous and vindictive deity. Her festivals were arranged in such a manner that local people were forced to make a clear and unambiguous statement of their territorial loyalties once every year. Should a group of satellite villagers choose not to attend the annual festival in Ha Tsuen District this was tantamount to a declaration of independence and was viewed as such by the Teng.

The territorial exclusivity of land-based cults did not affect the boat people who lived along the Ha Tsuen coast (see Ward 1965). Tianhou festivals that catered primarily to the floating population were often staggered to allow devotees to attend Flower Cannon competitions in several locations. In the New Territories these observances sometimes occurred two or three weeks after Tianhou's accepted *dan* date. Fishing specialists occasionally participated in the festivals held at the Tianhou temple in Ha Tsuen District but, if they were not permanent residents of the district, they were not expected to bring an altar. Once they settled on land, however, these fisherpeople were treated like any other group of clients and they were 'encouraged' to pay exclusive allegiance to the local temple.

Orthopraxy and the Suppression of Rival Cults

In researching the social history of Ha Tsuen District, it became clear to me that the Teng were not interested in what dependents thought about the Tianhou cult or what they said about the goddess; as long as these beliefs were not translated into action, Teng enforcers did not intervene.

The Teng maintained social control through the imposition of a surveillance system that monitored the behaviour of dependents. A special category of young toughs, known as 'guardsmen' (J. Watson 1985), was employed to collect crop-watching fees in the district and to ensure that satellite villagers participated in district-level rites, especially the decennial *jiao* and the annual Tianhou festival. In order to comprehend the full implications of this surveillance system we must examine its semantic underpinnings: my informants always used the Cantonese term *cham-ga* (Mandarin *canjia*) when discussing their involvement in religious rites. The term, usually framed as an active verb, can be translated as 'to participate' or 'to take part in'. The proper mode of questioning is to ask, 'Did you participate in the Tianhou festival or not?' The answer, yes or no, reveals nothing whatsoever about the respondent's inner feelings, nor her/his beliefs regarding the deity. Furthermore, one cannot ask – in colloquial Cantonese – the equivalent of the English question, 'Do you believe in Tianhou?' Rather, one must ask: 'Do you worship [Cantonese *baai-sahn*] the goddess?' These are neutral questions eliciting value-free information; to discover what is behind these responses one must dig deeper and risk alienating even the most open and friendly of informants. My own research among Cantonese villagers leads me to conclude that older people do not draw a sharp distinction between what many speakers of English might call 'belief' and 'action' (cf. Needham 1972). What matters most is public behaviour.

Teng guardsman also operated from these premises and, accordingly, they became guardians of orthopraxy (correct practice) rather than orthodoxy (correct belief). Satellite villagers were allowed to develop their own myths and harbour their own visions of the gods as long as they participated in district-level rites. This method of control – privileging orthopraxy over orthodoxy – was by no means unique to the Teng. As argued elsewhere (J. Watson 1993) it was the principal means of achieving cultural unity in pre-revolution China (see also D. Johnson 1989). Imperial officials did not try to legislate beliefs: as long as proper ritual forms were observed, including the worship of approved deities, the state did not intervene. The system that evolved in Ha Tsuen District was a microcosm of the general Chinese approach to social order.

Teng guardsmen were quick to oppose any deviations from accepted religious practice in their territory. Satellite villagers were allowed to build and maintain small temples, but only to the extent that these activities did not interfere with participation in district-wide Tianhou cult. Furthermore, many satellite villagers supported their own *jiao* – but with one important feature missing: they were not permitted to conduct a procession outside the premises of their own village. Only one deity, Tianhou, could be paraded through the district and the Teng enforced this monopoly with great vigour. Even in the 1970s, long after the circumstances had changed, satellite villagers dared not intrude into Tianhou's domain. 'We don't want to cause trouble by "walking the district" [leading a procession] with our deity', explained one villager. 'The Teng are very powerful and would not like it. So we just carry the statue around our village and then return it to the temple.'

Thus, from the guardsmen's point of view, it was inconsequential whether satellite villagers internalised Teng views of the

Tianhou cult or rejected them. What mattered was action and any evidence of a (physical) challenge to the status quo was swiftly opposed. The Teng were primarily concerned with maintaining political control of their traditional territory.

Conclusions

Periodic rituals associated with the Tianhou cult are carefully orchestrated and monitored by the Teng of Ha Tsuen District. Much like the masquerade studied by Cohen (1993), the *jiao* and especially the annual *dan* celebrations are represented as spontaneous displays during which violence, or the spectre of violence, is never far from the surface. In both the masquerade and the Tianhou rites great efforts are made by political elites to channel this violent energy into acceptable, manageable forms of political activity.

The Cantonese case also highlights the ambiguity of rituals that build on images of violence: who are the intended targets? As demonstrated in this paper, the Teng reinforced the centrality of their own *jiao* by the clear threat of physical violence aimed at former tenants who lived in nearby satellite villages. Refusal to participate was tantamount to a declaration of independence – necessitating reprisals.

In this sense, therefore, the violence was projected inward, within the district. The obvious goal was to maintain control over territory. In another sense, alluded to briefly in this paper, the potential violence of the *jiao* was directed outward toward rivals in neighbouring districts. Unlike satellite villagers, these rivals were the status equals of the Teng; they were members of powerful, landowning lineages. Many were affines of the Teng (see R. Watson 1985).

The *jiao* procession was, in part, a demonstration that the Teng were willing and able to protect their territory if required to do so. Interlineage warfare was an ever-present fact of life in this region until the British put an effective end to such confrontations in 1899 (see Baker 1968). *Jiao* processions often became the catalysts of these violent outbursts, resulting in death and serious bodily injury for dozens of men on both sides. The histories of these violent encounters are consciously and defiantly re-enacted in the *jiao*. Since the 1960s lineages have substituted operas for battles. As noted at the beginning of this chapter, a central feature of the *jiao* rituals is a series of operas held every ten years. A vast amount of time and money is invested in the production of these operas. Professional troupes of performers are invited to stay in the community for the entire period, over a week in many cases. The expenses are enormous and require years of saving and mobilisation of resources. Over 2,000 people attend these performances which last over five full days and nights. The theme of violence is carried through in the operas themselves, with elaborate productions based on military exploits and violence of all sorts. In my view, this is not a coincidence. The performance on stage parallels the political performance enacted in other aspects of the Tianhou rituals.

This case demonstrates the enduring value of Abner Cohen's contribution to social anthropology. In all of his major works he has paid close attention to the template of historical consciousness that conditions political awareness. Following Cohen's lead, the study of politics can never again be separated from the analysis of ritual.

References

Ahern, Emily. 1975. 'The Power and Pollution of Women', in *Women in Chinese Society*, Margery Wolf and Roxane Witke (eds). Stanford: Stanford University Press.

Baker, Hugh D.R. 1968. *A Chinese Lineage Village: Sheung Shui*. Stanford: Stanford University Press.

Cohen, Abner. 1969. *Custom and Politics in Urban Africa*. London: Routledge.

——. 1981. *The Politics of Elite Culture*. Berkeley: University of California Press.

——. 1993. *Masquerade Politics*. Berkeley: University of California Press.

Johnson, David. 1989. 'Actions Speak Louder than Words: The Cultural Significance of Chinese Ritual Opera', in *Ritual Opera, Operatic Ritual*, David Johnson (ed.). Berkeley: Publications of the Chinese Popular Culture Project, Center for Chinese Studies, University of California.

Johnson, Graham E. 1971. 'From Rural Committee to Spirit Medium Cult: Voluntary Associations in the Development of a Chinese Town', *Contributions to Asian Studies* 1: 123–43.

Needham, Rodney. 1972. *Belief, Language, and Experience*. Oxford: Basil Blackwell.

Sangren, P. Steven. 1988. 'History and the Rhetoric of Legitimacy: The Ma Tsu Cult in Taiwan', *Comparative Studies in Society and History* 30: 674–97.

Saso, Michael R. 1972. *Taoism and the Rite of Cosmic Renewal*. Pullman: Washington State University Press.

Strathern, Andrew. 1971. *The Rope of Moka: Big-Men and Ceremonial Exchange in Mount Hagen, New Guinea*. Cambridge: Cambridge University Press.

Ward, Barbara E. 1965. 'Varieties of the Conscious Model: The Fishermen of South China', in *The Relevance of Models for Social Anthropology*, Michael Banton (ed.). London: Tavistock.

Watson, James L. 1975. *Emigration and the Chinese Lineage: The Mans in Hong Kong and London*. Berkeley: University of California Press.

———. 1982. 'Of Flesh and Bones: The Management of Death Pollution in Cantonese Society', in *Death and the Regeneration of Life*, Maurice Bloch and Jonathan Parry (eds). Cambridge: Cambridge University Press.

———. 1985. 'Standardizing the Gods: The Promotion of T'ien Hou ("Empress of Heaven") along the South China Coast, 960–1960', in *Popular Culture in Late Imperial China*, David Johnson, Andrew Nathan, and Evelyn Rawski (eds). Berkeley: University of California Press.

———. 1993. 'Rites or Beliefs? The Construction of a Unified Culture in Late Imperial China', in *China's National Identity*, Samuel Kim and Lowell Dittmar (eds). Ithaca: Cornell University Press.

Watson, Rubie S. 1985. *Inequality Among Brothers: Class and Kinship in South China*. Cambridge: Cambridge University Press.

Young, Michael W. 1971. *Fighting With Food: Leadership, Values and Social Control in a Massim Society*. Cambridge: Cambridge University Press.

CHAPTER 10

Cultural Performance and the Reproduction of the Anaguta Symbolic Universe

Adrian Collett *

Introduction

The Anaguta are little-known subsistence farmers with a strong tradition of hunting who occupy about sixty square miles to the north and east of Jos, Northern Nigeria. They number about 18,000 and live in five large village areas each consisting of scattered compounds surrounded by their own farmland. Many have moved to the town of Jos itself but retain farmland in their villages of origin. Until well into the colonial period the Anaguta lived in superbly defended hill 'towns' that enabled them, together with neighbouring societies with whom they joined forces, to resist the attempts of the Bauchi Emirate to subdue and Islamicise them. To a large extent, the Anaguta also resisted attempts at missionisation during the colonial period, there being only a handful of Christians by the time of independence in 1960.

Specific procedures for the maintenance and reproduction of what Berger and Luckman (1967) call the 'symbolic universe' are

---

* The original fieldwork among the Anaguta in 1981/82 was funded by grants from the School of Oriental and African Studies and the Central Research Fund of the University of London.

particularly important when, as in the Anaguta case, political power in the village still derives to a significant extent, not from economic status and the ability to use legitimate force, but directly from the symbolic universe. The power of senior elders is directly proportional to their ability to invoke the power of the divine order and the demonstration of this power legitimises their definitions of reality. Procedures for demonstrating this power, thereby reproducing the conditions necessary for its existence, and for controlling access to esoteric knowledge are, therefore, essential.

This is particularly important now because, inevitably, there are competing symbolic systems, often reinforced through superior access to economic goods and external forces of influence and control, such as local and central government. Individuals or groups seeking power may introduce deviant versions (heresy – ibid.: 124) of the Anaguta universe. Borrowed systems may be introduced: for the Anaguta, this has often been successful where it has dovetailed with, rather than threatened, existing power relations. There is considerable evidence that the Anaguta symbolic universe is in any case highly syncretic and owes much to the dominant Hausa culture of the region as well as the many other neighbouring societies.

One example of this are the *night spirits* which are referred to in more depth below. Where the introduction of Christianity and of education is concerned, the relationships between these competing ideologies is an uneasy one in which senior elders are constantly trying to demonstrate their superior powers by invoking supernatural sanctions against Christians living in the village and against children and families of children who have been sent to school. Until independence children did not have access to schools unless they became Christians. Even Christianity is sometimes received syncretically, as the dual allegiance of Sani Maguda (see below) demonstrates.

In this chapter I examine ways in which the Anaguta symbolic universe is maintained, reproduced and legitimised through various types of cultural performance. The fable which follows provides a conceptual map to what Crick (1976) calls the 'moral space' of the Anaguta, and is a powerful tool for socialising children and young people into the accepted norms and values.

One evening my wife and I were sitting in the compound of Sani Maguda, with his two wives and three children, on a brief return visit in 1984. Sani had been our host, mentor and adoptive brother during the original fieldwork trip.[1] As often happened we were joined by various neighbours and their children, as well as people on their way to or from the beer parlour in Babale. On this particular evening ages ranged from about five to forty years. The story tellers were Sani Jah our nearest neighbour and Sani Maguda. Both Sani Maguda and Sani Jah were of a generation which should have been elders, but because an age-grade promotion ceremony had not been held for a long time they were still warriors (see Spencer, this volume).

At that time Sani Maguda was the only Anaguta living in the village who could read and write, being literate in Hausa, the second official language of the area, and English. He was essential to the community for keeping records of meetings of local committees, writing letters and recording the details of land transactions. He is a Christian and a follower of the local animist religion and quite consciously keeps a foot in both camps. He is, therefore, one of the few Anaguta men who can negotiate the boundary between the village and the town. It is Sani Maguda who tells the following story.

The Fable of the Hare and the Hornet

One day, Azomo the hare came to the compound of Chinchoro the hornet and said to him:

'Whenever I come to your compound to see you, I never find you at home. Where do you go?'

Chinchoro said:

'I always go to see my girlfriends. We have parties every evening. In fact, I am going there now.'

Azomo said:

'How can I come with you? I don't have wings like you.'

Chinchoro said:

'OK, if you really want to go with me you will have to bring a big ram; then I will make you fly.'

Azomo rushed away and soon returned with the biggest ram he could find. Then Chinchoro prepared some food – gruel and guinea corn dough. He put the gruel up one nostril and dough up the other. Chinchoro said to Azomo:

---

1 Sani and I taped much of the material in this chapter together. Sani then translated it in his own inimitable way and he and many other Anaguta friends interpreted the meaning for us. I have stuck as closely as possible to their interpretation of the events, adding only the theoretical framework. Sani spent six months with us in England during 1983 and met Abner Cohen.

'OK, now you can climb on my back.'
And off they flew to the place far above the sky where they met many people playing and drinking local beer and beautiful girls dancing.

Chinchoro didn't know how to play the drum, but Azomo was a very good drummer. They were standing watching the beautiful girls dancing and the drummers drumming when Azomo took one of the drums and started playing it and singing:
'Chinchoro with the gruel up his nose; Chinchoro with the dough up his nose.'
Chinchoro was very upset. He said:
'Azomo, I brought you here and you are trying to disgrace me in public, saying that I carry my food up my nose.'
He was so very annoyed that he went back home and left Azomo there.

When midnight came, all the inhabitants of the place above the sky went to their compounds. Azomo, being a stranger there, had no place to go. Everywhere he went people would chase him away saying:
'Go away; go away; we don't know you.'
Eventually Azomo came to the compound of an old woman who was so feeble that she could not even hold a stick to beat somebody. Azomo said:
'Open the door! open the door!'
The old woman said:
'Who are you?'
Azomo, trying to disguise his voice, said:
'I am your friend.'
So the old woman told Azomo to enter.

Azomo entered the parlour and said to the old woman:
'Please, if anyone comes and asks if there is a stranger here, don't say anything, all right? I will just hide in one of your big pots for the night and in the morning I will give you a very nice present.'
The old woman opened one of her biggest pots and Azomo climbed inside.

During the night a large animal like a man-eating elephant began moving around the town asking in a deep frightening voice:
'Are there any strangers in this town? Are there any strangers in this town?'
The creature went to all the compounds asking this question. When he came to the compound where Azomo was hiding, Azomo, trying the imitate the old woman, replied in a high quivering voice:
'There are no strangers in this town.'
The creature seemed to be satisfied with this and moved on to the next compound. But Azomo knew that it would return again and might not be so easy to convince next time. So he said to the old woman:
'This thing wants to eat you and me, so let's try to kill it when it comes this way again. This is what you will do. Go and collect some round stones and plenty of firewood.'
The old woman did as she was bid. She made a fire and put the stones on it so that they became red hot. Then they heard the creature coming in their direction once again. So Azomo said to the old woman:

'Please, make a hole in the pot so that I can put my hand through it and pick up the stones.'

Soon, the creature arrived at the compound roaring in its frightening voice:
'Is there a stranger in this town?'
Azomo replied:
'Yes, there is a stranger in this town.'
The creature rushed towards the pot and opened its mouth to try and swallow it. But Azomo was too quick. He took a red hot stone and threw it straight down the creature's throat. The creature charged off towards the river with its stomach on fire, but as soon as it got there it rolled over and died. Azomo was still hiding in his pot.

Very early in the morning, when the women of the town came to fetch water from the river and found the creature, which had terrorised them for so long, lying dead, they ran back shouting with joy and relief. When the Village Head heard the news he called all the people to assemble in the town square. Then he questioned them saying:
'Who killed this animal? If any of you can show that you killed this creature I will give him a handsome reward.'
They all looked at each other and said:
'No, I am not the one; I am not the one.'

At that moment, somebody found a shoe that the Village Head made everyone try on. But it did not fit any of the people there. Then the Head said:
'I heard that there was a stranger who came here last night and started playing the drum. Is he still here, or has he gone?'
The villagers said they didn't know, and they told the story of how they kept on chasing the stranger away. Then somebody said they thought he had stayed in the old woman's compound, so the Village Head sent a messenger to go and call Azomo.

At first, Azomo refused to come out, but they begged him and begged him until eventually, and with feigned reluctance, he entered the town square. The Village Head said to Azomo:
'Are you the one who killed this creature which has terrorised us for so long?'
Azomo said:
'No, I am not the one.'
The Village Head repeated the question saying:
'Please, we beg you, if you are the one who did this brave deed, tell us so that we can give a suitable reward.'
Azomo continued to deny it until the Village Head asked him to try on the shoe that turned out to fit him perfectly.

Then everyone was very happy with Azomo, and the village head asked him what he needed as a reward. He was even offered the most beautiful girl in the town as a wife. But Azomo said:
'No, I only need a nice drum; a drum which makes a good sound.'
So the best drum in the town was brought for Azomo and the head asked how he was going to get it back to his own town in the world below the sky. Azomo said:

'Well the only thing you can do to help me, my Chief, is to bring me a very long rope which will reach from here to there.'

The rope was brought and tied tightly round Azomo's waist. Azomo gave instructions that they were to listen very carefully, and if they heard a drum beat it meant that he had landed safely on the earth. Then they could cut the rope. On no account should they cut it until they heard the drumbeat.

Azomo left the place above the sky and started coming down, down, down, down on the rope which had been provided for him. On the way he met the sun who said:

'Please, can you lend me your drum so that I can play it for a little while?'

Azomo refused. Then he met darkness who made the same request. Again Azomo refused. After this he met the moon who wanted to borrow the drum. Azomo said: 'No!' Then he met a very powerful and dangerous eagle who repeatedly asked to play Azomo's drum, and each time Azomo refused, because he was still very far from the ground. The eagle grew angry and said:

'If you will not lend me your drum, I know what to do.'

So he swooped down on Azomo and hit the drum with his wing. The Village Head, listening in the place above the sky, heard the sound of the drum, thought Azomo was safe, and cut the rope. Azomo fell out of the sky, down, down, down, down, down.

Azomo was very lucky. He fell into a lake. But the fish there were hungry, and they rushed to eat him. But Azomo, still with his wits about him, said:

'Wait! Wait! Hang on! I have been sent by the Village Head to circumcise your children. The Chief said that you should find a cave for me and bring your children to me one by one to be circumcised.'

(Until this point there had been no interruptions. But here Sani was about to miss out an important part of the narrative, and was corrected by Sani Jah and another near neighbour. The children were listening with rapt attention.)

When Azomo had been installed in his cave, he said he was hungry. The fish brought him a big bowl of gruel made from the yellow powder in the locust bean pod. When this particular gruel has been freshly boiled it is extremely hot, much too hot for normal mortals to drink. They said to Azomo:

'If you have really been sent by the Village Head to do circumcision, drink this gruel straight away.'

Azomo sipped the gruel and it was indeed very hot. He said:

'For the love of God, I cannot drink cold gruel. Take it and put it in the sun to warm it up.'

So the fish did as he bid them, and later returned with the same bowl of gruel which was now thoroughly cool. Azomo drank it down in one gulp, proclaiming his satisfaction that it was now really hot.

Now the fish started to bring their sons to him one by one. Each time, after the parents had gone, Azomo would cut the child up and eat it. After he had eaten all the children except one, he said to the parents:

'Go and prepare a nice leather skin for each of your children so that I can send them out for the circumcision ceremony.'

When they brought the skins Azomo told the parents to wait outside the

cave. Then Azomo went inside and one by one he put the skins on the one remaining child, brought it out and asked:
'Whose child is this?'
Each time a parent would recognise the skin and reply:
'That is my child.'
Azomo continued until he had dealt with all the skins. Then he said to all the parents who were assembled outside the cave:
'Now I want you to come and collect your children. But you must not enter the cave until after I have gone.'
The parents nodded their approval.

Azomo came out of the cave, climbed up the bank and ran off as fast as he could into the bush. When the fish found out that they had been tricked they started to chase Azomo, shouting to anyone they saw to stop him. Azomo came upon a deaf person farming his land. Azomo shouted into his ear that he should carry him and run as fast as he could. The deaf farmer picked Azomo up and started running. Every time the pursuing fish shouted to the deaf man to stop, Azomo would slap him and say:
'They are telling you to run faster; run! run! run!'
Eventually they left the fish far behind and Azomo escaped.

After this our neighbour, Sani Jah, told two other stories, one about *The Hare and the Farmer* and the other about *The Hare and the Hyena*. The former is a typical Tar Baby story (Greenway 1964: 71–105) in which Azomo, who has been stealing a farmer's groundnuts, attacks the effigy of a beautiful girl made from resin and finds himself inextricably stuck to her. He is beaten to death by the farmer. There were many interruptions and corrections during the telling of this story.

Discussion

The Hare and the Hornet embodies a whole range of ideas. The older Anaguta believe that the sky is like an inverted bowl and that there are seven layers above it which are reflections of this world. It is in one of these layers that the spirits of the ancestors live. The souls of sorcerers are said to be able to ascend to some of these levels and bring back food in times of shortage. The souls of the most powerful may even visit the land of the ancestors, and they return to this world in dust devils (small whirlwinds) which occur frequently during the dry season. In this story Azomo assumes some of the attributes of a sorcerer, even to the point where he falls out of the sky on his return. But Azomo's powers are limited. Chinchoro the hornet may go back and forth nightly, but Azomo can only get to the place above the sky with Chinchoro's help. Azomo is Anaguta but Chinchoro is probably an outsider with resources which Azomo cleverly exploits to achieve his own ends. There is no suggestion in this story, however, that either Azomo or Chinchoro got to the land of the ancestors.

For the Anaguta there is no clear distinction between those who are credited with powers of sorcery and those who are not. Sorcerers, like others, are vulnerable to supernatural attack and the vicissitudes of the natural world, although they may be better equipped to deal with them. Azomo is thus a metaphor for all Anaguta men; usually wily and breathtakingly quick-thinking; possessing seemingly limitless powers of endurance; sometimes fatally stupid; and often displaying the skills attributed to sorcerers. *The Hare and the Hornet* is also a metaphor for the ability of the Anaguta to cross cultural boundaries and survive in the world outside their own. Boundary permeability is a constant theme of discourse and of kinship, and is summed up in the proverb 'the Anaguta are like a basket of water'. One minute they are visible, there in the basket; but as soon as you pick the basket up, they disappear.

The extraordinary network of interaction, of hares and hornets, eagles and man-eating elephants, even fish, of the worlds below and above the sky, and, it seems, of the people in both these worlds, of the sun and the moon and darkness, all this is comparable to the liminal interchange detailed also, but for a time centuries earlier, by Fisher (this volume). That even a deaf man not only hears Azomo, but must also be prevented from hearing the cries of the pursuing fish, highlights the dramatic possibilities of almost unlimited discourse.

Azomo is also a skilled drummer; this is something all Anaguta men strive to be, creating considerable competition among them. The instrument itself is of symbolic importance, whereas beautiful girls can be found anywhere. Furthermore, the best way of attracting a beautiful girl is to be a good drummer and to own an instrument which makes a really good sound. The symbolic significance of the drum is further emphasised by the fact that the instrument which Azomo has been given is so much sought after by the powerful occupants of the universe which he meets on his way back to this earth.

Hunting is an important ritual activity for the Anaguta. Men who have killed many dangerous wild animals, or who have taken many heads in war, have a specially made decorative pot placed on a tall rock at the head of their graves. The same distinction is shared by powerful sorcerers and the ritual leader of the village.

Again, this theme is explicit in Azomo's slaying of the beast which had been terrorising the town in the place above the sky.

Another aspect of the Anaguta value system is illustrated by Azomo's coyness in coming forward after killing the monster. To have admitted that he was the hero would have been seen as boastfulness and arrogance. He may also be reluctant to reveal his identity because he is a stranger in an alien land. Even today, when they travel outside the territory in which they are known, many Anaguta will not reveal their true cultural identity.

The significance of the circumcision ceremony in Anaguta thought is also clearly illustrated in *The Hare and the Hornet*. The fish accept, almost without question, that Azomo has been sent by the Village Head to circumcise their children. They only think of testing his powers, and thus his credentials, to perform this vital task when Azomo says he is hungry. In the days before 1930, when the last proper circumcision ceremony was held, it was performed by the ritual leader of the village, who would be qualified for the office partly on the grounds of possessing powers of sorcery.

The other incidents in the story illustrate how important it is to be calm in dangerous situations; to be able to work out a plan of action quickly and to take advantage of natural resources and people in order to survive. On the other hand *The Hare and the Farmer*, briefly alluded to above, illustrates how the cleverest of men, even one who is attributed with powers of sorcery, can be fatally blinded by arrogance and conceit.

The Anaguta say that fables are instructive and that a person can learn from them how to behave in dangerous situations, how to trick people and so on. In short, they are about lifemanship in Anaguta society; a powerful form of cultural performance, expressing a message not political only, but related to every aspect of society.

Riddles, proverbs, aphorisms and indirect speech are other common forms of, often highly ambivalent, discourse used by the Anaguta. The following incident illustrates the dramatic possibilities of enigmatic forms of speech and how these may be exploited to maintain and consolidate political power.

The Case of the Special Drum

In June 1982 the village of Andigwong in which we lived arranged a 'cultural show' in our honour. During the show young men of the warrior age-grade, elders, senior elders and women from our village and from other Anaguta villages performed various types of dance. Many of the dances would have been, when put in context, of ritual significance. Two of the instruments used, a small drum and a whistle, were said to have been captured from the Fulani during the decisive battle in 1873 when the Emir of Bauchi's army was defeated by the Anaguta and their allies. Another was a large and very old drum used for the senior elders' dance during the circumcision ceremony. This drum had been brought across the range of hills which divided the village of Andigwong into an upper and lower area, apparently for the first time. All the senior elders from Andigwong enjoyed playing it, dancing and drinking the sorghum beer which we had provided; there seemed to be no problem.

Later Wari Rhugu, the chairman of the permanent Andigwong village welfare committee which had organised the 'cultural show', heard a rumour that the senior elders were not entirely happy. So he went and asked them if there were any problem. They said no, there is no problem. On two more occasions the elders were asked if there were a problem and each time the reply was the same. About two weeks after the event, Sani Maguda met a man who was drunk (or pretended to be) who said to him: 'You are doing very well Sani; everyone is talking about you; everybody is saying how clever Sani is; I wouldn't like anything bad to happen to you.' Later the same evening Sani met another senior elder who told him that two weeks ago something very bad had happened: the special drum had been brought across the hill for the first time. He also said that Sani had done very well in organising the show. But, had he paid his fine for bringing the drum across the hill? Had the other villages danced the circumcision dance? Why had Andigwong alone danced?

This type of talk is a bad omen for an Anaguta. It means that people are jealous of you, and that you or your family will become the target for witchcraft or sorcery.

The following Sunday we went to Wari Rhugu's house. Wari is a devout Christian; he has a salaried job and lives in Jos, but has a house and land in the village. Most of the senior elders of the village arrived, and a large ram was tethered by the kitchen area ready to be slaughtered. The elders were clearly not happy with the soft drinks provided by the host, so Sani and I went to the beer parlour to buy some local beer. The following is an abridged transcript of the recording I made of the dialogue which took place.

Italics indicate words and phrases particularly emphasised by the speakers.

> Dundu (the 'big' senior elder of the village): 'We have come to spend the day with you because you have done something good. We are very happy. You should not be *too* worried – is that right [to the other elders]?'
> Wari (the host): 'You said I should not be worried, but I am shocked because this is the first time you have come to my house like this. I am too young [he is at least 40], and I might have done something wrong to you without knowing it. That is why I am worried.'
> Dundu: 'There is no problem. We have just come to see you because you have done something good. We have come to remind you so that you should go on doing good things. So there is no problem – no problem!'
> Wari: 'Please be patient. Another thing which makes me worried is that you ought to have called me to come to you, because I am too young to call you in our tradition. You ought to call me and give me advice and correction.'
> Taru (the same age grade as Wari): 'As young men we may have a quarrel, and we forget about it in five minutes. But you elders – it is very difficult for you to forget something which has happened recently.'
> Dundu: 'Even if you go to court for something you have done wrong it will have an end; so no problem. We are praying to have people who will do things wrong.'
> Taru: 'What we want nowadays is that, when we do something wrong, you should tell us before it is too late.'
> Jhinjhi (a senior elder said to be a powerful sorcerer): 'Senior elders, you see each of us has a compound in which we live; we elders are few and these young men are our helpers. Whenever we have a problem we call on them to come and help us. *So we are just praying for you people to have more children so that they can do good and bad to you, just as you are helping us now... The conclusion is a prayer which I pray to have a new person after today's gathering.*'
> Dundu: 'Things have changed now – it is not like before. Nowadays, if your son does something bad and you fail to tell him, it means that you have dug your grave. That is all; that is all.' [If your son dies because you haven't warned him there will be nobody to help you.]

At this point some of the senior elders were sent by Dundu to go and see the ram which had already been cut up for cooking.

> Tureki (another senior elder said to be a sorcerer): 'There is a bird called a rock partridge which always goes in a group. If one of them flies up it means that he is telling the others that something is going to happen. Now senior elders, open everything up and make it clear. Is that correct? Everything is settled now so there is no problem [because they had seen the ram]. Wherever any of the young men go they should be bright like moonshine.'
> Wari: 'Thank you; thank you!'
> Sambo (a young man who lives in the town of Jos): 'I am happy to see you elders. If any of us has a problem, it is easy for us to say it out as we are with our elders today. And as you say there is no problem, then I am very very grateful.'

Dundu: 'Don't worry, no problem. If anybody has a problem he will say it out. And everybody said no problem, so you should not worry at all.'

Junior Priest Chief of Andigwong: 'Sambo, whenever you hear elders talking there must be something wrong ... because of the Anaguta indirect speech. If you do something wrong to them it is hard for them to open it clearly to you ... but ... *Somebody who has a room must know where the roof leaks!*'

After this point the speeches became longer and more rambling as the local beer began to have its effect.

Discussion

Anaguta senior elders often speak in riddles and proverbs when debating the correct course of action in a given situation, or when responding to the sacrifice of a goat or ram for some violation of a social rule. Fables, proverbs and riddles are ambiguous and can be interpreted in many ways according to the context in which they are enunciated. Senior elders, in particular, have endless arguments and discussions about their meanings. Similarly, elders and young men will discuss and interpret the meaning of various proverbs and riddles they have heard at a meeting attended by senior elders, 'an example of how ambivalence can be used to mediate between categories and form the basis of a new classification' (Hamnett 1967: 388, on the function of riddles; see also Bourdieu 1977: 88-9).

The enigmatic speech of Jhinjhi, the senior elder said to be a powerful sorcerer, at the meeting at Wari Rhugu's house, caused much discussion and led to many interpretations among the younger men on the way home from the event.

In this context inverted speech, riddles, proverbs and aphorisms are clearly a mode of discourse or idiom for interpreting and reinterpreting the Anaguta symbolic universe and for negotiating power relations. It is quite likely that, during these arguments and discussions, aphorisms and the like are invented to suit the purpose of a particular power play. In the case of the big drum above, the younger men tried to negotiate for the elders to be more open in telling them when they have done something wrong. One of them explains that now many Anaguta live in Jos it is easier for them to make mistakes. The senior elders appear to agree to this until one of them points out that they cannot take what is being said at face value because of the Anaguta form of indirect speech.

This attempt to re-negotiate the way in which senior elders exercise power is one example of the way in which cultural performances are modified over time (see, for example, Herskovits and Herskovits 1958: 116) to reflect transitions and transformations in the moral universe much as maps are modified to reflect changes in the topography of the land they describe. Crick makes the point that 'Religion and political structure are often quite explicitly aspects of a single coherent ideology, so that "government" is not a separate sphere but merely a dimension of a total symbolic classification' (1976: 119).

Abner Cohen constantly refers to the dialectic between symbolic and power relations (see, for example, his introduction to Cohen 1981 and 1979: 105). A large number of Anaguta have become Christians and moved from the village into Jos although all still retain land and extended family ties. Most of the town dwellers have salaried jobs, many of them in local government where they can be influential as gatekeepers. This challenges the 'traditional' power of the senior elders economically, politically and spiritually. The elders' strategy for maintaining the balance of power is focused on creating opportunities for redistribution of wealth through fines which increase in size depending on the perceived affluence of the players, and the influence they can exert through perceived metaphysical or actual threats to the extended family in the village.

We witnessed many events similar to the meeting at Wari Rhugu's house, and listened often to indirect speech, riddles and aphorisms. In this particular case, however, the drama led to a tragic dénouement. It is clear that somebody had advised Wari that there was a problem and that the best thing to do was to apologise and give the elders meat. It is possible that, initially, there was not a problem, but that afterwards something inauspicious had happened, such as sickness. This would have indicated that the spirits were angry because of what had happened. Alternatively, some of the elders, annoyed at not having been consulted about moving the drum, had stirred up trouble after the event. It could also have been a form of blackmail – a way of extracting beer and meat from younger men. My wife, who spent the day with the women who were preparing the food, says that they were very cynical about the elders' motives, and thought they were just out for a good feast and plenty of beer. The most likely explanation would seem to be a combination of all three.

The precise connection between paying a fine to the elders and the appeasement of the spirits is not clear. When I asked Sani he replied 'I don't know; only the senior elders can know this!' It seems probable that appeasement of the elders is a pre-requisite to them performing the appropriate ritual.

However, eleven days after the feast for the elders we heard that the leader of the senior elders' dance, an important office, was very ill. This was the dance for which the big drum was used at the 'cultural show'. We went to his compound and were really shocked to find somebody who appeared fit and well three weeks previously, had wasted away completely and was on the point of death. He died soon after we left the compound and it is significant that not one of the other senior elders of the village visited him. It is impossible to tell whether there was any causal connection, psychosomatic or otherwise, between the events surrounding the drum and the death of this senior elder. Many people in the village were convinced that there was a causal connection. Even if it was a complete coincidence the fact remains that the death underlined the power of the senior elders thus reproducing the conditions necessary for its existence. That is, fear of what could happen if the senior elders were offended and not adequately appeased.

Sudden and dramatic death is a common occurrence in the village. There is no requirement for a death certificate to be issued and burial takes place within hours. Many are attributed to supernatural causes such as witchcraft, offences against the senior elders and against accepted norms of the society. It is a constant theme of discourse about the past and the present.

The Night Spirits

An Anaguta ritual performance which clearly illustrates what Cohen (1981) calls 'The Dramaturgy of Power' is the ritual of the *night spirits*. A woman had been sick and had consulted the leader of the *night spirits*. The leader is not himself a spirit, but he is the person who controls access to them. On his instructions she went to a particular native doctor (whom we knew) and was given some medicines with strict instructions on how to use them. However, the sickness continued, and on this particular evening she came back to the *night spirit* to find out what the problem was and what she should do about it. The ceremony took place in a large compound in the neighbouring village of Andrigiza. We arrived at about eight o'clock in the evening and there were probably a hundred or more people in and around the compound.

Many were women and children of all ages ranging from young babies to teenagers of both sexes. Many of the older people were already drunk and considerable quantities of local beer were being consumed. There was much laughter and joking and all were obviously enjoying themselves.

Inside the compound itself the women and girls were dancing and singing in a circle which moved in an anti-clockwise direction, while the men and boys danced round the outside in a clockwise direction. When the drumming and dancing stopped a very loud high-pitched voice was heard which seemed to come from a dense circle of cactus opposite the entrance to the compound. Inside the compound the leader sat on one side of the door of the entrance parlour and his assistant, who acts as interpreter for the secret language of the *night spirits,* sat on his right. The interpreter told the gathering that the *night spirit* said people were not paying enough respect and that the spirit would not help unless they showed more respect. Then one of the *night spirits* said that they should dance and sing a certain song.

When they had finished a different, lower pitched, voice was heard which appeared to be coming from another place in the compound. This was the voice of a higher level in the hierarchy of *night spirits.* Again the voice was interpreted as saying that people were not paying enough respect and that they should sing another song. When this had finished an extraordinary big booming sound came from somewhere inside the compound. This was the voice of the most important of the *night spirits* appropriately translated as the 'big sound'. This voice asked the sick woman to stand in the middle of the dance arena. It told her that the *night spirits* know everything and are never wrong. It was going to tell her what had happened and if what the spirit said was correct she should say 'yes'. Then the spirit told her, through the interpreter, that she had not used the medicines as she had been instructed. She agreed and asked what she should do to get better. The spirit said that she should pay a fine of a goat and then use the medicines strictly as instructed by the native doctor. A goat which she had brought with her was then produced and given to the leader. After this everybody sang more songs and danced.

When the *night spirit* is speaking it is forbidden to try and find out where the voice is coming from or to see the person doing it. Everybody keeps their heads down discreetly and although we were privy to many secrets, we had no inkling of who the *night spirits* were or who the leader was. The whole proceedings had the feeling of a court which, in spite of the gaiety surrounding it, was dealing with a very serious matter.

The voices produced by the *night spirits (anabur)* are most extraordinary and projected in such a way that it is impossible to detect where they are coming from. They are certainly meant to create awe and fear, and this was clearly the case, particularly for young people in the audience. There is also a spirit which travels in the day *(ushuhu)* which is said to be the wife of the *night spirits*. The appearance of *ushuhu* is also accompanied by powerful dramatic performances which leave strong impressions. These include the whipping, voluntarily accepted, of young men which can leave physical scars for the rest of their lives.

It is clear that these and many other ritual performances which we witnessed underline the quasi-supernatural powers of the elders and ritual leaders and the normative values of respect associated with the gerontocratic system. The *night spirits* and *those which travel in the day* derive their potency from a number of sources. They represent the spirits of ancestors, powerful sorcerers who have not been reborn into this world. They have played powerfully affective roles during primary socialisation and they continue to play affective roles during adult life. Sanctions for lack of respect or disobedience are often quite dramatically demonstrated by the death of the offending person, or a member of the family.

Interestingly, there is strong evidence that the *night spirits* were borrowed by the Anaguta in the 1920s from neighbouring societies (see Conant 1960 and 1963). They were then in direct competition with the unique and major Anaguta shrine, *Upwing Kping*. Now however, the Anaguta speak of these spirits as if they have always existed and they are well integrated into the symbolic universe. This has probably been made possible by the weakening of the leadership of the *Ujah* or Priest Chief of *Upwing Kping* due to the former colonial administration's attempts to persuade the holders of this office to take up more secular duties.

Conclusion

Some cultural performances are also living, creative and topical art forms and new fables, songs, aphorisms and riddles are being composed all the time. For example, during a visit to the fieldwork village in 1984 we heard two new songs composed that year. Both of them accuse living people of being witches. We heard both songs during a large gathering one evening near Babale just north of Jos. These gatherings were a frequent occurrence, and they often followed a ritual event such as a farming work party to mark a stage in the farming calendar. But they also happened at other times as purely social occasions. On this particular evening there were several hundred people present from the village of Andigwong and surrounding villages. A large circle of perhaps a hundred women, many with children on their backs, danced and sang whilst a group of drummers swooped in different directions to emphasise the refrain sung by different sections of dancers. Lit only by a few oil lamps, the whole atmosphere was highly affective.

One of the songs is about Anjelina and her boyfriend Wasco. It was composed in 1984 when the whole village of Amanza in which they lived were convinced that they had killed many people with witchcraft.

> Refrain: *Anjelina Wasco ...*
> You are not even married Anjelina, you look black in complexion and wicked to people.
> *Anjelina Wasco ...*
> No-one will want to marry you. You should have behaved well to people rather than being so wicked.
> *Anjelina Wasco ...*
> Therefore you will continue to stay unmarried forever. Who do you think will want to marry you as you proved to be a witch.
> *Anjelina Wasco ...*
> You are not beautiful; you look like a black canarium.
> *Anjelina Wasco ...*
> You are wonderful; you haven't got a child and if it happened you killed all the people. Who do you think will bury your body when you die?
> *Anjelina Wasco ...*
> A big unmarried wizard staying with her parents.
> *Anjelina Wasco ...*
> People are afraid to come near you.
> *Anjelina Wasco ...*
> She is wonderful in witchcraft.

We heard the same music played and danced to by young men of the warrior age-grade. On these occasions the words are not used, but everybody in the village will be aware of the unsung narrative. This is an example of collective social action which is not orchestrated or specifically legitimised by the senior elders. It seems to have occurred quite spontaneously as a reaction to arrogance or some other social failing of Anjelina and Wasco.

To conclude, in Anaguta society political power in the villages is still fundamentally derived from, as well as legitimised by, the symbolic universe, the ideology of respect implicit in the gerontocratic system, the ability of the senior elders and ritual leaders to harness the powers of the supernatural, and by the closeness of the senior elders to becoming ancestors or blessing the living by being reincarnated. Reproduction of the conditions of existence of the social order, therefore, makes maintenance of the symbolic universe vital. This is achieved through socialisation; continuous repetition of normative values – such as respect for the elders; and the affective drama of ritual performances.

Perhaps the most powerful performance for secondary socialisation – the initiation of young men into the warrior age-grade – had, at the time we lived in the village, not been performed for about fifty years. The fact that the gerontocratic ideology is still very much in evidence, despite competing power and symbolic relations, indicates that the alternative procedures for socialisation and universe maintenance, and in particular powerful affective cultural performances similar to those described in this paper, are still working effectively.

References

Beidelman, T.O. 1961. 'Hyena and Rabbit: a Kaguru Representation of Matrilineal Relations', *Africa* 31: 61–74.

——. 1963. 'Further Adventures of Hyena: the Folktale as Sociological Model', *Africa* 33: 54–69.

Berger P. and T. Luckmann. 1967. *The Social Construction of Reality*. Great Britain: Penguin Press.

Bourdieu, P. 1977. *Outline of a Theory of Practice*. Cambridge: Cambridge University Press.

Black, W. 1883. 'The Hare in Folk-Lore', *Folk-Lore Journal* I: 84–90.

Cohen, Abner. 1979. 'Political Symbolism', *Annual Review of Anthropology* 7: 87–113.

——. 1981. *The Politics of Elite Culture*. Berkeley and London: University of California Press.

Collett, A.C.A. 1984. 'The Making of a Patrilineal Ideology: a Study of Continuity and Change in Social Organisation Among the Anaguta of Northern Nigeria', PhD thesis, SOAS, University of London.

Conant, F.P. 1960. 'Dodo of Dass: a Study of Pagan Religion of Northern Nigeria', PhD thesis, Columbia University, New York.

——. 1963. 'The Manipulation of Ritual Among the Plateau Nigerians', *Africa* 33 (3): 227–36.

Crick, M. 1976. *Explorations in Language and Meaning.* London: Malaby Press.

Finnegan, Ruth. 1970. *Oral Literature in Africa.* Oxford: Clarendon.

——. 1977. *Oral Poetry.* Cambridge: Cambridge University Press.

Greenway, J. 1964. *Literature Among the Primitives.* Hatboro, Penn: Folklore Associates.

Hamnett, I. 1967. 'Ambiguity, Classification and Change: the Function of Riddles', *Man* (NS) 2: 379–92.

Herskovits, M.J. and F.S. Herskovits. 1958. *Dahomean Narrative.* Evanston: NW University Press.

Isichei, E. (ed.). 1982. *Studies in the History of Plateau State, Nigeria.* London: Macmillan.

——. 1984. 'Anaguta Songs', *West Africa* 4 June 1984: 1170–1.

Johnston, H.A.S. 1966. *A Selection of Hausa Stories.* Oxford: Clarendon.

Kluckhohn, Clyde. 1965. 'Recurrent Themes in Myths and Mythmaking' in *The Study of Folklore,* Alan Dundes (ed.). Englewood Cliffs: Prentice Hall.

Rattray, R.S. 1913. *Hausa Folk-lore,* 2 vols. Oxford: Clarendon Press.

Skinner, Neil. 1968. *Hausa Readings.* Madison, Milwaukee and London: University of Wisconsin Press.

Yai, Olabiyi. 1989. 'Issues in Oral Poetry: Criticism, Teaching and Translation' in *Discourses and its Disguises,* K. Barber and P.F. de Moraes Farias (eds). Birmingham University African Studies Series I.

CHAPTER 11

Dance and the Cosmology of Confidence

Paul Spencer *

Introduction

The general avoidance of dance as a topic for anthropological study reflects the problems of interpreting the art-forms of other cultures, let alone expressing these forms in terms intelligible to our own. The adepts themselves find it difficult but also unnecessary to articulate their feelings or any inner meaning, except through the medium of dance itself. Choreologists have argued that the anthropologists should learn the technicalities of body movement as a preparation for fieldwork, yet the aim of such training is to record dance as a museum piece rather than as a performance. It offers no bridge towards an inner understanding, breaking through the cultural barrier on the one hand or the problem of articulating inner feelings on the other. The distance between observer and performer is preserved and dance remains unapproachable for social anthropologists in general, neglected in their training, thereby perpetuating the neglect of this topic and encouraging the field-worker to look elsewhere for significance. Yet dancing is frequently a central spectacle of ritual and other public occasions,

---

* My fieldwork among the Samburu was principally undertaken between 1957–60 and made possible through the award of the William Wyse Studentship by Trinity College Cambridge, supplemented by a grant from the Colonial Social Science Research Council.

and to search elsewhere is to overlook this point, like the proverbial psychologist who turns in his seat at the theatre to peer at the audience. The central preoccupation of the participants is problematic, and the lateral approach, looking elsewhere for significance and understanding, becomes mainstream. This expedient has certainly paid dividends, but there remains the incongruity of *Hamlet* without the prince.

It is widely recognised that dance has an especially important role in pre-industrial societies. Its exotic nature has led various commentators who are well versed in dance as an art-form to search for its remote ancestry. Various books on the social significance of dance have an early chapter on its primitive origins – the title deeds as it were – leading up to the present (Sachs 1933, Rust 1969, Lange 1975, Royce 1977). This suggests a certain sterile parallel with the early history of anthropology. However, before dismissing this approach out of hand as unrewarding conjecture, it is worth pointing to one attempt of this sort that has had great influence on the development of social anthropology: Emile Durkheim's *The Elementary Forms of the Religious Life* (1915). In his search for the essence of religion, Durkheim drew attention to what he regarded as the most primitive form. Dance as such is scarcely mentioned in his account, yet if one turns from the most memorable passages of his work concerning the effervescent euphoria of collective gatherings among Australian aborigines to the sources on which Durkheim relied, one finds that incessant dancing, singing and processing were constant features in these (Durkheim 1915: 218; Spencer and Gillen 1904: 375–92). In other words, dance as a form – even an elementary form – of religious experience has its place implicitly in these passages. In looking beyond the dancing, like so many of his anthropological successors, Durkheim's argument comes close to an interpretation of inner understanding. He did not see the rhythms, stamping and the build-up of dance itself as relevant enough to his argument to elaborate on these; but dancing seems to have been a necessary vehicle for generating the collective sense of occasion that he was trying to convey. Durkheim's insight becomes memorable in drawing attention to the collective source of energy and experience vested in the interaction of the group – through the dancing. This contrasts with some more recent commentators on 'primitive dance' who have tended to look towards the dancer as a performer whose experience comes from inner resources, almost to the exclusion of the social context.

There is in dance a certain autonomy that is perceived in its purest form as an expression of the inner self rather than as a product of interaction with others. This was most explicit in Curt Sachs's monumental *World History of Dance* (1993), which treats the topic as a form of degeneration. In its pristine state, he saw dance as the purest and most private form of religious experience wholly devoid of society or social context, rather like Colin Turnbull's description of a lone Mbuti pygmy dancing in the forest or a popular view of some child wrapped up in its own play. Sachs expressed an extreme viewpoint, but this has lingered implicitly and even colours the more perceptive treatment by such major figures as Susanne Langer (1953: 175–84). This view also seems to be shared among dancers who maintain that the essence and inspiration of dance lies in some inner spirit that refuses to be classified or bound by convention or circumstance. In this chapter, it is precisely the 'spirit' of dance with which I am concerned. The point I wish to pursue is that the success of Durkheim's work was that the thrust of his argument did not rest on evolutionary speculation. He was looking towards relatively undifferentiated societies for an understanding of religion rather than towards some hypothetical ancestor. In doing so, his work provides us with a penetrating model for approaching performance, which also is embedded in its social context and extends beyond inner feelings to a shared awareness of the powerful forces of collective gatherings projected onto a cosmological plain, colouring the perception of time, space and the experience of life.

This is to place dance in the mainstream of social experience and hence of society itself. However, Abner Cohen (1993) has drawn attention to another aspect that is more subversive. His work has been concerned with the powerful forces of culture, through music and dance performance, in mobilising a popular awareness of underlying political and economic interests. In elaborating this theme in the present chapter, I wish to consider the extent to which the ebb and flow of tides of the popular expectation generated through dancing have a cosmic dimension. Such performances may be considered as collective representations in a Durkheimian sense. They express and promote the growth of a certain confidence, a mutual credibility, a gathering will to succeed, that is as relevant to understanding subversive popular movements as it is to understanding the dynamics of the market in the mainstream domain of economics. Ultimately, and notably to the extent that performance impinges on the popular perception of time, space and collective possibilities, it reaches towards the fundamental experience of society itself.

The Samburu Initiation Dance and the Spirit of Performance

To elaborate the argument further, I propose to discuss two contrasting examples of dance in Africa that convey the essence of the 'spirit' and 'meaning' of dance, and reveal a heightened perception of the forces of society at large that transcend normal everyday life.

The first example examines the role of a particular dance in cultivating an awareness of the passage of time among the Samburu, a pastoral Maasai-speaking people of northern Kenya. Like the Maasai, the Samburu are characterised by the young men who parade as *moran* or 'warriors'.[1] With an enforced peace under colonialism early in the twentieth century, warriorhood as such has become an anachronism. The fact that these young men have continued to adorn themselves and behave as *moran* has to be seen in the wider context of the interests of older men, who can retain their monopoly in polygyny only by delaying the marriages of these young men. In playing for time in this respect, the elders are also playing for wives, and a certain loss of control over the activities of their juniors is the price that they have to pay. In terms of the distribution of power with age, control over women, cattle and marriage is shifted towards the upper end of the age scale; and this creates a power vacuum lower down the scale, within which *moran* have their own lifestyle and ideals. These are associated with warrior values, close identity with their peers as a society apart, and concern for notions of honour and prestige, notably with regard to unmarried girls who pair with them as mistresses. There

---

1 The Arusha, discussed by Philip Gulliver in this volume, and the Samburu are both Maa/Maasai-speaking peoples with characteristics similar to the Maasai. The *moran* whom I discuss here, for instance, are similar up to a point with the *murran* discussed by Gulliver, although I have retained the concept of 'warriorhood', because this was expressed clearly by the Samburu themselves and posed an anomaly to which my study among them was addressed (Spencer 1965: xxi, 99–100, 102. Qv. Gulliver note 11, p. 133 in the present volume). A comparison of the Samburu and Arusha age systems leading to an alternative interpretation of Arusha has been published elsewhere (Spencer 1976).

is in this also an underlying anger that erupts from time to time in a delinquent lifestyle, extending to stock theft, feuding among themselves between clans, and illicit adultery with the wives of elders. The *moran* besport themselves in their distinctive regalia, always aware that they are the focal topic of interest and concern. Boys look forward to their period as *moran* with unsuppressed enthusiasm. Elders regard the *moran* with mistrust, amounting at times to a fury over their adulteries, and yet remember their own past *moranhood* with affection. Women of all ages dote on the idea of *moranhood*: as girls with *moran* lovers, as mothers with *moran* sons, and as younger wives who should avoid *moran* but are constantly suspected of adultery. The *moran* respond to this attention, conscious that their every movement is watched and interpreted by onlookers. The widespread interest in their performance extends beyond their dances to the total array of their activities throughout their period of *moranhood*. There is in this display a certain timelessness that extends from the first initiations of one age-set to the next over a period of some fourteen years. The *moran* are marking time during this period, with no sense of career until they can marry and settle down to elderhood; but dominating this is their pride in their coveted position. The oldest *moran*, aged thirty or more, may be ready for marriage by the time their period of *moranhood* has run its course. However, younger *moran*, who feel cheated by their late initiation into *moranhood* are still in their mid-twenties and have no intention of relinquishing their position voluntarily.

It is in this situation that we may now turn to the position of the uninitiated boys who are eager to become the next age-set of *moran*. Their promotion to *moranhood* is a coveted ambition, and their dancing is an expression of this desire, as they begin to flex their muscles in anticipation. The unfolding of events is geared to the rate at which boys mature and at which seasoned *moran* are prepared to settle down, which in turn is geared to the rate at which elders are prepared to relinquish their monopoly over marriage. There is no exact synchronisation of this process and no counting the years. The period of transition is one of adjustment to the inevitable in which the boys' performance provides one of the more significant signals.

Some three to five years before the new set of initiations, there is a certain restlessness among the older boys. At this stage, there would be no question of openly defying the *moran* in a premature display of warriorhood and risking a beating. However, a number of boys may muster to dance at night in villages where they are well represented, and the spirit of restlessness spreads. They process from village to village after the day's herding, singing and dancing their initiation dance, *lebarta*. As it is already dark, the salient aspect of their performance is in their singing and this can be heard throughout the neighbourhood; but the physical assertiveness projected in this display is an aspect of their performance as a group, which for Samburu also implies dancing. *Lebarta* has not been performed since the last period of initiations, and is only half remembered from an earlier period of their childhood when they were mere onlookers. At first they are unpractised in the idiom and few have voices deep enough to convince the community at large that they are yet fit for *moranhood*. The tune, rhythm and dance movements will be uncertain and variable. Displaying themselves at too early a stage merely exposes their immaturity and risks general ridicule. But it is a beginning.

This gathering spirit may then be interrupted by a dry summer season when there is a general dispersal and the initiative fades. The summer may even be followed by a period of extended drought inhibiting any renewed build-up of their dancing and expectations. Even so, they are still growing in number and stature to become an increasingly intrusive presence when conditions improve. As their voices, confidence, and style develop, so they take heart and use this song and processional dance to recruit other boys to join them. The developing timbre of their singing combined with the panache of their dance display is a measure of the mounting strength of feeling and unity among the boys and an indication of the passing of time. They have to demonstrate their credibility as potential *moran* before they are allowed initiation, and they can only do this by performing their dance and achieving a convincing degree of coordinated assertiveness as they mature physically and as their numbers increase.

For the *moran* of the previous age-set, the gathering assertiveness of this dance is a signal of their own impending elderhood. Sooner or later the boys will be able to stand up to their seniors physically and at that point they are fit to take over the coveted role. The older *moran* do not want to risk the humiliation of having been hounded into elderhood by mere 'boys', and it is in their interests to stand to one side before this point is reached. The elders too realise that they cannot hold onto their monopoly over marriage, denying the *moran* wives indefinitely. Even less do the elders want to be seen to have aged to the point where they have lost control over the situation as fighting breaks out between ageing *moran* and overgrown boys. The timing of the change-over with a new spate of initiations is therefore a matter of widespread concern. Many factors are relevant and give clues to the timing, but it is the display of the boys' dancing that is popularly regarded as particularly telling. It is the calibre of this dancing, that informs popular opinion of the passing of time during this crucial phase of the age-set cycle. In one particular cycle, for a variety of reasons, confidence among the boys may be slow to build up and the period will extend well beyond its normal span. In another cycle, it may be reduced. Either way, it is the boys' dancing that substitutes for a precise time reckoning. It evokes the growing into manhood of a new age-set with all that this implies for more senior age-sets. Insofar as one can write of the 'meaning' of the boys' dancing among the Samburu, the sight and sound evoke a range of vivid associations extending from a sense of the aesthetic charm of *moranhood* as a time of carefree display to a popular awareness of the passage of time, the process of ageing, and ultimately the progression of generations as power slips from one set of *moran* to the next, and at a higher level from ageing men to a new cohort of young elders.

Even rather young girls play their part in this process. Normally, all unmarried girls share in the general admiration for *moran* two or three times their age, joining in their dances and pairing with them as lovers. However, as the boys mature and older girls are married off, so the younger girls begin to hold back. They now see the *moran* as on the brink of marriage and elderhood, and this breaks the charm of the established *moran* over these girls who dread the distant prospect of an arranged marriage to a much older man. They are aware of a growing body of maturing youths closer to their own age and poised to take the central arena, and they expect to look towards these for their future lovers and companions. In this way, as the dancing of the boys builds up in confidence, so the dancing of the established *moran* loses a measure of support from the girls, and this loss of admiration brings their realisation of the inevitability of elderhood another step closer.

I have elsewhere elaborated more fully on the dancing of *moran* and of married women among the Samburu, both of which are more spectacular than the dancing I have described here (Spencer 1965: 120–7; 1985: 143–61). However, both *moran* and wives are locked almost timelessly into their condition, and their dances provide further insight into these conditions rather than into the passage of time itself. The boys' *lebarta* dances are less spectacular, especially in the early stages when they take place at night. But in marking the passage of time, there is an ominous ring in the way in which they develop into a concerted performance. The boys' dancing is the rehearsal for their own *moranhood* when they will take over the central arena of display among Samburu. It is not a matter of whether they will achieve this transition, but when and with what panache. As their time for initiation approaches, eligible boys are increasingly allowed to free themselves from herding, and it then becomes possible to build up a visible and concerted performance during the daytime as they tour the region, processing and dancing, mustering their numbers.

Initiation among the Samburu, as among Maasai, has various symbolic similarities with birth, as though the initiates are 'reborn' in *moranhood*. Correspondingly, there is a deeply held belief that like unborn and newly born infants, initiates are especially close to God as the ultimate giver of life (Spencer 1988: 39–42, 61–3). As the time of initiation approaches, boys can perform their *lebarta* further afield with impunity, even beyond the boundaries of Samburu. At such times, it is held, no request should be refused and anyone who harms an initiate would risk divine retribution, even former enemies of Samburu who share similar beliefs, such as the Booran. The time of change-over to a new age-set in this way becomes tinged with a sense of religious awe. Between periods of initiation, the *moran* are held in a timeless state of social suspension, and this provides a back-drop to their delinquencies. The period of change-over involves an end to this impasse and implies a general promotion in roles, for boys, for ageing *moran*, for their parents, and a radical shift in the pressures for marriage affecting girls and men of all ages. To this extent, the experience of ageing and hence of time itself moves in a sequence of radical steps, and the sense of sanctity and awe associated with initiates during the period of change-over appears to be a response to this liminal period of transition. It is an expression of the anxieties provoked by the periodic reminder of ageing on a cosmic scale.

I first became aware of the *lebarta* dance building up during the spring rains of 1958. This was in an area where the Samburu clans were interspersed, but each village tended to be associated with just one clan, and the clan above all was the focus of social discourse and identity. Here, it was Pardopa clan (Lorogushu) in particular that were well represented, and their local network of affiliation became the focus of my study at this stage. The brunt of the daily herding was undertaken by boys, and they would be dispersed with their family cattle for long hours without respite. In the late evening, when the scattered pastoral villages seemed to have settled for the night, spells of dancing with singing could build up among boys or at other times among *moran* and girls. The *moran* were not tied down to herding as the boys were, and the locus of *moran* activity and their dancing tended to shift around the area, reflecting their image as itinerant warriors who were expected to range widely and remain generally vigilant, avoiding involvement in village life and keeping their own company. It was during the late evenings, especially when *moran* activity seemed quiescent locally, that the boys would dance among themselves, an outer ring clapping and singing catchy rhythms without words as the inner ring of dancers jumped in time. Then, within these performances, as a certain spirit and cohesiveness built up, they might start performing *lebarta*, with less emphasis on rhythmic dancing and more on the assertiveness of their singing, voicing their claims to warriorhood, and throwing an implicit challenge to onlookers the louder they sang.

One night, a contingent of perhaps twenty boys from elsewhere processed through the area from village to village performing this dance and creating a greater sense of occasion and confidence than I had heard before, and other boys from the locality joined them. In the days that followed, the *moran* of Pardopa clan locally discounted the event. They had been involved in their own affairs elsewhere, and the boys would not dare to sport their dances and certainly not *lebarta* when *moran* were around. As matters stood, the initiations of these boys still seemed quite distant: it was the *moran* who still had to perform a major ceremony, their '*ilmugit* of the bull', before there could be any further initiations, and popular attention was still firmly fixed on the *moran* and the prospect of this major ceremony. This relaxed view seemed consistent with the fact that there had normally been about fourteen years between successive age-sets in the past, and the existing *moran* had only been initiated ten years earlier. The elders of Pardopa, however, were more sensitive to the significance of these boys' dances. It was they who pointed out to me that the boys were building up a sense of their own strength. The visiting performers, had been from other clans, and rather as initiation itself was expected to be a pan-Samburu event, inaugurating a new age-set that cut across all clans, so the mustering of the boys was conducted in this spirit, in contrast to the parochial concern for clanship among both *moran* and elders. Rather as the roving spirit of evening dancing among *moran* linked village life to the wider region, so these boys appeared to be following a similar pattern, independent of the *moran*, except in so far as they avoided them.

Over the next few weeks, I heard *lebarta* performed on this scale perhaps three more times, breaking the stillness of the night and aware of what appeared to be a gathering momentum. Let the *moran* perform their *ilmugit*, suggested the elders, and then it will be the boys' turn: times are changing and the *moran* should settle down to elderhood sooner than in the past to make way for the boys. It was as if a change-over to a new age-set was imminent. The boys had created a certain sense of expectation, or at least an awareness that their time would come, even if this was discounted by the *moran*. In fact, it was a further four years before the new initiations took place in Pardopa clan, and the existing age-set of *moran* held their position for a full fourteen years. The apparent momentum behind the boys' *lebarta* was not sustained during the dry season that followed.

Ostensibly, it was a prolonged drought that delayed new initiations, but beyond this, it was the elders who prevaricated. Delay was always to their advantage: both in keeping the ageing *moran* as just *moran*, and the boys as just boys. Individual elders locally in 1958 expressed a willingness to contemplate early initiations, encouraging the boys with a carrot (and indeed encouraging the anthropologist to stay longer to see these initiations). However, collectively in delaying any decision, the Pardopa elders were playing for time and, I have suggested, for wives. The elders had lost their own youthfulness, but it was in their interests to hold high the ideals of youth, encouraging the boys as they also encouraged *moran*. The persistence of tradition in Samburu society, in spite of the demise in inter-tribal warfare, was the persistence of the gerontocratic ideal of polygyny among elders. This ideal brought the vigour of youth, notably through dance, to the centre of the popular stage. It punctuated the sense of time among Samburu, but it also remained geared to the ultimate interests of elders throughout their careers from the time they retired from *moranhood* to marry and build up their families until they grew old and stopped taking on further wives.

Throughout the present century, when the whole tradition of Samburu society has been in question, the performance of the boys' dances seems to have provided an important sign of the capacity of the next age-set to follow in this tradition. This has led to an awareness of the progress of time in a historical sense, when future life courses may not replicate the past, and the boys have been confronted with the contradictions between persistent tradition and unstoppable change. The messages are mixed and it has often not been clear how far current symptoms have been temporary set-backs or signs of more radical transitions.[2] In the performance of *lebarta*, the implication for other Samburu is that they are growing older and this implies change. However, these songs are also an assertion among the boys that they intend to follow the pattern of their forebears in resisting change; and this is music to the ears of polygynous elders for whom change is acceptable only in so far as it does not threaten their cattle herds or their further marriage prospects, which stem from the persistence of *moranhood*.

The Cult of Bori Spirits and the Success of the Market Among the Hausa

Having examined the way in which Samburu awareness of the passage of time, linked to personal development and ageing, is shaped by a particular dance, we may turn to the cosmological implications of a different type of dance performance among the Hausa of northern Nigeria, especially as recounted by *Baba of Karo* to Mary Smith (1954).[3]

The Hausa year is divided between the farming season from April to October, and the oppressive dry season which brings a variety of illnesses and epidemic conditions together with a general movement of the population towards the villages and towns where they turn to trading and other non-farming activities. It is in this urban situation, of trading on the one hand and maladies on the other, that the pagan cult of *bori* spirits occupies an ambivalent position in exploiting the gaps created by the formal state hierarchy, which rests on the premises of Islamic orthodoxy and male dominance. Officially, the cult is not recognised, but the power of

---

[2] The change-over of age-sets around 1912 and 1936 in Samburu seemed to indicate a breakdown of the system under modern conditions, but led to a recovery (Spencer 1973: 157, 163). Aspects of Samburu society considered here seem to have been as relevant to these earlier times as they were to the times of my visits over a period from 1957 until 1976.

[3] Abner Cohen (1969: 58, 163–4) has also noted the existence of the *bori* spirit possession cult, and the history of this cult is considered by Renée Pittin, in the present volume.

the authorities does not extend to a control over popular belief or to the acclaim on which a sense of fulfilment within an urban community ultimately rests. At a popular level, this fulfilment is associated with the benevolent presence of the *bori* spirits, whose activities are believed to mirror the moral order of Hausa society, publicly spreading gossip through their adepts and punishing wrong-doing with illness. Popularly, the spirits are held to have a passion for community living and the people have a deep attachment to the local spirits; but with the authorities there is a certain mistrust. The adepts are predominantly women who fall short of the Islamic ideal and are marginal to Hausa society, notably prostitutes and unattached divorcees between marriages. The spirits are thought to manifest themselves in the vigorous dancing of these adepts, and this provides an opportunity for privileged licence in which women, normally secluded within their compounds, can display themselves and their grievances in public (Smith 1954: 25, 155, 222; Onwuejeogwu 1969: 278–80, 282–3, 289–91).

Each *bori* spirit has its own guise, such as a prince, a slave or a lame woman, echoing the status structure of Hausa society, and each has its characteristic dancing rhythm and movements portraying its attributes. It is held that the spirits can only be seen by adepts, and that a spirit possesses an adept by mounting her head, at which point the dancing becomes that of the spirit itself. The higher the reputation of an adept, the larger the number of the spirits who might on different occasions possess her (or occasionally him) and the more versatile the range of performance (Smith 1954: 21, 221 ; Onwuejeogwu 1969: 285–6, 288).

Special *bori* dances may be mounted in times of crisis, such as famine, epidemic, or loss of confidence in the local economy. The adepts make known the demands of the spirits, for alms or for concessions; and the authorities are expected to respond, or the opportunity to obtain the benign protection of the spirits will be lost, or worse still they may vent their anger bringing further misfortune. On such occasions, famous adepts may be employed to dance day and night over a continuous period, to attract the spirits and voice their demands. When the extended session is over and the adepts leave, it is hoped that the spirits will have settled down and will remain as spiritual patrons to the town (Smith 1954: 64, 175, 188, 220; Onwuejeogwu 1969: 287).

Here, I wish to focus on the role of *bori* dancing in the context of the market as a vital feature of Hausa urban existence.

According to popular belief, a thriving market town attracts a flourishing community of *bori* spirits and it becomes a place for festivity. It belongs as much to the spirits as to the people, and the town grows as more people come to live there. By attracting the spirits to settle, the town will grow and its market will grow as confidence builds up. A successful market implies one that is in a sense possessed by an assembly of dancing *bori*, and there is no clear distinction between the success of the market as an economic venture and its success as a centre for the *bori* cult. It is the benign presence of the *bori* spirits, made manifest in the dancing, drawing the crowd of onlookers, that is felt to reflect but also to create the community spirit and the thriving market. How far it is the success of the market enterprise that draws the crowd, or the presence of the crowd that spurs the dancers and musicians to excel, or the performance of the dancers that contributes to the success of the market and the drumming is perhaps impossible to answer. The market, the dancing and the swelling of the crowds are entwined in the popular sense of occasion. Market confidence, popular participation, and the belief in dancing spirits themselves are all part of a total performance that cannot be clearly divided between aesthetic, economic and religious aspects, even though *bori* dancing and commercial enterprise (and the formal Islamic aspects) are conducted by separate people in separate spheres of activity (Smith 1954: 220–2).

These parallel activities are elements of a joint venture that only succeeds to the extent that it captures the popular imagination at the expense of neighbouring market towns. It is this rivalry between towns, competing for success, that provides the division that is more decisive than the specialisations within any town. Each market has its own particular day for trading to allow traders and craftsmen to circulate between towns. Similarly, some adepts, like the traders, may move freely within a region. To attract *bori* spirits on a local market day, drummers beat out the rhythms, tempting the spirits to possess the adepts, and working up their performance in response to the dancers and the crowd.[4] When the spirits are called by their own drum rhythm, they are expected to come and take possession. Sometimes the atmosphere fails to build up, and the performance then lapses. On such occasions, the spirits are assumed to be preoccupied elsewhere, perhaps at another market

---

4 Philip Jaggar, in the present volume, elaborates on the relevance of drumming displays in this region and notes an overlap of beliefs with *bori*.

where the rhythms are more compelling or possibly treating this as a day of rest after a particularly energetic performance in another town. In this way, the commercial rivalry between towns encompasses a wider range of activity than just trading. Successful markets tend to generate successful *bori* displays and vice versa. If any of these wilt in the competition and falter over a period, for whatever reason, the spirits are felt to be deserting the market as the sense of enterprise deserts the town, trade falls off, the dancing itself subsides. Silence is the hallmark of a town without a market, whose people go elsewhere to trade and ultimately to live (Smith 1954: 20, 63, 189, 227).

The music and dancing of *bori* can be viewed as a symbolic expression of the concentration of popular concern in space. Crowds respond on market days as the sense of occasion spreads. Within the wider region, the timbre of the drumming with contending rhythms from different market centres diffuses the awareness of the distribution of *bori* activity and market success, rather as a form of gossip. Like the charismatic qualities of leadership, some towns have the quality of success, breeding confidence and drawing crowds, and some do not. Those that have success must constantly strive to retain it, for in popular dance as in any economic venture and community life more generally, the element of confidence shifts insidiously. There is an element of uncertainty in any dance that is well expressed by the notion of capricious possessing spirits whose whims shift unpredictably. This uncertainty makes a market enterprise, linked to *bori* dancing, all the more spectacular and memorable when it comes off and all the more dismal when it fails. In dance as in any performance or enterprise, nothing succeeds quite like success.

Conclusion: the Dynamics of Performance Through Dance

The analysis of the context of dance provides a variety of themes that are familiar in the anthropological study of ritual, belief and emotional expression. Thus while the literature tends to be silent on the dancing itself, it at least provides the wider social context that gives meaning to the activity. Dance, after all, is just one aspect of the more general performance of ritual with all its symbolic connotations. Each of the two dances I have discussed reveals a world of projected emotions conceived in terms of a cosmology that extends to a spirit world in Hausa and the experience of maturation and ageing in Samburu, and corresponding to the dynamics of confidence that builds up and extends over time and space.

In the Samburu example, the calibre of dance performance is viewed as an indicator of the passing of social time, reminding the population at large that as the age cycle progresses, a future age-set of boys are coming of age and they all are growing older. There is also a spatial dimension in so far as the growing calibre of the dancing is unevenly distributed. In certain areas, the boys will have built up their performance and mustered confidence ahead of other areas where there is no incipient challenge to the established *moran*. The process towards new initiations is perhaps patchy at first, but it builds up to a sense of the inevitable and the notion that the initiates are protected by God, raising expectations of a change-over to a higher level throughout the country.

In the Hausa example, the distribution of *bori* spirit activity, revealed by their dancing, may be regarded as a symbolic representation of local concentrations of popular acclaim and charismatic success in space. Here, the dimension of time has a relevance in the local cycle of market days and the seasonal aspects of trade, but above all in the rivalry between towns that leads to shifts in the distribution of success over a region as the success of markets rise and fall and *bori* spirits are felt to move their allegiance capriciously.

Dance performance displays a very public message. It is not just gossip that is broadcast to humiliate those in authority by making public their peccadillos, as occurs in *bori*, or the boasting of the Samburu boys in their dancing which may tease the raw sensitivities of others. Beyond this, there is the message of the panache of the community represented by these dancers and an awareness of a wider audience who stand to gain when the performance faulters: this is the more far-reaching gossip. Confidence, betrayed by performance, shifts over time and over space, and it has a significance for dynamics of power, however these may be interpreted within any culture.

Contemporary specialisation within anthropology seems to point towards an anthropology of dance through such topics as ethno-musicology and various approaches towards the cross-cultural study of aesthetics and of the body. Dance could have an honoured place in any of these, and yet somehow it fits awkwardly with less attention paid to it or to the dimension of performance than one might otherwise expect, rather as Durkheim appears to have overlooked the role of dance in his analysis of religion. Had Durkheim turned his pen to the topic in a search for *The Elementary Forms of Performance* that illuminate the essence of our own experience, and had he chosen for his example of an undifferentiated people a group such as the Samburu, then he might have noted that dance, music, song, aesthetic expression and bodily display and decoration are inseparable. They are all subsumed under the general concept of dance. The various specialisms reflect our own disciplinary boundaries and our own process of differentiation. To the extent that the Samburu may be typical of other parts of Africa and further afield in this respect, the omission of ethnodance from anthropological curricula seems to provide a further insight into our own classificatory system at the expense of underrating the central importance of dance in the conceptual systems of peoples whom we study. However, the value of including such a subject would surely lie in extending the search beyond the form in which dance is presented, to consider aspects of the performance and the spirit of the occasion. The major problem of dissecting and interpreting the art-form is avoided by turning attention to the context and the social dynamics of performance.

References

Cohen, A. 1969. *Custom and Politics in Urban Africa*. London: Routledge and Kegan Paul.

——. 1993. *Masquerade Politics: Explorations in the Structure of Urban Cultural Movements*. Berkeley: University of California Press.

Durkheim, E. 1915. *The Elementary Forms of the Religious Life*. Translated by J.W. Swain. London: Allen and Unwin.

Lange, R. 1975. *The Nature of Dance: an Anthropological Perspective*. London: Macdonald and Evans.

Langer, S. 1953. *Feeling and Form: a Theory of Art*. London: Routledge and Kegan Paul.

Onwuejeogwu, M. 1969. 'The Cult of the Bori Spirits Among the Hausa' in *Man in Africa*, M. Douglas and P.M. Kaberry (eds). London: Tavistock Press.

Royce, A.P. 1977. *The Anthropology of Dance*. Bloomington: Indiana University Press.

Rust, F. 1969. *Dance in Society: an Analysis of the Relationship Between the Social Dance and Society in England From the Middle-Ages to the Present Day.* London: Routledge and Kegan Paul.

Sachs, C. 1933. *World History of the Dance.* Trans. B. Schonberg, 1937. London: Allen and Unwin.

Smith, M. 1954. *Baba of Karo.* London: Faber and Faber.

Spencer, B. and F.J. Gillen. 1904. *The Northern Tribes of Central Australia.* London: Macmillan.

Spencer, P. 1965. *The Samburu: a Study of Gerontocracy in a Nomadic Tribe.* London: Routledge and Kegan Paul.

——. 1973. *Nomads in Alliance: Symbiosis and Growth Among the Rendille and Samburu of Kenya.* London: Oxford University Press.

——. 1976. 'Opposing Streams and the Gerontocratic Ladder: Two Models of Age Organisation in East Africa', *Man* (N.S.) 11: 153–75.

——. 1985. *Society and the Dance: the Social Anthropology of Process and Performance.* Cambridge: Cambridge University Press.

——. 1988. *The Maasai of Matapato: a Study of Rituals of Rebellion.* Manchester: Manchester University Press.

CHAPTER 12

Possession and Dispossession:
Changing Symbolic Structures and Meanings in Contemporary Nigeria

Renée Pittin

Introduction

In *Masquerade Politics*, his most recent book, Abner Cohen demonstrates through the use of the Notting Hill Carnival, the integral and dynamic relationship between politics and culture. 'The cultural is continuously interpenetrated by the political and is thereby transformed into ideology, whether of the so-called "dominant class" or of a collectivity opposing it. Meanwhile the political is constantly expressed, articulated and objectified in terms of cultural forms and performances... the phenomena that we deal with are simultaneously both cultural and political' (Cohen 1993: 8). Earlier, Cohen notes that 'social relationships are ... also relationships of power ... when considered throughout the extent of the polity' (ibid.: 7).

It is this linkage and interaction between the cultural and political, and the demonstration of the pervasiveness of power in various contexts, which inform this chapter. It deals with the practice, changing meanings, forms and political presence of *bori*, now often termed the Hausa spirit-possession cult.[1]

---

1 We have already made a political statement in symbolic terms, in the language employed. A cult is described, e.g., as 'a particular form of religious worship' (*Shorter Oxford English Dictionary*, 1973) and is, in that respect, not a substantive religion *per se*. This already improperly undermines *bori*, which has represented and underscored Hausa lifestyle, the people and the state.

Bori in Katsina: A Historical Perspective

Bori is cultural performance *par excellence*, from the public spectacle of a group of men and women possessed, or seemingly possessed, by the spirits which are themselves culturally constituted, to the actions of individual adepts working in their own homes, summoning or seeking the spirits, and drawing upon their received knowledge of medicine, pharmacology and psychology to help troubled or sick individuals seeking assistance. In both cases, *bori* is theatre and performance, and profoundly evocative. As the music calling forth the spirits is played, and some in the arena 'play' at *bori*, others may be possessed, all unwilling, by the spirits. The sight of a nursing assistant shuddering in the first stages of possession, and muttering that she knew she should not have come near the music, as a friend 'greets' and calms the spirit through gently touching the trembling woman, is an indication of the continuing effect of the cult on many local people, and the power of the rites.

In this chapter, I will focus in particular on the players in this cultural performance, and on the political relationships and ideological contestation represented by and through *bori* over the course of time. *Bori* has provided an arena in which political struggles have been waged and reflected. Support and contravention in relation to the polity have been symbolised and played out through *bori*, while the conception of the polity itself has shifted. *Bori* is also a site wherein power and representation in relation to gender have been demonstrated, defined and revised. *Bori* has been the subject of considerable interest among recorders of Hausa culture, although it has received less attention as its political importance has waned, its rites have become less open or frequent, and its extensiveness has been reduced. This chapter does not deal with *bori* generally, but rather focuses on the participation in and practice of *bori* in the Nigerian city of Katsina.

Bori must be specifically located, as its relevance and significance in different Hausa communities and states has followed different trajectories. The structural and political positioning of the rites, functionaries and adherents must be localised and contextualised, as are even the very spirits (Hausa: *iska*, pl. *iskoki*) of *bori*.

Katsina City, the capital of Katsina State since the creation of the State[2] in 1987, has a lengthy history. According to the Bayajida

---

2 'State' has different meanings in this chapter. For clarity, when this most recent entity, Katsina State, created in 1987, is intended, the term 'state' is capitalised. When not capitalised, this is the polity at the time: the kingdom (pre-1807) or the emirate, post-1807.

legend, and to a series of 'king lists',[3] Katsina was founded by Kumayo, son of Bawo and grandson of Bayajida and the Queen of Daura. Historical sources suggest that Kumayo founded the state around the twelfth century AD. He and his descendents, known as the Durbawa, established themselves west and southeast of the present Katsina City. The Durbawa were eventually overcome and a new dynasty arose led by Korau, whose name is still commemorated in the epithet accorded to every subsequent ruler of Katsina, Magajin Korau (successor of Korau). According to Barth (1857-58) and some other historians, the accession of Korau occurred in the middle of the thirteenth century. The beginning of Habe rule about two centuries later is marked by the accession of the first of the Muslim Habe kings, Muhammadu Korau.[4]

Of particular interest to us are the possible changes in state-associated religion from the reign of the Durbawa. According to Usman (1981: 16-17), the nature-linked religious system on which *bori* is based, centring around the shrine of Inna or Uwa (Hausa: mother), and signifying (mother) earth, was more relevant to the increasingly cosmopolitan Katsina-area population than the more restricted ancestor-focused worship of the Durbawa:

> The very heterogeneity of the settlements in terms of descent, religion and occupation, was a condition favoring the growth of a political authority standing above the old kinship, religious and occupational groups. The shrine of Inna (Mother Earth) provided a more suitable foundation for such a political authority... (Usman 1981: 17)

The link between rulers of Katsina and the spirit-based religion was sealed with the death of Korau: he became one of the spirits in the pantheon, a son of Inna. Usman notes that '[the] close identification of Korau with Mother Earth provided an important religious basis for his authority, and that of his successors' (ibid.: 19).

---

3 The term 'king list' is used advisedly, as these very lists point to all the earliest rulers of Daura being women (see, e.g., Palmer 1928, vol. 3; and Hogben and Kirk-Greene 1966).

4 Y.B. Usman presents Korau and Muhammadu Korau as the same individual, and places his reign at 1445-1495 AD. He rejects Barth's and others' contention of a new dynasty, the Habe, and suggests that the ruling group were rather the diverse but related 'grand-children' of Korau (1981: 63). Katsina kinglists are rather problematic in relation to dating and analysis (see, e.g., A. Smith 1971, for an overview and relevant references).

It is clear that *bori* has been closely associated with the kingdom of Katsina for centuries. The personnel, the performance of rituals, and the ritual of performance have been an integral part of the structure and validation of the rulers and of their regimes. Identification with the system of belief in spirits shored up the power of the ruling regime, while also implanting the seeds of its destruction via the increasing strength of Islam.

For centuries, the relation between the spirit-based religion and Islam was not one of strong polarisation or opposition, but indeed to varying degrees one of coexistence or possibly symbiosis. After the mid-fifteenth century,[5] many of the Katsina kings professed Islam, while not necessarily disowning their involvement in or debt to the spirit-based religion. Indeed, the installation of a Hausa king was legitimated through the religion, and this linkage 'remained a permanent feature of the political system closely identified with the dynasty' (ibid.: 28). Most of the Hausa kings patronised shrines of the spirits, personally or through their representatives. Islam and supporters of Islam were recognised within the pantheon of the spirit-based religion, and until now, Muslim and non-Muslim spirits may be invoked. The spirit-based religion reflected and responded to the dynamics of cultural and political realities and perceptions.

For individual rulers, the contradictions between the belief systems may have become overwhelming. Usman notes (ibid.: 69–70) the 'schizophrenic' behaviour of Sarkin Katsina Gozo (1795–1801), who refused the 'fetishistic' traditional installation ceremony, yet later became a worshipper of the spirits, and was incorporated into the spiritual pantheon on his death. At the same time, he was a supporter of Islam and a builder of mosques.

---

5 An important figure in the increased Islamic influence in Katsina in the late fifteenth century was the scholar al-Maghili, who was in Katsina in the 1490s and who 'exerted his influence both forcefully and directly' (Usman 1981: 21). See too the chapter by Humphrey Fisher in this volume: al-Maghili is an actor in this scenario also. Katsina was on and part of the West African trade routes and broader political activity, subject also to the blandishments and teachings of the powerful Muslim scholars and functionaries moving throughout the region, and availing itself through some of its aristocracy of the benefits of a strengthened Islam. Fisher notes that demonstrative acceptance or active proselytisation of Islam further validated several West African rulers and regimes at this time, while the acceptance of Islam by the state or its functionaries could serve to increase the legitimacy of the religion among the populace.

According to Usman, the conflict between the two cosmological systems for political order and legitimacy was becoming overwhelming, even while some integration was still possible. During Habe rule, before the Jihad of 1804–09, as Abdullahi Smith points out: 'Politically, the *bokaye* [*bori* priests] came to share power with the *malamai* [Muslim teachers], and the *sarki* [chief] to occupy an uneasy position of leader of both groups' (1971: 197).

However equally, if not even more prominent in *bori*, was the role of royal women. Thus, Usman notes that in Katsina, from around the sixteenth to the nineteenth century: 'The palace ... remained a stronghold of various cults of the *iskoki* under the Maidaki, and other senior wives and concubines ... it is likely that most of the Sarakunan [rulers of] Katsina ... patronised shrines of the *iskoki*' (1981: 28).

Women, Authority and *Bori*

In many of the savannah states, a tradition of women's political power is reflected in the mythology of the states, and of the groups of people who, through migration and/or conquest, became associated with the larger political entities. Control over the state appears to have been infrequently exercised by women, or perhaps is selectively remembered. In the Hausa states, there was a general pattern of women's power, supported by the myth of origin, similar gender-based offices, and a framework within which the state religion was mainly the preserve of female devotees, led by a woman or women of the ruling class. The continued success of the realm was held to lie in large measure in the efficacy of the rites conducted, with fortune ultimately reposed in the person of the ruler, usually but not always a male. Women's political power probably reached its zenith around the sixteenth century, with women ruling in some of the Hausa kingdoms and Borno.

In Katsina, women's titles and politico-religious authority were becoming firmly established (ibid.: 24). The terminology in the various states differed, but the women usually exercising political power included, among others, the 'queen mother' (not necessarily the mother of the incumbent king), and the sister(s) and/or daughter(s) of the ruler. The 'queen mother' was known as Iya in Katsina; the royal sister or daughter was called Magajiya. So evident was the power of royal women in the Hausa states, that this very situation was used by Shehu Usman dan Fodio in his call for *jihad* to demonstrate in part the un-Islamic nature of the regimes, suggested by this passage in the *Kitab al-Farq*: 'One of the ways of their governments is that (a man) puts the affairs of his women into the hands of the oldest one, and every one (of the others) is like a slave-woman under her' (Hiskett 1960: 567 [parentheses in the text]).

The most important consequence of the successful waging of the *jihad* for women may have been the loss of their ritual authority, a prime base of the political power which they had formerly exercised. As *bori* lost its political legitimacy, so did its adepts suffer a similar fate.

Yet while overt political power declined, with some sharp breaks such as that caused by the *jihad*, the involvement of aristocratic and other women with *bori*, and the linkage of *bori* to political and supernatural power, has been maintained in various ways. The very practice of *bori* in Katsina became a symbolic form of confrontation between the ideologically legitimate, and male, political structure, and the submerged traditional system, with a more active role for women. By the 1970s, it was said that *bori* was officially banned in Katsina, probably based on a pronouncement by the then Emir, Usman Nagogo. Thus, *bori* was tacitly accepted as a non-legitimate activity on an ideological basis, and on the basis of direct political decree. Even at that time, it was questionable whether the practice had been curtailed; it appeared to be flourishing.

The rumours which circulated regarding the reason for the prohibition of *bori* are indicative of the subversive nature attributed to the cult. Thus, one explanation relates that the practice of *bori* disturbed the Emir at his prayers, and the second that the *bori* adepts insulted one of the Emir's wives. The first version is symbolically accurate enough, with *bori* portrayed as an antagonistic force with regard both to the present political hierarchy, and to Islam. The second version is rather more interesting, for it appears to be an attempt to destroy part of the political rationale behind *bori* by removing its traditional support by female members of the aristocracy. That the ban had not been effective was clear from the fact that a group of *bori* adepts continued to perform their rituals and ceremonies deep within the palace. This group, the *'yan kwarya*, are in fact historically linked with the environs of the palace, and their spatial and political proximity to the aristocracy is of continuing relevance in relation to their access to those in power, and their own demonstration of authority.

The 'yan kwarya are one, but not the only group of *bori* practitioners in Katsina. During the 1970s, *bori* in Katsina manifested itself in two distinct forms. The differences were both material and ideological, and were reflected in the participants and spectators attracted to each, as well as in the distribution of the ceremonies in place and time. These two main categories of *bori* adepts are the 'yan kwarya, noted above, and the 'yan garaya; each group was named in relation to the musical instruments[6] which are played to summon the spirits in their respective sects. Neither group denies the validity of the other, but in certain respects tends to promote the authority and purity of its own *bori vis à vis* its counterparts.

An additional and important distinction is that between 'public' and 'private' *bori*, which is often implicitly extended to distinguish between *bori* as a profane public display and *bori* as an efficacious and religious art. Others, however, do not negate the efficacy of *bori* whatever its form (see, e.g., Guy Nicolas 1975), a point I return to below. Public and private *bori* are sometimes treated as synonymous with the distinction between city and village (see, e.g., Onwuejeogwu 1969, and Barkow 1973); in Katsina, however, both forms of *bori* coexist.

The 'yan garaya are associated primarily with public *bori*. The group includes both men and women, although the number of women far exceeds that of men. The 'yan garaya attend and participate at gatherings which include both sexes. In the past, wherever a major celebration was being held, one could expect to find a contingent of 'yan garaya. At the present time, the occasions at which *bori* music is played are much more limited, with both increasing fundamentalism and severely constrained budgets among the majority of the population.[7] The 'yan garaya associate themselves with the more Westernised elements of the society, and indeed their rites are sometimes referred to as *borin bariki*, the *bori* of the

---

6 A *kwarya* is any calabash. The calabash is turned upside down and drummed; it may be set in water to increase the resonance. A *garaya* is a stringed instrument which is plucked or strummed. It is topped with a metal strip edged with rings to produce a jingling sound. Other instruments played by men include the *goge*, also a stringed instrument, and drums.

7 The kind of market *bori* discussed by Baba of Karo, and noted by Paul Spencer in this volume, a central and centralised event which signaled and reflected the vitality of the town, has not been evident in Katsina over the past two decades. The meaning and use of *bori* in urban and administrative centres is quite different from that in the rural areas.

'modern sector'. The *'yan garaya* include among their membership most of the 'courtesans', or *karuwai*, who participate in *bori*, although the majority of women are not *karuwai*.

Private *bori* in Katsina has been much more the sphere of the *'yan kwarya*. The *'yan kwarya* have considered themselves to be the more proper or legitimate of the two groups of *bori* adherents, with a following of only women, most of whom are either married, or respectably non-married, i.e., not practising 'courtesanship'.[8] However, it is not only because of the respectable roles of the participants that the *'yan kwarya* claim a superior position to the *'yan garaya*. They note also the spatial propriety and the receptive rather than aggressive nature of their rites. The *'yan kwarya* engage in *bori* only within houses, for and with women. They do not seek ceremonies and occasions at which to act: they are sought. Only by invitation do they appear at a non-adept's house.

On the other hand, this *bori* is also an eminently public ritual, a communal rite, albeit within an excluding space. Thus, it is virtually on the basis of greater morality and probity that one group of practitioners of *bori* claimed the spiritual high ground, disputed of course by the other. According to the *'yan kwarya*, they have access to more spirits than the *'yan garaya*, and they can invoke the spirits more frequently and with more ease than the latter. The *'yan garaya*, on the other hand, believe their spirits to be 'stronger' than those of the *'yan kwarya*, and therefore more efficacious.

The claim to supernatural power made by a group which recognises its own lack of overt political power is a feature noted in relation to a number of possession cults, especially among those patronised by women in particularly male-dominant cultures, or by other politically marginal or marginalised categories of persons. Women do continue to play an important part in *bori* in its present form. Support and/or participation in *bori* is evident in all echelons of Hausa society, among differing classes and in relation to different backgrounds, although the more wealthy and educated are more likely to patronise than participate in *bori*, if they are involved at all. Other groups active in *bori* include, for example, sexually marginal men such as transvestites and homosexuals.

Bori does provide both authority and an at least temporary liberation from the total control of the dominant ideology and its representatives, while nevertheless fiercely binding its adherents to

---

8 In his Ibadan study, Cohen noted also that the majority of the female initiates and supporters of *bori* were not *karuwai*, but rather 'respectable' women (1969: 58).

its own strictures and requirements. Possession indeed permits the 'dispossessed' possessed to confront and to challenge ostensible authority figures, structures and mores, and to make demands through the mediation of the possessing spirits. The very forms of movement, the tactility and closeness, the transformed modesty and presence of *bori* adepts, creates a world removed from everyday Hausa society. Even so, the behaviour and challenges are themselves controlled within the latitude permitted the spirits and their mounts. While riding roughshod over prevailing mores in the external, non-*bori* world, the mounts, or horses, are themselves ridden. Yet even from within the confines of possession, challenges may be and are delivered, possessed to possessed, possessed to non-possessed, to and in both the *bori* and the external authority structures.

One must recognise not only the possibilities of authority and expertise, and thus forms of local power which may be created through the access to exclusive knowledge within *bori*, but also the possible historical and at times concurrent authority and obedience of participants in the subject group, who themselves act on the basis of differing identities and interests. A number of the *'yan kwarya* live within the environs of the palace (Cikin Gida), and their authority is said, by them, to be derived from one of the wives of the late Emir, whom they describe as a 'patroness' of their group. Equally important, a number of the *'yan kwarya* are themselves linked to the administration of the feudal system through senior and very powerful hereditary positions held by husbands, fathers or other relatives. The *'yan kwarya* are among the likely spiritual descendants of the adepts of the early *bori* cult, in which ritual and political power were inextricably linked, and in which the various actors and beneficiaries of the feudal system were equally active in its maintenance. In addition, it is the *'yan kwarya* who not only have access to but also have legitimate positioning within the palace, and thus have 'played the palace' long after the ostensible banning of *bori* rites.

For some of the *'yan kwarya*, the authority of *bori* may have replaced the lost trappings of power of the *ancien regime*; perhaps particularly, but not uniquely, for those whose nominal class position in terms of the feudal hierarchy was low, yet whose attributed rank, through kinship or conjugal affiliation, was high. Other considerations, other positionings, may be equally instrumental in an adept's continued involvement in *bori*. However, the very bases on which people participate may change, and the relevant identities of the actors also vary, as particular identities are forefronted depending on place, purpose and context.

With regard to the power exerted by and on the actors, we would note, following Foucault, that individuals 'are always in the position of simultaneously undergoing and exercising power. They are not only its inert and consenting target; they are also the elements of its articulation... Individuals are the vehicles of power, not its points of application' (1980: 98). The reflection of and association with temporal power, and the holders of that power, was of ongoing importance for *bori* adepts. The passivity, restraint and modesty proclaimed by the *'yan kwarya* is not apparent in either the structure of *bori* or its practice. With a hierarchy of offices even more detailed than that of the *'yan garaya*, and with a physical and historical location in the centre of the traditional ruling group, the *'yan kwarya* have manifested a continuous, personal and immediate interest in the trappings of local power.

Structuring Bori

Each of the *bori* groups maintains a set of titled officials, important for their symbolic significance rather than for their substantive input. Other than the title of Sarkin Bori (Chief of *Bori*), the titles do not necessarily denote a particular role or responsibility, and titles in *bori* reflect the extant traditional and increasingly, government, ruling hierarchies, as well as popular figures within them. Trends and changing power relationships in the temporal world are reflected in the hierarchy of *bori*. The significance of the titles themselves, the ways in which the titles are chosen or bestowed, and the possible linkage between the titled *bori* adepts and their namesakes are the operative considerations.

Titles may be given to *bori* adepts by the titleholders themselves (this is particularly appreciated), or may be adopted by an adept who comes from the titleholder's house (as relative or servant), or may be unilaterally adopted, if there is no objection. A title requested may also be refused, if the *bori* adept who holds the title is still living, even if s/he has moved from Katsina. If the temporal titleholder is promoted and given a higher position, his namesake could also take the new name. *Bori* adepts sometimes perform ceremonies at the time of or subsequent to receiving their titles, as do their namesakes, although this is not required and was already beginning to fall into disuse by the 1970s. At that time, among the 'yan kwarya, most of the senior titles in the traditional hierarchy: the emir's council, senior administrators and senior district heads, were or had at some time been taken by *bori* adepts. Twenty-four titles were named, although some titles were vacant. The *'yan garaya* had a much smaller titled group, of nine persons. The titles in the two groups overlapped, reflecting the most powerful positions particularly in traditional Hausa society, and the most supportive titleholders.

By the 1980s, the titles in both groups were changing, with the strengthening and greater local relevance of Katsina State, and international linkages. Thus, titles such as Gwamna (Governor) and Ambasada (Ambassador) had been incorporated into the structures of the *bori* groups. It must however, be noted that the value and significance of title-holding in the broader Hausa society is rapidly changing: particular historical titles maintain their significance, but a plethora of new titles from surrounding traditional states and empires are presently being imported and bestowed on citizens who have gained fame (and, usually, wealth) in other areas of endeavour. State and federal governments have demonstrated a dual policy towards the maintainance of feudal titles, trappings, obligations and perquisites, ostensibly shoring up the system through the demonstration of respect for and support of the title-holders, while concurrently increasing the number of positions and titles, thus reducing the relative importance of the former incumbents and increasing internecine conflict and competition among them.

For the *bori* adepts, there were and are also clear instrumental reasons for adopting particular titles: an openhanded wealthy temporal titleholder is a likely source of some modicum of support or assistance for his namesake. This is particularly the case if the titleholder supports *bori*, which is now openly treated by some of the elite as a part of traditional culture, a panoply of songs, dances and music to be enjoyed, recognised, and documented. There are other purposes for which the elite, and others, value and use *bori*, discussed further below. But in relation to overt reaction to and association with *bori*, the treatment of *bori* as 'cultural form' is now, at least among some of the more sophisticated of the elite, a legitimate response. In this way, *bori* may thus be taking on for some a function as indication of Hausa tradition and shared culture, which probably remains wholly anathema to many Hausa, but which presents the possibility of a revalidation of ethnic identity via historic and contemporary ritual representation.

Power continues to be contested, although less strongly, between the 'yan ƙwarya and the 'yan garaya. In terms of temporal power, despite the historic association of the 'yan ƙwarya with the palace, the 'yan garaya probably have an edge, not only through the group's closer association with a range of political authorities, but also through the influence of the individual men[9] and women who constituted the group. It appears that as a group, by the late 1980s, the 'yan ƙwarya were losing ground to the 'yan garaya in terms of the invitations and requests they were receiving. 'Entertainment' *bori*, and representation on that basis, remains the preserve of the 'yan garaya, who can also perform 'real' *bori*. On the other hand, the perceived spiritual associations and therefore strength of individual *bori* adepts among the 'yan ƙwarya remains, and these have been, possibly increasingly, sought out.

Renewed Authority: Bori in Contemporary Context

By the end of the 1980s, *bori* had taken on, for some, a new look, more professionalised and better suited to the changing needs and pressures of the times. With increasing fundamentalism in Katsina and in Nigeria in general, it is said that there is less tolerance for *bori per se*. On the other hand, the very pressures of contemporary life demand individual or group response, and *bori* remains a significant route to the release or redirection of such pressures. While *bori* has particular significance and provenance for its adepts, it also remains important, as it always has, in the broader community.

Bori, and the effects and benefits of *bori*, have always been an area fraught with ambiguities. The situating of *bori* within Hausa society has changed dramatically over time in terms of its political positioning, and the responses of the populace to *bori* have also been and remain diverse, as noted above. There can be few who do not accept the existence of spirits, and the spirits, whether called *bori*, *iskoki*, or *aljannu* (from genies, or *jinn*), are

---

9 The patron and prime mover of the 'yan garaya is a man well-known, or perhaps, notorious, in Katsina. His actions are often in conflict with the custom or indeed law of the area, but with his contingent of followers, he commands too much support to be treated high-handedly by the authorities.

generally perceived of as dangerous beings, which must be propitiated.[10] Illnesses may be brought by the spirits, as may be other misfortunes.

Bori has never disappeared, and may now be gaining renewed recognition. To some extent, *bori* is being 'rehabilitated' because of and through its remedial effects. *Bori* is recognised as traditional medicine (*maganin galgajia*). The recognised purveyors and exponents of traditional medicine are not all *bori* adepts, and not all *bori* adepts will be eligible for certification as practitioners of traditional medicine, with the renewed legitimacy this confers. This latter-day overt recognition is consistent with the broad revaluation and enhanced profile of traditional medical expertise reflected in, e.g., the re-examination of traditional pharmacopiae taking place throughout Nigeria and elsewhere in Africa, and given support by some senior medical personnel. It is also consistent in terms of the reinforcement of association between the local authority structure and the *bori* functionaries, this time even in writing via certification.[11] On the other hand, the acknowledgement of the value of these alternative rites is somewhat surprising in view of the antipathy to *bori* by some Muslim scholars, functionaries and preachers. It may be that the resort to and association with *bori* is sometimes more implicit than explicit in the recognition of a practitioner's skill and success.

As a route to healing, *bori* has always had a significant clientele. While this may have diminished through, for example, access to and use of Western drugs, medicines and medical facilities, the possible resort to *bori* has remained. Indeed, at present, hospitals and clinics are themselves far more problematic than was the case a few years ago. With Structural Adjustment, funding has been cut for health and medicine, as for other social services. Even in the past, some *bori* clientele would first seek treatment in the hospital, and then resort to *bori* when the hospital treatment failed to yield success. At present, hospital facilities, equipment and services are

---

10 Perhaps the most evocative discription and discussion of the *bori* spirits is that of A.J.N. Tremearne, writing in 1914. Using the medical analogy, he describes bori performances as 'comparable to innoculation', rendering the adepts safe from the otherwise evil and dangerous effects of the 'demons' (1914: 20). The very title of the book combines for him consecration, devotion and possible destruction. He notes that 'to ban a spirit is to bind it, to prevent it from doing harm' (ibid.: 429).

11 The certificates are said to be signed by the Emir, the District Head of Katsina, and one of the hospital doctors.

poor, where available at all. Drugs must be bought, and in fact the quality of the drugs themselves is often suspect, through the effects of dumping, bootlegging and fraud. The cost of treatment through the supplication and propitiation of *bori* spirits has never been cheap; *bori* is not a low-cost alternative to Western medicine, but may now be seen as providing, at the very least, a more trustworthy route to cure than the Western equivalent.

Propitiation and the active seeking of assistance from the spirits are used for more than illness. Any concerns or crises may be ameliorated through *bori*, and in periods of stress or pressure, many persons seek such help. Students seek assistance for help in exams; workers hope for better jobs, more pay, avoidance of transfer (in government positions), or resolution in their favour of workplace conflict. A wide range of personal and structural tensions are believed to be subject to the influence and mediation of *bori*. Thus, people turn to *bori* to ward off or discover the causes of misfortune, to act against an enemy or threat, to ensure success in some enterprise, or for other reasons. Some of the *'yan kwarya*, known for their healing and spiritual power, and thus for their successful treatments, are heavily patronised. Lack of money among the masses, with the predations caused by structural adjustment, has reduced casual expenditure on *bori*. However, the treatment of illness and the possibility of gaining a supernatural edge on employers, co-wives, and other significant persons in positions of power or authority, are not luxuries, but rather valid and justifiable expenditure in defence of optimal or at least improved maintenance of daily life.

However, it is important to note that for these very purposes people may also turn to Islam and the Koranic teachers, or malams. Using different methods, the malams also provide supernatural aid, especially through the use of amulets, or 'medicine' made by washing verses of the Koran from the Koranic board. Not all malams traffic in charms and counter-charms, but many do (see also McIntyre, in this volume). The decision to resort to a malam or a *bori* adept has perhaps less to do with the supplicant's religious convictions, than with the reported efficacy of the individual religious practitioner's product. Thus, both *bori* and Islam offer alternative or additional means by which the individual can cope with or influence an otherwise neutral or hostile environment. Here again, Islam and *bori*, through their respective functionaries, continue to compete with each other for the support of an often canny Katsina clientele.

Conclusion

In his excellent work concerning the Hausa community in Ibadan (*Custom and Politics in Urban Africa*, 1969), and in the more theoretical *Two-Dimensional Man* (1974), Cohen demonstrates how a group may reconstitute itself on different bases, how new identities are forefronted to maintain cohesion, and how this new focus can become a basis for mobilisation and transformation of the community. In his analysis of the Hausa community of Sabo, he argues cogently that the group reestablished its solidarity through its recognition of and adherence to a particular form of Islam, as the reference to ethnic solidarity became increasingly less viable.

The religious context may of course also permit or encourage the reflection of alternative positions or interests within the community. The religious arena has been described, correctly, as constituting an ideological space, with aesthetics, morality, and symbolic referents and codes of action, in which dominant and subaltern groups may engage in 'cultural negotiation'.[12]

In this chapter, I have focused on the changing historical and contextual significance of one religious institution, that of *bori*. Previously expressing the power and authority of the polity and its affirming link with earth and nature, the former religion and now 'spirit-possession cult' of *bori* has been transformed over the course of centuries, while its ties with its past are in certain respects maintained, and new referents are created. The purposes and bases of *bori*, and the political positionings of its adherents have in some respects changed, while yet retaining symbolic linkage with former structures and historic strength.

Bori is taking on new significance at present both in relation to its perceived efficacy, and to its importance as performance, as reflection and exemplification of traditional Hausa culture. Islam in Katsina has at the same time been fractured into a series of factions and sects, with an expanding number of Friday mosques and increasing division and disagreement among clerics and laity. Most, if not all, *bori* adherents in Katsina are Muslims: *bori* does not deny Islam, and indeed it has been noted that *bori* has incorporated Muslim as well as Western and other elements into its pantheon and into its rites. It is likely that in this post-modern

---

12 C. Coulon, 'Les itinéraires politiques de l'Islam au Nord Nigeria', in *Les Mediations Religieuses en Afrique noire*, Jean-François Bayart (ed.). Paris, 1991. Paraphrased in J. Ibrahim 1991: 128.

world of difference and multiple positionings, perceptions and truth claims, *bori* will continue to survive, in modified forms and with multiple purposes for its adherents, as it has done for centuries.

References

Barkow, J.H. 1973. 'Muslims and Maguzawa in North Central State, Nigeria: An Ethnographic Comparison', *The Canadian Journal of African Studies* vol. VII, no. 1: 59–76.

Barth, H. 1857–58. *Travels of Discoveries in North and Central Africa*, 5 vols. London: Longman, Brown, Green, Longmans & Roberts.

Cohen, A. 1969. *Custom and Politics in Urban Africa*. London: Routledge & Kegan Paul Ltd.

Cohen, A. 1974. *Two-Dimensional Man*. Berkeley and Los Angeles: University of California Press.

Cohen, A. 1993. *Masquerade Politics: Explorations in the Structure of Urban Cultural Movements*. Berkeley and Los Angeles: University of California Press.

Foucault, M. 1980. 'Two Lectures' in *Power/Knowledge: Selected Interviews and Other Writings 1972–1977*, C. Gordon (ed.). New York: Pantheon Books.

Hiskett, M. 1960. 'Kitab al-Farq: A Work on the Habe Kingdoms Attributed to Uthman Dan Fodio', *Bulletin of the S.O.A.S.*, University of London, vol. XXIII, Part 3: 558–79.

Hogben, S.J. and A.H.M. Kirk-Greene. 1966. *The Emirates of Northern Nigeria*. London: Oxford University Press.

Ibrahim, Jibrin. 1991, 'Religion and Political Turbulence in Nigeria', *The Journal of Modern African Studies* 29 (1): 115–36.

Nicolas, G. 1975. *Dynamique Sociale et Appréhension du Monde au Sein d'une Société Hausa*. Paris: Institut d'Ethnologie, Muséum National d'Histoire Naturelle.

Onwuejeogwu, M. 1969. 'The Cult of Bori Spirits Among the Hausa' in *Man in Africa*, Mary Douglas and Phyllis M. Kaberry (eds). London: Tavistock Publications.

Palmer, H.R. 1928. *Sudanese Memoirs*, 3 vols. Lagos: Government Printer.

Smith, Abdullahi. 1971. 'The Early States of the Central Sudan' in *History of West Africa*, vol. 1, J.F. Ade Ajaye and M. Crowder, London: Longman Group Ltd.

Smith, Mary F. 1954. *Baba of Karo: A Woman of the Muslim Hausa*. London: Faber and Faber Ltd.

Tremearne, A.J.N. 1914. *The Ban of the Bori: Demons and Demon-Dancing in West and North Africa*. Reprinted by Frank Cass & Co., Ltd., 1968.

Usman, Y.B. 1981. *The Transformation of Katsina: 1400–1883*. Zaria: Ahmadu Bello University Press Ltd.

CHAPTER 13

Cultural Performance and Economic-Political Goals:
an Ethnographic Study of Blacksmiths in Kano (Northern Nigeria)

Philip J. Jaggar *

Introduction

This chapter explores the dynamic relationship between socio-cultural formations and the articulation of exclusive group identity within a traditional community of specialist blacksmiths in

---

* I am grateful to numerous individuals and institutions who have contributed to this chapter: to all my friends in Kano City and Tamburawa, especially the blacksmiths, for the kindness and informed co-operation they afforded me at all times, and to Abner Cohen, my thesis supervisor at the School of Oriental and African Studies (SOAS), University of London. Lionel Caplan, Humphrey Fisher, Judy Sterner and other colleagues at SOAS, as well as James Vaughan, also offered constructive comments on previous drafts, all which have materially benefited the final product. A pre-final version was presented at the Institut für Historische Ethnologie, Johann Wolfgang Goethe-Universität, Frankfurt am Main, Germany, January 12, 1994 (supported by a grant from Johann Wolfgang Goethe-Universität), and I am grateful to those who attended for thoughtful suggestions and stimulating discussion. The analysis developed here does not necessarily represent the views of any of the above individuals. I would also like to thank Catherine Brown and Doreen W. Jaggar who patiently helped me with the task of typing up initial drafts of the fieldnotes which provide the empirical baseline for this study. The original fieldwork (1970–71) was made possible by funding from SOAS and the Central Research Fund, University of London. Finally, I am profoundly indebted to my late father, David Holdsworth Jaggar (1922–92) – a skilled and much-respected metallurgist himself – for his knowledgeable concern and selfless support throughout all stages of my postgraduate research.

developed in studies by Cohen (1969, 1974, 1981, 1993). The unifying focus of these studies centres on the dialectic between Tamburawa, a Muslim Hausa town about ten miles south of Kano City, northern Nigeria, using the conceptual and analytical model culturally-distinct symbolic forms/activities and their economic and political functions within society, an instrumental relationship which Cohen considered to be a key problem for social anthropology. I will profile the main strategies deriving from traditional culture – relating to marriage, kinship, and ritual – employed by the Kano blacksmiths as a means of defining and legitimating their monopolistic, occupation-based sub-culture, demonstrating that these distinctive cultural elements cater for a range of collective human needs.

Despite the substantial corpus of ethnographic data on the socio-economic (and historical) aspects of pre-industrial craft specialisms in Hausaland (see Jaggar 1994 and references therein), and with the marginal exception of Echard (1965, see below), no comparable in-depth study is available of the unifying symbolic forms that express and govern interpersonal relations within any of these ancient occupations. In the existing literature on the cultural aspects of blacksmithing amongst the Hausa and other Chadic-speaking groups in northern Nigeria, e.g., Pilaszewicz (1991 and references therein), Sterner (1993), Sterner & David (1991), there is little or no hard information on the kinds of kinship-based organisational features and (marriage-linked) collective rituals detailed in this chapter. Echard's (1965, 1983) important papers are a rich source of ethnographic data on an elaborate array of magico-religious phenomena among the smelter-smiths of the ethnic Hausa (non-Muslim) Asna Masafa community in the Ader region of the neighbouring Niger Republic, but because her descriptions focus mainly on ritual dramas surrounding the smelting sequence, they contain no (quantified) documentation on comparable cultural forms, structural arrangements and their manipulation. The present chapter thus helps to fill a conspicuous gap in our ethnographic knowledge of the Hausa socio-cultural sub-system.

The description and analysis derive from data collected in the field in 1970–71 and relate quite specifically to conditions prevailing at that time. The overall research focus centred on the causal factors which determined the demand-led expansion – during the colonial and post-colonial periods – of the traditional craft of blacksmithing in Kano City (Jaggar 1973a, 1994). The fieldwork techniques included a collection of individual case histories through informal discussion, comparative-historical research, and a statistical-social survey of all adult blacksmiths and associated metalworkers, in addition to the (sometimes participant) observation of the ceremonials elucidated below. I subsequently extended the scope of the study to include the well-known cluster of Tamburawa blacksmiths and discovered that many of the archaic craft customs which had disappeared in Kano City continued to thrive in the more rural setting. Owing to a gradual erosion of the socio-symbolic phenomena associated with the traditional craft under urban conditions, the ritualisation of ironworking has diminished amongst the City craftsmen, but still persists in well-defined forms in outlying rural Hausa communities like Tamburawa.

Tamburawa Blacksmiths: Special Features of Communal Identity

Cohen (1969: 201–14, 1974: 69ff.) has observed that the exclusive identity of a group can be informally articulated by various cultural formations and activities, with different groups combining idioms in different proportions, and the major diagnostic mechanisms which the Tamburawa smiths use to confront the basic organisational problem of maintaining their monopoly over craft production and externalising their distinctiveness include:

1. Common residence and paternally driven occupational membership.
2. Special collective performances and public dramas, especially those celebrating the strongly ritualised first marriage of a blacksmith's son.
3. Unique markings.

We shall see that these salient organisational patterns and modes of symbolic behaviour are articulated to fulfil a number of interrelated functions for the smiths, including economic-political, expressive, integrative, and recreational, and the paradigmatic features of following description – with the exception of the distinctive facial markings which, to my knowledge, are unique to the Tamburawa smiths (see below) – generalise to smithing communities throughout Hausaland, with regional groups exhibiting some variability in detail.

Common Residence and Patrilineally-framed Craft Membership

A Hausa blacksmith (*maƙerin baƙi/babbaƙu*, lit: forger of black [iron]) can be operationally defined as a man who manufactures crucial specialist products in iron (*baƙin ƙarfe*, lit: black metal), e.g., farm implements, domestic utensils, weapons etc., and who uses in the productive process the following core artefacts and raw materials of metalworking: fire, charcoal, an open hearth, a rooted iron anvil, tongs, skin bellows, and a variety of striking devices.[1]

In 1971 there were thirty-two tax-paying (adult) blacksmiths actively working in Tamburawa, spread across seven different agnatic descent groups, and representing about four percent of the total workforce of 805 tax-paying males in Tamburawa, the majority of whom were farmers (1970/71 Tamburawa Tax Register). Males become liable to pay tax (*haraji*) on craft earnings in their late teens, by which time young smiths will have broken away from their father's (or senior relative's) anvil (*uwar maƙera*, lit: 'mother of the forge'),[2] and become their own viable productive units, planning and working independently. Blacksmithing represents the most important and potentially high-earning traditional craft industry in Tamburawa – other (non-agricultural) craftsmen include butchers, potters and tailors, and craft specialisms such as cloth dyeing, weaving and tanning have all declined or disappeared.

The blacksmiths themselves are most obviously distinguished from other groups by their concentrated residence – a discrete cluster of fifteen compounds, the largest of which embraces an extended grouping composed of the elementary families of several paternally-related craftsmen – two full-brothers, one half-brother, a cousin and nephew to the two full-brothers, plus six wives and ten children, with each individual family occupying its own partitioned section. They live and work in close spatial proximity to each other, occupying the Makeri ('Blacksmith') sub-section of Zango ward (population 2,168) of the town (total population

---

1 All (non-proper) Hausa words are *italicised*, 'hooked' (lower/upper case) ɓ/Ɓ, ɗ/Ɗ, ƙ/Ƙ are glottalised consonants, ' represents a glottal stop, and *c* = English 'ch'.

2 Notice the genderisation and personification of the anvil in Hausa, encapsulating its centrality – see Herbert (1993: 98ff.) for an interesting comparative discussion of the attribution of humanness and gender to ironworking artefacts.

4,056),[3] conveniently located near the market-place where they dispose of some of their products for local consumption (Tamburawa has a well-provisioned and busy alternate-day market). This residential propinquity serves to facilitate internal communication and economic co-operation within the craft and intensifies informal group interaction in the context of the daily routine and work situation, and fellow smiths will sometimes pool their resources, conduct personal transactions for each other and check on supply and demand conditions in the large Central Market of Kano City (as well as the Rimi and Sabon Gari markets), where they have a regular and lucrative year-round outlet for their export products.[4] This is especially the case with older smiths who are less able to endure the rigours of travel (by push-bike, bus, or donkey), and so become increasingly dependent upon younger relatives to dispose of their craft output in Kano City and also purchase important materials for them, e.g., scrap industrial steel, wooden handles etc. The craft is basically a domestic industry, practised by domestic (man plus boy) labour-units in or near the home (there are twenty separate forges with one or more anvil and labour-unit), each unit manufacturing largely on its own account, and it remains within the (near) monopolistic control of a few families. The smiths are thus members of a highly localised face-to-face community which is held together by a framework of interlocking social and economic relationships. The community thus functions as an informal interest group, constantly exchanging business information and sharing common economic goals.

Institutionalised endogamy, whereby men neither give women to other groups in marriage nor take women from them, is not exploited as a major articulating principle of corporate identity amongst the Tamburawa smiths, who freely inter-marry with other groups (polygamy is common and homogamy is the norm). Out of a total of forty-four marriages involving smiths and still holding

---

[3] At the time of fieldwork, the population of the entire Tamburawa Yamma administrative are a (including outlying locations/wards) was 11,010 (1970/71 Tamburawa Tax Register). Tamburawa is so named because it houses the royal drums of the Emir of Kano (*tambura*, sing. *tambari*).

[4] See Jaggar (1994: Ch. 6) for a detailed account of the extensive inter-community contractual links between the 'client' (*yaro*) Tamburawa smiths and their 'patron' (*maigida*) metalware dealers in the Central Market area of Kano City. Large orders from the Kano City ironware merchants are regularly farmed out amongst a group of Tamburawa smiths.

in the wet season of 1971, only eight were with Tamburawa smith women, and none involved partners of the same descent group – in fact more unions (ten) were with women whose fathers were primarily farmers. Elsewhere in Hausaland, M.G. Smith (1959: 249) writes about a general 'tendency towards class-endogamous marriage' between traditional Hausa occupational groups, and also refers to 'traditional marriage alliances' between Koranic teachers and blacksmiths, though I found no evidence of this in the Kano area. Mary Smith (1954: 102) reports a similar pattern of 'class-endogamous' marriage between smiths and farmers in the Zaria area (southwest of Kano), and Echard (1965: 357) notes that marriages between blacksmiths and non-blacksmiths amongst the Asna Masafa of Niger 'are not rare' (despite this, Echard (p. 367) chooses to talk of a 'caste forgeronne').

Conversely, there is no norm which states that being the female relative of a blacksmith is in any sense a prohibition to marriage with non-smith men – of the twenty-eight marriages I recorded involving smith women in Tamburawa, only six were with blacksmiths. These low ratios of intra-group marriage are also repeated in Kano City itself, where women from smithing and other occupational categories are free to move in either direction (there are, however, cases of Kano City and Tamburawa smiths solidifying their economic interdependence through marriage ties). Shea (1983: 109–11) describes comparable alliances within and between different craft groups in rural Kano. In general, therefore, Kano Hausa smiths are well-respected, fully integrated, and often prosperous, members of the community who practise their ancient craft specialism, provide indispensable services in the traditional subsistence economy, and are valued for their expertise and mastery of valuable skills. They have distinctive magico-religious activities (see below), and are ranked neither above nor below the group of farmers into which they regularly marry.

Although in no way sufficiently endogamous to qualify as a casted occupational group,[5] over the generations there has been a degree of intermarriage between the relatively small agnatic descent groups – many are linked by overlapping relationships based on blood and/or marriage, and these ties act to consolidate the network of economic relationships.

---

5 Herbert (1993: 27) misconstrues the analysis, therefore, when she writes that in an earlier paper (Jaggar 1973a: 21–3), I had claimed that (Kano City) blacksmiths 'lean toward ... *strictly endogamous* occupational groups' (my emphasis).

Cohen (1969: 202–3) has noted that, in the absence of strict, formalised in-group endogamy, i.e., the relatively loose situation encountered amongst the Kano Hausa smiths, a descent-based mechanism can act as a compensatory vehicle for preserving and articulating corporate identity, and membership of the smiths' group is also defined via strong adherence to a principle of a patrilineally transmitted occupation.[6] This practice is also motivated by economic-political factors. In a self-sufficient and relatively poor community which lacks formal, institutionalised (guild-like) associations, kinship affiliation – the elemental mechanism of social organisation – is mobilised to ensure that essential specialist roles are filled over time (see also Vaughan 1970: 89ff., MacEachern 1990, and Sterner & David 1991: 361ff.). Thus, of the thirty-two enumerated smiths in Tamburawa, twenty-eight had inherited the craft directly through their smith fathers, two matrilineally, and of the remaining two, one shares a non-smith mother with two smith half-brothers (his father is a farmer), and the other is the son of the non-smith husband of a smith's younger sister; both these craftsmen had been taken on as young apprentices (a substantial repertoire of expertise is required to master the complicated technology of traditional metalworking). However, although craft membership is in theory fluid and flexible, and there is no stated norm as such which reserves the knowledge and practise of the traditional craft for smithing families, this is essentially the situation in reality. Conversely, although not every son is obliged to step into his father's shoes, older smiths could recall only about ten men in living memory who had decided to permanently abandon the family occupation and leave Tamburawa to take up unrelated occupations – another indication that on the ground there is strong hereditary attachment to the profession.

Apart from solving the problem of supplying a critical resource from generation to generation in a predominantly agricultural society (the hoe is the most important utilitarian tool), it is important to bear in mind that craft attachment is also driven by economic and political self-interest. Compared with many occupations, both traditional and modern, smithing can be a potentially lucrative and stable profession for an energetic and opportunistic craftsman. In 1971, for example, some of the more

---

6 See also Madauci et al. (1968 [1982]: 59). Tambo (1976: 13) reports that smithing amongst the Angas and Birom of the Jos Plateau area is also basically hereditary.

industrious Tamburawa smiths were earning as much as N20/- or N£1 (Nigerian shillings/pounds) per day clear profit from wet season craft production, i.e., N£7 per week, computed as follows: working from 8 a.m. to 6 p.m., a smith can produce ten large (ribbed) hoes (*garma*) which sell at 4/- each, making 40/- in total sales, less about 20/- production costs (scrap, charcoal and wooden handles). It is instructive to compare these relatively high earnings with the daily (1971) rate for hired farm-labourers (*'yan kwadago*) of 5/- (= 3/- for work between 8 a.m. and 2 p.m., plus 2/- for the afternoon 3 p.m. to 6 p.m. session). Hill (1972: 117) estimated average £N6-10 *monthly* earnings for farm labourers in the village of Batagarawa (six miles south of Katsina City) in the late 1960s (a number of Tamburawa smiths employ *'yan kwadago* labourers during the wet season, when craft manufacturing is at its peak), and Lubeck's (1986: 173–4) wage data for factory employment in Kano City, where the cost of living is generally higher than in rural areas, also places the potentially high (daily) earnings of the Tamburawa smiths in perspective: he notes that the minimum factory wage for an eight-hour day in 1972/73 was between N8/9d and N9/- shillings, and documents the case of man earning N6/- a day making bricks, and a maximum N12/- a day as an apprentice mason.

With this in mind, it is easy to see how assigning responsibility for iron-working to a few descent groups is an obvious and effective means of maintaining a near monopoly on a relatively significant source of income, thereby satisfying common corporate interests. This strategy is a prototypical instance, therefore, of Cohen's (1969, 1974, 1981, 1993) major insight – an informal group manipulating a (kin-framed) cultural form to achieve economic-political goals. Smiths will also rationalise their choice of profession with comments like 'apart from smithing what else can we do?', 'this is what God has ordained for me', 'if I leave, who will help my father when he grows old, and who will take over when he dies?' etc. Many also feel a strong moral obligation to continue catering for their regular customers.

Marriage and Cultural Performance

A number of anthropologists, especially Gluckman (1942), Turner (1957, 1974, 1983), as well as Cohen himself, have emphasised the sociological significance of exploring the political nature of ritual norms and cultural performances, and amongst the Tamburawa blacksmiths, such ceremonials can be viewed as an vehicle for enhancing the defining boundaries of the group within an extensive network of intersecting social relationships. Cohen (1993: ix) neatly summarises the instrumental link-up between political action and cultural expressions when he defines 'masquerade politics' as 'politics articulated in terms of non-political cultural forms such as religion, kinship, the arts' (see also Fisher, in this volume).

In Hausa culture, a young man's first marriage is the most important rite of passage in his life. Most youths get married in their early twenties (girls in their early teens), marriage confers adulthood, and blacksmiths publicly celebrate this key change in status in their own dramatic communal way, manipulating a number of symbolic techniques.[7] They also exploit the ceremonial to manufacture important work-tools.

The smiths' marriages always take place at the end of the hot period of the dry season (*bazara*) or at the beginning of the wet season (*damina*), typically in April/May through September – there were four such (first) marriages during the 1971 wet season. This is the time of year when the smith is at his busiest, forging essential agricultural implements in readiness for the farming season (farming is done entirely with hoes), and so he is best able to meet the necessary marriage expenses. Those smiths who have spent some of the dry season months working elsewhere will have returned home to smith, farm, and participate in any seasonal rituals.[8] In the 1970/71 dry season (roughly October/November through March), for example, twelve Tamburawa smiths (the majority in

---

[7] In addition to the all-important rite of passage of first marriage, the special naming-day (*ran suna*) and circumcision (*kaciya*) ceremonies for first-born sons are sometimes accompanied by similar rituals amongst blacksmiths, though instances of this are nowadays relatively rare. A child is given his/her Muslim name on the seventh day after birth. Circumcision is obligatory for all Muslim males, and most Hausa boys are circumcised around the age of seven.

[8] For those smiths who elect to spend the dry-season at home, it is a period of increased specialisation, and much of the surplus production is for urban consumption. Craft products typically manufactured during the dry-season include matchets, knives, tweezers, sickles, axes, small bells, harvesting and cutting tools, and some smiths cast aluminium handles for knives and swords, employing a technique comparable to the *ciré-perdue* use of hardened clay and beeswax (these weapons are extremely popular with nomadic Fulani in the area). Even in the relatively slack dry-season months, therefore, there are still considerable opportunities for Tamburawa smiths to acquire a reasonable income through craft production – perhaps N£5 per week net profit – which is geared largely to metropolitan needs (see Jaggar 1994: Ch. 6, esp. 82ff.).

their twenties or thirties) were working away from home (*cin rani* 'eating the dry season'). Most of these men were lodging together and trading animals (sheep and goats), and occasionally metalware, in Kaduna, a large town about 140 miles south-west of Tamburawa. Many of these dry season migrants returned to Tamburawa in the wet season of 1971.

On the evening before the legal marriage ceremony (*ɗaurin aure*) is performed, and two days before the wedding party (*bikin aure*) itself, a group of drummers and associated praise-singers assemble in the blacksmiths' quarters, where they stay at the expense of the groom's father, or bride's blacksmith father/guardian in the case of a non-smith groom. These six or so professional musicians are all from Kura, a large town thirteen miles south of Tamburawa, and they perform mainly for the smiths of the Kura/Tamburawa area (occasionally also for silver and goldsmiths), as did their fathers before them. Essentially they are the blacksmiths' special drummers who play the *dundufa* drums for them (sometimes for tanners and dyers), and no performance is complete without these musicians. These highly expressive communal dramas thus have an important social dimension – as Cohen (1993: 7) notes in the context of an analysis of the Notting Hill Carnival, aesthetic forms like dance and music are also 'techniques that develop and maintain the cultural forms of social relationships' (see also Spencer in this volume).

A party may be arranged to celebrate the first marriage of a smith's son or daughter, though the smiths claim that the father/guardian is under less obligation to arrange a wedding ceremonial for a daughter, attributing this to the fact that she will never be a productive unit and hence as much of an economic asset as a man. However, all four daughter marriages in the wet seasons of 1970 and 1971 (to non-smithing grooms) were celebrated in traditional fashion, an indication of the enduring importance of these rituals. Occasionally, a groom with a more distant craft association is accorded the honour of a ceremonial. At one such celebration in 1971, the groom was the non-smithing son of the elder sister of an active blacksmith who arranged and paid for the celebrations himself, and another performance was organised for a young farmer/fisherman whose maternal uncle and grandfather were smiths.

Great importance is attached to providing the son of a blacksmith with a true 'send-off' on the occasion of his first marriage, and the father or senior relative is expected to make sure that all the necessary arrangements are made, especially the invitation of the drummers, and he thereby gains in prestige himself. The overall cost can be quite substantial, however, and in 1970/71, the father could face a total bill of as much as £N30 – equivalent to several weeks' average income (profit) from craft activity. It is a poor and/or miserly smith indeed who fails in this duty without adequate reason, and I heard of only one instance of this happening in living memory in Tamburawa. External factors can also interfere with these ritual arrangements. In the late 1950s, for instance, the Emir of Kano imposed a levy of 30/- per performance on praise-singers and drummers in Kano Emirate, and this decision had a direct impact on the *dundufa* players who were unable and/or unwilling to pay what they considered to be an unfair fee; and the devastating cholera epidemic of 1971 caused the tragic death of several Tamburawa smiths and forced the cancellation of some wedding celebrations.

The drums themselves do not start up until the morning after the arrival of the musicians, in a convenient open space in the smiths' quarter, and a little before the marriage itself is solemnised at the house of the local *imam* or judge. It is mainly the women and children of the smiths who join in the dancing at this stage, the women being allowed out of purdah for such occasions (adult women are normally in full Muslim seclusion during daylight hours). Female friends and/or relatives from other families in the neighbourhood/town also attend the festivities as onlookers or performers. The real entertainment does not begin until the following day, however, when the existence of the smiths as a distinctive occupational group receives symbolic public expression. The performance always takes place in a convenient space near the groom's (father's) house, even if he is not of a smithing family and the bride is, and smiths explain this by saying that the craft then 'follows her to her new home' and honours the groom and his family (Hausa marriage is virilocal, and often patrilocal if it is the groom's first marriage).

An interesting dimension to the performance is the forging of several key work tools (see below). The necessary props for this task include an anvil, bellows, tongs, hammers, charcoal and large pieces of iron,[9] and provision of these items is a collective effort, though the smith groom's father/guardian contributes the most

---

9 See Jaggar (1973b) for a description of the technology and vocabulary of smithing.

(he normally donates some industrial scrap and charcoal). The principal actors in this public drama are younger smiths, together with the drummers and praise-singers, in addition to some of the senior smiths, including the father of the groom and/or bride, though usually as spectators only. One senior smith takes an active part in all wedding ceremonials, however, a member of the descent group in which official craft titles were formerly invested, and by virtue of his title (Madakin Kira) he directs the smiths' activities. It is he who holds the tongs on the anvil, decides when the iron is to be withdrawn from the fire, how it is to be tempered, and he also prevents spectators from encroaching on the dance area by threatening them with red hot pieces of iron. The groom himself takes virtually no part in the activities, but simply appears for a short while in the later stages, accompanied by a few close friends. He remains seated with head and shoulders covered with a shawl, is greeted as 'emir, king' (*sarki*) by the musicians, and looks generally embarrassed as people approach and give him small gifts of money to 'help him in his new life'. The bride will only make an appearance if she is of a smithing family, but there is no contact between the two since their initial relationship is constrained by feelings of modesty/shame (*kunya*). Otherwise, cultural expectations forbid her from attending.

Some of the revellers are craftsmen from surrounding towns and villages like Kura, Kumbotso and Kofa – smithing communities which have strong relationships of friendship and goodwill (*zumunci*) with the Tamburawa smiths, based upon common occupation and sometimes consolidated by marriage. The guests also often include several Tamburawa-born blacksmiths who have migrated permanently to other areas within Kano State to set up anvils and ply their craft in communities without resident smiths. The smiths attach great importance to maintaining good inter-community relations, and these are supported by strong moral imperatives. During the 1971 wet season, an argument flared up between young Tamburawa and Kura smiths attending a wedding ceremonial in Goron Dutse, a small hamlet close to Tamburawa, as a result of which the Kura smiths at first refused to invite their fellow craftsmen to a similar performance later on, and it was only after determined intervention from the senior smiths in both communities that the conflict was curtailed, good relations were restored and the celebrations went ahead as planned. These powerful ceremonial performances thus fulfil an important integrative function, providing a public forum for social interaction and cultural cohesion, where common craft values and traditional sentiments are regularly reaffirmed. In this way, the exclusiveness of the blacksmiths is articulated via cultural performances that are based on primary ethical imperatives.

As soon as the fire is glowing and the drumming has started, two large bars of iron are placed in the fire, and when one of the pieces is red hot it is withdrawn and beaten on the anvil by two smiths in turn. This change in activity is accompanied by a simultaneous change in the drumming rhythm (*take*). The drums usually consist of a large *dundufa*, a smaller ('daughter') *'yar dundufa*, plus a *kuntuku* drum hung around the neck, and the main function of the drums is to spell out the special praise-songs (*kirari*) and rhythms. The two young smiths hammer away to the beat of the drums and if they appear to be flagging are immediately harangued by the singers. Between the smiths and drummers and praise-singers there is constant banter and fun-poking, the musicians urging the smiths on to greater efforts, and the smiths complaining that the correct drum-beat is not being maintained. When the two youths have completed this initial hammering (*dukan karfe* 'beating the metal'), they drop their hammers and dance within the circle formed by the onlookers, and up to the musicians, whereupon another pair takes their place until as many as ten pairs have all had their turn and the piece of metal has taken on a recognisable shape.

The members of the audience in the meantime present the young revellers with small gifts of money which they press onto the sweating brow of the kneeling dancer. They also give money to the praise-singers, especially their 'master of ceremonies' who makes most of the announcements and states the names of the donors. Most of the praise-songs are for the benefit of the smiths (see also Pilaszewicz 1991: 255–9 and references therein). The singers mention them by name and pedigree, emphasising their virtues and generosity and extolling their ancestors. All the money collected remains with the musicians.

The most dramatic and entertaining part of the ritual occurs when one of the smiths begins to play with the pieces of red-hot incandescent iron (*wasan/cin wuta* 'playing with/eating fire'), drawing them without any observable damage over various parts of his body which he has smeared with special protective medicine (*maganin wuta* 'medicine against fire'). The atmosphere of the occasion – the constant frenzied drumming, dancing, fire-games and the smell of singed flesh – now has something emotive, frantic and at times dangerous about it. Smiths have only to make one slip while handling the irons and they can be burned, but I have witnessed smiths drawing irons across their open eyes without apparently damaging them in any way. The whole ceremonial is emotive and frenzied, with each young smith deriving pleasure from joint participation in a highly charged and agitated atmosphere. In this way – like solidarity rituals amongst the Ndembu (Turner 1957) – the consciousness of common identity and collective exclusiveness is heightened. Conversely, the margins defining the smiths as a distinctive group are reinforced in a highly visible public arena via society's perception and understanding of their exclusive ceremonials and associative functions.

These rite of passage celebrations also have an important pragmatic component. The end-product of the day's exertions usually consists of several large (40–45 cm.) rolled hammers (*masaba, mundu*), and occasionally a new anvil, and these implements are presented to the newly-wed young smith. Although cultural performances are often analysed as essentially non-rational, non-utilitarian symbolic activities, it is recognised by the smiths themselves that these special symbolic activities also have an important material pay-off, since the manufacture of such large items is impossible without collective effort and technical co-operation. If the bride (but not the groom) is of blacksmith descent, any tools forged at the ceremonials will be shared amongst her younger blacksmithing kin, e.g., a cousin who may act as her guardian (*wali*) and represent her at the marriage ceremony (she does not attend). In such cases too, any blacksmith (from Tamburawa or outside) is in fact free to use the collective workforce and bring along to the ceremonial such heavy work as may necessitate a co-operative effort. In June 1971, for example, a group of smiths from a nearby village took advantage of such a celebration and had some large hammers produced. In addition to their expressive role of publicly validating the exclusive identity of the group, these public ceremonials thus have an important economic function, representing joint enterprises which are expressed in the ritual idiom, mobilising the requisite labour force required for production of heavy work tools. In this context, therefore, we can observe the dynamic interaction between a ritual sub-system and material-utilitarian requirements.

Amongst some non-Muslim Hausa (Maguzawa) rural smithing communities, pre-Islamic rituals which have largely disappeared in Muslim Hausa areas still accompany another important communal undertaking – the setting up of a new (stone) anvil and wooden log (*turu*) into which the anvil itself is rooted.[10] The selection of the stone and log is highly ritualised and is accompanied by the same dramatic unifying activities described above for weddings, in addition to the sacrifice of black goats and cocks to propitiate the spirits (*iskoki, aljanu*), and thereby ensure that success and prosperity flow from the anvil. The Muslim authorities tend to consider these practices as a form of religious deviance, however, considering it shameful for respectable Muslims to attend such boisterous and unrestrained events, and have largely suppressed them, especially in urban Hausa areas, a fact which, as suggested above, might also explain the deritualisation of ironworking in Kano City and other urban centres. The last such ceremonial in Tamburawa took place during the Second World War, and the administrative head (ɗantuɓe) of Tamburawa rarely, if ever, attended blacksmithing rituals. Some of these same spirits are also worshipped by female practitioners of the pre-Islamic *bori* spirit possession cult in Hausa society (Cohen 1969: 58, 163–4; see also McIntyre, Pittin, in this volume), and certain ritual features of Maguzawa metalworking have been incorporated into the cult's activities (Greenberg 1966 [1946]: 34ff., Rogers 1990: 90–1). Implements specially forged by blacksmiths, for example, are offered to certain spirits, e.g., ɗan Gajere Mai Baka receives small arrows, Sarkin Noma farm-tools, and Kure is given knives.

The informal articulation of communal distinctiveness is also actualised through certain semi-secret activities. In common with many other peoples, the Hausa believe iron – and by extension the men who work it – to possess certain occult powers which may be exploited for good or bad purposes, and fire mastery plays an important part in the ritual activities of Hausa smiths. The belief that the blacksmith is a 'master of fire' has of course been current at various times in central Europe, Asia, and North and South America, as well as Africa, and the immunity of certain people to fire, e.g., the shamanist communities, has been a constant source of wonder, nervousness and bafflement to observers of the phenomenon for centuries (both Plato and Virgil recorded instances of people walking unscathed on hot coals).

Fire-handling rituals amongst the Hausa blacksmiths involve dancing and chanting, and participants work themselves into a

---

10 See Herbert (1993: 98ff.) for discussion of the ritualisation surrounding the manufacture of basic ironworking tools, e.g., anvils, hammers, in sub-Saharan Africa.

state of entranced frenzy, applying the technique of mind over matter. The genuineness of the blacksmiths' powers is never in doubt, even though there is perhaps no rational scientific explanation of their fire-handling feats and immunity to fire. The Hausa themselves characterise fire-handling as a combination of magic (*rufa-ido*) allied to dexterity/skill (*dabara*), but it is so old and widespread (globally) that we need to confront the fact that certain people have the natural and mysterious ability to handle fire with immunity and without any mechanical trickery being involved.

The true Hausa blacksmith, because he possesses expert and privileged knowledge of the mysterious properties of iron and fire, is still ambivalently regarded as an object of awe and admiration by most people today. Apart from being highly skilled craft specialists, blacksmiths are experts in the esoteric preparation of medicinal concoctions which are believed to contain magical properties, e.g., the protective substances applied to the body before the ritual playing with fire (noted above), and the necessary ingredients for the herbal formulas can only be supplied by the smiths themselves who jealously guard these trade secrets (see also Taylor & Webb 1932: 213, Mary Smith 1954: 97, Madabo 1979: 10, and de Maret 1980). The smiths will travel some distance into the 'bush' to collect the necessary organic herbs, leaves, tree bark and roots which they then grind into a powder before mixing with water and applying to their bodies.

Other (benevolent) medicinal substances are prepared with the by-products of ironworking, e.g., slag and clinkers from the fire, pieces of old goatskin bellows, including special anti-burn preparations, diagnostics and curatives for syphilis, anaemia and leprosy, antidotes for poison (including snakebites), protective medicines for hunters, boxers and warriors, and charms to ensure success in bride-seeking and business ventures (see also Herbert 1993: 70–4). (One Kano City blacksmith is so renowned for successfully treating burns with his medicines that he is sometimes invited to assist with burn victims at the City Hospital!) Some charms, e.g., amulets (small leather packets), and secret devices prepared with iron shavings from an anvil, are anti-social and can be used to harm people, inducing illnesses and madness. The smiths claim that the production and use of these substances date from the pre-Islamic era, though in time they have come to be combined with some Islamic elements, such as mixing the potions with ink from Koranic writing boards, reciting sections from the

Koran. Control over metallurgy, therefore, invests practitioners of the skill with unusual and esoteric powers.

Like the (marriage-based) cultural performances described above, all these interactive formations represent both the symbol of, as well the instrument for, the expression of corporate cohesiveness, further enhancing the exclusiveness of this monopolistic group. This legitimacy is also predicated on the general public's perception and acceptance of their long-established distinctive roles, as articulated in the various cultural forms.

Facial Markings

Another permanent – and to my knowledge unique – way in which most Tamburawa blacksmiths objectify their collectivity is the use they make of distinctive 2/2+3/3 facial markings (*aska/tsaga*), involving two small horizontal cuts at both sides of the mouth plus three small vertical cuts on each temple, markings they share with some local groups of Agalawa. The Agalawa (sing. Ba'agale) are long-distance (salt/kolanut) traders of Tuareg slave origin, whose original homeland was on the southern (Sahel) fringe of the Tuareg commercial orbit (Lovejoy 1980: 75ff., and personal communication, 1994). Many Agalawa have settled as farmers in parts of northern Nigeria and neighbouring Niger, and they are the joking relations (*abokan wasa*) of Hausa blacksmiths, trading institutionalised insults back and forth – Cohen (1974: 24, 47, 89, 134) considers institutionalised joking relationships to be another stylised pattern of activity which, together with ritual and ceremonial, help to define the boundaries of a group's unique subculture or life-style. There has also been a considerable amount of intermarriage between the two groups in Tamburawa.

The incisions themselves are normally made by a barber-doctor (*wanzami*) a few days after the child's birth (on the naming-day or soon thereafter). In 1971, twenty-two out of a total thirty-two smiths showed the complete 2/2+3/3 cicatrisation pattern, and all twenty-two had inherited the craft patrilineally. Of the remaining ten smiths, five simply had the 2/2 mouth Hausa markings common to the area, three had the 3/3 mouth pattern favoured by some Agalawa, and two (matrilineally inherited smiths) had no markings at all. This difference is attributable to the fact that it is the child's father (sometimes in consultation with the paternal grandfather) who usually determines the markings to be given to his child – usually the same markings he has. Although I have no exact data on females, my impression was that there is also a strong preference for these same markings amongst the daughters of the Tamburawa smiths.

An indication of the corporate value attached to these visible marks of identification is provided by the case of two smith children – a boy of nine and a girl of seven – who felt excluded because they had only been given the 2/2 mouth markings at birth. They both desperately wanted to share this tangible and directly symbolic form with their peers and so secretly paid a barber-doctor to perform the painful operation and add the 3/3 temple incisions necessary to complete the pattern – *sabo da gado* 'because of inheritance/tradition' the boy explained to me. This seemingly trivial yet important social drama underlines the expressive and integrative function of this particular cultural form and patterns naturally with other phenomena considered above – the children's action stemmed from a desire to articulate full group identity and so consolidate shared values and sentiments.

Conclusion

This chapter has profiled the primary mechanisms which the Tamburawa blacksmiths manipulate to sustain their craft monopoly and objectify their distinctive identity, highlighting the politico-cultural dynamics of the social situation to which the customs and performances refer. The corporate boundaries are maintained in terms of symbolic forms and activities that are articulated around primary kinship relationships within a communally organised occupational group, and wedding ceremonials are seen as an especially salient and effective means of expressing group identity. The ethnographic description and elucidation of such boundaries and interests is essentially a contribution to the sociological analysis of the way in which groupings exploit informal means to pursue economic-political goals, an important and fruitful research front which derives much of its stimulus from Cohen's penetrating insights into socio-symbolic interdependence.

References

Cohen, Abner. 1969. *Custom and Politics in Urban Africa: A Study of Hausa Migrants in Yoruba Towns*. London: Routledge & Kegan Paul.

———. 1974. *Two-Dimensional Man: An Essay on the Anthropology of Power and Symbolism in Complex Society.* London: Routledge & Kegan Paul.

———. 1981. *The Politics of Elite Culture.* Berkeley & Los Angeles: University of California Press.

———. 1993. *Masquerade Politics: Explorations in the Structure of Urban Cultural Movements.* Berkeley and Los Angeles: University of California Press.

Echard, Nicole. 1965. 'Note Sur les Forgerons de l'Ader (Pays Hausa, République du Niger)' *Journal de la Société des Africanistes* 35: 353–72.

———. 1983. 'Scories et Symboles: Remarques Sur la Métallurgie Hausa du Fer au Niger', in *Métallurgies Africaines: Nouvelles Contributions,* Nicole Echard (ed.). Paris: Société des Africanistes.

Gluckman, Max. 1942. *Analysis of a Social Situation in Modern Zululand.* Manchester: Manchester University Press.

Greenberg, Joseph. 1966 [1946]. *The Influence of Islam on a Sudanese Religion.* (Monographs of the American Ethnological Society 10). Seattle & London: University of Washington Press.

Herbert, Eugenia W. 1993. *Iron, Gender and Power: Rituals of Transformation in African Societies.* Bloomington & Indianapolis: Indiana University Press.

Hill, Polly. 1972. *Rural Hausa: a Village and a Setting.* Cambridge: Cambridge University Press.

Jaggar, Philip J. 1973a. 'Kano City Blacksmiths: Precolonial Distribution, Structure and Organisation', *Savanna* 2(1): 11–25.

———. 1973b. 'A Kano Blacksmith's Vocabulary', *Kano Studies (New Series)* 1(1): 99–109.

———. 1994. *The Blacksmiths of Kano City: A Study in Tradition, Innovation and Entrepreneurship in the Twentieth Century.* (Westafrikanische Studien, Frankfurter Beiträge zur Sprach-und Kulturgeschichte, vol. 2.). Cologne: Rüdiger Köppe Verlag.

Lovejoy, Paul E. 1980. *Caravans of Kola: The Hausa Kola Trade 1700–1900.* Zaria, Nigeria: Ahmadu Bello University Press.

Lubeck, Paul M. 1986 *Islam and Urban Labor in Northern Nigeria: The Making of a Muslim Working Class.* Cambridge: Cambridge University Press.

MacEachern, A.S. 1990. 'Du Kunde: Processes of Montagnard Ethnogenesis in the Northern Mandara Mountains of Cameroon', PhD dissertation, University of Calgary.

Madabo, Musa Husaini. 1979. *Ciniki da Sana'o'i a Kasar Hausa.* Lagos, Nigeria: Thomas Nelson.

Madauci, Ibrahim, Isa Yahaya and Bello Daura. 1968 [1982]. *Hausa Customs* (7th edition). Zaria, Nigeria: NNPC.

de Maret, P. 1980. 'Ceux Qui Jouent Avec le Feu: la Place du Forgeron en Afrique Centrale', *Africa* 50: 263–79.

Pilaszewicz, Stanislaw. 1991. 'The Image of Hausa Smiths in Some Written Sources', in *Forge et Forgerons* (Actes du IVe Colloque Méga-Tchad, vol. 1), Yves Moñino (ed.). Paris: ORSTOM.

Rogers, Peter A. 1990. 'The Social Dynamics of Local Iron-Working in Nineteenth-Century Hausaland', MA thesis, University of Wisconsin-Madison.

Shea, Philip J. 1983. 'Approaching the Study of Production in Rural Kano', in *Studies in the History of Kano*, Bawuro M. Barkindo (ed.). Ibadan: Heinemann Educational Books.

Smith, Mary F. 1954. *Baba of Karo (A Woman of the Muslim Hausa)*. London: Faber & Faber. [Reprinted, 1981, New Haven & London: Yale University Press.]

Smith, M.G. 1959. 'The Hausa System of Social Status', *Africa* 29: 239–52.

Sterner, Judy. 1993. 'Transformers Transformed: the Blacksmith/Potter Category in the Mandara Region of Cameroon and Nigeria', unpublished ms., Department of Anthropology and Sociology, SOAS.

Sterner, Judy, & Nicholas David. 1991. 'Gender and Caste in the Mandara Highlands: Northeastern Nigeria and Northern Cameroon', *Ethnology* 30(4): 355–69.

Tambo, David C. 1976. 'Pre-Colonial Iron Working on the Jos Plateau', paper presented at the Seminar on the Economic History of the Central Savanna of West Africa, Bayero University Kano, Nigeria, 5–10 January 1976.

Taylor, F.W. and A.G.G. Webb. 1932. *Labarun Al'adun Hausawa: Accounts of Conversations Describing Certain Customs of the Hausas*. London: Oxford University Press.

Turner, Victor. 1957. *Schism and Continuity in an African Society*. Manchester: Manchester University Press.

——. 1974. *Dramas, Fields and Metaphors: Symbolic Action in Human Society*. Ithaca & London: Cornell University Press.

——. 1983. 'Carnival in Rio: Dionysian Drama in an Industrializing Society', in *The Celebration of Society: Perspectives on Contemporary Cultural Performance*, Frank E. Manning (ed.). Bowling Green, Ohio: Bowling Green University Popular Press.

Vaughan, James H. 1970. 'Caste Systems in the Western Sudan', in *Social Stratification in Africa*, Arthur Tuden and Leonard Plotnicov (eds). New York: The Free Press.

CHAPTER 14

Pilgrims and Genies:
A Case Study in the Liminality and Masquerade Politics of Cultural Performance, from the History of Islam in West Africa, c. 1500

Humphrey J. Fisher *

The Setting

The setting is the Songhay empire, encompassing the Niger bend roughly from Timbuktu in the west to Gao in the east, late in the fifteenth century. Sonni Ali had been its outstanding ruler. Eccentric and wayward, causing many of his subjects, particularly the Muslims, great anxiety and distress, he had nonetheless proved a very effective warrior-ruler. He professed himself Muslim, and even his harshest critics never went so far as to dub him an outright *kafir*, or unbeliever. Sonni Ali died somewhat mysteriously (pp. 250–1) in 1492; his son, Sonni Baru, succeeded him. Early in 1493, the *sonni* dynasty was overthrown in an internal coup d'état, and the first of the *askiya* dynasty, Muhammad, seized power. A little later, perhaps in the period 1496–8 (see n.15), Askiya Muhammad undertook the pilgrimage to Mecca, with several clerics from the imperial court at Gao; the cream of the Islamic establishment at Timbuktu abstained from this pilgrimage, remaining aloof still

---

* My thanks to Lionel Caplan, Murray Last, Andrew Manley, John Peel, Richard Rathbone, Andrew Roberts and others, for helpful comments on earlier drafts. Surviving errors and eccentricities remain my own.

from the usurper at this stage.[1] On pilgrimage, the *askiya* himself, or members of his entourage, had several encounters, with the Abbasid *khalifah* in Cairo, with the *sharif* of Mecca, with *jinn* (singular *jinni*, whence the English genie) in the Egyptian desert, dramatic cultural encounters significantly affecting the *askiya*'s political status.

The Purpose of the Exercise

My purpose is not straightforwardly historical (for historical analysis, see Blum and Fisher 1993), but rather concentrates on the various pilgrimage encounters, trying to understand better how these were perceived by the participants, or by later local commentators. Owing to this focus upon local perception and interpretation, an evolving story, accumulating accretions from oral tradition and other wellsprings of the imagination over centuries, is positively grist to the mill, however unreliable as 'hard' historical data. We begin with a series of passages concerning the *askiya*'s installation, on pilgrimage, as the leading Islamic authority for western Africa; this series culminates in the *Tarikh al-fattash*, which describes events (as far as we are concerned here) in the late fifteenth century, was written in Timbuktu in the seventeenth century, and significantly revised (for local purposes – i.e., legitimation of Masina, a fledgling Muslim theocracy initiated by a later Islamic coup d'état) early in the nineteenth century.[2] The late *Fattash* revision provides also our other main heading, the desert encounter of pilgrims and genies. Quantitatively, the historical data are sparse, but, for events alleged to have occurred 500 years ago in Egypt and Arabia, unrecorded there but described in western Africa over the following 300 years, unexpectedly vivid and detailed.

---

1 An example of Gulliver's 'conflict avoidance' (in this volume), here not built into customary cultural performance, but interrupting even so deeply rooted a performance as the *hajj*.

2 Mahmud Ka'ti/Ibn al-Mukhtar, *Tarikh al-fattash*, ed. and tr. O. Houdas and M. Delafosse, 1913–14, reprinted Paris: Adrien-Maisonneuve, 1964. Hereafter cited in the notes as *T/F*. For the nineteenth-century revisions, see Levtzion 1971: 571–93.

My principal tools, in this analysis of perceptions, are anthropological, firstly the late Victor Turner's concept of liminality,[3] and secondly Abner Cohen's 'masquerade politics', an exploration of the political significance of ritual and dramatic enactment.

Masquerade Politics

(i) Definition

The term 'masquerade politics' comes from Cohen's latest book, *Masquerade Politics: Explorations in the Structure of Urban Cultural Movements* (1993),[4] chiefly about the Notting Hill Carnival, held yearly in London since 1966. Cohen defines politics, somewhat circularly, as 'the distribution, maintenance, exercise of and struggle for economic-political power' (1993: 8). Masquerade politics is 'politics articulated in terms of non-political cultural forms such as religion, kinship, the arts' (ix), with special attention in this interesting and thought-provoking book to 'seemingly frivolous, playful cultural movements like carnivals, fairs and festivals' (1). 'These two components of social reality [politics and culture] differ fundamentally from each other. Political action is intended and rational. Cultural action is unintended and non-rational' (8). (The demarcation seems too sharp – for example, surely politics can sometimes be tragically non-rational, while Jaggar in this volume shows the rational pay-off in first-marriage rituals among Kano blacksmiths.) Yet cultural forms and political issues are also 'dynamically interrelated', with 'continual interplay' between them (7, 79). Politics is crucial in this relationship – 'a cultural movement is *ipso facto* also a political movement' (154), with various cultural forms being

---

3 Criticism of Turner, particularly in pilgrimage studies, is presently fashionable. Eade and Sallnow (1991), for example, set a new agenda (2–3), with pilgrimage an arena of competing, conflicting discourses, 'a tangle of contradictions, a cluster of coincident opposites' (52). This seems unduly to promote the anthropologist's analytical overview, at the expense of the pilgrim's own individual experience. Some scarcely concealed Turnerian insights survive even in Eade and Sallnow (1991), such as baptismal symbolism signalling the 'fraternal equality [of the sick] with other pilgrims at Lourdes' (ibid: 62), and in general I find Turner's liminality more relevant to the askiyan material than are the new agenda's contradictory discourses.

4 See also Cohen 1981.

created, revived, modified, mobilised and integrated 'to deal with rapidly changing economic-political conditions' (148). Nevertheless, an event like carnival is

> ... a cultural form *sui generis* and cannot be reduced or explained away in terms of politics alone. Once developed, it becomes an intervention, not just an expression (7).

In such an event, culture and politics are 'melted down into a transcendental aesthetic unity', having its own 'autonomy and authenticity', albeit 'never completely realised', and 'continually subverted by the dynamics of power relations' (146–7).

(ii) The Investiture

There are various references in the chronicles, from Timbuktu and elsewhere, to the *askiya*'s pilgrimage as a kind of inaugural ceremony. Probably the most accurate report historically, the only one 'that fully made sense' (Hunwick 1990: 85), is that reproduced by an early eighteenth-century Moroccan historian, from an otherwise unknown author called *al-imam al-Takruri*, the Takruri (i.e., the West African) *imam*. According to the *imam*, the *askiya* met the 'Abbasid *khalifah* in Egypt

> ... and asked him to authorise him to rule the *bilad al-sudan* and to be a vice-gerent (*khalifa*) for him there. The Abbasid caliph delegated to him authority (*al-nazar*) over the affairs of those regions and made him his lieutenant over the Muslims [who dwelt] beyond him (88, Hunwick's insertions).

This is straightforward, lacking both liminal overtones and the ceremonial of masquerade politics. Indeed, the *askiya*, having requested the title of *khalifah*, is apparently appointed only lieutenant, *na'ib*, a significantly less prestigious rank.

In later elaboration of the event, liminality and ceremony are introduced. An initial fillip to such embroidery may have come with the final demise of the Abbasid caliphate, at the Ottoman conquest of Egypt in 1517, just a few years after the *askiya*'s visit. The anchor of precise historical context being thus lost, the creative imagination floated more freely.

The account in the *Tarikh al-sudan*, another seventeenth-century Timbuktu chronicle, is recognisably based upon the same material as the *imam* used, but with trimmings. The setting is 'that blessed land', sounding rather like Arabia, although adjacent events in the narrative sequence seem clearly Egyptian. The installer is 'the Abbasid *sharif*': the Abbasids were *sharif*'s, but *khalifah* was their more common title, and we may suspect some preliminary assimilation to the *sharif* of Mecca. The *askiya* requests caliphal status in Songhay; the *sharif* agrees, ordering the *askiya*

> ... to divest himself for three days of the position in which he was, and to come to him on the fourth day. He did so, and he [the *sharif*] made him his *khalifah* and placed upon his head a bonnet and turban of the *sharif*'s own. And he was truly a *khalifah* in Islam (Al-Sa'di 1964: 73 [Arabic], 120 [French]).

The transition has clearly become liminal. First, separation from the royal structure. Next, three days in ambiguous, even dangerous, liminality, which may indicate either the crucial distinction between traditional kingship and new-broom Islam, or – perhaps even at the same time – the possibility of chaos and disorder when for three days there is, in fact, no government at all.[5] And finally, integration into a new caliphal structure. Masquerade politics also appears with the separation, but still more with the ceremonial bestowal of the *sharif*'s own bonnet and turban, like Elijah's mantle, upon the *askiya*, cultural elements relating to the political situation at home, underlining the new beginning, with the contaminated past discarded like a garment.

The *Tarikh al-fattash* makes four distinct references to the investiture. Three, probably from the seventeenth century, specify the *sharif* of Mecca, rather than the Abbasid caliph. Various titles, in one account or more of these three, are bestowed upon the *askiya*: *amir, amir al-mu'minin, na'ib, khalifah*.[6]

The fourth *Fattash* passage, almost certainly from the early nineteenth-century revision of the chronicle, draws perhaps on other sources, such as oral tradition:

> As for the Hassani *sharif*, Mawlay al-'Abbas, he was with the Prince of the believers and the *khalifah* of the Muslims, Askiya al-Hajj Muhammad, sitting near the Ka'bah [in Mecca]. The two were talking, and the *sharif*, Mawlay al-'Abbas, said to him, 'O you who are here, you are the eleventh of the *khalifah*'s of whom the Apostle of God (may God bless him and grant him peace) spoke. But you have come to us as a king, and kingship and caliphate are incompatible.' And he [the *askiya*] said to him, 'How is that, my master [*sayyidi*]?' Mawlay al-'Abbas said to him, 'There is only one way, and that is that you come out of that in which you are.' The *askiya* obediently agreed with him. He sent away from him all his ministers. He collected all the insignia of power

---

5 Cohen 1993: 3 mentions 'forbidden excesses' allowed during carnival. The ambiguity of symbols is a recurrent theme in the book, for example ibid.: 27–8, 125–6.

6 68 (Arabic), 131 (French); 86 (lines 11–6, Arabic), 162 (French); 329 (French only).

and the riches thereof, and put that, in its entirety, in the hands of al-'Abbas, being thus self-deposed. Mawlay al-'Abbas entered into *khalwah* for three days. Then on Friday he came out. He called Askiya al-Hajj Muhammad, and sat him in the mosque of the noble town of Mecca. He placed on his head a green bonnet and a white turban, and gave him a sword, and the congregation [*jama'ah*] there present bore witness that he was *khalifah* for the country of Takrur, and that everyone who disobeyed him in that country disobeyed thereby God most high and His Apostle (12 [Arabic], 16 [French – see also 15]).

The story's evolution, from source to source, usefully warns us against too readily trusting even written records. Elements of masquerade politics and liminality have been gradually elaborated and enhanced, and titles, themselves a component of masquerade politics, distributed with generous and somewhat inconsistent – almost carnival-like – largesse.[7] In the final text, 'the Hassani *sharif*, Mawlay al-'Abbas' is an historical amalgam, merging echoes of the long-defunct Abbasid dynasty with the now far more telling Meccan association. The *askiya* is Prince of believers and *khalifah* of the Muslims without (it seems) the *sharif* of Mecca having done more than acknowledge this as a fact. When the *sharif* does finally intervene, after the pregnant three days, he appoints the *askiya* merely *khalifah* of Takrur. To be assigned such an out-of-the-way corner of the Islamic world, after having been heralded as *khalifah* of all the Muslims, and penultimate *khalifah* of the Prophet's chosen twelve, seems rather a come-down, only partly compensated for by the authority, tantamount to that of God and the Prophet, given the *askiya* within Takrur. The investiture enjoys the full panoply of masquerade politics: on Friday, in the mosque at Mecca, a sword added to the bonnet and turban, a crowd of witnesses. Similarly, the liminal transition, from former kingship to true *khalifah*-hood, first sketched in the *Tarikh al-sudan*, now appears full-blown, with a mass of detail including *khalwah*, which will recur in a moment at the outset of the desert encounter.

The Desert Encounter

(i) The Original Source

The encounter descriptions so far considered, amongst which we have attempted to trace a sequence, all involve established Middle

---

7 See also Jaggar (in this volume), and the Kano blacksmith who is addressed at his first-wedding celebration as *sarki* – emir, king.

Eastern authorities, the Abbasid *khalifah* in Egypt and/or the *sharif* of Mecca. Let us now turn to a different encounter, that with the genies or *jinn* in the desert near Alexandria. For this, only one description survives, in the *Tarikh al-fattash* (65–7 [Arabic], 126–8 [French]):

> And he [the *askiya*] marched with his companions until he came to a broad oasis between Alexandria and Cairo, and he spent the night there with his troops. In the middle of the night Alfa Salih Jawara went out alone to offer supererogatory prayers[8] in *khalwah*.[9] Hearing raised voices he turned towards them, and, as he approached, he saw lanterns around which students [*talabah*], who were *jinn*, were reciting the Book [i.e., the Koran]. He went round them and saw that they were the people[10] of Shamharush, who were returning with him[11] from the *hajj* [pilgrimage to Mecca]. He [Shamharush] was in the midst of them, and the *jinn* students were reciting to him. Alfa Salih Jawara went towards him, and, on reaching him, greeted him with the greeting of Islam, and shook hands with him. The people [*raht*] began to greet him [Alfa Salih] and to shake his hand.
>
> Their voices were raised on this account, and were heard by Alfa Muhammad Tal [t.l], who had come out to offer supererogatory prayers. He recognised the voice of Alfa Salih Jawara among the others. Fearing lest Alfa Salih Jawara were quarrelling with one of the companions of Askiya Muhammad, he went towards them. When he came to them he found them to be the people [*raht*] of Shamharush the *jinni*. Alfa Salih Jawara was near Shamharush, asking him questions. He [Alfa Muhammad] came and greeted Shamharush and his people [*raht*], and sat down to talk with them.
>
> While they were thus engaged, Musa, the son of Alfa Salih Jawara, then a lad of six years, came out. Hearing the voice of his father he went towards it, and came to them and found his father and Alfa Muhammad Tal amongst the *jinn*, the people [*raht*] of Shamharush the *jinni*, and he sat down by his father.
>
> Shamharush said to the two *faqih*'s [jurisconsults], 'Who are you?' They said, 'We are of the people [*qawm*] of the Prince of the Believers [*amir al-mu'minin*], Askiya Muhammad; he has come out on pilgrimage and we have come out with him.' Shamharush congratulated Jawara, and said, 'Askiya Muhammad is a righteous [*salih*] man. I have heard the Prophet, may God bless him and grant him peace, speak of twelve *khalifah*'s, each *khalifah* among them of the Quraysh, and I think that he [the *askiya*] is among them. Ten of them have passed away, and two remain; perhaps[12] he is the eleventh. The last of them will come in the thirteenth century [1786–1883]. The Prophet, may God bless him and grant him peace, has informed me that I shall live until the ninth of the centuries, that I shall meet the eleventh of the *khalifah*'s, who will

---

8 The verb here is *tanaffala*, to offer such prayers.

9 The French translation here for *khalwah* is *un endroit écarté*, a remote place; I shall suggest below an alternative and more precise meaning.

10 *Raht*; this could also mean 'kindred'.

11 I follow the French here; the Arabic reads *ma'ahum*, 'with them'.

12 Arabic *la'alla*; the French gives *sans doute*, which seems too strong.

judge between the *jinn* and humankind. Then I shall die.' They said to him, 'Have you seen the Prophet, may God bless him and grant him peace?' He said, 'Yes, and I have studied with him.' They rejoiced at this.

While they were thus engaged, a *jinni* slave came to them and said, 'A shepherd of yours beat a servant of ours into unconsciousness, and we appeal to the *shari'ah* against you.' Al-Faqih Alfa Salih Jawara said, 'How did a shepherd of ours beat a servant of yours, since we cannot see you?' The slave said, 'The servant took the form of a snake.' Shamharush, their *amir*, said, 'The blood of him who changes his form may be shed without retribution.'

Then they arose, bade them farewell, departed and returned to their companions.

(ii) Layered Liminality

Meeting the *khalifah/sharif* was primarily an exercise in masquerade politics, although we did see there the emerging development of a liminal element. The encounter with the *jinn* reverses these priorities. Masquerade politics is still present (though, see p. 252, of a somewhat inept kind), but liminality has taken over. The desert encounter is a positive onion of liminality, layer upon layer. The pilgrimage is itself a liminal act *par excellence*, each departing pilgrim separating from his or her former structural status, sharing the *communitas* engendered by the rigours and comradeship of travel,[13] and epitomised in the ecstacy of an undifferentiated body of worshippers. And then reintegration. In cases of guilt and penance – a major theme to which we shall return – pilgrimage seems ideally suited for winning absolution. The structure within which any grave, motivating sin was committed may have been thereby irrevocably compromised and contaminated, but through liminal separation all this is left behind, the structure into which the liminar is later reincorporated being like a room fumigated and sterilised after illness.[14]

On the night of the *jinn* both clerics, and the lad Musa, go out – the verb is *kharaja* – individually from the structure of the pilgrimage caravan camp. Observe how a grand liminal exercise, such as the pilgrimage, may generate within itself quite precise structures – a pilgrim caravan, for example, might be highly organised, with an hierarchy of officials: Ibn Battutah became *qadi* of such a caravan in the fourteenth century – from which

---

13 The first two chapters of Eade and Sallnow (1991) comment on the bonding effect of travel to and from Lourdes.

14 For a brief discussion of penitential Christian pilgrimage, see ibid.: 107.

then lesser, so-to-speak interior acts of separation might occur. Salih Jawara went out to perform his supererogatory prayers specifically *bi-khalwah*, in *khalwah*. This may mean a deserted or desert place, but within the context of Muslim worship, as here, a kind of spiritual 'retreat' or withdrawal exercise (see, for example, Triaud 1988), as in the *Fattash* investiture account (pp. 241–2), seems far more likely.

There is chronological liminality also. The *askiya*'s pilgrimage took place about 903,[15] close to the fault-line of two centuries. The significance of the date is heightened inasmuch as the Prophet has told Shamharush that he, the *jinni*, will live until 'the ninth of the centuries', that he will see the eleventh *khalifah* (who is the *askiya*), and then die. When Shamharush (apparently) learned from the two clerics that the *askiya* had come, that was the *jinni*'s death sentence. Dying is highly liminal. The prediction about the twelfth *khalifah* also hints at the turn of a century.

Another liminal dimension, certainly the most diversified and probably the most interesting, is the intersection of several distinct realms of being. Whether we regard trans-boundary *association* as part of the intense *communitas* of the liminal situation, or a result of the heightened awareness and capacity which that situation evokes, or whether we concentrate on trans-boundary *movement*, itself a liminal act, trans-boundary links are often part of the overall liminal experience. In the desert encounter, the two realms chiefly involved are those of humankind and of the *jinn*. Fraternal greetings exchanged between Salih Jawara in particular and the *jinn*, their friendly conversation, express *communitas*. Concerning the maltreated *jinni* servant, Shamharush judges between humans and *jinn*; the eleventh *khalifah*, who is the *askiya*, will do likewise.

Beyond the desert encounter *per se* – which surely is to be understood within a wider context, not as a one-off, free-standing incident – we find other noteworthy and related *jinn*/human links, in oral traditions. According to these, the *askiya* was himself son of a *jinni* father, while his mother was Kassey, Sonni Ali's sister. Additionally it is the *jinni* parent who gives the sword with which Muhammad later strikes off the head of the *sonni* ruler (Ali, or perhaps his son and successor), who was at that moment

---

15 *T/F*, 127 n. 2. The chronicles differ slightly over these dates; see Blum and Fisher 1993: 66 and nn. 4–5.

leading the festival prayers at Gao at the end of Ramadan (Rouch 1953: 187). According to another tradition, while on pilgrimage Askiya Muhammad promised to send the Meccans thirty virgin slaves. After returning home he did so. Unfortunately, *en route* the slaves fell in with some *jinn*, and arrived in Mecca seven months pregnant. The Meccans sent them back. The women gave birth in the Sahara, where their children remained and became the Tuareg, whose descendants later spoilt Songhay (ibid.: 194). Kassey and the slave girls are the only women in our story: marginality is emphasised by the sexual liaisons with male *jinn*; danger, by the violence in which, sooner or later, the offspring engage.

Returning to the desert encounter, there is also communication between the living and the dead. This was clearly the case with Shamharush in his association with the Prophet, whom he had seen, been addressed by, from whom he had received various prophecies, and with whom he had even studied. Furthermore, Shamharush was nearing his own life's end.

Salih Jawara had an extraordinary experience a little later in connection with links across the river of death. After the pilgrims' return home to Songhay, the *askiya*, wishing to launch formal *jihad* against the neighbouring Mossi people, asked Salih Jawara about the appropriate procedures, and then sent him to the Mossi ruler with a summons to convert. The ruler and his ministers, before replying, went to consult the ancestors. After offerings had been made, an old man appeared, before whom all prostrated themselves. The ruler explained the situation; the old man emphatically advised against conversion, favouring war to the last man. Salih Jawara, observing all this, was able afterwards to have a private word with the visitor, and asked him who he was. He obligingly explained that he was the devil, Iblis, deliberately misleading people so that they might die in unbelief (*T/S*: 74 [Arabic], 121-3 [French]). The story is also an interesting, if grotesquely partisan, commentary on the interaction between Islamic intervention and the claims of the ancestors.

The desert encounter also incorporates interaction between *jinn* and animals, in the metamorphosis of a slave *jinni* into a snake. Sonni Ali, as we shall see (p. 251 below), enjoyed a similar gift.

Musa, Salih Jawara's small son, though not an active player in the desert encounter, may nonetheless have contributed to its liminality. Young children, not yet fully incorporated into the structures of human society, perhaps still trailing clouds of glory from some prior home, may have a particularly numinous liminality.[16] The next episode in the *Tarikh al-fattash* illustrates this. Two nights after the desert encounter, a member of the caravan died. At the funeral, in another instance of the living/dead connection, only Musa saw angels remove the body, leaving an empty litter behind (67 [Arabic], 128 [French]). The deceased had been guiltily associated with the previous dynasty. Was the immediate and urgent angelic attention a sign of divine favour, the pilgrimage intention having expunged past misdeeds, or of imminent retribution? Ambiguous symbolism.

Next the caravan ran out of water, amid a parching wind. The *askiya* begged Salih Jawara to pray to God for rain, for the sake of the Prophet. The cleric, declining to invoke so great a name as Muhammad's for so worldly a need, did appeal direct to God, for the sake of the people on the spot, sinners though they were. Salih Jawara had not finished speaking before thunder sounded and rain deluged down (*T/F*: 67–8 [Arabic], 129–30 [French]).

Colleagues have raised two important questions about my handling of liminality here. Firstly, while the interaction amongst these various spheres may seem to us trans-boundary, can we be sure that they were not locally understood as parts of a single continent? And secondly, since various scholars, including Douglas, Leach, and others – though not, I think, Turner – have argued that liminality occurs only or primarily where there is *dangerous* unclarity of categories, overlap, and the like, is this c. 1500 material genuinely liminal?

I think that the answer to both questions is yes. Whilst there may indeed be some ultimate, ideal harmony of the spheres, such as is expressed by many worldviews (see also the conclusion of this

---

16 The passage in Wordsworth's *Ode: intimations of immortality*, beginning with the words, 'Our birth is but a sleep and a forgetting', explores this beautifully. The role of children as intermediaries between the living and the dead, or between persons far apart, is startlingly described by E.W. Lane in Chapter XII, 'Magic, astrology, and alchymy', of his *The Manners and Customs of the Modern Egyptians* (1923); interestingly, in the procedures Lane witnessed, *jinn* were also invoked. When Dame Julian of Norwich, in the fourteenth century, was thought to be dying, her confessor came bringing a child with him; I do not know the significance of this.

The Arabic says Musa was a *sudasi*, a 'sixer', which the French translates as six years old. However, *sudasi* may also describe height, 'six spans from the ankle to the top of the ear ... corresponding to an age of about 12 to 15' (Nachtigal 1980: 216).

chapter), and an enhanced awareness of which may be a touchstone of liminality, too many details here point to the present existence of serious boundaries. The pilgrims emphasise that *jinn* are normally invisible to humans. When the pilgrims hear of Shamharush's intimate association with the Prophet, they say (in this text) nothing about the *askiya* being (perhaps) a *khalifah*, but they do rejoice in Shamharush's special relationship with the Prophet – Salih Jawara, asked to pray for rain, does not himself venture to cross that particular boundary. The unique perceptions of young Musa, concerning the angels, clearly imply a boundary crossable only by special categories of people. Further, in oral tradition, the union between human and *jinni* parents of the first *askiya* is clearly an extraordinary event, leading to extraordinary offspring. All this, and more, implies the existence of significant boundaries.

Danger and ambiguity abound (see p. 241 and n. 5). Shamharush rejoiced in the fulfilment of Muhammad's prohecy about the *askiya* as the eleventh caliph, but the *askiya*'s coming also signalled the imminent death of Shamharush. In oral tradition, with a weapon from the *jinni* world, the *askiya* murders his own uncle (or cousin), at the acme of Islamic devotion, violating both kinship and religious fellowship. The illegitimate, half-*jinn* offspring of the slave girls sent by the *askiya* to Mecca will ultimately overturn Songhay, the *askiya*'s own empire. The masquerade performed by Iblis, the devil, appearing to Mossi suppliants as spokesman of their own ancestors, and leading them to death and damnation, is a vivid instance of perilous ambiguity: the extent to which the Mossi had been deceived is underlined by the use of the root *s.j.d* for their prostration before the devil – such prostration is in Muslim opinion offered only before God Himself (Fisher 1993: 72–88). Musa sees the angels carry off the corpse: for torment or salvation? The noteworthy ruling at the end of the desert encounter, concerning metamorphosis, again highlights extreme ambiguity, plus acute danger: those indulging in such adventures become outlaws, bereft of all protection.

These boundary incidents, united by the single figure of Salih Jawara common to them all, constitute a powerful network of interlocking realms of being: humans (specifically including children) and *jinn* and animals and birds (see p. 251), the living and the dead (including, in an ominous way, 'the ancestors'), angels, the devil, the Prophet, God. The intersection of so many boundaries, the arena of so many links, exchanges, so much crossing over (sometimes without living humans involved at all), is liminal indeed; an actor upon such a stage is subject to many power sources, some complementary, some conflicting.

Were this network not unusual and arresting, would its details have been remembered and/or elaborated for three hundred years, before being lodged in a local chronicle?

(iii) Masquerade Politics

Ahmadu Lobbo, the Twelfth Caliph

The desert encounter is certainly dramatic entertainment. One after another, three individuals abandon the security of the caravan camp, plunging into darkness, unable perhaps to *see* anything. Each is guided by what he can *hear*, Salih Jawara by the sound of the *jinn*'s voices, Muhammad Tal particularly by the voice of his friend and colleague, Musa by his father's voice. Lit by lanterns, many *jinn* are chanting the Koran, a haunting sound in the desert night. The magic of the scene is enhanced, the theme of seeing or not seeing is reinforced, by the fact that the *jinn*, on this occasion so approachable, are normally invisible to human eyes: how can we have beaten a *jinni*, asks Salih Jawara, when we cannot see you? And the whole dramatic impact is immeasurably intensified by the liminal dimensions already explored.

Within this cultural performance, three major political messages – three examples of masquerade politics – are acted out. A trailer for Ahmadu Lobbo of Masina as the twelfth *khalifah*, another variation on the installation theme, is one. In a sense this is the most important of the three, given the extensive revisions made to the *Tarikh al-fattash* early in the nineteenth century specifically to gild Ahmadu Lobbo's contemporary status. Despite this, the only detail given about the twelfth *khalifah* is that he will come in the thirteenth Islamic century, i.e., 1786–1883. Indirectly, of course, anything which strengthened the *askiya* strengthened also his successor and emulator, Ahmadu Lobbo, who three centuries later implemented his own successful Islamic coup d'état. The fact that, directly, so little is said about Ahmadu Lobbo, while other matters are handled so much more extensively in the desert account, lends credible support to the hypothesis that the early nineteenth-century revisers were drawing substantially upon alternative, already established, information, quite likely oral tradition.

Absolution

The second of the three important political issues explored and expressed by the masquerade politics of the desert encounter – and the most elusive and speculative of the three – concerns the *askiya* as usurper, possibly even regicide, who had overthrown the legitimate dynasty (which he had himself served), and one of whose reasons for so prompt a pilgrimage after the successful coup d'état may have been to seek absolution for any wrongdoing involved. We have already touched above upon the absolving potential of pilgrimage as a liminal ritual. That pilgrimage was regarded theologically as sufficient penance for even serious misdeeds is clear from other instances in the chronicles. In the fourteenth century, Mansa Musa, ruler of Mali, unintentionally killed his mother, and was advised to seek the intercession of the Prophet; he did eventually go on full-scale pilgrimage (*T/F*: 33 ff. [Arabic], 56–7 ff. [French]). In the sixteenth century Askiya Dawud of Songhay received the same advice after his unintentional killing of a *sharif*, a descendant of the Prophet; being old, Dawud paid six hundred slaves as blood-money instead (*T/F*: 116–17 [Arabic], 212–3 [French]). One incident may be copied from the other, but that would rather confirm than discount the view that exculpation has been a popular way of regarding the pilgrimage.

Absolution, however, in the 'great' tradition of the Muslim pilgrimage, is not part of the desert encounter script. What is there is something far more enigmatic, yet, I believe, directly relevant to the *askiya*'s immediate needs (whether as he perceived them himself, or as they were attributed to him later). It is Shamharush's rather high-profile assurance – the final point in the whole elaborate encounter description – that the blood of one who metamorphoses himself cannot be avenged. To assess this more fully, albeit still tentatively, let us look back at Sonni Ali's death.

The *Tarikh al-fattash* reports that Ali died suddenly, cursed by several Muslims whom he had wronged. His body was hurriedly buried, and his troops marched on without the local people being aware of his death. The location of his grave is unknown.[17] The *Tarikh al-sudan* says he drowned, and that the body was disembowelled and the cavity filled with honey against decomposition. His burial is unmentioned (*T/S*: 71 [Arabic], 116 [French]; cf. Rouch

---

17   51 (Arabic), 98–9 (French).

1953: 185–6). Oral tradition describes a direct physical attack, at the festival prayer ending Ramadan, by the usurping *askiya* upon the ruling *sonni*: outright regicide.[18]

These fragmentary and contradictory accounts are puzzling, particularly since Sonni Ali died while still at the helm of state, and was succeeded, albeit briefly, by his son. The chronicles are insufficiently detailed to impose a tight rein on subsequent development of oral tradition, and the two have grown apart: prayer-ground assassination, for example, is not drowning. Another metamorphosis reference invites speculation. Oral tradition attributes to Sonni Ali (and his horse) the power to metamorphose himself into a vulture (Rouch 1953: 183–4). We may, perhaps, imagine some cataclysmic final confrontation, emerging in oral tradition and folk memory, a confrontation during which Sonni Ali, hard-pressed, resorts to the final weapon of metamorphosis. Despite this, he is slain. And the ruling of Shamharush clears his slayer of all responsibility. If there be any truth in this, admittedly very hypothetical, reconstruction, the apparently marginal incident of the *jinni* who, having rashly changed himself into a snake, was roughly handled by one of the pilgrims, becomes in reality a sweeping acquittal of the usurping *askiya*. The presentation of the incident confirms its importance. The initial accusation against the pilgrims focuses our attention; the plaintiff's appeal to the *shari'ah*, the Islamic law, shows that the matter is profoundly serious; and the ruling of Shamharush, who has studied with the Prophet, is unassailable.

Two further details, subsequent to the pilgrimage, lend further credence to this emphasis upon guilt and exculpation. Firstly, the visiting scholar, al-Maghili, *ex post facto* apologist for the coup d'état, laboured intently to prove Sonni Ali worse than an unbeliever (see, for example, Hunwick 1985: 78). And secondly, when the *qadi* (or judge) of Timbuktu reminded the *askiya* how the latter had put his hand into that of the *qadi*, begging to be saved from hell, the *askiya* acknowledged that it had been so (*T/F*: 61 [Arabic], 117 [French]; see also Gomez 1990: 18). Absolution by *hajj*, by *jinn*, by al-Maghili, by Timbuktu.

The quest for absolution reminds us of the power struggle between the usurping *askiya* and the *ancien régime*, tying in closely with *Masquerade Politics* (Cohen 1993: 4): although an artistic

---

18 Rouch 1953: 187–8; see also Ba 1977: 133.

spectacle, carnival 'is always political, intimately and dynamically related to the political order and to the struggle for power within it'.

The Investiture

The third political issue being acted out is the installation of the first *askiya* as an outstanding Islamic notable. The presentation of this in the encounter is odd, even clumsy. The pilgrim visitors tell Shamharush they are followers of the *amir al-mu'minin*, the Prince of the Believers. It is highly unlikely that Askiya Muhammad laid claim to, much less enjoyed, any such title at this very early date. Rather, to acquire such status was one important reason why he went on pilgrimage at all; there is certainly, as we have seen, considerable evidence, some quite early, about the *askiya*'s attempt to enhance his standing once he had arrived in Cairo or Arabia. The encounter advances his right to the title of the eleventh *khalifah* with curious diffidence. 'I think, *azunnu*,' says Shamharush, 'the *askiya* may be a *khalifah*; since ten have already died, he may perhaps, *la'alla*, be the eleventh'. This hesitancy is difficult to understand: did not Shamharush have a hot-line to the Prophet, who would assuredly have been able to speak authoritatively? Further, such reticence is out of keeping with the emphasis, quite heavy, at many other points in the chronicles on this and other titles for the *askiya*. Nor can it be said that, in the desert encounter, promotion of the *askiya* as the eleventh *khalifah* is secondary to the promotion of Ahmadu Lobbo, in the early nineteenth century, as the twelfth, for Lobbo receives even less attention than does the *askiya*.

Masquerade Politics, Liminality, and the Aesthetic Imperative

In fact, all three political issues in the desert encounter – preparing a highway in the desert for Ahmadu Lobbo, absolving the *askiya*, saluting his status – are in one way or another rather marginal, rather carelessly handled. The gradual, utilitarian elaboration of the inaugural theme, and of the *askiya*'s titles, so clear in the passages examined at the beginning of this chapter, and fitting so well into the framework of masquerade politics, are in the desert encounter overshadowed by liminal emphases. Of course, masquerade politics and liminality are interwoven: the inaugural scenario does include a distinctly liminal shift by the *askiya* from kingship to *khilafah*, and the desert encounter has its share of masquerade politics, speaking symbolically to political concerns at home in the West Africa of 1500 and of 1800. Nonetheless, the informing emphasis has shifted. The link between masquerade and politics has been loosened: pride of place has moved away from the practical utilitarianism of the inaugural sequence, and instead we have liminality responding to what we may call an aesthetic – or perhaps even a metaphysical – imperative, a sense of how things ought to be.

I have argued earlier in this chapter that the trans-boundary aspects of the desert encounter, and of the associated data clustered around the figure of Salih Jawara, were genuinely liminal movements between one sphere of being and another, often highlighted by ambiguity and even danger. However, despite the fissures and frustrations implicit in such ambiguity and peril, the underpinning intention of this body of data, the aspiration of the human spirit which it embodies, is I believe towards the overall harmony of all being: the ultimate truth, which passes all understanding, is holistic.

To some extent, this overarching aesthetic or metaphysical imperative corresponds to the conclusions of *Masquerade Politics*. We have already noticed above Cohen's awareness of 'a transcendental unity' emerging from the fusion of culture and politics in masquerade situations, a unity having its own 'autonomy and authenticity'. Elsewhere (1993: 120), discussing again the insufficiency of politics as a single cause, Cohen remarks:

> Despite the crucial part played by politics in shaping the structure of the cultural event, it is futile to try to explain, or explain away, the cultural in terms of the political. Indeed, cultural symbols and the communal relationships they express and sustain are so powerful in their hold on people that political formations everywhere, including the state, always attempt to manipulate them in their own interests.

The tension remains unresolved: the 'transcendental unity … is continually subverted by the dynamics of power relation', yet the aesthetic isolation of politics is 'a process continually converting… the desires of the individual to the duty towards the collective, particularity to universality' (ibid.: 146–7).

What I intend by the metaphysical imperative is something more elusive, yet at the same time more independent, more permanent, more self-contained (if that description may be applied to a mystery containing in itself all things), and ultimately better glimpsed through the insights of liminality, helpful though the analyses of *Masquerade Politics* have been throughout my argument. Masquerade politics and liminality can both be powerfully integrative, but the former tends to emphasise the exclusive group (see for example, Jaggar, in this volume), while liminality is potentially all-embracing.

The desert encounter exists today only in a single description, apparently added to the *Tarikh al-fattash* early in the nineteenth century. If my guess is correct, that the material was in significant measure simply transfused from oral tradition into the written record at that time, then perhaps the greater stress on liminality and the aesthetic imperative, in contrast to more pragmatic masquerade politics, may reflect some basic distinction between oral tradition and the written record.

Cohen (1993: 152) seems to point to a somewhat similar distinction, between the first formulation (in our case, the earliest written descriptions of the encounters) and the later development (in our case, maybe, the evolution of oral tradition):

> It is important ... in discussing the processes of politico-cultural dynamics to distinguish between the original creation or adoption of a new cultural formulation and its dissemination among the membership of the collectivity.

We all, in one way or another, subscribe to the aesthetic/metaphysical imperative. In moving from one draft to another of this chapter, my major yardstick for judging progress is whether the overall argument has become more coherent, more unified, more holistic. Maybe life is really like that: maybe a coherent argument in any writing is in some sense a reflection of the truth: maybe existence does ultimately embrace, as one, all the different spheres of being illustrated in the desert encounter and the associated material. Or, maybe this is all theory, idealism, a search for the Garden of Eden, a chimera – while life, real life, with masqueraders scrambling for political ends, lurches chaotically from one crisis to another, from disaster to triumph and back again.

References

Ba, Adam Konari. 1977. *Sonni Ali Ber*. Niamey: Etudes Nigeriennes No. 40.

Blum, Charlotte and Humphrey Fisher. 1993. 'Love for Three Oranges, or The *askiya*'s Dilemma: the *askiya*, al-Maghili and Timbuktu, c. 1500 A.D.', *Journal of African History* 34: 65–91.

Cohen, Abner. 1981. *The Politics of Elite Culture: Explorations in the Dramaturgy of Power in a Modern African Society*. Berkeley: University of California Press.

——. 1993. *Masquerade Politics: Explorations in the Structure of Urban Cultural Movements*. Berkeley: University of California Press.

Eade, J. and M.J. Sallnow. 1991. *Contesting the Sacred: the Anthropology of Christian Pilgrimage*. London and New York: Routledge.

Fisher, Humphrey. 1993. '*Sujud* and Symbolism: a Case Study in the Ambiguity of Symbolic Ritual Action in the Quran and in Western Africa', in *Threefold Wisdom: Islam, the Arab World and Africa: Papers in Honour of Ivan Hrbek*, Otakar Hulec and Milos Mendel (eds). Prague: Oriental Institute.

Gomez, Michael. 1990. 'Timbuktu Under Imperial Songhay: a Reconsideration of Autonomy', *Journal of African History* 31: 18.

Hunwick, John O. 1990. 'Askia al-Hajj Muhammad and his Successors: the Account of al-Imam al-Takruri', *Sudanic Africa: a Journal of Historical Sources*, University of Bergen 1: 85–9.

Hunwick, John O. 1985. *Shari'a in Songhay: the Replies of al-Maghili to the Questions of Askia al-Hajj Muhammad*. Oxford: Oxford University Press.

Ibn al-Mukhtar/Mahmud Kati. 1913–4 [1964]. *Tarikh al-Fattash* (ed. and translated by O. Houdas and M. Delafosse). Paris: Adrien-Maisonneuve

Lane, Edward William. 1923. *The Manners and Customs of the Modern Egyptians*. London: Dent.

Levtzion, Nehemia. 1971. 'A Seventeenth-Century Chronicle by Ibn al-Mukhtar: a Critical Study of Tarikh al-Fattash', *Bulletin of the School of Oriental and African Studies* 39 (3). Reprinted in Levtzion, 1994, *Islam in West Africa: Religion, Society and Politics to 1800*, Aldershot (Hampshire) and Brookfield (Vermont): Variorum.

Nachtigal, G. 1980. *Sahara and Sudan*, vol. ii: *Kawar, Bornu, Kanem, Borku, Ennedi*. (translated by A.G.B. and H.J. Fisher), London: Christopher Hurst.

Rouch, Jean. 1953. *Contribution à l'Histoire des Songhay*. Dakar: Mémoires de l'Institut Français d'Afrique Noire, no. 29.

Al-Sa'di, 'Abd al-Rahman bin 'Abd Allah. 1913–4 [1964]. *Tarikh al-sudan* (ed. and tr. O. Houdas). Paris: Adrien-Maisonneuve.

Triaud, Jean-Louis. 1988 '*Khalwa* and the Career of Sainthood: an Interpretative Essay', in *Charisma and Brotherhood in African Islam*, Donal B. Cruise O'Brien and Christian Coulon (eds). Oxford: Clarendon Press.

CHAPTER 15

A Cultural Given and a Hidden Influence:
Koranic Teachers in Kano

J.A.McIntyre *

Introduction

If one walks past a Koranic school in Kano, northern Nigeria (there is one or more on almost every street), one will see pupils being taught how to read and write the Koran by a Koranic teacher or 'malam'. This activity is what the word 'malam' refers to. There is however something else involved in being a malam, something I shall call 'medico-spiritual' activities, which are not designated by the word 'malam'.[1]

Malams' traditional social status is equal to that of merchants and second only to traditional political rulers; they are closely associated with both groups and are very influential. Their individual

---

* The research on which this article is based was originally (1974–5) funded by the Social Science Research Council, London and by the Central Research Fund, London University. I then worked for three years in Bayero University, Kano, from 1975–1978. Since 1978, I have visited Kano on several occasions and learned more about the 'medico-spiritual' theme. A first version of this paper was presented on 19 October 1994 to the Department of African Languages and Cultures, Warsaw University, during a visit organised as part of the partnership agreement between Warsaw and Hamburg universities.

1 'Malam' is derived from Arabic *mu'allim* and designates a 'teacher' – not a 'medico-spiritual' practitioner.

and (occupational) group status is formally understood (both by themselves and others) to be based on their role as educators; this role is legitimated by the long and difficult educational process they themselves have undergone. The part played by medico-spiritual activities in the formal group definition of malams is less clear.

The highly visible Koranic schools are not only centres of teaching and learning, they are also, informally, mosques where the five daily prayers, led by a malam, may be performed. Furthermore, the malam's function of prayer-leader (or *imam*) is often complemented by his performance of rites-of-passage rituals for the community he serves as teacher. This is the 'cultural given'. Medico-spiritual activities – ranging from the administration of herbal medicine to the invocation of spirits on behalf of a client – are known and available to all. Many Hausa people avail themselves of this in the course of their lives, but it is a very private sphere and a good deal of secrecy surrounds it. This is the 'hidden influence'.

The purpose of this chapter is to describe the relationship between educational and medico-spiritual activities. It draws on the work of Abner Cohen who, in his latest work, explores the relationship between the Notting Hill Carnival and the political aspirations, needs etc., of its participants, a relationship he calls 'masquerade politics': 'politics articulated in terms of non-political cultural forms such as religion, kinship, the arts' (1993: ix). This article is an attempt to extend Cohen's theory, describing a relationship in which education is seen as the 'cultural event' which 'masks' the medico-spiritual activities. The following differences between this approach and Cohen's can be identified: firstly, Koranic education is not a 'cultural event' in the same way as the London carnival; it is however a daily event, legitimated by Islam and well established in the culture. Secondly, both Koranic education and medico-spiritual activities are religious; neither is 'frivolous' or 'unintended' (1, 8); each is a 'cultural form sui generis' (7). Thirdly, neither Koranic education nor medico-spiritual practice is directly political: malams as an occupational group do not engage directly in 'the distribution, maintenance, exercise of and struggle for economic-political power' (8); they are not in political competition with the people they teach or for whom they undertake medico-spiritual activities.

One fact parallels Cohen's view of carnival and 'the struggle for economic-political power' in Notting Hill: despite the 'masking' function of education, there is a dialectic of mutual consolidation, a kind of unity is achieved (ibid.: 146–7): the malams' status and much of their influence derive primarily from their educational activities; the medico-spiritual activities are legitimated through this 'mask'; they, in their turn, consolidate the malam's status. It must also be said that malams are not entirely non-political: there are two ways in which they have a 'say' in politics: 1) as a group they can defend their own interests when necessary (a brief example is given); 2) their 'hidden influence' is often used to further the interests of individual politicians. They are not, however, in competition with these people; the malam's influence is put at the disposal of such people.

The chapter is organised as follows: 1) a brief outline of Koranic education and the place of the Koranic teacher in his community; 2) an outline of medico-spiritual activities; 3) Koranic education as a mask for medico-spiritual activities; 4) malams and economic-political power; 5) conclusion.

The 'Cultural Given': Koranic Education

The aim of this section is to describe Koranic education, highlighting aspects of the system which contrast with Western education: the centrality of the Koran, individual pacing, authority structures, personal choice of teacher, learning medico-spiritual knowledge and the personal definition of the conclusion of one's education. The interaction of these factors makes personal relationships rather than bureaucratic definitions the cement which holds the system together. The malam's relationships in the community he serves, both as teacher and medico-spiritual practitioner, are also typified by personal relationships.

The Koran is centripetal in Koranic education. It is the point of departure and the point of return. The Koran is read and learned by heart in its entirety by many students; it is understood to be, quite literally, the word of God.[2] Not all Koranic students learn the whole text by heart; many specialise in *Ilimi*[3] – the general word for

---

2 One could say that the text of the Koran is held to be sacred not just semantically but also phonologically. (cf. *Encyclopedia of Islam*, V: 400–2, where the meaning of verse 18, Sura 75, is discussed.)

3 Tone and vowel length of Hausa are not marked here. Hausa has four 'glottalised' consonants written ɓ, ɗ, ƙ and 'y.

other branches of learning. Even here, some subjects, (e.g., *Tafsiri*, 'exegesis', *Fikihu*, 'jurisprudence') concentrate almost entirely on the Koran or constantly refer back to it. Students specialising in the Koranic text will learn the other subjects later: *Tafsiri, Fikihu* or for example *Nahawu* (grammar). Young students learn songs in Hausa about the five pillars of Islam, including how to pray, how to wash beforehand etc.; older students read local texts, but the Koran is always central. The Koran has a central place in the learning process and therefore in the definition of what a malam is and does, including his medico-spiritual activities.

The structure of Koranic education is not formal or bureaucratic. Most malams recognise three learning groups (in ascending order): *'yan kotso, titiburai, gardawa*; however, no terminology is accepted throughout the Hausa language area; some malams simply refer to *kanana* (little ones) and *manya* (big ones, adults).[4] Learning groups are not defined according to age, each student moving through them at his or her own pace; this leads to a high fluidity of group-definition. The gender boundary is much less fluid: girls and boys sit separately inside the first two learning groups; the more advanced students (*gardawa*) seen on the street are all male – older female students learning with other women or with their husbands inside their homes.

Education begins at home for most students but many fathers send their sons to a malam in another town. For those students who proceed to higher studies, the choice of malam becomes their own, fellow students or malams advising each other. Such students often go to Borno (N.E. Nigeria); at first this may be only during the dry season, the students coming home to help with the harvest. Later, they will leave home completely, living in another town, begging and/or farming to support themselves, but always able to rely on the malam for support if things get difficult. The student owes his malam respect and obedience and will take his malam's advice in many things, including advice on which malam to learn a new book or subject with. In the dry season advanced students will leave the malam they are staying with to go further into the bush or desert in order to study even more intensively. Malams often stress the hardships involved: long hours of studying, heat, hunger,

---

4 Sometimes the *'manya'* are referred to as *'yan kasuwa*, 'traders'. These are the students who come in the evening – after the 4 p.m. (*la'asar*) prayer; many of them really are traders.

thirst, travelling on foot and attacks by wild animals or thieves. Motorised transport has lessened these hardships to some extent.

Knowledge of medico-spiritual activities is gained during the later period of study; a student favoured by his teacher may simply be told that the particular passage he is reading in the Koran is useful for a particular illness or social problem; this information, freely given, is regarded as a gift or as *sadaka* (alms) from the teacher to the student. The student may give something (it may be money) for such knowledge; however the exchange is regarded as *sadaka* and not as a monetary transaction. Over time, the student (or teacher) builds up his own collection of charms,[5] etc., including some which may for example help the student learn more quickly or improve his memory. Written collections pass from father to son.

If, occasionally, a student may be required to return home due to family circumstances, the end of one's education is normally a personal decision. The gifted student is free to make his own decision as to when to start working – as an assistant or an independent malam or in some other trade. This often coincides with his first marriage. Patronage – the support of one or more patrons – is crucial if the malam is to set up his own school (see McIntyre 1982).

The Koranic School in the Community

A Koranic school is a very distinctive neighbourhood feature. Each school exists in its own right, often taking place in or in front of the malam's house where children of both the rich and the poor are taught. (Traditionally, there is no residential separation of rich and poor.) Authority in the school is age-based: the malam is *the* authority in his school;[6] this is legitimated by his knowledge. Ranking and power are very visible and reputations spread even over national boundaries. The school is visible as a school during school hours and is the centre of a number of non-school activities.

---

5 Concerning the exchange of gifts or money for such knowledge, Reichmuth (1993: 172) says: 'Teachers pass on "formulae" of prayers and charms to trusted students and clients; a specific gift or price is often prescribed.' Concerning collections of charms, he says (ibid): 'In the course of time, every malam makes his own "loose-leaf" collection (Hausa *kundi*); he expands this constantly und uses it to gradually build up his own "clientèle".' (my translation).

6 As a man, I had no access to the many schools run by secluded women.

Many malams undertake functions associated with the role of *imam* (prayer leader); this includes leading the daily prayers, conducting naming and wedding ceremonies as well as funerals. Such activities are closely associated with malams and contribute in a small way to their livelihood. As is the case with medico-spiritual activities, this role is not 'named' in the term 'malam' (see note 1); nevertheless, it is a highly visible role, contributing to the centrality of the malam and his school in the community. His central place in the community is consolidated by what we might call 'social work': the personal relationship with parents or guardians of pupils entails giving advice on their behaviour – this may involve truancy, bed-wetting or educational prospects. A malam will often use his contacts to help adult students find work. He may also be involved in giving practical, day-to-day advice on how to solve problems, for example with neighbours, co-wives or colleagues – often situations where competition exists. Giving such advice often overlaps with his use of medico-spiritual knowledge.

Malams do not 'earn' their living through education: the gifts of money or in kind which they receive as teachers are not regarded as payment but as gifts of *sadaka* (alms). Furthermore, these gifts are small: the *kudin Laraba* (Wednesday money – Wednesday is the last day of the working week in the Koranic school) given by each child varies according to what the family can afford but is a token amount. Other gifts to the malam – again, regarded as *sadaka* – are given at the successful completion of various stages of the education and are given in kind – an animal or bird or a gift of cooked food – rather than money (see note 18). Such gifts are given to the malam to be distributed at his discretion to his household and/or students.[7] Another gift for malams is the annual *zakka* (the tithe to the poor prescribed by Islam) given by parents and/or patrons; again this is regarded as a gift rather than a payment. He may also receive gifts for performing 'rite-of-passage' ceremonies but all these gifts together will not guarantee a decent livelihood. Many malams have a parallel 'profession' to help them support themselves;[8] many benefit from the support of a patron or patrons – support which is often given in return for medico-spiritual help.

---

7 Many malams have students living in either the malam's house or in rooms he has rented or rooms made available by one of his patrons.

8 See Paden (1973: 57): 'It has been customary in Kano ... for many malams to support themselves through other occupations, especially trade, tailoring, and farming.' One could add: 'or medico-spiritual activities'.

To sum up, the following factors – rather than formal or bureaucratic structures – hold the Koranic educational system together: i) the central place of the Koran in the curriculum, in the learning process and in the definition of what a malam is and does (including his medico-spiritual activities); ii) the malam as teacher and *imam*: his educational role *and* the personal relationship (including medico-spiritual activities) he enjoys with the parents and/or guardians of his pupils. One might add the following: iii) the personal contact between malams who have studied together.

The Hidden Influence: Medico-Spiritual Activities

Medico-spiritual activities range from the practice of herbal medicine to the invocation of spirits.[9] Many but not all malams undertake such activities; to my knowledge, they are undertaken by malams who have specialised in learning the Koran by heart rather than by those who specialised in *ilimi* (see p. 259 above).

Traditional medicine is widely used in Hausa society (see Kleiner-Bossaller 1993: 90 ff.). Herbalists (who do not claim to be malams) can be found selling their wares (leaves, bark, animal bone, skin, hair, potions and salves) in the market; a pre-Islamic spirit cult, the *bori* cult (see Besmer 1977; Monfouga-Nicolas 1972; Onwuejeogwu 1969; also Jaggar, Pittin and Spencer in this volume), offers remedies similar to those of the herbalist and the malam. Despite ideological differences (malams reject the *bori* cult on the grounds of its pre-Islamic origins and beliefs), each recognises the abilities of the other.[10] A malam's knowledge of herbal

---

9 The secrecy surrounding this very private sphere (see the section 'Koranic education as mask' below) makes it difficult to investigate. My own knowledge comes from various sources. It is a topic I have often discussed with my friend and former neighbour, Alhaji M. Sa'idu, alone or with his colleagues and/or advanced students. One condition of such conversations is that no names or dates are mentioned; nor are any precise details of ritual readings, etc., given; these are 'trade secrets', secrets which M. Sa'idu keeps to himself.

10 One malam told me that, to cure the itching caused by the *gizaka* caterpillar one can go to a ɗan tsubbu (a herbalist with some Koranic learning, associated with the *bori* cult); he added disparagingly that the ɗan tsubbu only wants money. Malams (like everyone else) refer to a 'stroke' as *shanyewar Inna* 'the drying of Inna', a spirit of the *bori* spirit cult; they accept that a good *boka* (*bori* practitioner) can cure a stroke. There are malams who claim to cure it by rubbing on a salve and/or perfume.

medicine is therefore just one of a number of traditional choices available to Hausa people.

The 'spiritual' part of medico-spiritual activities is commonly referred to as *addu'a* or 'supererogatory prayer'. This seems to be a euphemism for a variety of practices which include numerology (*hisabi*), astrology (*duba*) and 'working with the Koran' (*yi aiki da ƙur'ani*) – or parts of it – or with other Islamic books. Some malams refer to occult Islamic knowledge as *Ismil Azim*; strictly speaking, *Ismil Azim* is the names of God in the Koran which are not known by everyone. Another word, *siddabaru* (see Adamu 1987), seems to be a general word for 'the unexplainable': this includes the miracles recounted in the Koran, Torah, Gospels or other books[11] as well as activities which are clearly forbidden. Some of these activities would come under the rubric 'magic'[12] or 'conjuring'[13] in our culture.

Numerology involves the occult study of numbers and is used to select appropriate times for particular activities; astrology has a similar function. Traditionally, these services were used by traders in order to set an auspicious day for setting out with the caravan. Texts (*laƙani*) may be used in various ways: they may be written, recited or read.

Written texts may be drunk as a medicine or used as an ointment or salve.[14] Short written texts may be worn in a leather-bound charm, the general name for which is *laya*. Children often

---

11 I have often been asked if Europeans have a book from which their 'malams' derive technology.

12 When Europeans hear about such phenomena, they often ask if it is 'magic'. Hausa people reject this word. Adamu's paper (1987) lists the different kinds of *siddabaru*. Most of these activities are not allowed by Islam: communication with spirits (*tsafi* or *sihiri*), three kinds of conjuring (*rufa ido, damfara, dabo*), uttering charms (*surƙulle*), fortune telling (*duba*) and the *bori* spirit cult. Although the author lists *duba* under things which are forbidden, he says there is a kind of *duba* which some malams undertake in accordance with Koranic principles.

13 I have witnessed a malam literally 'making' money; I took this to be a conjuring trick (*dabo*, see note 12) which I did not 'see through'. Belief in the reality of this is widespread; I have heard it said that one should use such money quickly before it returns to its original state (in the case I witnessed: newspaper). Similar activities are recorded in Woblai (n.d.), an autobiographical account of a pagan magician in 'Yola, N. E. Nigeria, before he became a Christian.

14 I have seen a malam writing out a section of the Koran (from memory, of course!) onto a small writing-board, rinsing the board (the written text) into a bowl and smearing the liquid onto his eyes. This was a medicine against an eye complaint.

wear a *laya* against illness; adults may wear them for a number of reasons; Abraham (1962: 617) suggests that they are used against 'fever, evil spirits and thieves' and as an 'antidote' against *sammu*, 'evil charms'.[15] One of the areas in which malams use *laya* is in their treatment of marriage problems. A woman may go to a malam to request his help when she feels her husband is not happy with her (she may feel he is neglecting her – in favour of another wife).[16] Such activities may overlap with the malam's 'social worker' activities for he may simply be able to give advice without resort to medicine or spiritual activities.

Recitation of a *laƙani* may be used where one wishes to achieve a specific end. A businessman, for instance, may recite a *laƙani* given by his malam when going to meet another businessman to sign a contract: he will recite it while approaching his opposite number to shake hands, his intention being to create a climate in which a favourable conclusion is reached.

When the Koran or another book is read, it often involves more than one reading and more than one person. It involves not just a particular text but also a ritual number of readings read at particular times – often at night. The malam will undertake such a reading either with colleagues and/or with advanced students. It is a time-consuming activity, one which binds malams to those with whom and for whom they undertake it. The pilgrimage to Mecca may also be undertaken as part of an *addu'a*; the malam may undertake it; it will be paid for by the person asking for the *addu'a*. The malam and his client share a common interest in the success of *addu'a*: the client has his private reasons, the malam his professional interest.

'Spiritualism'

'Spiritualism' is a particular part of what I have called the *addu'a*-related activities of some malams. (Whether there is a clear distinction between 'spiritualism' and other *addu'a*-related activities, I cannot say – due to the privacy associated with this sphere.)

---

15 Professor Joanna Mantel-Niecko, Dept of African Languages and Cultures, Warsaw University, said (personal communication) that traditional Ethiopian priests also make such charms; she found many parallels between Koranic and traditional Ethiopian Christian educational and medico-spiritual practises.

16 There are *layoyi* (sing. *laya*) which are believed to enhance sexual pleasure; they can be worn round the waist or kept under the pillow.

The English word 'spiritualism' normally implies communication with the spirits of the departed; Hausa 'spiritualism' involves the invocation of spirits of another world. For this reason, I leave the word in inverted commas.

'Spiritualism' seems to be widespread and is believed to be very effective. Belief in the existence of spirits is a part of everyday life. Words such as *iskoki, aljannu, dodanni* and *rauhanai*[17] are everyday words for spirits. Spirits may be asked to induce illness, injury, madness or even death but this kind of invocation can be a dangerous activity; sacrifice (*zub da jini*, 'spilling blood') will be required to make sure that the illness or injury does not strike the malam or his client.[18] Many Muslims reject such activities out of hand, referring to them as *hila* 'subterfuge' or *camfi*, 'superstition'; Adamu (1987) clearly says that such activity is forbidden by Islam (see note 13). Even malams who engage in such activities admit that it is not really allowed in Islam and that they only do it *in extremis*.[19]

Hausa people are absolutely convinced that *addu'a* works – and very convincing.[20] However, the close relationship malams enjoy with their influential patrons (see below) raises an interesting

---

17 The fact that malams are readily associated with *rauhanai* can be seen in the dictionary entry for *rauhani* where the term *mai rauhani* (lit. 'one (associated) with night-spirits') is considered as an equivalent to *malami*, 'malam': (*pl. rauhanai*) (1) *mai rauhani* = *malami*. (2) *ya nemi rauhanai* he invoked night-spirits to carry out his wishes (*if mistakes are made, it is considered there is risk of madness or even death*) (Abraham 1962: 727)

18 The fear that one may risk madness or death in such activities is so widely accepted that some people interpret the gift of an animal or bird to the malam for having reached a certain point in the study of the Koran as a sacrifice (it will be slaughtered and eaten) to avoid such a possibility. The reasoning is that the student has just read a passage which may be used for such an invocation. Other people insist that this gift is simply alms, presented to the malam to show thanks for his help. Prof. Ibrahim Yaro Yahaya of Bayero University (personal communication) insisted on the second interpretation.

19 On the other hand I have heard it said that certain activities such as smuggling – a malam can help smugglers with charms such as *layar zana* (a charm which renders a person invisible) – are not considered to be against the law of God: borders were not drawn by God, but by colonialists.

20 In one notorious case (concerning the reduction of a prison sentence by an appeal court judge), I was almost 'laughed out of court' (pardon the expression!) for expressing my incredulity at the judge's reducing the sentence and, apparently, accepting a large amount of money for doing so – it was, after all, a public act. I was told that the judge had *no choice* but to reduce the sentence *and* take the money. The explanation was that some malams had 'done *Yasin* on him [the judge]' – a literal translation of '*an yi masa Yasin*'. Yasin is a chapter of the Koran which, read under certain circumstances, is believed to be very effective.

question: are *addu'a*-related successes achieved through medicine, prayer, 'spiritualist' activities or, perhaps, through these very contacts? I suspect that the malam's patrons often play a role in helping to get someone a hospital bed, a marriage partner or a job.

Koranic Education as 'Mask'

The central argument of this chapter is that Koranic education masks the medico-spiritual activities. The secrecy surrounding the performance of *addu'a*-related (especially 'spiritualist') activities is crucial to this argument. We have seen that many Muslims condemn these activities and that even those who practice them admit that they are not really allowed. This and the privacy associated with these activities are sufficient reason for secrecy. There is, however, a paradox which has to be explained: the existence of these activities is common knowledge! For instance, writing boards (smaller than those on which students or malams normally write) on which *addu'a* are written if one wants to drink or smear the 'medicine' (see note 14; also Jaggar, in this volume) can be seen in almost any Koranic school. (It is said that young students are preferred to write such texts as they are considered more innocent in the eyes of God). Again, the vocabulary of such activities is part of normal speech; such themes even appear in humorous tales.[21] If these activities are common knowledge, why the secrecy? The reasons are simple and have been mentioned: *addu'a* is too private and often involves practises forbidden by Islam (see note 12). Any investigator must be sensitive to these facts.[22] Everyone 'knows'

---

21 One funny story (see Ahmad, n.d.) called *Addu'a ba ta ci* 'The prayer doesn't work' tells of a man constantly coming to visit an emir, eventually asking the emir to give him an *addu'a* which, he has heard, the emir has and successfully uses. The emir gives him the prayer (presumably a written text, perhaps with instructions) but tells him that 'it is not acceptable (to God)' (*ba karɓaɓɓa ce ba*): the emir used it to ask God to stop this man coming – and here he is again!

22 (See note 9) Only one malam (not Sa'idu) ever mentioned a specific case and a name; this involved a man's marrying a woman who had many suitors. One friend and Koranic teacher, Alhaji M. Jinjiri (he taught in his elder brother's school) flatly refused to talk about the subject when I first broached it. We had known each other for over two years and still maintain contact; but I never asked him again, nor did he ever volunteer any information on the subject. However, I once witnessed a small girl coming to Jinjiri to ask him to do *addu'a* for her brother who seemed to be lost. She handed him 1 Naira – I presumed this was *kuɗin kafin alkalami*, an initial payment. Jinjiri's elder brother, Alhaji M. Badamasi is a malam of some influence in Gwammaja quarters. It is unlikely that he does not perform *addu'a*.

that they occur and can quote examples – even personal examples, but they are not openly discussed. Giving details of *addu'a* – even of the ritual number of prayers, the times, etc. – would be a betrayal by the malam of his hard-won knowledge and, of course, of his client – rather like passing on industrial secrets or the secrets of confession; this is especially true of 'spiritualist' activities. (I have no detailed examples of a malam's undertaking such activity although everybody 'knows' where to find a malam who could do such things!)

Given the secrecy surrounding medico-spiritual activities, the idea that something might function as a mask is not surprising; this mask is education. Three factors indicate this: 1) medico-spiritual activities are carried out in the malam's school; 2) medico-spiritual practitioners 'earn' more from their medico-spiritual than from their educational activities; 3) there is no specific term for the malam as medico-spiritual practitioner.

1) The school is the centre of medico-spiritual activities: the client goes to the malam in his school to ask for *addu'a* to be done; it is here that the malam conducts his medico-spiritual activities using the small boards he has there or conducting the *addu'a* with students or fellow malams according to what is needed in a particular case.

2) The masking function of education is underlined by the fact that the malam cannot rely on education to 'earn his living' (see note 8). Firstly, Islam forbids payment for teaching the Koran; secondly, as I have mentioned above, the amounts given are small. The fact is that the malam undertaking *addu'a*-related activities receives more from them than from his educational activities. When a client approaches a malam asking him to perform *addu'a* for him he must bring a gift: *kuɗin kafin alkalami* (lit. 'the price of applying the pen'); if the wish has been granted (Hausa: *bukata ta biya*), a further gift will be given to the malam. Gifts are given according to what the client can afford. M. Sa'idu has made the pilgrimage to Mecca a number of times; he could not afford these journeys from what he receives as a Koranic teacher; they are probably paid for by patrons and may well be *addu'a*-related. M. Jinjiri's brother (see note 22) has influential patrons: his first car was a gift from a businessman; the extra rooms for his 'living-in' students (see note 7) are paid by a patron. One malam (see note 24) told me that he financed his first marriage through his role as a go-between in the 1964 election (between a politician and malams doing *addu'a* for him; his client won).

3) If the words 'malam' or 'imam' clearly depict a status and an associated activity, the status associated with *addu'a*-related activities is not separately named, i.e., not 'labelled' with a noun.[23] Non-islamic medico-spiritual practitioners, however, are clearly named: the *boka* (*bori* practitioner) and the *ɗan tsubbu* (see note 10). I relate this to the secrecy of *addu'a*-related activities. Paradoxically, the word 'malam' can, in context, be used to mean 'medico-spiritual practitioner' (this, despite the fact that not all malams undertake such activities!) and the malam regularly undertaking such activities may even be referred to as the *ainihin malam* ('real malam')[24] of the person on whose behalf he performs it! This euphemism is a mask, one which clearly indicates what is being masked and what the mask is!

One consequence of this masking function is that the role of malam as medico-spiritual practitioner is ambivalent: is he a patron or a client? In Hausa there is no technical term for 'patron'. The term '*mai gida*' ('house owner', 'landlord'; also used by a wife to mean 'husband') is often used to express this role, its meaning being context-bound rather than lexicalised. Similarly, the malam in his role as medico-spiritual practitioner is simply referred to as '*malam*', the context making the meaning clear. The term *ainihin malam* ('real malam', see above) clearly casts the malam as 'patron'. The malam's clients are referred to with a context-bound euphemism: *mutum* (plural: *mutane*), 'person (people)'.

Malams' relationships with parents and other members of the community they serve are patron-client relationships in which the malam is most often the patron. Reichmuth (see note 5) describes the person seeking help from a malam as 'client'. This is certainly true of his relationship to less wealthy clients: they come to the Koranic school to learn and/or pray; they come for advice about their sons and daughters and for the kind of help expected from

---

23 This is an interesting sociolinguistic phenomenon: verbs and nouns are found at opposite poles of a time-stability scale in language, with verbs depicting 'rapid change' while nouns depict 'entities ... which do not change their identity over time (or change it rather slowly)' (Givón 1979: 14). Medico-spiritual activities are described, verbally or with an action-noun: e.g., *yi aiki da ƙur'ani* (work with the Koran), *addu'a* (praying).

24 Alhaji M. Abubakar Bashiru (a Tijaniya malam whom I got to know through his involvement in the sale of Islamic mss. to Bayero University, Kano) told me this.

addu'a; the term 'big man' describes the malam's position very well. Officiating as *imam* for prayers or rite-of-passage ceremonies consolidates this position.

With wealthier people, however, the relative statuses become ambiguous: Paden (1973: 57) describes the malam as 'client' in his relationships with important personages. Economically, the malam is the client, performing a service for someone who supports him. On the other hand the malam wields power in the secret realm of *addu'a* where the patron is dependent on his (the malam's) abilities and success.

Malams certainly see themselves as the equals of their patrons. M. Sa'idu expressed himself very clearly on this point, saying that while his patrons[25] were 'wealthy men' (*masu kudi*), malams were 'learned men' (*masu ilimi*) – a pointed way of putting them on an equal social footing. The fact that the malam is obviously the patron in his relationships with less wealthy clients can only reinforce this. Perhaps too the fact that any monies or goods given to the malam are regarded as *sadaka* (alms) and not payment also plays a role in this ambiguity: the malam is not being *paid* for his services. Furthermore, the idea that the malam who performs *addu'a* is the 'real malam' of the person for whom it is done, implicitly casts the latter as 'student' – whatever his status.

Malams and Economic-Political Power

In this section I shall describe malams' connections with merchants and politicians. This is an important fact and deserves to be mentioned in its own right; it is also important to show that malams as an occupational group are not in competition with merchants and politicians.

One need only sit with malams for a short while to hear how many 'names' they know: that 'so-and-so' is the patron of the school (see note 25); that one of their wives is the younger sister (etc.) of 'so-and-so'; that they will ask 'so-and-so' to help a client. M. Jinjiri (see note 22) mentioned Alhaji Audu Lukat and Alhaji

---

25 He was referring specifically to my late landlord, a leading contractor in Nigeria, with a minor political title in Kano; he played a decisive role in Sa'idu's becoming the malam of the area I lived in (1975–78), building a mosque and appointing Sa'idu as the imam; it is also Sa'idu's school (see McIntyre 1982).

Sani Mashal (both well known in Kano business circles and beyond) in connection with his brother's school.

Malams' links with the political classes of Hausa society are well documented; Paden (1973: 57) says:

> ... each major government figure in Kano has a circle of personal malams to advise him and *pray for* him. The madaki may have as many as ten malams; the waziri may have six. These malams *pray for* the success of the government official and have a personal *client* relationship with him. [My italics]

Malams are themselves represented on the emir's council, only businessmen and traders being better represented (see Paden 1973: 417, 419–20).

Malams and their *addu'a*-related activities are simply part of the traditional political fabric of a city such as Kano. The close links between malams and the political classes – including present-day politicians at both state and national level – are best summed up by a Koranic teacher friend, M. Muhtari, who told me (September 1993) how former president Babangida had 'robbed us [malams] of our livelihood' by not allowing civilian (party) politics. He was referring to Babangida's cancelling the June 1993 election:[26] Babangida had also 'cancelled' the *addu'a*-related activities performed for politicians.

As a short coda, it is worth mentioning an example of malams defending their own interests. This relates to the question of the introduction of Universal Free Primary Education (UPE) announced in October 1974. The lives and livelihood of malams would have been directly affected by UPE: the establishment of Western education for every child would weaken their influence, reducing the numbers of Koranic students and probably affecting their 'income', at least in a small way. Any reduction in student numbers or in contact with students' parents and/or guardians could reduce the scope of their medico-spiritual activities and weaken the masking function of education. The malams were able to use their influence to defend their own interests. Once this was achieved, however, they did not go on to establish a permanent party or influence-group.

---

26 President Babangida handed power to an 'interim president' (Shonekan) on 26 August 1993 after cancelling the June election, assumed by many to have been fairly won by the southern candidate, Abiola, against his northern opponent, Tofa (a Kano man).

Conclusion

Malams achieve their status primarily in education: they are formally understood to be teachers and derive their status and identity from it; this is the cultural given. During their education many learn medico-spiritual knowledge, the hidden influence. The Koran is central to their education and important to their medico-spiritual knowledge. The malam's identity as teacher legitimates his place in the community. From this 'place' he may practice medico-spiritual activities, activities which give rise to a number of ambiguities: some of these activities are not allowed in Islam; the role associated with these activities is not named; they are more important to the malam's livelihood than education, cementing his relationship to wealthy patrons and consolidating his status in the community. Thus from this strong position of legitimacy – as educationalists – malams can allow themselves room to manoeuvre in a sphere whose legitimacy is less clear.

Although malams are closely connected to wealth and power, their hidden influence is not used in the group interest. Ongoing group interest as described by Cohen (1969a, 1969b, 1974, 1980, 1981), where a non-political identity is used to further political ends for the group itself, is not a permanent feature of the malams' identity. Malams can defend themselves when threatened (as in the case of UPE) but they do not seek to consolidate ongoing group power, political or economic; their *addu'a*-related activities are performed for others. Malams are not in competition with merchants or politicians, they work *for* them. Although individual malams may achieve power and influence in the spheres of both educational and *addu'a*-related activities, malams play a subsidiary role in the political sphere. Perhaps their very identity – as people who pray (apparently, successfully) for the success of *others* – limits their potential to develop into a group which understands itself as having an ongoing political identity. Perhaps too malams are simply content with their 'behind the scenes' work, enjoying many of the benefits and avoiding many of the risks associated with political struggle.

Although the relationship between education and medico-spiritual activities is not one of 'politics articulated in terms of non-political cultural forms' (Cohen 1993: ix), nevertheless, the masking function of education parallels Cohen's idea of 'masquerade politics': here, the legitimacy of one cultural form, education, functions as a mask for an activity whose legitimacy is not clear, allowing it to subsist. Performing this half-hidden activity for wealthy and powerful people guarantees the high status and influence of malams.

References

Abraham, R. C. 1962. *Dictionary of the Hausa Language* (2nd edn). London: University of London Press.

Adamu, Muhammad Tahir. 1987. 'Siddabaru a Kasar Hausa: Yadda Yake da Kuma Yadda Ake Gudanar da Shi', Unpublished paper presented at the Fourth Conference on Hausa Language, Literature and Culture, Bayero University, Kano, September 1987.

Ahmad, Alhaji B. n.d. (?1958). *Ban Dariya. Funny Stories.* Zaria: North Regional Literature Agency.

Besmer, F.E. 1977. 'Initiation Into the Bori Cult. A Case Study in Ningi Town', *Africa* 47: 1–13.

Bosworth, C. E, Evan Donzel, B. Lewis and Ch. Pellat (eds), assisted by F. Th. Dijkema and Mme S. Nurit. 1986. *Encyclopaedia of Islam* (New Edition), vol. v. Leiden: E. J. Brill.

Cohen, Abner. 1969a. *Custom and Politics in Urban Africa (A Study of Hausa Migrants in Yoruba Towns)*. London: Routledge and Kegan Paul.

——. 1969b. 'Political Anthropology: the Analysis of the Symbolism of Power Relations', *Man* (N.S.) 4: 215–35.

——. 1974. *Two Dimensional Man (An Essay on the Anthropology of Power and Symbolism in Complex Society)*. London: Routledge and Kegan Paul.

——. 1980. 'Drama and Politics in the Development of a London Carnival', *Man* (N.S.) 15: 65–87.

——. 1981. *The Politics of Elite Culture*. Berkeley and Los Angeles: University of California Press.

——. 1993. *Masquerade Politics (Explorations in the Structure of Urban Cultural Movements)*. Berkeley and Los Angeles: University of California Press.

Encyclopedia of Islam. 1986. see Bosworth et al.

Givón, Talmy. 1979. *On Understanding Grammar.* New York: Academic Press.

Kleiner-Bossaller, Anke. 1993. 'Zur Stellung der Frau in der Hausagesellschaft: Ein Brüchig Gewordener Konsens', in *Muslime in Nigeria: Religion und Gesellschaft im Politischen Wandel Seit den 50er Jahren,* Jamil M. Abun-Nasr (ed.). Beitrag zur Afrikaforschung, Universität Bayreuth.

McIntyre, J.A. 1982 (unpublished). 'The Malam in the Community: Functions, Wealth, Patrons and Clients', Paper presented to Department of Anthropology and Sociology, SOAS, London University.

Monfouga-Nicolas, J. 1972. *Ambivalence et Culte de Possession: Contribution à l'Etude du Bori Hausa*. Paris: Editions Anthropos.

Onwuejeogwu, M. 1969. 'The Cult of the Bori Spirits Among the Hausa', in *Man in Africa*, M. Douglas and P.H. Kaberry (eds). London: Tavistock Publications.

Paden, J. 1973. *Religion and Political Culture in Kano*. Berkeley: University of California Press.

Reichmuth, Stefan. 1993. 'Islamische Bildung und ihr Verhältnis zum Staatlichen Bildungswesen', in *Muslime in Nigeria: Religion und Gesellschaft im Politischen Wandel Seit den 50er Jahren*, Jamil M. Abun-Nasr (ed.). Beitrag zur Afrikaforschung, Universität Bayreuth.

Woblai, Joel. (n.d.). *Tarihin Boka*. Yola, Nigeria: L.C.C.N. Bookshop.

BIOGRAPHICAL NOTES ON CONTRIBUTORS

Ifi Amadiume is Associate Professor of Religion and African Studies at Dartmouth College, USA. Her publications include *Male Daughters, Female Husbands: Gender and Sex in an African Society* (1987), which was the Winner of Choice Magazine Outstanding Academic Book Award 1988–89, and *African Matriarchal Foundations: the Igbo Case* (1987). She is also a published and award winning poet.

O.A.C. Anigbo is a Senior Lecturer in the Department of Sociology/Anthropology, University of Nigeria, Nsukka. He has a Doctorate in Dogmatic Theology from Rome, Urbaniana, and a PhD in Social Anthropology from the School of Oriental and African Studies, University of London. Dr Anigbo has published *Commensality and Human Relationship among the Igbo* (1987) and *Igbo Elite and Western Europe* (1992).

F.G. Bailey is Professor of Anthropology (Emeritus), University of California, San Diego. His most recent books are *The Prevalence of Deceit* (1991), *The Kingdom of Individuals* (1993), and *The Witch-Hunt* (1994).

Sandra T. Barnes is Professor of Anthropology at the University of Pennsylvania. She is the author of *Patrons and Power: Creating a Political Community in Metropolitan Lagos* (1986), for which she received the Amaury Talbot Prize, and *Africa's Ogun: Old World and New* (1989). Her research and publications have focused on African urbanism, religion, politics, and history. She is currently preparing a study of cultural and social pluralism in precolonial West Africa.

Lionel Caplan is Professor of South Asian Anthropology at the School of Oriental and African Studies, University of London. He has conducted research in Nepal and urban South India. Author of *Class and Culture in Urban India: Fundamentalism in a Christian Community* (1987), and editor of *Studies in Religious Fundamentalism* (1987), his most recent publication is *Warrior Gentlemen: 'Gurkhas' in the Western Imagination* (1995).

Adrian Collett worked for many years in commerce. In 1987, at the age of 41, he resigned from Unigate Dairies to do a first degree in Law and Social Anthropology at SOAS, then went on to complete a PhD in Social Anthropology, doing fieldwork in Northern Nigeria. He now runs two thriving businesses in partnership with his wife and his son, and writes when he can find the time. Publications include 'Authority in rural African communities south of the Sahara' and (with Sani Maguda) 'The Anaguta of Northern Nigeria: a rural case study', both published in *The Courier*, No. 99 (1986).

Elizabeth Colson is Professor Emeritus, Department of Anthropology, University of California, Berkeley. She has carried out long-term research in Southern Province, Zambia, beginning in 1946 when Zambia was still the colonial territory Northern Rhodesia, and has also done research among Native Australians and in the Northern territory of Australia. She is the author of *The Social Consequences of Resettlement: The Impact of the Karib Resettlement upon the Gwembe Tonga* (1971), *Tradition and Contract: The Problem of Order* (1974), and senior author of *For Prayer and Profit: The Ritual, Economic, and Social Importance of Beer in Gwembe District, Zambia, 1950–82* (1988).

Humphrey J. Fisher has taught at the School of Oriental and African Studies since 1962. He has written extensively on the history (chiefly the Islamic history) of sub-Saharan Africa, and on religious phenomenology and the processes of religious change there. His major single publication is the four-volume annotated English translation of Gustav Nachtigal's *Sahara und Sudan* (1980), putting for the first time this German work, one of the most outstanding African accounts from the nineteenth century, into the hands of African scholars and readers.

P.H. Gulliver is Distinguished Research Professor of Anthropology, Emeritus, York University, Toronto. He has conducted field research in eastern Africa and the Republic of Ireland. His publications include *Disputes and Negotiations* (1979), *In the Valley of the Nore* (1986), and *Merchants and Shopkeepers, A Historical Anthropology of an Irish Market Town* (1995).

Philip J. Jaggar is Senior Lecturer in Hausa, School of Oriental and African Studies, University of London, and during 1994–95 was a Visiting Scholar at the Nigerian Studies Institute, Indiana University, Bloomington, USA, preparing a *Hausa Reference Grammar*, and a *Hausa Newspaper Reader*. Recent publications include *An Advanced Hausa Reader with Grammatical Notes and Exercises* (1992), and *The Blacksmiths of Kano City, Nigeria: Tradition, Innovation and Entrepreneurship in the Twentieth Century* (1994).

J.A. McIntyre is Lecturer in Hausa at the Seminar für Afrikanische Sprachen und Kulturen, at the University of Hamburg. After a year's research in Kano on Qur'anic schools, he taught in Bayero University, Kano from 1975–78. Since 1978, he has taught in Hamburg, and from 1984–94 at the University of Cologne. Recent publications have been concerned with Hausa language: verbo-nominalisation and lexicon. They include, with Hilke Meyer-Bahlburg and Ahmad Tijani Lawal, *Hausa in the Media: A Lexical Guide. Hausa-English-German; English-Hausa; German-Hausa* (1991).

Onigu Otite is Professor of Sociology at the University of Ibadan. After completing his PhD at the School of Oriental and African Studies, he was a Government Administrative Officer before becoming an academic. Professor Otite was Visiting Research Professor at the Centre for Development Studies, University of Bergen, Norway in 1986; Visiting Professor of Sociology, University of Pennsylvania, Philadelphia in 1987; and Senior Social Development Research Fellow, ACARTSOD, Tripoli, in 1991. His publications include *Autonomy and Dependence: The Urhobo Kingdom of Okpe in Modern Nigeria* (1973), *The Urhobo People* (1982 – ed.), *Ethnic Pluralism and Ethnicity in Nigeria* (1990), and *On the Path of Progess: A Study of Rural Immigrants and Development in Nigeria* (forthcoming).

David Parkin is Professor of African Anthropology at the School of Oriental and African Studies, University of London, and a Fellow of the British Academy. He has carried out fieldwork in Kenya, Uganda and Zanzibar among such peoples as the Giriama, Digo, Luo and certain Swahili-speakers on topics covering religion, including Islam, indigenous uses of space and environment, local medicines, cross-cultural semantics and informal politics. His books include *Sacred Void, The Cultural Definition of Political Response, Palms, Wine and Witnesses* and *Bush, Base; Forest Farm*.

Renée Pittin is Associate Professor in Women's Studies, in the Women and Development Programme, Institute of Social Studies, The Hague. Her most recent publication is *Confronting State, Capital and Patriarchy: Women Organising in the Process of Industrialisation*, co-edited with Amrita Chhachhi, and shortly to be published. She is presently completing a volume entitled *Women, Work and Ideology in Nigeria*.

Paul Spencer is Professor of African Anthropology, specialising in the Maasai-speaking peoples and other pastoralists of East Africa. This has led to a particular interest in age organisation and the perception of maturation and ageing more generally. His approach towards dancing, discussed in the present volume, stemmed from fieldwork among the Samburu (1957–60, 1962). Recent publications include *The Maasai of Matapato: a Study of Rituals of Rebellion* (1988).

James L. Watson is Fairbank Professor of Chinese Society and Professor of Anthropology at Harvard University. He taught previously at the School of Oriental and African Studies (University of London), University of Pittsburgh, and the University of Hawaii. His publications include *Emigration and the Chinese Lineage*, *Asian and African Systems of Slavery* (ed., 1980), and *Death Ritual in Late Imperial and Modern China* (ed., 1988). He is currently working on a book entitled *Fast Food Transnational: MacDonald's in East Asia*.

Pnina Werbner is a Senior Lecturer in Social Anthropology at Keele University and Research Administrator of the International Centre for Contemporary Cultural Research at the Universities of Manchester and Keele. Her publications include *The Migration Process: Capital, Gifts and Offerings among British Pakistanis* (1990), *Black and Ethnic Leaderships in Britain: The Cultural Dimensions of Political Action*, co-edited with Muhammad Anwar (1991), and *Economy and Culture in Pakistan: Migrants and Cities in a Muslim Society*, co-edited with Hastings Donnan. She is currently the director of a major research project funded by the Economic and Social Research Council, UK, on 'South Asian Popular Culture: Gender, Generation and Identity'.

INDEX

Aborisade, Oladimeji, 21, 25, 27, 38, 39, 40
absolution, forgiveness, 153, 244, 247, 250-2
Abuja, 53, 54, 56
actors, 12-3, 27, 32, 89, 90, 202, 206, 207-8, 228
addu'a, 264; see also *dawas*
aesthetics, xxxv, 62, 187, 193, 196; community, 90-2; domain, xxiv-v, 82, 84-5, 96-7, 213; artistic unity, 5, 11, 32; 'transcendental unity', 240, 247, 252-4
African National Congress (ANC), Zambia, 68-9, 70, 77
age-grade, 133-6, 140-2, 163, 170, 177-8, 184, 185-91, 195, 278; ageing, 278
agriculture, farming, 7, 12, 50, 53, 58, 66, 68, 70, 75, 76, 78, 86, 92, 104, 106, 108, 110, 111, 117, 132, 133, 152, 161, 167, 169, 177, 191, 220, 222, 223, 224, 225, 226, 233, 260, 262, 278; cash crop, 66, 133; fertilizer, 53; subsistence, 50, 69, 161, 222; shifting cultivation, 136-7
Ahmadu Lobbo, 249, 252
alcohol, xvii, 33, 125-6, 138, 141, 163, 164, 170, 172, 173, 175, 276, 278

Amadiume, Ifi, xxvi, xxxiii, 13, 41-59, 275
Amaury Talbot Prize, ix, xi, 275
ambiguity, ambivalence, xxxiv, xxxvi, 88, 97, 152, 157, 169, 172, 179, 210, 232, 241, 247-8, 250-1, 253, 255, 270
America, USA, x, xviii-ix, xxix, 49, 61, 71; suburbia, xxix, 129-32, 136, 141-2
Anaguta, xxiv, xxxiv, 161-79
ancestors, 102, 104, 106, 134, 146, 150, 152-3, 167-8, 176, 178, 201, 229, 246, 248; *see also* dead
Anderson, Benedict, 'imagined communities', 13, 17, 41, 65, 67, 77, 90, 96
anger, 14, 43-4, 185, 192
Anigbo, xxxv-vi, 101-114, 275
animals, xxxii, 4, 7, 85-9, 91-2, 108, 147, 163-9, 170-2, 175, 178, 221, 226, 231, 244, 246, 248, 262, 266; talking, 87
anthropology, anthropologists, xxviii, xxxiv, xxxvi-viii, 40, 42, 81-3, 92-3, 127, 181-2, 190, 195-6, 224-5, 239, 255; American, x, xviii-ix, 83; British, xvii, xix, 83; cultural, xviii-ix, xxxvii; social, viii-x, xvii, xxxvii, xxxix, 101, 181, 218

Arab Border-Villages in Israel, viii, xvii, xxxviii, 19, 39, 83
Arabs, viii, xi, xxxviii; Arabia, 238, 240, 252; Arabic, xxxiii
archaeology, 62-3
Ardener, E., xxxvi, xxxviii; Shirley A., x, 44, 57, 58
arts, artist, xx, 67, 73, 97, 98, 176, 181-97, 205, 225, 239
Arusha, xxviii, 133-6, 139, 140-3, 184
Asia, South, xxv, 84, 85, 90, 96
Askiya Muhammad, xxxii, 237-55; A. Dawud, 250
audience, 3-4, 8-11, 13, 22, 34-5, 83-4, 87, 90, 92, 94-5, 97, 112-3, 120, 148, 176, 189, 205, 227-9, 233; congregation, 119; jama'ah, 242
Australia, 99, 182, 197, 276
authenticity, 11-4, 16, 41, 62, 240, 253
autonomy, 23, 42-3, 44, 50, 62, 72, 102, 104, 106, 113, 131, 136, 140, 183, 240, 253, 255, 277
avoidance, xxviii-ix, 125-43, 181, 190, 237-8; dispute a., 126-41; conflict a., 126-7, 141-2
Baba of Karo, see Mary F. Smith
Babangida, Gen. Ibrahim (1985-93), 45, 48, 49, 51, 55-7, 271; Maryam, 48-57
Bailey, F.G., ix, xvii, xx-xxi, xxxviii, 1-17, 41, 275
Bantu Botatwe, xxvii-viii, 61-80
Barnes, Sandra T., xxiii, 19-40, 73, 113, 275
Bayart, Jean-François, 21, 27, 32, 38, 39
belief, xvii, xviii, xxiv, xxv, xxviii, xxix, xxx-xxxi, xxxiii, xxxv, 2-4, 16, 67, 119-20, 156, 159, 192, 193, 202, 231, 243, 252, 264, 266; unbelief, 237, 246, 251
Bemba, xxvii, 66, 67, 68-9, 71, 72, 74, 75
birds, 88, 92, 166, 168, 171, 248, 251, 262, 266
Bisipara, xx-xxii, xxxiv, xxxvi, 6-20
black, xiii, 84, 92, 94, 99, 100, 177
blacksmiths, xxx, 217-36, 239, 242
Blum, C., and H.J. Fisher, 238, 245, 254
bori, xxx, xxxii-iii, xxxv, 58, 191-6, 199, 215, 231, 263, 264, 269, 273-4
boundaries, borders, 19-20, 92, 98, 100, 188; cultural, xxxvii, 37, 81, 115, 120, 163, 168, 233-4; descent, 108; economic, xxxviii; ethnic, 83, 93; international, xi, 70, 261, 266; liminality, 245-9, 253; local, 28, 104, 149; permeability, 20, 168
boundedness, groups etc., xxiv-xxvi, xxviii, 42, 50, 61-2, 74, 102
Bourdieu, Pierre, 31, 39, 93, 98, 172
bourgeoisie, xxi, 35, 44, 46
Brecht, Bertolt, xxi-xxii, xxxvi, xxxviii
Britain, ix, xiii, xxiv-v, xxix, 29, 44, 61, 81-100, 163; *see also* colonialism, British, *and* anthropology, British
Buddhism, 152
bureaucracy, 25, 26, 28, 29, 30, 35, 36, 44, 95, 259, 263
burial, 95, 168, 174, 177, 247-8, 250-1, 262; tombs, 150
business, manufacturing, industry, 22, 27, 28, 29-31, 33, 45, 51, 72, 76, 86, 94, 117, 118, 123, 126, 146, 154, 221, 224, 232, 235, 265, 278

Cameroons, 23, 40, 58, 235-6; Adamawa, 30; Mandara, 235-6; Yola, 264
capital, 22, 31, 100, 117, 278; symbolic, 20, 23, 31, 32
capitalism, xxv, xxxvii, 44, 50; Global Finance C., 44
Caplan, Lionel, xxiii, xxxviii, 41, 217, 237, 276
carnival, 5, 239-40, 241, 242; *see also* Notting Hill
caste, xx-xxi, xxx, xxxviii, 5-17, 222, 236
cattle, herding, xi, 85-9, 123, 184-5, 188, 189
Chaudri Muhammad Amin, 85-96
checks and balances, 22, 25, 28, 44
chiefs, xxiii-iv, xxvii, xxxvi, 19-40, 73-66, 79, 108-14; predictions concerning, 26-7, 32
children, 4, 69, 70, 103-4, 116, 133, 137, 162-3, 166-7, 175, 177, 186, 220, 227, 233-4, 248, 260, 264-5, 269, 271; as innocent intermediaries, 188, 195, 246-7, 267; child birth, 149; disabled, 54; not-yet-born, 104; 'of God', 10-1; *see also* family, kin, wives
China, Chinese, xl, 146, 153, 156, 278
choice, xxix, 129, 141, 264
Christianity, xxvii, 45-6, 46, 53, 55, 62-3, 75, 114, 117, 120, 149, 162-3, 170, 173, 239, 244, 255, 264, 265, 276, 278; missions, 53, 68, 114; Dame Julian, 247; YWCA, 45-6
circumcision, 166-7, 170, 225
citizens, 9, 10, 12, 22, 23, 37, 69-70, 96, 97, 121-2
clans, 15, 43, 185, 188-9

class, 20, 42, 44, 45-6, 55, 56, 92-4, 130-2, 159, 199, 203, 206, 207, 222, 235, 276
cleric, Muslim, xxx, xxxi-iii, 85, 91, 202, 211, 213, 237-8, 243-9; *ulema*, 88; see also *malams, maulvi, imam,* etc.
clients, xii, 24, 146, 211, 212, 221, 261, 268-9
Clinton, Hillary, 49
Cohen, Abner, viii-xiii, xv-xxviii, xxix, 1, 19, 39, 41-3, 44, 57-8, 61-2, 74, 83-4, 96, 101, 115, 123-4, 125, 145, 157-8, 163, 173, 183, 191, 199, 206, 213, 217-9, 223, 224-5, 226, 231, 233-4, 239, 253-4, 254-5, 258, 272
collective, 56, 89-90, 92, 182, 183-4, 190, 218-9, 227, 233
Collett, Adrian, xxiv, xxxiv, 161-79, 276
colonialism, ix, 37, 39-40, 43-4, 83, 133, 266; British, xxiii-xxv, xxxviii, 15-6, 20, 25-6, 38-40, 42, 45, 48, 58, 67-8, 72-4, 77, 80, 109, 146, 157, 161, 176, 184, 218, 276; land reform, 146; French, 25-6, 38, 40
Colson, Elizabeth, xxvii, 26, 61-80, 276
commensality, xxxv-vi, 101-114; *see also* food
conflict resolution, xviii, xix, xxviii-ix, 7, 23, 26, 28, 29, 82, 118, 127, 212, 228
Copperbelt, copper, 66, 68, 69, 70, 71, 72, 82
cosmology, xxxv, xxxviii, 181-97, 203
courts, royal, chiefly, 2, 24, 106, 110, 237
credit, xi, 70, 76
Creoles, ix, xxvi, 42-3, 45, 46, 65

cultural performance (especially the dialectical relationship between power and symbolism), xv-xvi, xx, 19, 42, 62, 83-4, 173, 183-4, 199, 218, 234, 239-40
custom, xi, xiii, xv, xxvii, xxxiv, 106, 107, 111, 210, 234, 236, 238; *see also* tradition
Custom and Politics in Urban Africa (1969), ix, xi, xv, xvii, xxvi, 19, 42, 47, 61, 65, 83, 123, 206, 213, 218-9, 223, 224, 231, 247
dance, xix, xxx, xxxiv-v, xxxviii, 52, 56, 104, 105, 107-8, 112, 119-20, 164, 170, 174, 175, 177, 181-97, 209, 215, 226-9, 231; dragon, 150; fire, 229-30; Kalela, xvii, xxxix, 82-3; *lebarta*, xxxv, 186-91
dawas (Muslim supplications, in this case *against* someone, amongst Punjabi Muslims in Manchester, from the Arabic *du'a'*), 88; see also *addu'a*
dead, xxxix, 42, 95, 104, 148-9, 246-88; ghosts, 147, 149; *see also* ancestors
death, 8, 113, 148, 149, 157, 159, 174, 176, 202, 227, 237, 245-6, 248, 250, 266, 278; execution, 22, 167; mourning, 8, 149; suicide, 22; *see also* murder
debate, dialogue, 8, 20, 21, 22, 47, 49, 51, 76, 82, 89, 91, 92, 95, 96, 98, 170-4
decision-making, xxi, 20, 107, 136
deconstruction, 41, 56
democracy, democratisation, 12, 21, 40, 48, 58, 72, 77, 86, 89, 91, 92, 93, 97, 110, 116, 143
deposition, 22, 28, 33
Derridaemonic confusion, 11

descent groups, descendants, 24, 43, 62, 102, 108, 111, 116, 118, 146, 201, 207, 220, 223, 224, 228, 246
desert, xxvi; Sahara, xxxii, 238, 242-50, 252-4, 260; Sahel, 233
development, xii, 27, 38, 52, 53-4, 69, 73, 77, 122, 124, 278; aid, 44, 53
devil, Iblis, demons, xxxix, 211, 215, 246, 248
dialects, 66, 68, 80, 116
diaspora, xii, xxiv-vi, 42, 45, 63, 81-5, 88, 94, 96-7
Diop, Cheikh Anta, 43, 56, 58
diplomatic service, 29-30, 49-50, 126, 209
discourse, 26, 32, 34, 36, 82, 84, 90, 94, 168, 172, 174, 239
drama, dramaturgy, social drama, ix, xi, xii, xv, xvii, xviii-ix, xx-i, xxxii, xxxvi, xxxvii, xxxix, 1-17, 31, 35, 41, 73, 74, 85, 89, 104, 116, 119-21, 168-9, 173, 174, 176, 178, 218-9, 225, 228, 231, 234, 238, 239, 249
dress, xxv, 33-4, 46, 55, 87, 117, 118-20, 123, 151, 185, 228, 241-2; cloth, 34, 118, 120, 220; dyeing, 87, 220; tailoring, 118, 123, 220, 262
drums, 34, 164-6, 168, 169-74, 175, 177, 193, 205, 221, 226-9
Durkheim, xxix, xxxiv, 42, 62, 182-3, 196
Eade, J., and M. J. Sallnow, 239, 244, 255
ecology, environment, xxvi, 82, 102, 116, 201, 213, 278
education, xxiii, 25-6, 29, 44, 46-7, 49, 50, 68, 70-1, 76, 87, 95, 148, 162, 206; primary, 271; secondary, 30, 65, 67, 70-1, 75, 77, 80; university,

29-30, 31, 65, 75; fees, 31, 271; students, 212, *jinn*, 243; teachers, 7, 70-1; Islamic, xxxi-ii, 257-74, with Prophet, 243-4, 246, 248, 251
Egypt, Cairo, xxxii, 238, 240, 243, 247, 252
elders, 121, 133-5, 147, 149-53, 162, 169-174, 176, 177-8, 184-91; *Onyeishi*, elder (pl. *Ndiishi*), 104, 106, 107, 110-1, 112
elections, xxiii, 9, 26, 30, 52-3, 55-6, 65, 70, 72, 73, 76-7, 79, 85-7, 94, 108, 109, 121, 268; annulled (12.vi.93), 30, 35, 55-6, 271
elite, ix, xi, xxvi, xxxiii, 19-21, 23, 26, 41-8, 53, 56, 59, 67, 71, 74, 77, 80, 110, 131, 146, 157, 209, 275; mystique, cults, 41-2, 44-5, 56
emir, emirate, 30, 44, 161, 170, 204, 207, 209, 211, 227, 228, 242, 267, 271; *amir al-mu'minin*, 241-3, 252
empowerment, xxxvii, 21, 36, 38, 74, 82, 83, 96
English language, 10, 67, 71, 94-5, 163, 238
Epstein, A.L., xvii, xxxix, 62, 78, 83, 98
equality, inequality, xxviii, 9, 10, 14, 35, 74, 159, 239, 270
essentialism, xxviii, xxx, xxxvii, 81
ethnicity, x, xi, xii, xiii, xv, xxiii, xxiv, xxvi, xxvii-xxix, xxxvii, xxxix, 12 19, 20, 37, 41, 42, 45, 48, 53, 61-80, 81-100, 116, 121-4, 209, 213; ethnogenesis, xxvii, 235
ethnography, ix-x, xviii, 57, 63, 126, 128, 214, 217-36

Europe, Europeans, Europeanisation, 35, 37, 38, 44, 45, 46, 67, 71, 73, 114, 231, 264, 275
Evans-Pritchard, E.E., xii, 82, 98
fables, folklore, xix, xxxix, 19, 43, 80, 85-9, 92, 162-9, 172, 176, 178, 179
facial markings, 133, 219, 233-4
family, household, xviii, xxiii, xxxiii, 6, 15, 22, 29, 30, 33-4, 35, 50, 70, 71, 97, 101-14, 116-8, 122, 130, 136-7, 162, 170, 173, 176, 190, 220-3, 227; *see also* children, kin, wives
famine, hunger, xxvi, 114, 167, 192
festivals, festivity, xv, xx, xxxv, xxxix, 6, 8, 91, 102, 104-8, 111-2, 119, 151-5, 239, 246
feudalism, 15, 207, 209
fire, xxx, 104, 228-33, 236
First Lady, xxxiii, 48-9, 52, 54, 56
fish, fishing, 71, 119, 147, 155, 159, 166-7, 168, 226
Fisher, Humphrey J., xxxi-iii, 41, 168, 202, 217, 225, 237-55, 276
food, feasts, xvii, xxv, xxxv-vi, 6-7, 12, 17-8, 33-4, 50, 85, 86, 95, 101-114, 117, 119-20, 147, 159, 163-4, 166, 167, 170-4, 278; drink, 6, 104, 110; fasting, 88; Holy Communion, 114; vegetarian, 147, 149, 151; *see also* alcohol, meat
Foucault, xvi, 208, 214
Freemasons, 42, 65; see also *Politics of Elite Culture*
friendship, xii, 24, 28, 34, 45, 94, 107-8, 120, 227, 228
Fürer-Haimendorf, Christoph von, ix, 128, 130, 132, 142
Gandhi, xxi, 6, 10-1, 15, 17
Geertz, Clifford, 13, 17, 84, 96, 99

gender, xxxiii, 40, 42, 43, 48, 57, 93, 98, 200, 203, 220, 235-6, 260, 275, 279; politics, 43
generations, xxxii, xxxv, 27, 110, 187, 222-3, 279; *see also* age grade
geomancer (Hong Kong), 148-9
gerontocracy, 110, 116, 118, 176, 178, 197
Ghana, ix, 22, 30; Asante, 40
gifts, 7, 12, 31, 34, 40, 94, 100, 105-6, 119, 152, 192, 226, 228-9, 261, 268, 270; *sadaka*, 261-2, 270
Gluckman, Max, vii, xvi-ix, xxxix, 97, 99, 224
God, Allah, xxxi, 3, 10, 86, 87, 88, 106, 120, 188, 195, 224, 241-2, 247, 264, 266, 267; *Orise*, 120
goddess, xxiv, 43, 146; 'mammy water', 120
gods, 6, 150, 152-3; earth-god, 150, 201-2
government, elected, *see* elections; local, 14, 16, 19-40, 67, 72, 76, 85, 90, 94-5, 109 10, 112, 114, 121-2, 162; *see also* police
grassroots, 20, 26, 28, 29, 32, 37, 38, 52, 65-6, 82, 83, 85
guests, hospitality, 7, 32, 34, 105, 114, 151-2
Gulliver, P.H., xxviii-ix, 125-43, 184, 238, 277
Gwembe, 61, 65-7, 70, 71, 72, 73, 80, 276
Habermas, Jurgen, xvi, 20, 35, 40, 89, 97, 99
hajj, 238, 243; *see also* pilgrimage
Hamlet, xx, 2, 13, 182
hands, 243, 245, 251, 265
Harijan, 10-1, 14-5, 16
Ha Tsuen district, xxiv, 145-59
Hausa, xi, xxiv, xxvi, xxx, xxxi, xxxii, xxxv, 42, 45, 58, 65, 118, 122-4, 162-3, 179, 191-2, 195-7, 199-215
healing, disease, xxvi, xxx, xxxiii, 30, 50, 70, 120, 123, 137, 173-5, 191-2, 200, 211-2, 229-30, 263-7, 278; cholera, 227; herbal, 120, 232; leprosy, 232; madness, 232, 266; *see also* 'medico-spiritual'
hegemony, xvi, xxiv, 8, 9, 93, 146
hierarchy, xxiii, xxviii, xxxi, xxxvi, 8, 10, 23, 25, 33, 42, 54, 55, 75, 97, 131, 141, 142, 154, 175, 191, 204, 207-9, 244
Hinduism, Hindus, xxi, xxxviii, 7, 10, 15; see also *neelkanth*
Home Front, The, 49, 54-5, 57
Hong Kong, xxiv-xxv, 145-59
honour, dishonour, 86, 88, 149, 151, 184
Humanism (Zambia), 73, 78, 79
hunting, gathering, xxix, 75, 132, 141, 168, 232
Ibadan, xi, xii, xxiv, 65, 122-3, 206, 213; University, 30, 277
identity, x, xxviii, xxxv, xxxvii, xxxix, 37, 41, 45, 46, 56, 62, 67, 69-70, 72-6, 77, 78, 81-100, 102, 105, 107, 110, 115, 116, 117, 121, 151, 169, 202, 204, 207-8, 209, 213, 217, 221, 223, 230, 234, 279
ideology, xxv, xxx, xxxix, 19, 37, 38, 42, 43, 56, 62, 67, 73, 90, 94-6, 131, 162, 173, 178, 199-200, 204-5, 206, 213, 278
igbe religion, 118-21, 123
Igbo, xxxv-vi, 43, 44, 48, 57, 58, 101-114
Ila, xxvii, 4, 21, 62-6, 68, 73, 74, 75, 77, 78
imam, 88, 227, 240, 258, 262-3, 269-70

income, 66, 87, 118, 170, 173, 223-5, 227
independence, post-colonial, ix, xi, xxiii, 10, 16, 20, 19-40, 41-59, 65, 66, 68, 69-70, 73, 79, 81, 84, 109, 133, 161-2, 218
India, Indians, xx-xxi, 5-17, 132, 276
initiation, xxxv, xxxviii-ix, 107-8, 112-3, 133, 178, 184-91, 273
installation, *askiya*, xxxii, 238, 240-2, 245, 249, 252-3; chief, 32-5; king, 202
intellectuals, 67, 75, 79, 84, 91, 93
international, global, x, xxv, xxvi, xxviii, xxxii, xxxvi, xxxvii, 35, 37, 44, 71, 74-5, 81, 83, 85, 89, 94, 97, 99, 209
International Monetary Fund (IMF), 50, 58, 76
interpretation, exegesis, xxxvi, 13, 19, 145, 163, 172-4, 175, 181-4, 238-9, 260; interpretive community, 90
Iqbal, Muhammad, 86, 88, 92
Ireland, 125-8, 132, 141, 143, 277
iskoki, 200, 203, 210, 231, 266; see also *jinn*, spirits
Islam, *see* Muslims
Israel, viii, xi, xii, 98
Jaggar, Philip J., xxx, xxxii, 193, 217-36, 239, 242, 254, 263, 267, 277
jiao, renewal rites, xxiv-v, 145-59
jinn, (sing. *jinni*, whence genie), xxxii, 110, 231, 237-55; *aljannu*, 231; Shamharush, 243-6, 248, 250-2; see also *iskoki*, spirits
joking, laughter, 83, 91, 175-6, 229, 233, 267
Jos, 161, 170, 171, 172-3, 177, 223, 236
judge, judicial, 28, 30, 35, 73, 227, 251, 260, 266; *see also* law

justice, injustice, xxi, 57, 104, 142, 152
Kaduna, 45, 58, 59
Kano, xxx, 217-36, 239, 242, 257-74
Kapferer, Bruce, xvii, xxxix, 81, 96, 99
Katsina, 200-215
Kaunda, Kenneth, 68, 73, 78
Kenya, 59, 132, 184, 278
khalifah, caliph, xxxii, 238, 240-5, 248-9, 252-3
khalwah, 242-3, 245
kings, xxvii-viii, xxxii, 15, 24, 26, 36, 37, 72, 74, 116, 202, 228, 241-2, 252-3, 277; *see also* royalty, *sarki*
kinship, xv, xix, xxxix, 15, 19, 22, 23, 43, 62-3, 70, 76, 94, 104, 116, 118, 121, 123, 137-9, 143, 159, 168, 201, 207, 218, 223, 224, 225, 234, 239, 243, 248; *see also* children, family, marriage, etc.
knowledge, xxxvii-viii, xxxix, 25, 90, 100, 261, 264
kola, xi, 33, 106, 114, 123, 233
Kolanut, N.C., 114
Koran, xxx-xxxi, xxxiii, 212, 232-3, 243, 249, 255, 257-74; *Yasin*, 266
labour, jobs, 10, 28, 66, 67, 70-2, 76, 94, 111, 114, 130, 170, 173, 212, 262, 267; workers, xvi-vii, xxvi, 7, 12, 50, 82, 86-7, 97, 116-7, 126, 146, 212, 146, 221, 235
Lagos, 22, 26, 28, 32-4, 37, 39-40, 46-7, 49, 53
land, xxiii, xxiv, xxxviii, 7, 15, 28, 40, 62, 68, 74, 75, 86, 104, 113, 116-7, 167, 170, 173; property rights in temple, 12; reform, 146

language, xvi, xix, 32, 37, 61-80, 117; multi-lingual, 48; *see also* individual languages
law, 5-7, 9-10, 12, 35, 123, 127, 142-3, 146, 153, 210; chiefs, 27, 28, 30; court, 14, 135, 140, 175-6, 266; Islamic, 251; lawyer, 28, 29; outlaw, 248; *see also* judge
learning, xxi, xxxi, xxxiii, xxxv, 95, 107-8, 169; *Lehrstück*, xxii; *see also* education
legitimacy, xxxi, xxxii, xxxiii, xxxv, 28, 61, 89, 92, 202-3, 204, 207, 209, 211, 218, 233, 250, 258-9, 272-3
Lenje, xxvii, 63-6, 68, 73, 74, 77
Lewis, I.M., xii, 44, 58, 132, 143
life-styles, xxvi, 42, 55, 75, 89, 117-8, 123, 184-5, 199, 233
liminality, xxxii, xxxvi, 188, 237-55; danger, 247-8, 253
lineage, xxiv-xxv, xxxv, xi, 82, 101-14, 126, 134-6, 140-2, 145, 147-8, 150, 153-4, 157, 159
linguistic analysis, loyalties, 62-6, 69; *see also* languages
literacy, illiteracy, 29, 37, 67, 86, 163
literature, writing, 11, 30, 67, 68, 73, 77, 91, 179, 211; *see also* poetry
London, ix, xii, xiii, xxxiv, xxxv, 94, 239; University, viii, x, 101, 161
love, 43, 46, 101, 114, 120
Lozi, or Barotse, xxvii, 66, 71, 72, 73, 74-5
Lusaka, 65, 66, 68, 71, 77-8, 79, 80
Maasai, 133, 184, 188, 197, 278
'mafia clubs', 44-5, 58, 59
al-Maghili, 202, 251

Maguda, Sani, 162-3, 166, 170, 173, 276
malams, xxxi-ii, 203, 212, 222, 257-74; as occupational group, 258-9, 263, 265, 268; patrons or clients, 269-70; with merchants and politicians, 270-1; *see also* clerics
Manchester, viii-ix, xix, 39, 85-96; 'Manchester School', viii-ix, xvi, xvii, xviii, xx, 83
marginality, xii, 21-2, 29, 81, 92, 192, 206, 230, 246, 252
markets, xi, xii, xxxv, 16, 24, 28, 35, 67, 68, 69, 70, 75, 76, 95, 105, 117-8, 123, 183, 191-5, 205, 221, 227, 263; market women: 46, 51
marriage, viii-ix, xii, xviii, xxx, xxxi, 42, 104-5, 107-8, 111, 177, 184-8, 207, 218-9, 221-34, 239, 242, 261, 262, 265, 267, 268; adultery, 185; bridewealth, 134; divorce, 192; endogamy, 221-3; exogamy, 104, 113; homogamy, 221; inter-marriage, xxvi-vii, 71, 122-3, 221-2, 233; polygamy; 221, polygyny, 184, 190
Marx, Marxism, xvi, xvii, xix; Communism, xxix, 146
Masina, xxxii, 238, 249
masks, xxxii, xxxv, xxxvii-viii, 104, 105, 107-8, 112-3, 258-9, 267-70
masquerade, xxxv, xxxvii, 34, 104, 248
Masquerade Politics (1993), x, xi, xv, xxxvii, 1, 19, 61-2, 74, 83, 115, 157, 183, 199, 218, 224-6, 239-44, 249-54, 258
masses, mass action, etc., 47, 48, 51, 56, 85, 97, 212
matriarchy, xxxiii, 43, 56, 57, 58

maulvi, cleric, 85, 86-7, 93
McIntyre, J.A., xxxi, xxxiii, 212, 231, 257-74, 277
meat, 106, 119, 147-8, 173; butchers, xvii, 220; slaughtering, 170-1; *see also* food
Mecca, xxxii, 237-8, 241-3, 246, 248, 265, 268
media, xx, xxii, xxviii, xxx, xxxiv, 22, 29, 34-5, 42, 46, 47, 54-6, 67-8, 72, 86, 147, 152, 277; free press, 76
mediation, xxiii, 7, 82, 84, 172, 128-9, 139, 141, 207, 212; arbitration, 7, 128, 135, 140; intermediaries, xxiii, 20, 24, 62, and children as i.
metamorphosis, xxxii, 244, 246, 248, 250-1
micro-history, micro-politics, xvii-xviii, xx, 116
migrants, strangers, population mobility, xi, xii, xvii, xxxi, xl, 22, 24, 43-4, 46, 62-3, 65-6, 71, 74, 75, 78, 82, 83, 84, 86, 96, 97, 99, 100, 102, 104, 105, 107, 108, 111, 115-24, 147-8, 154, 159, 161, 164-5, 168, 169, 191, 193-5, 202, 203, 226, 228, 260-1, 279; *see also* diaspora, settlers
Mitchell, J. Clyde, xvii, xix, xxxix, 61-2, 63, 79, 82-3
models, 1-2, 5, 11, 12, 15, 16, 41, 46, 159, 178, 183, 218
modern, xxiii, xxxiii, 27, 38, 40, 42, 81, 83, 116, 191, 223; modernism, postmodernism, xvi, xvii, 84, 91, 93, 98
monopoly, xxiii, xxiv, 122, 146, 156, 184-6, 218-9, 221, 224, 233-4
morality, moral, xxi, xxiv, xxv, xxviii, 4, 10, 15, 16, 42, 43, 74, 78, 81-100, 121, 131, 136, 140, 142, 192, 206, 213, 224, 228; 'moral space', 162
moran, murran, formerly warriors, xxxv, 133-6, 184-91
mosque, xxvi, xxxi, xxxiii, 85-8, 92, 93, 100, 202, 213, 242; Koran school as, 258, 263
motherhood, xxvi, xxxiii, 43, 46, 49, 56, 185, 201; matricide, 250
Mousetrap, The, xx, 2, 8, 12-3
Muhammad, Prophet, 93, 241-2, 243-8, 250, 252
multi-cultural, 45, 48, 79, 83, 276; -ethnic, 71, 115, 124; -national, 31, 278; -vocality, 5-11, 41
murder, xx, xxxii, 2, 3-4, 13, 16, 95, 177, 245-6, 248, 250-1
Musa, son of Salih Jawara, 243-4, 246-9
music, musicians, xxii, xxxviii, 7, 12, 33-4, 112-3, 151, 183, 196, 200, 209, 226; instruments, 176, 205; pop singers, 151; praise singers, 34, 226-9; song, xxx, 34, 52, 55, 77, 119-20, 164, 175, 176-7, 179, 182, 186, 189, 196, 209, 231, 260; *see also* dance, drums
Muslims, Islam, xii, xxiv, xxx-xxxiii, 42, 44, 47, 48, 53, 81-100, 161, 191-3, 199-215, 218, 230-1, 232-3, 237-55, 257-74, 278-9; *umma*, 94; pre-Islam, xxx, 230-2, 276
mystification, xvi, xxxvi, 15, 45
myth, legend, 16, 40, 43, 51, 52, 62, 91, 99, 156, 179, 203
naming, 225, 233, 262; baptism, 239; names of God, 264
National Council For Women's Societies (NCWS), 46-7, 49-53

nationalism, xxvi, xxxvi, 26, 67, 69-73, 77, 78, 79, 84, 92, 96, 97, 100
Ndembu, xvii, 4-5, 13
Ndendeuli, xxix, 136-143
Near and Middle East, x, xii, xxii, 242-3; *see also* Israel
neelkanth (lit. blueneck, originally a name of Shiva and Vishnu, used very differently here), 87
neighbours, xix, 28, 66, 70, 137-40, 143, 148-9, 162, 163, 166, 176, 227, 262, 263
networks, 31-2, 47, 53, 72, 74, 76, 89, 90, 93-4, 137-8, 140, 143, 188, 222, 225, 248-9
Niger, state, 55, 218, 222, 232, 235; river, 237
Nigeria, ix, xxiii, xxiv, xxvi, xxx, xxxi, xxxiii, 20-40, 41-59, 65, 101-14, 115-24, 161-79, 191, 199-215, 217-36, 257-74
night-spirits, anabur, rauhanai, 162, 174-6, 266
nomads, xii, xxvi, 132, 141, 143, 197, 225; *see also* migrants, pastoralists
non-violence, 6, 10, 12
Northern Rhodesia, xxxviii, 62-3, 66, 67, 78, 79, 80, 82, 276
Notting Hill Carnival, ix, x, xii-xiii, xv, xxxv, 62, 83-4, 145, 199, 226, 239
Nuffield Foundation, xiv
offerings, sacrifice, 6, 8, 104
oil palm, 104, 115-24; oil seeds, 86, 91
Okitipupa, 116, 118-9, 121-4
Omabe festival, xxxv, 107-8, 112
one-party state, 68, 70, 71, 72, 76, 77, 79
Onwuejeogwu M., 44, 58, 192, 205, 263
operas, xxiv-v, 145-59

oral data, xxiv, xxxviii, 179, 238, 241, 245-6, 248-9, 251, 254
orthodoxy, orthopraxy, xxiv-v, xxx, xxxii, 146, 156, 191
Otite, Onigu, xxvi, 115-24, 277
Oyo, 22, 24, 26, 32, 39, 40
Pakistan, Pakistanis, xxiv-xxv, 81-100, 279
palaces, 24, 32-4, 204, 207, 210
paradigms, xvi, l, 40, 219
Parkin, David, xv-xl, 278
pastoralists, xxvi, 132, 133, 143, 184, 189, 278; *see also* nomads
patronage, 39, 51, 52, 72, 76, 152, 192, 207, 221, 261-2, 267, 268-70
pay-off, 10, 14, 56, 230, 239
performance, xix, xx, xxvii-xxxi, xxxii-v, xxxvii, xxxviii-ix, xl, 1-17, 32, 34, 41, 51, 54, 83, 90, 97, 108, 112-3, 115, 121-2, 138, 147, 152, 158, 169, 183-97, 200, 202, 211, 213, 224-34, 249, 258
persecution, harassment, xxiii, xxvii, xxix, 47, 56, 94-5, 204, 207; *see also* women victims
pilgrimage, xxxii-xxxiii, 88, 154, 237-55, 265, 268; Lourdes, 239, 244
Pittin, Renée, xxx, xxxii, xxxiii, 191, 199-215, 231, 263, 278
play, xx-i, xxxix, 1-17, 75, 164, 172, 183, 200, 207; *see also* theatre
poetry, 81, 86, 88, 91, 92, 179; *see also* literature
police, 6-7, 9-11, 12-4, 47, 70, 95, 112, 126, 149, 153
political parties, 6, 21, 22, 28, 30, 47, 65, 68-9, 71, 76-7, 86-7
Politics of Elite Culture (1981), *The*, ix, xi, xv, xvii, 19, 42, 65, 83, 173, 174, 218, 224, 239

population statistics, 6, 25, 42, 65, 109, 113, 115, 118-9, 133, 145, 161, 220-1
post-colonial, *see* independence
pragmatism, xxi, xxxvi, 16, 41, 132, 230
prayer, xxv, 86, 92, 106, 120, 142, 171, 204, 243, 245-6, 247-8, 251, 258, 260, 262, 264-5, 267-8, 269-70, 272, 276; ablution, 260; *addu'a*, 264; *dawas*, 88; *namaz*, 86, 88; prostration, 33, 246, 248, 255
pre-colonial, 20, 23-5, 36, 44, 79, 133, 235, 276
processions, xxiv, xxv, 5, 145, 147, 149-51, 153, 156-7, 182, 186, 188-9, 197; Belfast Orange Day, 149
professions, xxiii, 22, 29-31, 42, 48, 51, 70, 91, 147, 158, 210, 226, 274
prophecy, xxxviii, 119, 245, 246, 248-9; divination, 120, 264; omen, 150, 170
'public sphere', 20, 22, 35, 36, 38, 40; public opinion, 20, 29, 32, 34, 35, 36, 38, 76, 187
punishment, 7, 12, 22, 28, 33, 244, 247; fines, 170, 173-4, 175; *see also* supernatural sanctions
Punjabi, 84, 86, 91-3
Pygmies, 132, 183
queens, 22, 40, 50, 201, 203
racism, anti-racism, xv, 83, 94-7
radio, 67-8, 72; *see also* media
rain, 75, 78, 79, 87, 247-8
rationality, xxvii, xxix, xxxi, xxxiv-v, 4, 11, 12, 14, 16, 35, 41, 45, 129, 212, 230, 239
reciprocity, 31-2, 105, 107, 137-40
religion, xv, xx, xxiv, xxvi, xxx-xxxiii, xxxv, 12, 19, 43, 45, 58, 78, 84-99, 104, 116, 120, 123, 173, 182-3, 188, 201-2, 212, 213, 218, 225, 239, 258, 276, 278; *see also* Muslims, shrines, etc.
renewal, rebirth, rites of, xxiv, 145, 188
rhetoric, xxiv, 3, 5, 51, 52, 68, 84, 85-9, 91, 92, 95-6, 97, 172
Richards, Audrey, 69, 72, 79, 101, 114
rights, 52, 78, 127; ethnic, 94, 96; human, 78, 100; property, 12; religious, 96
rites of passage, 225, 230, 258, 262, 270
ritual, rites, xii, xvi, xx, xix, xxii, xxiv, xxvi, xxviii, xxx, xxxiii, xxxiv, xxxvi, xxxix, 1, 8, 9, 13, 19-40, 42, 43, 62, 69, 72-5, 97, 100, 102, 116, 118, 119, 133, 137, 138, 145-59, 168-9, 170, 174-6, 177, 179, 181, 194, 197, 202, 204, 209, 218-9, 224, 233, 239, 250, 255, 268, 276, 278
Roberts, Andrew, 63, 65, 79, 237
royalty, 2, 13, 32-3, 34, 221; *see also* kings
rural, xxiv, xxvi, 37, 40, 46, 48, 53-4, 55, 68-9, 70, 71, 76, 115-24, 218, 222, 230, 235
sacrifice, offering, 6, 8, 104, 246, 266
sadaka, see gift
Sala, xxvii, 63, 66, 73, 77
Salih Jawara, Alfa, 243-9, 253
Samburu, xxxv, 181, 184-91, 195-7
sarki, 29, 202-3, 208, 228, 231, 242
Satanic Verses, The, 94
School of Oriental and African Studies, viii, ix, xiv, 101, 125, 161, 217, 275-8

schools, viii, 30, 45, 70, 72, 95, 162; fees, 31
secrecy, 122-3; esoteric knowledge, 147, 162, 231-2, 258-9, 263-7, 270; initiation, xxxv, 107-8, 112; invisibility, 89-90, 244, 248-9; language, 175-6; power cults, 45; ritual, xii; societies, 22, 33
segmentary theory, 82, 83, 84, 92-3, 108, 116
self, self-respect, etc., xii, 14, 15, 81, 98, 129, 135, 140, 183
settlers, 62-3, 68, 71, 73, 116-7, 123, 233; resettlement, 276; *see also* migrants
sex, xxxiii, 57, 206, 246, 265; sexual insult, 44, 57; dual-sex, 43, 44, 56, 58
Shakespeare, 2, 3-4, 5, 8
sharif, xxxii, 238, 240-4, 250
Shiva, 6-8, 10, 12-4; see also *neelkanth*
shrines, 75, 78, 150, 152, 176, 201-3
siblings, 70, 82, 88, 105, 111, 133, 203, 220, 245; classificatory, 127
Sierra Leone, ix, xxvi, 42, 44, 45, 46, 65
slaves, 24, 84, 126, 203, 204, 233, 244, 246, 248, 250, 278
slogans, 10, 62, 70, 77
Smith, Mary F., 191-4, 197, 205, 222, 232, 236
snake, xxxii, 232, 244, 246, 251
socialisation processes, 27, 162, 176, 178
sociology, viii, x, xii, 96, 178, 224, 234
Soli, xxvii, 63-6, 68, 73, 74, 77
solidarity, 11, 13, 15, 19, 34, 43, 68, 89, 90, 103, 105, 213, 230; *see also* unity

Songhay, xxxii, 237-55
Sonni Ali, 237, 245, 246, 250-1; S.Baru, 237, 245; dynasty, 247
Spencer, Paul, xxxii, xxxiv-v, xxxviii, 133, 163, 181-97, 205, 226, 231, 263, 278
spirits, possession, xxxii-iii, 58, 75, 107, 113, 119-20, 148, 151, 191-6, 199-215, 263-5, 274; spirits of dead, 149; spiritualism, 265-8; see also *night-spirits, iskoki, jinn*
sports, cricket, 91, 100
stage, xxi, xxii, 1-17, 32, 41, 151-2, 158, 190
standard of living, 70, 76, 120
Structural Adjustment Programme (SAP), 50, 57, 58, 76, 211-2, 258
succession, 27, 29, 30, 116, 201; hereditary, 23, 24, 36
suffering, community of, 55, 90, 96
supernatural sanctions, 88, 129, 148, 153, 154, 162, 168, 173, 174, 176, 188, 192, 212, 232; cursing, 250; endangering those who would use them against others, 266; *see also* punishment, *dawas*
symbolism, xi-ii, xv, xix, xx, xxii-iii, xxiv-vii, xxx, xxxiii-iv, xxxvi-vii, xxxix, 2, 7-8, 12, 14, 19, 22, 31-2, 37, 42, 45, 50, 52, 62, 69, 74-5, 91, 93, 97, 108, 114, 115-7, 120, 122-4, 188, 204, 208, 213, 218-9, 225, 227, 230, 233-5, 239, 241, 247, 255; emblems, 33, 94; symbolic universe, 161-79
Takrur, 240, 242
Tanzania, xxviii-ix, 132, 133-43
Tarikh al-fattash, T/F, 238, 241, 243-4, 245

taxation, 40, 220-1, 227; tribute, 24; *zakka*, 262
teachers, 7, 22, 257-274; *see also* education, malams
technology, technocrats, 45, 61, 73, 78, 117, 122-3, 227
template, cultural, xvii, xxiii-v, xxxiv, xxxvi, 158
temple, xx-xxi, xxxiv, 5-17, 145-59
Teng lineage, xxiv-xxv, 145-59
text, xxxi-iii, 1, 11, 16, 41, 264
theatre, xix-xxii, xxxiv, xxxviii-ix, 1, 3-5, 6, 11, 16, 120, 200; *see also* play
theft, 167, 185, 261, 265
Third World, xiii, 50
Tianhou, 'Empress of Heaven', xxiv, 145-59
Tijaniya Brotherhood, xxvi, 65, 269
Timbuktu, xxxiii, 237, 238, 240, 251, 255
titles, xxiii, 19-40, 43, 107, 116, 203, 208-9, 228, 240-2, 252; *see also* chiefs
tolerance, intolerance, xxix, xxxii, 37, 99, 210
Tonga, xxvii, 61-80, 276
Torrend, Father J., xxvii, 62-3, 80
tourism, xxxvi, 26, 74-5, 81
trade, commerce, xi, xii, xxiii, xxxv, 16, 24, 42, 50, 70, 117, 118, 191, 202, 235; merchants, 65, 95, 123, 146, 154, 233, 257, 260, 262, 264, 277
tradition, xxiii, xxvii-viii, xxxii, 27, 29, 38-40, 43-4, 46, 47, 53, 56, 74, 76, 77, 84, 90, 95, 98, 102, 104, 106, 107, 108-14, 116, 143, 171, 173, 190-1, 202, 203, 204, 208-9, 211, 213, 217-8, 222, 226, 229, 234, 235, 241, 265, 276; *see also* custom
translation, 155-6, 163, 247

trees, forest, 6, 104, 116-7, 143, 183, 278; jungles, 92; *see also* oil palm
tribes, tribal, xxix, xxxviii, 65, 68, 69, 77, 79, 82, 114, 190
trust, 27, 28, 37, 43, 45
truth, 2, 3, 8, 10, 84, 88, 89, 91, 214, 254
Turnbull, Colin M., xii, 132, 143, 183
Turner, Victor W., ix, xvii-ix, xxxix-xl, 4-5, 13, 224, 230, 236, 239, 247; *communitas*, 13, 244-5
Two-Dimensional Man (1974), x, xi, xv, xx, 19, 42, 61, 213, 218-9, 224, 233, 272
United National Independence Party (UNIP), 65, 68-72, 76, 80
unity, 51, 52-3, 86-8, 90-1, 93, 102, 103, 105, 106-7, 108, 110, 111, 114, 159, 186, 258-9; *see also* solidarity
Untouchables, xx-xxi, xxxiv, 5-17
Urhobo, xxvi, 115-24, 277
utility, 16, 230, 252-3
Vaughan, Olufemi, 19, 21, 28, 29, 30, 37, 40
villages, viii, xi, xxiii-iv, 6-17, 25, 46, 48, 54, 65, 66, 69, 71-2, 75, 87, 91-2, 101-14, 116-8, 121-3, 145-59, 161-6, 168-74, 185-9, 191, 205, 235; *see also* rural
violence, xx, xxii, xxiv, xxix, 14, 45, 95-6, 99, 100, 129, 132, 135-6, 140, 145-59, 185-6, 246; *see also* warfare
warfare, xx, xxvi, 15, 21, 24, 44, 66, 84, 147, 157, 161, 168, 170, 237; Nigerian civil war (1967-70), 109, 112, 133, 142, 190; *see also* violence

warriors, xxxv, 6-17, 32, 33, 133, 135, 163, 170, 177-8, 184-5, 189, 276
Watson, James L., xxiv-xxv, xl, 145-59, 278; Rubie S., 145, 157, 159
wealth, xxiii, 15, 16, 20, 21, 22, 23, 24, 29, 30-1, 47, 55, 107, 121, 150, 154, 206, 209, 270; redistribution, 30, 173; no distinction amongst Koran school pupils, 261
weapons, 6, 117, 220, 225, 248; guns, 112; swords, 242, 245
Weber, xxix, 141
Werbner, Pnina, xxiv-xxvi, 62, 81-100, 278-9
west, westernisation, xxi-ii, xxiii, xxx, xxxiii, 27, 44, 46, 50, 92, 123, 130, 205, 211-2, 213, 271, 275, 276
witchcraft, wizards, 120, 170, 174, 176-7, 275; sorcerers, 162-72, 176
wives, spouses, 33, 34, 45, 47, 48, 49, 52-5, 82, 103, 108, 117, 118, 126, 133, 137, 162, 165, 184-7, 190, 204, 207, 220-1, 268; co-wives, 118, 212, 262, 265
women, xxiii, xxxiii, 34, 41-59, 82, 88-9, 94, 103, 108, 116-7, 119, 154, 170, 175, 177, 184-5, 187, 199-215, 227, 234, 246, 273, 278; elite, xxxiii, 22, 34, 38, 40, 70-1; girls, xxxviii, 46, 184-5, 187-9; initiation, xxxviii-ix; officials, 24, 32, 47-8; organisations, xxvi, 91; pollution, 149; purdah, 208, 227, 260-1; victims, 43, 56, 126; *see also*, queens, wives, etc.
World Bank, 50, 58, 76

yams, coco-yam, 105-6, 108, 110, 111, 119
young men, xxxv, 171-2, 177-8, 184-91; 'guardsmen', 149, 151, 152, 155-6
Yoruba, xi, 38, 46, 115-24
youth, 52, 71, 95, 107-8, 112-3, 162, 175-6, 190
Zaïre, 62, 65, 132
Zambia, xvii, xxvii-xxviii, 61-80; University, 61, 75, 77, 79, 82, 276